Serbian Dreambook

New Anthropologies of Europe

*Daphne Berdahl, Matti Bunzl,
and Michael Herzfeld,
founding editors*

Serbian Dreambook

National Imaginary in the Time of Milošević

Marko Živković

Indiana University Press

Bloomington & Indianapolis

This book is a publication of

Indiana University Press
601 North Morton Street
Bloomington, Indiana 47404-3797 USA

iupress.indiana.edu

Telephone orders 800-842-6796
Fax orders 812-855-7931
Orders by e-mail iuporder@indiana.edu

⊖ The paper used in this publication
meets the minimum requirements of
the American National Standard for
Information Sciences—Permanence
of Paper for Printed Library Materials,
ANSI Z39.48-1992.

Manufactured in the United States of
America

Library of Congress Cataloging-in-
Publication Data

Živković, Marko.
  Serbian dreambook : national imagi-
nary in the time of Milosevic / Marko
Živković.
    p. cm. — (New anthropologies of
Europe)
  Includes bibliographical references and
index.
  ISBN 978-0-253-35623-9 (cloth : alk.pa-
per) — ISBN 978-0-253-22306-7 (paper :
alk. paper) 1. National characteristics,
Serbian—History—20th century. 2.
Milosevic, Slobodan, 1941-2006—Influ-
ence. 3. Imagination—Social aspects—
Serbia—History—20th century. 4.
Imagination—Political aspects—Serbia
—History—20th century. 5. Narration
(Rhetoric)—Social aspects—Serbia—
History—20th century. 6. Narration
(Rhetoric)—Political aspects—Serbia—
History—20th century. 7. Serbia—Social
life and customs—20th century. 8. Pop-
ular culture—Serbia—History—20th
century. 9. Political culture—Serbia—
History—20th century. 10. Serbia—Poli-
tics and government—1992-2006. I. Title.
  DR2050.Z4 2011
  949.71031—dc22

2010041410

1 2 3 4 5 16 15 14 13 12 11

For mother

CONTENTS

ACKNOWLEDGMENTS

This book has been long in coming. Some people influenced it directly by reading and commenting on the text as it slowly unfolded, others by providing models of how to think which I absorbed along the way, and still others by supporting and nurturing me in many material and non-material ways. Visibly or invisibly they are all present in the text.

I was blessed with extraordinary teachers. Miloljub Perić, my high school philosophy professor, gave me the first lesson in the art of teaching; Jovica Stanojević, my first aikido instructor, taught me about laughing; Dejan Razić taught me Japanese as if it were an easy language; Elémire Zolla, the master of delicate and luminous imagination, graced me with his friendship; and Kostas Kazazis, a Balkan linguist extraordinaire, guided my first steps in this project. Daphne Berdahl was my elder sister at the University of Chicago. They are no longer with us, but they are a part of who I became.

At Chicago George W. Stocking Jr. and Carol Stocking first took me under their wing. George guided me through my entire graduate career both firmly and with great generosity. He was the only one to steer my English toward greater economy (I am not there yet); his seminars were the best I ever had; and he fed me for more than a decade. His cooking is superb. With James W. Fernandez I found the most congenial way to practice anthropology. I basked in his and Renate Fernandez's abundant conviviality and partook of many a legendary garlic soup at their home. Raymond D. Fogelson kept me connected with psychology and lavished upon me his time and his encyclopedic mind. Susan Gal understood, often better than I could, what I wanted to do, and then helped me do it better. Victor Friedman, with his prodigious knowledge of all things Balkan, provided guidance and generosity that extended much beyond academic advising. Outside my doctoral committee, Don Levine was my Sensei and friend both on and off the mat. He gave me my first lessons in teaching Chicago-style in the College Social Science Core course Wealth, Power and Virtue, but it was in the Master of Arts program in the Social Sciences (MAPSS) where I polished the craft. Thanks to John MacAloon for taking me aboard this amazing ship. I also want to thank him and Ann Terry Straus, my MAPSS student Lisa Feder, and Jim and Renate Fernandez for standing by me during the trying times in 1999. Nada Petković-Djordjević, Miša, and Darja were my second family in Chicago.

Robert Hayden and Milica Bakić-Hayden have been invaluable friends from whose hospitality and unique combination of expert knowledge I benefited for more than twenty years. Maria Todorova, Susan Woodward, Martha Lampland, Joel Halpern, Dina Iordanova, and Hermine DeSoto helped me greatly with their encouragement and advice over the years. To my fellow students at Chicago I owe special gratitude for the mutual illumination only peers can provide: Vyjayanthi Rao, D. J. Hatfield, Robert Albro, Shao Jing, Tom Lyons, Keith Brown, Anthony Berkeley, Mary Scoggin, Chris Oliver, Baron Pineda, Margaret Bender, Stuart Rockefeller, Alaina Lemon, Elizabeth Vann, Matti Bunzl, Krisztina Fehervary, Miklós Vörös, Paul Silverstein, Emily McEwan, Robert Zanca, and Alexandra Hrycak. Dale Pesmen showed me a thing or two about ethnography, incoherence, and mixing metaphors. Thanks to Dejan Guzina, Eric Gordy, Maja Korać, Ana Dević, Ivana Spasić, Stef Jansen, Slobodan Naumović, Maya Nadkarni, Elissa Helms, and Xavier Bougarel, all fellow travelers pursuing similar projects, for companionship along the way. Special thanks to Marina Deleon, Radosav Pušić, Milan Vukomanović, Dejan Stamenković, and Vladimir Djurić-Djura for being not only my lifelong friends but also my guides in the field. Ivan Čolović has been an incomparable model and mentor.

Thanks to George Harp for offering shelter, to Anne Chi'en for all that she has done for me, and to the MacArthur Foundation for its generous CASPIC (Council for Advanced Studies in Peace and International Cooperation) dissertation fellowship (1995–1996). For sustaining me and Gordana in Portland I thank my colleagues at Reed College: Robert Brightman, Rupert Stash, Laura Hendrickson, Anne Lorimer, Michael Reay, Salah Khan, Lena Lencek, Darya Pushkina, and Jérôme Cornette. I thank, in particular, Paul Silverstein, my fellow student at Chicago and colleague at Reed, my landlord, driving instructor, and beer guru, my most staunch supporter in all things big and small.

Thanks to the University of Alberta Anthropology Department for taking me in and providing me with generous collegiality. I especially thank Lisa Philips for her unflinching support without which this book would have taken much longer, and Chris Fletcher and Andrew Gow for their wit and intellectual camaraderie. Finally, I thank my brother in Balkan studies, Srdja Pavlović—a great guy to have at your side.

Thanks to Matti Bunzl, Rebecca Tolen, and Michael Herzfeld for their faith in me, as well as my two readers for great comments. They, together with Bruce Grant and Nancy Ries, helped me make this into what I hope is a better book than it otherwise would have been. I am particularly grateful to Rebecca for taking care to preserve my voice in the text.

My wife, Gordana Živković, is the author of my portrait and my artistic adviser. She brought love, French fashion, and her inimitable laughter into my life. Our furry companions, Mao and Zizi, provide our daily sustenance of grace.

Portions of this book were previously published in Andrew Colin Gow, ed., *Hyphenated Histories: Articulations of Central European Bildung and Slavic Studies in the Contemporary Academy* (Leiden: Brill, 2007), 141–166; *Social Identities* 13 (5) (September 2007): 597–610; *Cahiers de l'URMIS*, no. 6 (March 2000): 69–84; *Balkanologie* 2 (2) (December 1998): 77–98; *Replika*, special issue (1997); and *Filozofija i društvo* 18 (2001): 73–110.

Serbian Dreambook

Introduction

When Tito died in 1980 it was as if his feeble successors tried to keep everything in Yugoslavia in a stasis by conjuring his ghost in the slogan "After Tito, Tito." The standard of life went downhill and almost forgotten shortages appeared again as foreign loans had to be repaid, and as the cogwheels of flexible capitalism started grinding against the ever so slow cogwheels of self-managing socialism. Because of its relative openness, the cogwheels of the outside world had much more purchase on the internal works in Yugoslavia than in the more closed people's democracies, but there was also a widespread feeling that the senile stasis of Tito's spectral rule would gradually erode and give way to something freer and closer to "Europe." The relative independence from the Soviet sphere also made 1989 a less cataclysmic event in Yugoslavia than elsewhere. At least at the level of popular perception it was not so much the superiority of Western goods across the Wall, the Mercedes-Benzes and bananas, nor the "living in Truth" that Havel (1986) projected over the Iron Curtain that broke the back of socialism, but rather the revamped, resurrected national narratives that drove the schizmogenetic national mobilization in all of the Yugoslav constituent republics. Socialist Dreamtime was supplanted by the National Dreamtime. In Serbia, that national dreamtime was dominated by the rhapsodizing of national bards over the ever recurring battle of Kosovo. This rhapsodizing, as one of the bards put it, "saddled the horse" that Slobodan Milošević rode to power in the late 1980s.

Yugoslavia dissolved violently in a well-documented sequence of events.[1] First a quick withdrawal of the Yugoslav National Army (JNA) from Slovenia after brief fighting in 1991, followed by a full-blown war in Croatia between the Serbian insurgents aided by the Serbified JNA. This resulted in the establishment of Serbian enclaves, and after a period of uneasy UN-brokered truce, ended in a massive expulsion of Serbs in 1995. The war in Bosnia between the Muslim, Croat, and Serbian forces started in 1992 and ended with the Dayton Peace Accord in 1995. In Serbia Milošević survived a series of popular protests in the late 1990s, and the escalation of the conflict in the Serbian autonomous region of Kosovo, with its overwhelming Albanian majority, led to the NATO bombing of Serbia in 1999. Milošević survived another year and was ousted in October 2000. He was sent to The Hague Tribunal by the new authorities, led by Prime Minister Zoran Djindjić. Djindjić was assassinated in 2003, and Vojislav Koštunica served as the president and prime minister until 2008. Milošević died in The Hague in 2006. Kosovo declared independence in 2008 and, in a sense, closed the circle of Yugoslavia's dissolution, which could be traced to disputes over its status in Serbia that brought Milošević to power and set in motion the process of national mobilization. This book focuses on that Serbian Dreamtime which served as a matrix for Milošević's rise, sustained his rule, and persisted after he was ousted, especially as Koštunica led the nationalist coalition that included the ultra-nationalist Serbian Radical Party and the most conservative currents of the Serbian Orthodox Church in the aftermath of Djindjić's assassination.

I was born and raised in Belgrade, where I studied clinical psychology at the University of Belgrade. After graduating in 1984 and serving my army term in 1984–1985, I slowly drifted toward anthropology. I had a long-standing interest in things Japanese, and I came to the Ph.D. program in anthropology at the University of Chicago in 1989 planning to do my research in Japan. I was taking an intensive Japanese language course in Ann Arbor, Michigan, when the fighting started in Slovenia in the summer of 1991, and was in Yokohama, studying Japanese, during the 1992–1993 academic year when the war spilled into Bosnia. It was at the midpoint of that year in Japan that I decided to change my dissertation project from Japan to Serbia, and it was in the summer of 1993 that I visited Belgrade, after three years of absence, with this project in mind.

When I returned in the summer of 1993 I was greeted by my urbanite friends' bitter complaints about losing their city to the newly arrived "primitives," most conspicuously typified by the new musical genre of "turbo-folk." The war in Bosnia was presented by the regime media as though it were taking place in a distant country, and it did not loom nearly as large in the consciousness of ordinary Belgrade citizens as the hyperinflation that was raging at the time. People were eager to talk about their woes or discuss world politics, and I soon started to notice recurring themes in such talk. I catalogued these themes, tracing their sources and genealogies, the logic of their combinations, and the ways they were used by identifiable social actors vying for power and legitimacy. At the most basic level, then, this book could be seen as a "glossary of commonplaces"—a list of the important themes and their characteristic inflections, a short history of past uses, the most prominent sources of dissemination, and, finally, their ideological and political pragmatics.

FROM IMAGINARIUM TO DREAMBOOK

I find it most useful, however, to talk about the Serbian imaginary, or "imaginarium," in the sense in which, as Ross Chambers notes, the French have been using the term *l'imaginaire* in recent generations. *L'imaginaire,* according to Chambers, "refers to the repertory of items (or images) that define what, for a given individual or collective subjectivity, it is possible to imagine."

> The advantage of this term is that one can coin a parallel term, argumentarium (French *l'argumentaire*) for that which it is possible to argue. Taken together, these two terms describe the idea that there are limits, cultural or psychological or both, on what it is possible to think. From the point of view of narrative, they permit me to describe narrative statements as the product of an imaginarium, on which they draw, and of an argumentarium that determines the disposition of imaginary elements according to a set of grammatical rules or regularities. The two terms thus define a topology of narrative, which would need to be completed by a pragmatics, corresponding to the question: what does narrative do and how does it do it? (Chambers 2001:100)

My usage is close to that of Marilyn Ivy's (1995) "national-cultural imaginary," which she derives from Anderson (1991), Castoriadis (1987), and Lacan, and even more to that of Ivan Čolović (2002), who uses "imaginarium" in precisely the French sense outlined by Chambers.

This Serbian imaginary presented itself to me as analyzable, up to a point, as a repository of local tropes that use certain idioms such as mud, slush, asphalt, or coffee. These idioms could then be seen to be organized in certain recursive, redundant patterns that may be deployed in a "quality space" (Fernandez 1986) or revolving around certain axes of symbolic geography (north-south, east-west), with the resulting patterns of concentric circles and gradients (of depreciation or relative barbarity/ civilization) and such second-order effects as feelings of in-betweenness. All of these in turn are embedded in larger patterns that are usefully analyzed as narratives. Finally, one can go to genres as supra-narrative gestalts, flexible, changeable, and yet stable enough to offer reference points and tools for strategies of intertextual linking that are demon-strably powerful tools of political rhetoric (Briggs and Bauman 1992).

Tropes and idioms are then organized by recursive dichotomies, axes, and continua of quality space. They enter into scripts, plots, and narratives of different shapes, the narratives dialogically intertwine (see Bruner and Gorfain 1984), and in turn fall into discernible genres. All of this could be seen as subject to a grammar of sorts, the Serbian argumen-tarium, and embedded in the Serbian imaginarium, an abstract total repository of all the grooves that the Serbian imagination can follow.

This book could then be seen as a glossary of commonplaces, as a so-cial life of stories in Serbia, or the "stories Serbs tell themselves (and oth-ers) about themselves," and as a morphology of the Serbian imaginary. There is, however, one more framework that I find useful and would like to invite the reader to use in reading the book—that of the dream.

The very idioms that people in Serbia used to figure out their social reality were often bizarre, outlandish, and strange. Amorphous sub-stances like mud, slush, gelatin, and mists, for instance, were often over-determined as metaphors—that is, they figured both the "opacity of the political life" and the peculiar in-betweenness felt so often in the periph-eries of Europe. This in-betweenness, in its turn, was expressed in various spatial idioms of symbolic geography and in temporal idioms of "missing the [Euro] train," "catching up," and, in the Serbian case, most often of being "stuck" in some sort of twilight state of "bad eternity." A peculiar sense of being in the neither-here-nor-there state was expressed in such a fairy-tale image as the "castle neither in the sky nor on the ground" (*čardak ni na nebu ni na zemlji*), the whole family of Half-Bakedness tropes, the notion of the Bearable Evil of Tito's communism and the images of slumber and fitful dream—neither fully asleep nor fully awake.

Moreover, various pastoral idylls and fables of the Serbian Golden Age I traced in Serbia abounded with uncommon bizarreness exemplified, for instance, in phantasmagoric mixing up of Byzantine High Culture, peasant astuteness, or barbarogenius, and theories about Serbs as the "most ancient people." These fabulations were propounded by eccentric painters, prime-time TV astrologers, "serious" academic and public intellectuals, by world-famous writers like Milorad Pavić (1988) of the *Khazar Dictionary* fame, and film directors like Emir Kusturica. All of them inhabited the mainstream rather than the fringe, and most of them indulged in some variant of a Balkan Magical Realism. Finally, the immense mythopoetic cluster anchored in the Battle of Kosovo, with the incredible hold it exerts on the Serbian imaginary, suggested that in a sense the Serbs are a "people of the Kosovo Dreaming," to draw an analogy with the Australian Aborigines.

Clues were thus gradually accumulating over time that many of these bizarre, outlandish, and strange ingredients of the national imaginary emerging in my research on Milošević's Serbia could be figured as the National Dream. There was an oneiric bizarreness to it all. The banal daily residues entered as a finite number of prefabricated elements as into the most fantastic combinations both in the discourses disseminated by the media and in the words of my informants. There was evidence of condensation, displacement, and overdetermination in this material. There was a sense of twilight states of consciousness. Above all, the natives themselves, as well as foreign observers, often resorted to explicit figuring of Serbian social reality as a species of dream experience—most often, and predictably, as a nightmare. In wrestling with all this material I experienced both the interpretive delirium and its frustration. And that tension between delight in finding patterns in madness and a sense of my ultimate failure to impose neatness and structure onto the Serbian imaginary finally recalled to me that I am in the position of a dream interpreter.

Taking this imaginary to essentially consist of narratives that are in turn taken as the most comprehensive organization of tropes, idioms, characters, and plots is to remain beholden to the textual or, more generally, verbal models, and one reason why the dream might bring a salutary enlargement of our epistemology is that it is notoriously the arena of the most varied transformations of the nonverbal into verbal, and vice versa. In *Dream Nation* Stathis Gourgouris makes an explicit argument for the benefits of seeing modern nations, and especially their historiography, as dreams rather than texts. "Attributing to the national imaginary the characteristics of an exclusively discursive formation is not fair to its complexity," he argues. "The emphasis must shift from nation-as-text to nation-as-dream, which is to say that those texts bearing the nation's mark may ultimately be seen as descriptions of the nation's dream thoughts, thus figural transcriptions (prone to disguise and occultation—secondary revision) of the nation's dream-work" (Gourgouris 1996:30). It is the ambiguousness and complexity of such concepts as secondary revision, and ultimately the fundamental unintelligibility of the dream, that draws Gourgouris to the dream as the most fruitful figure for understanding the nation. "The apparent readability of the dream," he says, "is pseudoreadability because the content of a dream is ultimately not a text but an *object,* whose textual intelligibility is but an affect made necessary by the demands of a thought-producing consciousness in its desire to emerge from sleep" (ibid.:29).

To see the Serbian imaginary as a dreamwork, however, is not just to note that the natives sometimes use dream metaphors when they talk about their situation. Dreamwork is also a potentially very fruitful model for the sociological mind when it grapples with such complex abstractions as national imaginaries.

The dream is a "machine for thinking" about our social world of such intricacy, complexity, and flexibility that it should be taken seriously in social theory. Moreover, social theory already possesses an intrinsic affinity to dream as a figure. This affinity comes from the necessity for the social sciences to posit some sort of opacity of the social, for if social reality were transparent there would be no need for social sciences and, consequently, none would have been invented. And if social reality were perfectly transparent for ordinary people, there would have been no need for them ever to produce all this rich figuration—the fetishes, totems, monsters, and dreams—that we anthropologists make it our primary business to decipher. In other words, most people in most circumstances will have a significantly inadequate, partial, and in some way distorted understanding of the functioning of society of which they are a part. Ordinary consciousness tends to endow objects with agency, engage in fallacies of misplaced concreteness, is inconsistent, contradictory, partial, and unsystematic. This is often expressed as the distinction between surfaces or facades, on the one hand, and what is variously seen as depth, essence, or a more fundamental level of reality, on the other. Social sciences are, then, all uncoverers of hidden, mystified, veiled reality.

The very positing of reduced, opaque, or deficient awareness, with its corollary of surfaces and depths (themselves metaphors), is conducive to using the dream as a figure and conceptual model. It is, however, when the opacity is seen as not just functional, or not just the way the savage mind's bricolage appears to the scientifically trained mind, but as malignantly deceptive, as in Marxist social theory, that the dream as figure becomes potentially much more pertinent. We can thread the dream through Marxist social theory, a major site of its most fruitful use—from its anticipation in Marx's varied figurations of modern capitalism's peculiar enchantments to its full development in the work of Siegfried Kracauer and Walter Benjamin.[2] Doing so reveals several ways that dream might function as a trope, a model, a figure for things social.

For one, dreaming offers one of the most complex, nuanced, as well as experientially impressive models of various modalities in which consciousness could be attenuated or modified. Since social theory by necessity relies on some notion of the opacity of the social, it is easy to see how dreaming could offer nuanced models for this state of affairs. A corollary is that when various levels of social unconsciousness are mapped, insidiously or not, onto various social groups, these gradations could be figured as "maps of slumber." One could then see how both internal and external others (lower classes, women, children, primitives, exotics, Orientals, etc.) could be seen as relatively more dreamlike, prone to confusing dream and reality, or, perhaps less insidiously, as in better touch with their dreams than ourselves.[3]

Second, dream interpretation is a most apt model for the hermeneutical practice in general. It offers the archetypal figure of the dream interpreter as a fascinating role model. Oneirocritics are embodiments of the ideals of total interpretability who at the same time depend for their continued authority on the irreducible mysterious reminders, the uninterpretable core labeled famously by Freud as the "navel of the dream."

Dreams are, furthermore, epistemological machines for modeling all sorts of different worlds, self-sealing paradigms, epistemes, or frames, as well as the traffic between them. They are particularly good for thinking the paradoxes attendant on switching between such incommensurable worlds, especially if these worlds are also pictured as multiply nested and looping back on themselves. The most complex way of figuring such paradoxes seems to exist in the vast and intricate corpus of Indian myths and philosophical parables presented in Wendy Doniger's *Dreams, Illusions, and Other Realities* (1984) that rely on the dream as their master operator. Western literature played with these paradoxes—from Aeschylus to Shakespeare, Pirandello and Calderon de la Barca, all the way to Lewis Caroll, surrealists, and Borges—and yet, as Doniger claims, "only intermittently and rather nervously." Reading Doniger one cannot but conclude that it is the Indians who are peerless masters of the genre. Indeed, a certain "critical amount" of exposure to Indian tales of monks dreaming of being kings who dream of being outcasts, and so on, through endless vertiginous self-including loops, can do strange things to one's brain. After being squeezed through enough nesting dreams one can attain some sort of mental runner's high and acquire, if for a moment, the facility of a champion vaulter in frame jumping.

It is this frame jumping that I propose to the reader of this book as a fruitful exercise. The exercise would be to try out a few different frameworks through which to see the material presented—as tropology that moves and persuades in a quality space, as a repository of dialogically entwined stories, as intertextually linked genres of speech, and, finally, as a sort of national dreamwork.

NATIVE ETHNOGRAPHY AND VOICE: BETWEEN DEPRESSION AND AMUSEMENT

During the 1990s people in Serbia were experiencing traumatic changes and a high level of general turmoil. A great deal of what had previously been taken for granted was thrown out of kilter. The familiar, in a word, became strange, and the "natives" could find themselves no less bewildered than outsiders. Even though a Belgrade native, I felt like a stranger when I commenced my research in 1993 after three years of absence, and yet not knowing what was really going on was a very native position to be in. Rather than go over the general epistemological and ethical predicaments of native ethnographers already explored in anthropological literature, I will just note the range of identities I did inhabit in the course of my research.[4] In other words, what categories did I fit into and what were their situational pragmatics?

Rather than confining me to either insider or outsider status, most of my interlocutors could easily inhabit a category that included us both as insiders or a category that made me an outsider—depending on what they wanted to convey. I was, nevertheless, able, if I so desired, to successfully sustain my insider line in most contexts and with most of my interlocutors. What mattered most for the communication was rather at what level I established this belonging together—was it as an (ex)Yugoslav, a Serb, a Belgrader, or as someone who attended this particular primary school or shopped at that particular farmer's market?

For most of my interlocutors, that I was living in the States was only one, and not the most salient, aspect of my identity. To the extent that it came to the fore, it usually elicited a vacillation between the among-ourselves and self-display mode that was a grist for my mills. If the conversation started in the mode of "let me tell you (relative) outsider what's really going on here," I could almost always also steer it to the full "among-ourselves" mode by invoking the kind of intimate knowledge only an insider would have. In practice, I often started at some outer ring of insiders and had to work to get more "inside," as opposed to someone who never left. Only in that nuanced way was I relatively speaking something other than a straightforward native.

In most situations the returnee part of my identity was easily negotiated; more pertinent were the finer distinctions among insiders—those of social status, education, age, and, perhaps most important, political positioning. Thus the most salient part of my identity was whether I belonged to what was often glossed as "Second Serbia." This category was elastic and could well be defined as all those who opposed Milošević from the civic, anti-nationalist and pro-European position. With those who, so to speak, were not entirely opposed, there was a way of avoiding certain topics that could preserve islands of commonality.

It would have been quite comfortable for me to inhabit the "Second Serbia" position, but I avoided any active public engagements or commitments along these lines. This was not because I didn't endorse the aims or ideology of various oppositional organizations and movements; it was rather because I felt it would have been disingenuous to claim the moral superiority of being an active opponent of the regime without actually experiencing the suffering or running the risks of those who lived there permanently. I was based in the U.S., and in Belgrade I was just an occasional visitor. I was thus a native in terms of intimate local knowledge, but not a native in terms of existential commitments.

Moreover, I wanted to be in a position to be at least somewhat reserved toward the idealization of "Europe," civil society, and liberal democracy that was implied in most of the anti-regime talk of the groups I would have "naturally" belonged to had I stayed in Belgrade. I do consider the idealization of Western democracy a much lesser evil than idealization of the ethnic nation, but I want to reserve the right to be critical about both.

As a result, I often assume a voice from nowhere, an ironic superiority, that I then try to undermine with further irony, and as a result my voice gets hard to pin down. Moreover, this voice changed over time, since the writing of this text spans some sixteen years. My anger and bewilderment, for instance, were different in 1994 than in 1997 or 2003. Be that as it may, what emerges here is my voice and at some point I want to cease trying to escape it. Rather than flatten it from a standpoint of detached neutrality of the present, I want to preserve some of the passion and anguish in my voice as a testament to what it was like for someone like me to write about Serbia at a particular point in time.

As Herzfeld put it when talking about irony, "some things wilt under excessive attention, and so are best left unsaid" (Herzfeld 2001:82). There is, nevertheless, a point about my ironic voice that I should address, since it has a direct bearing on what turned out to be my method in writing this book. My shifting and, admittedly, hard to pinpoint ironic voice was, among other things, a way I negotiated a tension between what, for lack of a better word, I call depression and amusement. By depression and amusement I mean the nauseating messiness of the situation, on the one hand, and the exotic, extravagant, and flamboyant, the picturesqueness of grotesque excesses, on the other. In the everyday life of those I studied, these two states were probably experienced as amalgamated in various proportions, but in my text there is a discernible tension between the two.

The amusement aspect was due partly to my method and partly to something happening on the ground. I was always on the lookout for felicitous condensations or crystallizations of the themes I wanted to explore, and I was particularly drawn to those incidents that encapsulated ambivalences and ironies that signaled nodes of tension, "switch-points," or "hinges." These were heightened moments, they often had comic elements, and they tended to exaggerate. Thus my method—collecting these—and my mode of presentation that relies on the unpacking of such "revelatory incidents" (see Fernandez 1986:xi) tends to privilege the exaggerated, the flamboyant, the ironic, and the amusing. But concentrating on the exaggerated, amusing, and picturesque is not just an artifact of my mode of presentation. Something in the situation, on the ground, in the reality itself was amusing, grotesque, and exaggerated.[5]

The regime as well as the opposition was constantly staging megalomaniacal spectacles, rallies, conferences, and carnivalesque protests. For instance, in the midst of hyperinflation and international blockade in 1992 a Serbian businessman, a flamboyant figure himself, managed to stage the Fisher-Spassky chess rematch on the Montenegrin coast. A festive atmosphere that oddly clashed with the grim reality of war, poverty, and hopelessness was actively promoted by regime-controlled media in order to project a rosy picture of reality. The incongruity between frivolous entertainment and grim reality, however, produced a widespread feeling of living in a surreal world. Local commentators as well as outside observers often referred to this state of affairs as "magical realism," or the "dreamworld."

Milošević's technology of rule, as is now quite clear, involved constantly provoking crises that ranged from dissolving the parliament to inciting yet another war. Subjected to this never-ending series of crises, in which the very foundation of their existence appeared to be threatened, the citizens of Serbia often had a heightened sense of being in the midst of "making history." These crises give adrenaline rushes but also drain the organism, and, to use the medical idiom, undermine the immune system. Thus the anomie, or depression, prevalent in Serbia was not so much like a stagnant pool of enduring hopelessness but more like bewilderment mixed with fatigue from the cumulative crises. If cataloguing the bestiary of picturesque creatures that populated the Serbian imaginary was one of my tasks, the other was somehow to account for this protean anomie.

Irony, however, was not only a way that I expressed my ambivalent positioning or vacillation between amusement and depression. I was drawn to irony in the voices of people in Serbia itself. I found it in the conundrums of their life, and I ended up using it in the way I presented my findings. Irony was thus both what I discovered on the ground and what constituted one of my tools.

IRONY AS METHOD: THE DREAMING COLLECTIVE AND THE IRONIC AWAKENERS

I have already mentioned that I was on the lookout for felicitous condensations that encapsulated ambivalences and ironies. I found them in the raw material of everyday conversations, but my best source turned out to be not "private voices" of ordinary citizens but a number of excellent social commentators who picked up things that were "in the air" and encapsulated them in deft turns of phrase or poignant anecdotes. Commentators were as immersed in everyday life as anyone else in Serbia but also, in their professional role, capable of detachment and the kind of reflection that is enabled by a more synoptic view of the situation. It is not that I believe that ordinary people are incapable of detachment and reflection. They are, but only under certain circumstances. Exigencies of everyday life make most people most of the time relatively tolerant of incongruities. On the other hand, those who have the leisure and the professional obligation to comment pounce on these incongruities, and if their genre is a weekly column of, say, a thousand words, then what more economic way of exposing them than sophisticated irony? "Perhaps no other form of human communication," as Booth observed, "does so much with such speed and economy" (1974:13). Economy, too, was what urged me to look out for the most pregnant nodes in the Serbian imaginary, and they turned out to be various incongruities, conundrums, contradictions, and paradoxes. To expose them almost always entailed irony. Commentators were masters of the genre, and as a meta-observer (observer of observers) I distilled their ironies into my own catalogue.

This book could then be read as a series of "isn't it ironic that" statements and their unpacking. Isn't it ironic that Gypsies, the most despised outcasts in our moral universe, are the very image of our soul and through their music the essential conduit for it (chapter 2)? Isn't it ironic that lowlanders have their own lowlanders, and highlanders their own highlanders (chapter 3)? Isn't it ironic that the most noble among us turn out to be criminals, that civilized women fall for the brutish, primitive males, or that the feminized West rules over us hyper-masculine Serbs (chapter 4)? Isn't it ironic that we Serbs tend to owe our most intimate soul to our worst historical oppressors, the Turks (chapter 5)? Isn't it ironic that the most ancient people are also the youngest of nations, no more than adolescents (chapters 5 and 6)? And isn't it ironic that Serbs still exist, since what defines them is a predilection for collective suicide (modeled on the Kosovo battle they lost in 1389)? Isn't it further ironic that their Kosovo Choice of Heavenly over the Earthly Kingdom is invoked precisely in very earthly territorial claims (chapter 7)? Isn't it ironic that the best thing to be is a (symbolic) Jew (chapter 8)? Isn't it ironic that the most marginal state is at the same time at the very center of world power contests in Serbian conspiracy theories (chapter 9)? And, finally, isn't it ironic that my best informant may turn out to be a fictional character (chapter 10)?

The encapsulations of Serbian imaginary I formulated or found ready-made in Serbia could also be read as a series of oxymorons: Magical Realism and Turbo-Folk, Noble Criminals and Reverse Pygmalion (or Female as Culture vs. Male as Nature), the Peasant-Cosmopolitans (cultured but in a natural way) and the Most Ancient Young Nation, the Muslim Jews, and the Remnants of the Slaughtered People.

An imaginary that bristles with such incongruities and oxymorons is dreamlike indeed. The dream can encompass so much—the whole tropology (see Hayden White 1999), the oxymorons, the mixed metaphors,[6] the ambivalences and ambiguities, the unities of contraries, the twilight states, the in-betweenness, the well-formed and the ill-formed narratives, the poetics of opacity, or the national historiography as secondary revision. But it cannot encompass irony. Only an "awakened" mind can say, isn't it ironic that X is taken for granted (by another consciousness that relates to mine as dream relates to waking) while I know that the exact opposite is actually the case. Of course, there is lucid dreaming. But the lucid dreamer is constantly under the threat of thinking he is awake while he may still be dreaming. The nesting logic of Indian tales of dreamers dreamt offers, in fact, a good model for the structure of indefinite irony—the irony that tries to undermine and even deny itself, that is hard to pin down, the irony of my voice in this text.

To be an analyst of incongruities of social life is to be an ironist and a dream interpreter. Some of the ironic commentators I draw upon were, moreover, positioning themselves not only as dream interpreters but also as awakeners of the dreaming collective. I refrain from the explicit role of an awakener, but I use irony not only to voice the impossibility of finding my own place to stand but also as an indicator of the similar difficulties people in Serbia experienced in finding their own bearings.

This book presents some of the stories Serbs were telling themselves and others during the period that is, alas, most precisely glossed as the "Milošević years." Individual chapters try to disentangle the threads of these stories and bundle them together into packages of semi-stable molecules made of narrative and imagistic particles held together by the logic I discerned in them. The subject is a somewhat disembodied realm of the Serbian imaginarium, or the national dreamlife, but the vantage point from which it is accessed is definitely Belgrade-centric. The particles and molecules of this imaginarium, or its flora and fauna, were in a sense collected by "botanizing the Belgrade asphalt." The first chapter, then, introduces the idiosyncratically selected urban fragments, a personal take on Belgrade, the Capital of Serbian Imaginary.

ONE

Belgrade

Those lucky to wake up this morning in Belgrade can assume
that they have accomplished enough in their life for today.
To insist on something else in addition would be immodest.

—DUŠAN RADOVIĆ, *Beograde, dobro jutro,* 1975

This is how one early July morning in 1975, from the top of the tallest
Belgrade building, the Beogradjanka (lit., The Belgrade Girl), poet and
writer Duško Radović greeted the city in what was going to become the
legendary radio show, a city's sound-signature, that left a lasting imprint
on Belgraders' self-understanding and everyday speech. The show was
called "Good Morning, Belgrade." Duško Radović was a Yugoslav institution, comparable perhaps only to Dr. Seuss in the U.S. Generations
grew up on his children's poetry. His rasping voice had a dark, almost
misanthropic drone, his aphorisms a bitter, ironic bite. For a while the
city had a true sage implanting pithy reminders of decency and common
sense into the ears of semi-awake parents preparing to go to work and
children packing their schoolbags. His friend and the illustrator of all
his books, Dušan Petričić portrayed him as a moody hen perched on top
of Beogradjanka in what became one of the truly iconic representations
of Belgrade (FIGURE 1.1).

The sentence pokes fun at Belgrade-centered myopia, at the arrogance and self-centeredness of those capital city dwellers on whose men-

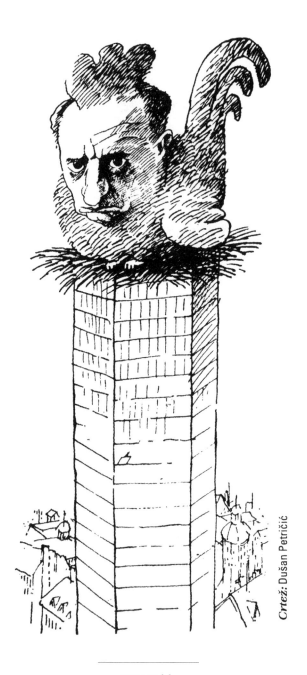

Crtež: Dušan Petričić

FIGURE 1.1.

Duško Radović perched on top of Beogradjanka.

DRAWING BY DUŠAN PETRIČIĆ

tal map the rest of Serbia is probably shrunk to a mere appendage, as in infamous U.S. maps drawn by New Yorkers, and criticizes the arriviste and social climber's superficiality and lack of perseverance. Radović here invokes a whole genre of laments over the shortcomings of native mentality—the propensity to rest on one's laurels or to stop any further efforts at the first sign of success (so fatal in soccer matches with Germans, where the brilliant Yugoslavs score early and then relax and lose to relentless, machine-like Germans who never give up). But underneath this dig there is also a genuine celebration of Belgrade as a good place to be, a grudging admiration that softens the irony's bite.

"He grew up on Belgrade asphalt" conveys concretely the identity of being nurtured by the city, as if literally having sprouted from it. To sprout from asphalt is to be streetwise, and products of Belgrade "asphalt jungle" are supposed to exhibit a peculiar combination of dangerous, violent temper, mischievous charm, and noble generosity that reaches its extreme and pure form in those legendary criminals who earn the title "Knights of Belgrade Asphalt."

Cobblestone is *kaldrma* in Serbian—a Turkish word that clatters crookedly over the tongue the way its bumps feel through the soles of your shoes or the way car tires rattle over it. Asphalt is opposed to the soil, the mud, the soft, fertile fields of village, the not-city. Kaldrma is internally opposed to asphalt. It is rough and unsophisticated, but it claims a longer urban pedigree.

The Street. The buildings stand one beside the other. They form a straight line. They are expected to form a line, and it's a serious defect in them when they don't do so. They are then said to be "subject to alignment," meaning that they can by rights be demolished, so as to be rebuilt in a straight line with the others (Perec 1999:46).

The characteristic dilapidation of surfaces, the variety of local building materials interacting with the local climate, and determinate periods of neglect produce unique patterns of peeling paint, bricks revealed by crumbled stucco, the rust spots, the patina of soot and grime, the broken façade ornaments, missing columns in balcony balustrades—Belgrade's peculiar *decay formula*. On top of that: the cacophony of roofs, the incongruity of architectural styles, slanted lines that unsettle the eye—a compounded crookedness (FIGURE 1.2).

FIGURE 1.2.

Belgrade roofs.

Seen from above, Belgrade appears angular, torn, gray, and hard, as if a staircase made of ten settlements piled one atop another, and all that in motion and ascending. You feel that incline as you walk the Belgrade streets: under your feet the ground wells up and demands that you climb it. Walls of Belgrade houses are rarely horizontal at the ground level or level in height; they either abruptly shrink, or grow, and sometimes it is almost grotesque how a house suddenly disappears into the ground or leaps out of it . . . Houses sit one on top of another because streets in many places carry each other on their heads . . . You enter a gate (kapidžik) of some little old house and the inner courtyard startles you: a miniature town on ten different levels, tall, short, hanging. When they demolish a tall building somewhere, three or four levels jump out from behind it. At the lowest a wooden Turkish shed (čatrlja) staring at you as if just dug it up. On the second level appear old, graveyardly calm trees. The third level is a plateau with a huge stone coat of arms in the middle. The fourth supports the foundation of some modern building standing in quite another city quarter. (Sekulić 2001:392) (translation mine)

Laundry is dried on strings or racks on balconies or outside windows. The intimacy of underwear and linen exposed to the public. This is below notice, in the realm of Perec's *l'infra-ordinaire*. Japanese dry their laundry the same way. That's perhaps one of the reasons why I felt so "normal" there. The Tokyo infra-ordinary is in many ways quite close to Belgrade's.

The bed is thus the individual space par excellence, the elementary space of the body (the bed-monad), the one which even the man completely crippled by debts has the right to keep: the bailiffs don't have the power to seize your bed. (Perec 1999:16)

Mattress, pillow, pillowcase, blanket, comforter, bedsheets (*dušek, jastuk, jastučnica, ćebe, jorgan, čarsav*) the infra-ordinary bed items, are all Turkish loanwords.

Turkish words for clock, stockings, slippers, soap, tap, coffeepot, sugar, spoon, boots, meat pie and yoghurt, money, pocket, change, small store, tobacco, bag, tavern, brandy, and carouser's ecstasy tend to map out the concentric worlds of the infra-ordinary.[1] Starting from the bed, utensils, and food, they spread out to activities that define that indefinite realm of neighborhood.

Neighborhood is *komšiluk* in Serbian, a Turkish word that carries a high charge of intimacy as opposed to its neutral-sounding Slavic equivalent *susedstvo*. The neighbor (*komšija*), it is said, is closer than the shirt. Serbian envy, as an endemic character trait, is to wish the *komšija's* cow to die (*da komšiji crkne krava*).

Komšiluk is, first of all, people who live in the same or adjacent apartment buildings. A typical apartment building will have an engineer, a national ballet dancer, a university professor, a policeman, a doctor, a postman, an electrician, a government clerk, a manual laborer, and a janitor (called *hauzmajstor*), living on the first floor, usually a jack of all trades who can fix plumbing, household appliances, the elevator, and the hall lights.

The range of people you call *komšija* could be extended beyond the extreme proximity of its primary reference, but not indefinitely. It runs the risk of appearing as fake familiarity as soon as it leaves the confines of what are mostly named city quarters or districts. Significantly, many of these named districts have Turkish names—*Čubura, Dorćol, Bulbulder*. A *Čubura* dweller is not, usually, a *komšija* to a *Dorćol* dweller.

The whole city could, however, at times genuinely feel as an intimate *komšiluk*. During periodic massive power shortages Belgrade would turn into an irregular patchwork of dark and light neighborhoods. Sometimes these blackouts would follow a planned pattern announced in advance; at other times they were unpredictable. "Serbian roulette" was said to be played by sticking your finger into a power outlet. Those without power would visit friends who had electricity across town, and those whose freezers couldn't work would throw parties in order to use up massive amounts of meat that would otherwise spoil. *Komšiluk* solidarity would then extend across the city. The ultimate feeling of citywide neighborliness came, according to those who experienced it, during the three months of NATO bombing in 1999.

There is one more highly significant Turkish word that maps a (conceptual) space as intimate and indefinite, as *komšiluk,* yet of a different order of magnitude. *Čaršija* originally meant the town square, market, or merchant's quarter. It now refers to a city's rumor mill, or "public opinion," but in a denigrating sense of small-town or village gossip, full of envy and backstabbing. To refer to Belgrade as *čaršija,* is to rhetorically reduce a capital of 2.5 million to a provincial town where public opinion is formed by men who sit, each clan in its own tavern, around the city square, enveloped in cigarette smoke. *Čaršija* is thus not a place but a creature that is part communicative practice/network, part a state of mind. Yet I have a clear image of a particular place in Belgrade as its physical locus. This is the square close to the city center surrounded by major media institutions (state radio and daily *Politika)* that boasts some of the most famous taverns (*kafane)* in Belgrade—*Pod Lipom* (Under the Linden), *Šumatovac, Grmeč.* A *kafana* is distinguished from a café (*kafić)*—a more recent, espresso-serving institution modeled on Italian cafes, even though you can drink coffee in it (usually Turkish); it is not exactly a "restaurant" either, even though you can eat there (sometimes quite well). When I picture the legendary node of the *čaršija* network—the tavern philosopher (*kafanski filozof)*—I picture him in *Grmeč.* Right next to *Grmeč* is a taxi stand where idle cabbies often play chess on the hood of a car. Taxi drivers are the mobile *čaršija.* As elsewhere some are talkative, others taciturn. They will often immediately switch into the intimate mode. One can engage in sociological analyses, friendly gossip, common lamentation, or political argument with a taxi driver.

The *kafana* is proclaimed with mystical awe (mostly by men) to lie at the core of "everything." A central unit of the *čaršija* rumor mill where tavern philosophers hold forth, this is where a certain unofficial, yet indispensable, "education" for young men is supposed to occur, where business is done, life, existence, and especially politics are discussed, and where, ultimately, the ecstasy of "*sevdah,*" which forms the core of the inexpressible Serbian soul, takes place.

It is often heard in Belgrade that *kafane* as well as cafés and restaurants are always full. This usually means, in mock or genuine shame before outsiders or in the mode of serious social analysis: "Who ever works in this city?" (there is pride, too—we know how to live). This is an old question. More pertinent, during the Milošević era, the question was: "Who has the money?" If it is noted that Belgrade *kafane,* cafés, and restaurants are, on the contrary, empty, this means: "If the *kafane* are empty, this is the end of the world as we know it." It's as ominous as saying that things are so bad even jokes have disappeared (FIGURE 1.3).

Once in Belgrade my feet immediately recognize how to compensate for the turns a bus would make on a familiar route.

FIGURE 1.3.

A Belgrade kafana scene.

Public transportation is buses, tramcars, and trolleys. Tramcars were Czech mostly, buses a mixture of Hungarian Icarus, and German MAN and Mercedes. The first trolley I remember was a clunky British Leyland. Some buses are of the accordion type with four instead of three doors. When opposition won in Belgrade in 1996, old and new buses were donated by European governments and even by Japan. Private buses of all conceivable types, shapes, colors, and states of disrepair were added to the mix. Japanese buses are painted yellow and adorned with a big red sun. Folklore has it that the Japanese stipulated that the city could keep the buses only on the condition that they were cleaned every day.

Careful observers will note variations in the intensity of body odors or strong perfumes, the quality of clothes and hairstyles, and passengers' general irritability according to the route, time of day, and social, economic, and political situation. One can also smell what people have been eating. That would vary according to the season.

Once a passenger, sitting above the wheel, fell through the rotting bus floor and was instantly killed. This happened in the late 1990s.

The young are supposed to give up seats to the elderly. Who counts as young and who as old is quite elastic and subject to dispute. When a young person remains seated, this is taken as a measure of general cultural and moral decline and gives the older person the right to openly castigate the young.

Public transportation routes tend to possess abiding characteristics. Bus No. 31 used to be No. 13 and may still be called the Dame (like the Queen in playing card). Bus No. 24 is elusive and rarely sighted. It manages to traverse the city center by squeezing through the narrowest of streets. The symbolically most pregnant is the tramcar No. 2, whose route describes the famous "Circle of Two" (*krug dvojke*) that supposedly encompasses the true civic, urbane heart of Belgrade. This magic circle either protects the true Belgrade from the barbarians that besiege it, or, in a more generous mode, transforms these barbarians, ever anew, into authentic city dwellers by some sort of alchemical osmosis.

The value of centrality is immense. What exactly counts as center is precisely the point of contention. A friend living very close to the "center" once declared that everything beyond Beogradjanka (and thus my neighborhood) is "periphery." A rather bold move (offending, of course, my pretensions to centrality), intended humorously, and exposing its own vulnerability—a more central "center" could conceivably be found that would relegate *him* to the periphery.

A young man is taking a pig on a leash across the main Belgrade square one murky December day in 1925. Behind him the National Theater; the pavement is predominantly cobblestone (*kaldrma*), numerous people on the street and no cars, but one person in something that could be a military uniform looks like he might be directing traffic. The photograph is being sold as a postcard on that same Republika square, in a Belgrade shop window—a store that specializes in more tasty Belgradiana aimed at the nostalgic Diaspora and foreigners.

Belgraders often comment that their city is in reality a "big village"... One constantly encounters small, but telling reminders that this is not the West, but rather some half-way station between Europe and the East, between the past and the present. Within five blocks of the National Theater the early morning hours are punctuated by the crow of roosters, and on the city streets one may be approached by a peasant in homespun dress offering a freshly slaughtered suckling pig which he has produced tail-first from a battered suitcase. (Simic 1973:70)

The smallness of the Belgrade airport, the tractors of the common sort used in villages that pull the luggage trailers, and plowed fields immediately beyond the single landing strip.

SOME IMAGES OF THE CITY

Children write compositions about "my native city" every year. An architect-philosopher, who was also the mayor of Belgrade (1982–1986), admiringly mentions one such composition that likened Belgrade to a perky little rooster. And it was the shape of the city, seen from a particular vantage point, that suggested this image—his tail is this part of the city, his wings that feature of its silhouette, his beak this prominent landmark. Belgrade is thus a little ruffled, small but cocky, alert, ready to fight. The city-philosopher admired the freshness of this image.

Phoenix rising from the ashes is a standard image of Belgrade—a city razed to the ground and rebuilt many times in its long existence. The image appears with tedious frequency in tourist brochures, popular histories of the city, and literary compositions young Belgraders write in grade school. Phoenix is invoked when Belgraders have to explain to visitors from Europe the absence of truly old architecture.

When Le Corbusier said that Belgrade was the ugliest city with the most beautiful location, he was looking at the result of centuries of destruction. Those who love and know this city today, know it not from what they have seen or touched. Its greater, perhaps finest part has disappeared without a trace and we shall never see, photograph or touch it again. But the part of it that is gone, that can never be reconstructed, belongs to history too, the history that is inside us. (Pavić 1998:1)

On the intimate side it is the sparrow who is the true bird mascot of Belgrade. Belgraders feel peculiar warmth toward sparrows because they are small, unpretentiously gray yet spirited, and they don't leave the city even in winter when all the avian traitors are gone to places where it's easier to live. A legend, not a widespread one, just an idiosyncratic literary fancy I came across, tells of how once, after one of those legendary battles for Belgrade, they found a sparrow shot through with three arrows under the Kalemegdan Fortress. In the *Mahabharata,* arrows fly so thick that they eclipse the sun. Here the hyperbola is of vastness in minuteness.

I experience Belgrade as a spine with ribs. The spine is a ridge of the main city axis and then you can descend along the ribs on both sides to the rivers. Like an upturned boat. The prow of that boat (now right side up) is the Kalemegdan Fortress, built by Celts and Romans, then Byzantines, Ottomans, and Austrians successively, jutting out and looking over the confluence of the rivers Sava (the largest Yugoslav river about 800 km long) and Danube. This is where, in the popular idiom, Sava and Danube "embrace." Matrimonial metaphors are also suggested by the fact that Sava is feminine and Danube masculine in Serbian. Danube is a carouser, a wanderer who passes through many countries before he snatches Sava under the Kalemegdan walls and takes her away. "Kalemegdan" is a Turkish word. Ottomans also called it *ficir bair*—a hill for contemplation.

This is traditionally the place one comes to in order to contemplate the city. If there is a unifying, core image to be discovered about this city, you are supposed to find it sitting at this promontory.

Kalemegdan is the place for pensioners who sit on benches and discuss local and global politics. You can hear snippets of such conversations as you pass by. Then mothers with children, young lovers, and grandparents with grandchildren. "To walk my grandchildren on Kalemegdan" is a phrase that sublimates the longing of Belgraders abroad, the ur-image of prodigal son of Belgrade's idyllic return.

This is a large park, with many a nook and cranny, perhaps a lover's paradise at night, but also a potentially dangerous place. There was once a genre of mugging there called "selling a brick." If you don't buy it, you get it in the head.

The fortress is the only part of the city that actually does have concrete remnants of Belgrade's long history. If the rest of the city is shallow or light in that respect, this prow is deep and heavy. It has a very deep Roman well. On the very tip of the promontory, there stands the obelisk of the Victor, perhaps the most prominent of Belgrade visual signatures.

In the 1970s the Bureau for Monument Preservation tried to negotiate with Belgraders who were pilfering the stones from the World War I military observation post left as a monument in the Pioneer Park right across from the Federal Assembly building. It was rumored that Belgraders found these stones perfect for pressing down the lids of the barrels where they fermented their cabbage in winter. Fermenting cabbage in the big barrel in your basement or cellar is a national pastime and pride. Every household head (*domaćin*) worth his salt boasts of secret procedures that make his cabbage the best. A key to the process is a good, heavy stone since by pressing the lid down it keeps the cabbage away from air. Apparently the monument offered exactly the perfect stones. This is a story as told by Dušan Radović of "Good morning, Belgrade" fame. He praises the Bureau for the sensible way it framed its appeal to Belgraders. It offered not money for stones returned but instead good cabbage-fermenting stones—for, Radović mused, a Belgrade *domaćin* doesn't need the money, he needs the stone. The success of this appeal, however, is unpredictable. So Radović suggests the following: Why shouldn't all Belgrade household heads get together and collectively ferment their cabbage. They could use the Roman well as the barrel and the statue of the Victor as the stone.

Vegetables and fruit are to be found in small, private grocery stores (*bakalnica* or *piljara*, both Turkish loanwords). It is hard, however, to divert Belgraders from open farmer's markets which they still consider the best place to get fresh produce. Markets are often quite big. A dense grid of covered stalls with heaps of seasonal produce. The vendors are a mix of peasants who sell their own produce and the middle-men (*nakupci*)—those who buy wholesale from peasants. It is often hard to tell the difference. There was a time when middlemen were feeling the pressure of official socialism's dislike for "speculators" (those who live not from producing but from buying and selling). They were also stigmatized as "inauthentic" peasants. Wholesomeness of produce is still directly associated with the concreteness of the authentic peasant standing in front of you at the stall. Any interpolation of monetary exchanges tends to spoil this aura of authenticity.

Haggling is expected and so is friendly banter when one is in the mood.

Otherwise very conscious of fine distinctions between urbanite and peasant, urbanites seem to enter into an egalitarian peasant-urbanite zone when shopping at the farmer's market. Attire can be very informal. This is where TV personalities, writers, opera singers, and other public personages can be seen wearing slippers and indoor clothing—worn out, shapeless clothes that should have been discarded long ago. Wearing such clothes outside one's apartment marks the territory of the most intimate *komšiluk*. Farmer's markets are usually a good walk, even a bus ride or car drive away from home, yet to these markets, too, is often extended the sphere of intimacy marked by home clothes.

Those of long urban pedigree (rare) indulge their romantic identification with idealized peasants as they are buying a kilo of potatoes. Those (almost everyone) who have recent peasant roots seem to be comfortable performing them in showing their farmer's market savvy (I can see through your peasant tricks—since I am one myself, ahem, under this urban veneer). Peasants or peasant-urbanite middlemen are urbane, too. They can switch that urbanity on or off as they read their customers. An urbanite buyer: "How much for this celery root . . ." Then, looking at it more carefully: "It's awful, it's all hollow." The peasant vendor: "You are hollow, you peasant!" (March 1995).

While big retail systems of socialism, such as department store chains, go out of business, or stand empty, the retail universe spills out onto the streets. The already empty sidewalks are further narrowed by rows of kiosks and stands—so Požeška Street, like many others, becomes a kind of Oriental bazaar (suk). Capilarization of retail brings about even smaller units—the hood (of a car) or a cardboard box. These could be considered a diminutive of a kiosk. The flea market spreads and becomes a panurban phenomenon . . . The kiosk is, without doubt, the most important architectural form of the Milošević era . . . The Keops pyramid or a Cathedral is built by those who have all the time in the world and believe that their complex edifices will retain their meaning in times to come. A kiosk is rigged up by the one who, based on previous experience, senses that his surroundings will as of tomorrow be devastated by floods, tornados, Huns, Avars, locusts, earthquakes, or volcanic eruptions, so he hopes to quickly get a few bucks and flee to somewhere a bit safer. (Prodanović 2002:109–110) (my translation)

What is sold in what kind of store got scrambled in the early 1990s. This mixing up, often totally unpredictable, of what properly belonged to separate established store genres would confuse and sometimes exasperate the natives. Some Belgraders felt this mixing very strongly as an abomination, yet another stomach-turning incongruity. The vehemence of such reactions points to a strong sense of propriety, of what a "normal" city should look like, a yearning for an "iron cage of rationality" that exhibits straight lines and puts things in their proper places.

SOME CITY TYPES

Since the city doesn't practice recycling of any sort, Roma have entered this empty niche and can be seen collecting cardboard and other recyclable materials from the street containers and hauling it in improvised carts to the peripheries where they sell it to a paper factory. Part of a disappearing urban soundscape is their yelling: "We buy scrap iron, we fix old umbrellas!" In the late 1990s strange vehicles appeared on the streets of Belgrade: some Roma have motorized their hand-pushed carts. A wonderful 2003 documentary, "Pretty Dyana," shows how Roma refugees from Kosovo lovingly rebuild Dyanas, the successors to the legendary Citroen CV2s, sometimes equipping them with radios, cigarette lighters, even miniature TVs, and rig them to their carts (Mitić 2003) (FIGURE 1.4).

Belgrade asphalt used to nurture a special breed of tough guy that is now lamented to have given way to new criminals without charm, dignity, honor, and magnanimity. Words like "ruffian," "hooligan," or

FIGURE 1.4.

A modified Dyana turned into
a cart on a Belgrade street.

"hoodlum" cannot quite capture the mix of mischievousness, a quick wit, and violence mixed with a soft, generous heart that is supposed to characterize the Belgrade *mangup, baraba,* or even *silos* (bully). Popular films often feature this type, with certain actors specializing in the role.

Sponsored girls (*sponzoruše*), a new type appearing in the mid-1990s, hang onto the arms of newly rich boys who park their luxurious cars and SUVs in the narrow street in Dorćol district, now known as "Silicon Valley"—thus named (with the gleeful anticipation of a foreigner's shock) after breast implants. *Sponzoruše* are a type that is defined not so much by outer looks but by the nature of the "contract" they enter into with their "sponsors." They are reputed to readily accept public humiliation and even physical abuse from their sponsors in return for expensive clothes and the "high life"—Belgrade style. *Sponsoruša* is a term of abuse; *sponsoruša* is always the other girl.

Pensioners playing chess on park benches and discussing politics are the abiding sight, a facet of *longue durée*. What is new is a shabbily dressed pensioner digging through the garbage container, an icon of utter degradation and misery.

Bride and groom exiting a church, followed by Gypsy bands, and departing in a convoy of horn-blaring, flower-and-towel-decorated, flag-weaving cars.

A Sunday mechanic under his twenty-year-old Fića in the street. A Fića was the true national car, the Yugoslav equivalent of the East German Trabant. This was a slightly larger version of the miniscule Fiat 500 "Topolino" boosted to 750cc that was produced between 1960 and 1985 by the same Zastava factory in Kragujevac that will later make Yugos. The Fića was so simple that almost anyone could fix it. Like a mule, it could take heavy abuse and carry unbelievable loads. When in the 1970s urbanites started building "weekend houses" (*vikendice*—the Yugoslav counterpart of Russian dachas), the bricks, cement, or cinder blocks for many of them were hauled, carload by carload, by the little car with a big heart. Souped up, fortified with roller-bars, and outfitted with Italian Abarth engine parts, the Fića raced in the special "National" Formula races and was immortalized in the cult movie *Nacionalna klasa* (Marković 1979) (FIGURE 1.5).

A WALK

My apartment is on the fourth floor. The building is new. My parents moved there a year after I left for Chicago in 1989. Together with a number of similar apartment buildings it was intended for government officials. The street is very narrow and used to be quiet and sleepy when it was the straightest route to my grade school.

The street is named after Hadži Milentije, an abbot of an important Serbian monastery, a participant in the 1804 uprising against Turks, a Belgrade Mitropolitan who had made a pilgrimage to Jerusalem, thus the prefix "Hadži" to his name. Most of its inhabitants are not likely to know all this (I had to look it up). Hadži as part of someone's name, however, exudes a certain Turkish aura and patina of the nineteenth century. It is divided in two parts by the steep, narrow Braničevska street. The second part ends at my grade school named after Svetozar Marković, turn-of-the-century socialist. This is the quieter part of the street now. One afternoon in 1995, sitting on my balcony, shots are heard from the

FIGURE 1.5.

A Fića on a Belgrade street.

direction of the school. A new restaurant has been built there recently
and is "frequented by mafia," they say. Drive-by shootings are happening
occasionally. Mitsubishi Pajeros often roar through the street in those
years. The vehicle of choice for the warlord Arkan and his gang, as well
as of those who aspire to that status. Arkan gets assassinated in 2000.

In the other direction, my street slopes gently down to the Karad-
jordjev park. Karadjordje, the leader of the First Serbian Uprising (which
Hadži Milentije fought in) camped there while besieging Turkish Belgrade in 1806. The whole lower part of the park, the core of my boys' gang
territory (we played cowboys and Indians, largely modeled on Karl May
novels) was emptied out in the late 1980s in order to dig the tunnel for
the metro. This part was later restored to its previous condition.

In February 1995, two days after I arrived in Belgrade, I marveled at
the entrance to the underground train station that appeared across the
street (Boulevard of the Yugoslav National Army, or JNA). There was a
metro sign, a map, a train schedule. It felt like a dream fragment or a

joke. It was that hard to imagine that Belgrade could ever have a true metro. The Belgrade Metro was the equivalent of the Golden Mountain, the Son of a Barren Women, a logical and empirical impossibility. Especially in Serbia in 1995.

The park is a long strip squeezed between the narrow Nebojšina Street and the wide Boulevard of JNA. They climb rather steeply to the highest Belgrade hill—the Vračar plateau that houses the National Library, the St. Sava Temple, and the monument to Karadjordje himself.

The National Library is a concrete building imitating a stylized traditional Serbian house. An acquaintance told me in 1995, in all seriousness, that one of the two German super digging machines (popularly called "caterpillars") "accidentally" got stuck right under the library while boring the metro tunnels. It must be that Germans have mined it and are waiting for an opportune moment to blast the library into the air. They tried, he said, and almost succeeded when they bombed Belgrade in 1941 destroying the old National Library in the process. Apparently they haven't destroyed some really important documents then, so they will try again. The very existence of these documents constitutes a deadly threat to Germans.

St. Sava Temple (Hram Svetog Save) resembles Istanbul's Agia Sophia. It is the third largest Orthodox temple in the world. Socialist authorities let the building, abandoned before World War II, recommence in 1985. In 1988 the shining brass dome, which had been constructed on the ground, was raised inside the building at the rate of two meters a day over a period of twenty days. In retrospect, the raising of the Temple coincided with the resurgence of Serbian nationalism through the cracks of the decaying communist ideology. The poet laureate of this new growth, Matija Bećković launched the phrase "The Temple is building us," inadvertently echoing a slogan of post–World War II communist rebuilding—"We are building the railway track, the railway track is building us."

At the tip of the park, several kiosks. One is of the old kind—selling cigarettes, lighters, playing cards, little one-deciliter liquor bottles, razors, soaps, shampoos, several other categories of small necessities and cheap toys. A newsstand kiosk selling only newspapers and magazines. In January 1994, just days before hyperinflation stopped, I used up a new 500 billion dinar banknote to buy newspapers at that stand.

Going downhill Boulevard JNA steeply, many low, rundown houses divided by narrow gates offer glimpses into inner courtyards. An empty lot overgrown with human-height weeds visible through a hole in the corrugated iron fence attracts my camera repeatedly, resulting in a photo collection spanning several years (FIGURE 1.6). The Boulevard finally enters Slavija, a circular intersection of no fewer than seven streets, a major city node, and one of the ugliest.

In the middle sits a circular lawn with a bust of Dimitrije Tucović, a prominent Social Democrat who died in 1914 in a war he vehemently opposed. His bones were moved under the bust from their original resting place in a remote Belgrade suburb by the new communist authorities after World War II. In the latest reshuffling of monuments, his will probably be returned to his distant suburb. Monuments of older national heroes are reconquering the city. Karadjordje and St. Sava already occupy the domineering height of Vračar plateau from where I descended. The St. Sava Temple, directly visible along St. Sava Street, dominates Slavija by appearing uncannily close, the eye tricked by its unsettling size.

Streets and squares already renamed during Milošević are getting renamed again. Two streets radiating from Slavija bear two names, and one bears three. Old names die hard since they are parts of people's mental maps. Those who knew Belgrade before World War II often continued to call streets by their old names even when they were massively renamed by the new communist authorities. Some streets and squares have reverted to these prewar names, some have acquired new ones, and a few have seen more than one recent change. Belgradians use a heterogeneous combination of these street names according to their age and personal spatial psychohistory undergirding their idiosyncratic memorization technique. Only taxi drivers have to know them all. Sometimes the street name you use acts as a code for your political orientation and may spark ideological clashes with your taxi driver.

On the ugliness of Slavija everyone agrees. It is considered unseemly, a scandal, and a shame that such a major thoroughfare is surrounded by low, dilapidated buildings. On the northeast corner, the so-called Mitić hole. A prewar businessman, Mitić planned to build the largest Belgrade department store there but was interrupted by World War II just as the foundations had been dug. Communist authorities deprived him of all his considerable property, and the hole remained. From 1946

FIGURE 1.6.

A hole in the fence.

to 1980 twenty-six plans were made for this space—none of which was realized. The architect-philosopher and mayor, Bogdan Bogdanović, filled the hole during his tenure (1982–1986) and made it into a park with a sundial. Criticized by experts and laymen alike, this is now seen as the best "temporary" solution of all.

Mrs. Dafina, a private banker who operated one of the two huge pyramid schemes during the hyperinflationary period of 1992–1993, destroyed the sundial in early 1990 to make space for a grandiose building. As she soon went bankrupt the accursed hole remained, and, surrounded again with the tall corrugated iron fence, it became a true weed jungle and gigantic junkyard inhabited at some point by several families of Roma refugees from Kosovo. The park is back, minus the sundial, and since Mitić's descendants dispute the land rights nothing is being built there.

On the eastern side, an empty parking lot and a few kiosks stand where once there was a movie theater famous for introducing Belgrade to soft porn, a bookstore, and the oldest city pharmacy. Another "transitional solution" lasting years. Kiosks came and went, huge billboards appeared in mid-1990, but shoeshine stands remained the same. They have colorful shoelace displays. Shoe polishers are traditionally Roma and can offer highly urbane, cosmopolitan conversations while they shine your shoes. Behind the emptiness of the parking lot a formerly dilapidated side of an exposed apartment building was painted over with an enormous yellow ad for coffee with a single window peeking out of a gigantic brown coffee bean.

During Milošević's years various kiosks proliferated around Slavija. Perhaps most prominent were the around-the-clock grill stands, at times densely packed into a whole miniature barbecue city whose smell gave the square its unmistakable signature. The smell of Serbian hamburgers, made with onion, of kebabs (ćevapčići) and other delicacies, clashed horribly for some with what they imagined a proper major square in a proper European city should look like. For those Belgradians, the barbecue city was an affront, yet another incongruity that could at times stand for all the other abominable categorical mixes of the Milošević era.

Marshal Tito Street was renamed during Milošević's rule as the Street of Serbian Rulers (Srpskih vladara) and renamed again as King

Milana Street (its pre–World War II name) after Milošević's fall. A friend
told me of an acquaintance who now collapses these many names and
calls it the "Marshal Milan" street. This is the route that forms the backbone of Belgrade—from Slavija through Terazije and all the way to Kalemegdan Fortress.

I will continue to call it Marshal Tito Street. It is lined with increasingly luxurious stores. Often glamorous, glittering windows set in low,
dilapidated buildings. The black obelisk of Beogradjanka now becomes
the dominant sight ahead. Right before Beogradjanka, on a corner with
Generala Ždanova (now Resavska), a narrow tramcar-bearing street
rising steeply toward St. Mark Church on the Boulevard of Revolution,
stands the Student Cultural Center. A cult place in the early 1970s when
for a brief period it was a major site of avant-garde artistic breakthroughs,
hosting such luminaries as Bob Willson, Josef Beuys, Oriana Fallaci, and
Petra Kelly, as well as Belgrade's own Marina Abramović who soon left to
become perhaps one of the world's most famous performance artists. In
1973, in what is now a legendary performance, Marina lay in the center of
a burning five-pointed star made of sawdust and almost died of carbon
monoxide poisoning.

When it was finished in 1974, Beogradjanka was a glittering epitome of modernity. The first four floors housed the largest Belgrade department store, the top was occupied by a local radio station, Studio
B. For at least a decade the department store held its high place in the
shopping hierarchy, a display case for comparative consumerist mu-
nificence of Tito's Yugoslavia. With the advent of Milošević's era it got
shabbier and gradually emptied out. The skyscraper itself continued to
be a major city landmark and a meeting place. More important than
the merchandise still displayed in the windows in the 1990s, both too
shabby and "socialist" to attract the newly rich, and too expensive for
the impoverished middle-class, became the hard currency dealers who
congregated in front. Usually young, strong, unshaven, leather-jacketed
men, the dealers conspiratorially hissed through their teeth: "*devize,
devize*" (currency, currency) which came out as *dzzzz, dzzzz*, probably
the most prominent sound-signature of the city during the years of the
UN-imposed blockade (1992–1995).

Two palaces, further down the street, used to house kings and
princes of both Serbian dynasties. From one of them King Alexander

Obrenović and his wife Draga Mašin were defenestrated in 1903 in an act of regicide that appalled Europe and contributed to the image of Balkan violence. The succeeding Karadjordjević dynasty demolished the palace and built a new one. In between the two palaces was a small park where the antiwar movement in Belgrade used to light candles in commemoration of those killed in the wars of Yugoslav succession, and to protest the politics issuing from the new palace that houses the Serbian Presidency and its main occupant, Slobodan Milošević. While undoubtedly a courageous symbolic gesture, this protest actually never provoked overt repression.

The street finally flows into Terazije, the true city center. Hotel Moscow and Hotel Balkan on one side, the first Belgrade arcade, Bezistan, on the other. Behind, St. Sava Temple still dominates the view down Marshal Tito Street; in front, the Albania Palace bifurcating the street into the promenade of Knez Mihajlova and Kolarčeva that leads to Republika Square.

Terazije (Turkish word for weighing scale) is an elongated square or a widening of the street. Felt as the heart of the city, and with sidewalks generous enough to support a significant crowd, Terazije belongs to that zone of highest symbolic import where a protest gathering carries weight. In March 1991 this is where students spent three days in protest and wrested significant concessions from Milošević just days after he managed to violently break the March 9 opposition rally at nearby Republika Square with the help of army tanks. This is where one could start drawing a map of Milošević-era Belgrade protests with the help of a convenient time line developed by the political scientist Slobodan Antonić (2002) that lists "seven crises" of the Milošević regime. The March 1991 protests would belong to the second crisis.

Kolarčeva, a short street that leads from Terazije to Republika Square, was, during the protest walks of 1996–1997 (fifth crisis), the site of a prolonged confrontation between the protesting citizens and the police cordon. When the opposition coalition "Together" (*Zejedno*) won major victories in the local elections, Milošević tried brazenly either to change the results or annul them as irregular wherever he lost. Protests in major Serbian cities started spontaneously around November 20, 1996. In Belgrade they lasted for two and a half months, where daily "strolls" (*šetnje*) in bitter cold winter had between one hundred thousand and two hundred thousand people on the street engaging in carnivalesque protests against the election theft. The protest was known as the "Yellow" or "Egg" Revolution, since pelting eggs at regime institutions was one of its weapons of choice. Republika Square was the center where "strollers" assembled every day after walking all over the city. When, after two months, the walks hadn't shown signs of abating, Milošević resorted to harsher police methods. In mid-January 1997 a cordon of heavily armored riot police started blocking the demonstrators in Kolarčeva and the battle of wills commenced. After loosing a few initial bouts in the wee hours due to fatigue, the police cordon was ordered to stay put round the clock with fresh reinforcements every two hours. Students, who led their own separate protests, then showed their stamina and ingenuity. For about a week students organized street theater, parties, and dances to the music of the "Blue Cordon" discotheque in front of the police lines. The blockade was finally breached on January 27, 1997, when Milošević dared not stop the Patriarch of the Serbian Orthodox Church leading the St. Sava Day procession through Kolarčeva.

When you enter Terazije you feel you have entered the city center. Yet Terazije is essentially a widened thoroughfare lined with hotels and stores. You are still propelled further. You can enter the Knez Mihajlova promenade, and that, in its own way, is a culmination of the Belgrade experience. If you continue past the Albania Palace through Kolarčeva you will enter Republika Square and feel that you have finally arrived. This is it, the central city square: a place to arrive at. It is a contained space, not inhumanly large yet just barely monumental for a capital's main square. One's eye quickly finds the essential element of a European city's central square—a larger-than-life, elevated horseman in a dynamic, forward-thrusting pose. The horseman is Knez Mihailo Obrenović (1823–1868), but the monument is known simply as "the horse." Predictably this is the most popular meeting place.

Republika Square is the place where citizens congregate for major events by default. At the culmination of the first crisis, this is where the opposition met on June 13, 1990, to pressure Milošević to hold the first multiparty elections under fair terms. Moving from the Square to the Federal Assembly where they found closed doors, the mass dispersed, but the staunchest thousand or so protesters were beaten by the police when they tried to demonstrate in front of the State TV in nearby Takovska Street, the main pillar of Milošević's propaganda machine. The State TV then became a prominent spot on the Belgrade map of protests, assuming the popular name of TV Bastille. TV Bastille, however, was always zealously guarded by the regime, and didn't fall until Milošević himself fell in October 5, 2000.

During the second crisis, the notorious March 9, 1991 demonstrations that were dispersed by police water cannons, tear gas, and, ultimately, army tanks, took place on Republika Square. Then, as in 1990, the storming of TV Bastille was planned and forcibly averted. The students then kept the protest going on Terazije over the next few days and managed to wrest concessions from Milošević.

The protests of the third crisis in 1992 focused on the Federal Assembly where between June 28 and July 5 opposition gathered some half-million people for the St. Vitus Day rally but to no avail. That year also saw the student protest that lasted almost a month and was centered on the Students' Square. This, and the subsequent fourth crisis, which extended, according to Antonić's time line, up to the Dayton Peace Accord in 1995, however, were marked less by protests than by the UN's total blockade of Yugoslavia that started with Resolution 757 in May 1992 and lasted until 1995, and by the hyperinflation of 1993. The most visible manifestations of this period lay further down the Boulevard of Revolution from the Federal Assembly that stands at its beginning—in improvised stands, cardboard boxes, and car hoods, where impoverished Belgraders foraged through goods that leaked through the blockade or brought their own to sell.

The icons of that period were the ubiquitous hard currency dealers hissing *dzzzz, dzzzz,* and plastic 1.5-liter Coke bottles used to sell gasoline on the streets, out of private apartments, and along highways. The major "pipeline" for smuggled gasoline ran through the stretch of the Serbian-Romanian border along the Danube between Veliko Gradište and Golubac—the "Serbian El Dorado," as it was called. Gasoline leaked from Hungary and Greece, too. "Super" smuggled from Greece was green, and "Shell Original" was red—both kinds were apparently preferred by discerning customers to gasoline smuggled from Romania. An enterprising citizen offered gasoline dyes to remedy this situation in the following ad in the daily *Politika* of April 21, 1995: "Boost your gasoline sales. Original (green, red) color. Fuel barrels."

Belgrade University (BU) doesn't have a campus. It is more an umbrella concept than a concrete something one can see or touch. What exists concretely are the Faculties—enclosed universes, each with its own building, dispersed throughout the city. Students' Square, a short walk from Republika Square, does, however, gather up a few Faculties around it (Philosophy, Philology, and Natural Sciences, as well as the BU Rectorate). The newest building is the Faculty of Philosophy that houses the Psychology, Pedagogy, Andragogy, Philosophy, Sociology, History, Art History, Archaeology, and Ethnology Departments. It overlooks a sizable plateau that at various times of the year accommodates restaurant tables, used-book sellers, and skateboarders. This is also the headquarters of student protests. Students are, without a trace of irony, referred to as "academic citizens," and there is a sense that they belong to a different order of existence, a separate academic state. Students tend to be seen as politically unsullied; they are sacred cows and there are some sixty thousand of them. Thus, when they mobilize, they represent a political power in its own right. The Faculty of Philosophy is often, though not always, the initiator of student mobilization. The plateau is a heavily symbolically charged place on that account, and it has been the major gathering point, as well as a stage for the student protests of the Milošević era (two major ones occurred in the summer of 1992 and the winter of 1996–1997). Sandwiched between the street that leaves Republika Square and the promenade of Knez Mihajlova, the plateau has become a major node in the circulatory flow. The plateau is now dominated by the bookstore ПЛАТО (Plato), the best in Belgrade, whose enterprising owners run a bar upstairs, and an excellent café restaurant that often features live jazz.

Knez Mihajlova is the main city promenade, a pedestrian-only zone familiar in Mediterranean and Balkan cities. Belgraders, especially those who self-identify as more urbane, may play a game when strolling together: whoever meets more acquaintances along the length of Knez Mihajlova wins. When acquaintances are met, this means that Belgrade is still its old self; when no acquaintances are met, it is lamented that "our kind of people" have all dispersed and the city is now filled with some other kind of people, the unfamiliar newcomers. Crises, changing musical tastes, and turns of political climate all find visible signs in Knez Mihajlova. Nationalistic and war-related kitsch appeared on improvised stands in the early 1990s, and disappeared when Milošević turned away from warmongering after his breakup with Bosnian Serbs in 1995. An exhibition of war kitsch appeared in a gallery on Knez Mihajlova only a short while after this ethnographic material disappeared from the street. After several years of domination, turbo-folk cassettes gave way to the music from the happy Tito years and pirated film DVDs.

Starting at the Albania Palace, where Terazije Square ends, Knez Mihailova passes by Republika Square, the Faculty of Philosophy plateau, and the Serbian Academy of Arts and Sciences and continues past British and German cultural centers to the Academy of Fine Arts at the end. Beyond it, across the tramcar tracks, lies Kalemegdan Park.

TWO

Serbia's Position in European Geopolitical Imaginings

Starting in the mid-1980s the dominant Yugoslav rhetoric of self-management socialism, brotherhood and unity, and non-alignment came to be increasingly upstaged by the narratives of national identity. These narratives fed off one another in an escalating spiral and provided the ideological justification for the wars that tore the country apart in the 1990s. In their tight dialogical embrace, the opposed narratives of breakaway republics and Yugoslavia's constituent nations often mirrored each other. Mutual grievances, resentments, and conflicting claims of these stories were woven out of local historical detail, but they were all framed by, and oriented toward, a wider European context—that of revived pre–Cold War narratives that emerged as the Iron Curtain dissolved and that replaced the symbolic geography of Yalta with the one long predating it. This wider symbolic geography never completely determined the Serbian imaginary in all its local detail and pragmatic workings, but it did, nevertheless, significantly constrain, frame, and shape it.

THE VIEW FROM THE KALEMEGDAN FORTRESS

The Kalemegdan Fortress is one of the first places Belgraders take their out-of-town visitors. For Belgraders themselves Kalemegdan Park is where they might have played hooky in high school, where they went for outdoor rock concerts or basketball games, where they kissed on the park bench, pushed babies in strollers, and, finally, walked their grandchildren. That Kalemegdan is the privileged spot from which to contemplate the city may rarely come to everyday consciousness, but it is true that there is something about two large rivers coming together under an ancient fortress, the plains opening to the north, the rolling hills on all other sides, that may invite thoughts about how this place relates to more distant lands and ages past.

Kalemegdan was taken precisely as such a "hill for contemplation," a *ficir bair*, as the Turks called it, in a book published in Belgrade in 1938, reprinted in 1991, and again in 1992 by the Belgrade City Library, itself situated at the point where the main promenade of Knez Mihailova flows into Kalemegdan Park. The book is titled *A View from the Kalemegdan Fortress: An Essay on the Belgrade Man,* and was written by Vladimir Velmar-Janković (1895–1976), a dramatist, novelist, critic, and psychologist who studied law in Budapest and Zagreb, and who worked in the Ministry of Education in Belgrade between the two world wars.[1]

Velmar-Janković contemplates Belgrade as the center, the model, and the microcosm of the nation. Belgrade is the avant-garde, both in the sense of prefiguring the changes that await the whole nation and as a literal military outpost, the forward shield (buttress) of the nation, "the last sharp wedge of highlanders' will for survival, thrust into the plains out of the mountain massif that always sustained us" (1992:20).

The book is a mix of Romantic national pathos, nuanced ethnographic detail, sober sociological analysis, and political conservatism. Velmar-Janković was a Serb educated abroad (in Central Europe) who decried the snobbish contempt that those like him felt for Belgrade's many failures to live up to European standards, but was equally critical of those who languished complacently in the comforts of its Balkan backwardness.

Belgrade is, for Velmar-Janković, a mill for producing the urbanite "psychological amalgam" out of the autochthonous peasant Serb from the mountains combined with the civilization washing over him from the northern plains, a mill that is "not up to speed, with new additives constantly tried out, the miller himself still at a loss, the grindstone not yet of the right weight and properly adjusted" (ibid.:32). What this imperfect grindstone produces is the "man of the Belgrade orientation," a transitory being with all the attendant flaws and advantages, which Velmar-Janković goes on, quite perceptively, to list and analyze. This

man is not just the literal inhabitant of Belgrade; he is what all the Serbs
are becoming.

Belgrade is both a part, and container, of oppositions and their
mediations that themselves tend to exhibit a nesting, fractal nature. It
mediates between the mountain hinterlands (which stand for idealized
peasant tradition, patriarchy, and Byzantine/Ottoman legacy) and plains
to the North from where the European civilization brings its suspicious
gifts. At the same time it refracts these larger oppositions between North
and South, East and West, Europe and the Orient, or mountains and
lowlands in its own internal idioms of mud (peasant) opposed to asphalt (urbanite) or, recursively, of asphalt (Western urbanity) opposed to
cobblestone (*kaldrma*) (Turkish urbanity). Belgrade is a wobbly, erratic
mill for grinding out the amalgamated, transitory beings out of disparate
and perhaps incommensurable elements.

From Kalemegdan Fortress Velmar-Janković worriedly surveys the
sources of precisely these elements that make up the main ingredients,
orientation points, or commonplaces of Serbian national imaginary. To
the South, the rolling hills and rich soil of Serbia's heartland rises to the
mountains of epic patriarchalism, the Byzantine frescoes, the afterglow
of the vanished Serbian Empire, and the Ottoman legacy. To the East,
in the distance, Moscow—the Land of the Slavic Soul but also of Communism as an alternative. And a gaze over the rivers to the northern
plains reveals the direction from which European civilization comes
to Belgrade. And it comes mediated by the Serbs educated, just like
Velmar-Janković himself, "over there (*preko*)," the so-called *prečani* (lit.,
"overthereians") who got their new ideas and their civilizational veneer
in the former Habsburg lands—the third-rate Europe, Velmar-Janković
quips alluding to wider European civilizational hierarchies.

HIERARCHIES OF CENTRAL EUROPE

Central Europe is a good place to start examining Serbia's position in
European symbolic geography. Historically it is Serbia's most proximate
source of (ambivalently received) "Civilization." Central Europe was,
moreover, a site of a major attempt to realign and reinterpret existing
cold war European geopolitical imaginings during the 1980s, and it did
provide some directly relevant contexts for internal Yugoslav realign-

ments, especially the Serbian-Croatian rivalry that I pursue here in some detail.

During the mid-1990s I tended to pass through Central Europe on my way from Chicago to Belgrade. One still could not fly directly to Belgrade because of the UN sanctions against Serbia. In the summer of 1993, and the winter of 1994, I flew from Chicago to Budapest and then took a minibus to Belgrade. In the summer of 1994 I flew with Czechoslovak Airlines, and we had an overnight stay in the hotel Kladno some 25 km from Prague. I took the metro downtown, and my first pilgrimage was to Charles University. I roamed the empty halls of the second floor where my grandmother studied English literature in the 1920s. I never met her, for she perished in the Croatian concentration camp just as Tito's partisans were about to liberate it at the end of the war. When this frail Jewish girl from Prague was about to marry my grandfather, a Prague-educated Jewish architect, and join him in his native Sarajevo, her Prague relatives were convinced that she was going to enter a *harem*. For them, Sarajevo was the city where they killed Archduke Franz Ferdinand and his wife in 1914—a city of killers and barbarians.

What citizens of the former Habsburg lands thought about Sarajevans or Belgraders in the 1920s or 1930s may seem largely irrelevant for the divisions of the Cold War. The Prague-Sarajevo axis belonged primarily to the North-South "gradient of depreciation," as I like to call it, while it was the West-East axis that ordered the Cold War symbolic geographies. As Larry Wolff argued, the rhetoric of the Iron Curtain and the Western representations of the socialist bloc countries relied for their persuasiveness on much older European imaginings that started with the Civilizational Maps of the French Enlightenment (Wolff 1994). A project of redrawing this map that started by realigning its West-East axis, however, ended up reactivating the old Central European North-South gradients.

The Berlin Wall was still standing firm, apparently indestructible, when a group of intellectuals from Eastern Europe embarked on a project of boundary remaking. Starting in the early 1980s with influential articles by Jenö Szüch, Czeslaw Milosz, and Milan Kundera, soon joined by Václav Havel and György Konrád, the old notion of Central Europe was revived in a new form as a realm defined in terms of carefully selected cultural traits and historical genealogies (see Schöpflin and Wood 1989).

In extricating themselves from Eastern Europe, the proponents of Central Europe defined their cultural zone in opposition to the rest of Eastern Europe, and transferred the odium they received from the West further to the East. While the project was still purely in the realm of imagination during the mid-1980s—"a search for a cultural identity, a mixture of Habsburg nostalgia and postcommunist utopia," as Jacques Rupnik (1994:92) put it—it was the Soviet Russia that stood as the most important contrastive other. Commenting on a passage from Konrád, Timothy Garton Ash was to observe, in 1986:

> We are to understand that what was truly Central European was always Western, rational, humanistic, democratic, skeptical, and tolerant. The rest was East European, Russian, or possibly German.
>
> The clearest and most extreme articulation of this tendency comes from Milan Kundera. Kundera's Central Europe is a mirror image of Solzhenitsyn's Russia. Solzhenitsyn says that communism is to Russia as a disease is to the man afflicted by it. Kundera says that communism is to Central Europe as the disease is to the man afflicted by it—and the disease is Russia! (Garton Ash 1989:184–185)

The Balkans were sometimes included in Central Europe, sometimes divided between Central Europe and Eastern Europe along the dividing line of Catholicism and Orthodoxy, and sometimes seen as belonging wholly to Eastern Europe together with Russia, but at that early stage Central Europe was not yet explicitly defined in opposition to the Balkans. It was only in the early 1990s, when the Central European project was "harnessed as an expedient argument in the drive for entry into the European institutional framework," that the Balkans "first appeared as a dichotomical opponent, sometimes alongside with, sometimes indistinguishable from Russia" (Todorova 1997:159–160).

The first to gain a foothold into the European institutional framework, and to be invited to join NATO, were precisely the three core countries of the Central European project: the Czech Republic, Hungary, and Poland. Though there is no denying that there were sound infrastructural, economical, and political advantages[2] that made these particular countries most eligible, one should not underestimate the power of European geopolitical imaginings that they were in the best position to exploit as symbolically the "Westernmost" and thus the highest in the East European symbolic pecking order.

During the time when the world was divided between the First and the Second, Yugoslavia opted for the Third, defined, however, not by its backwardness and poverty but as the progressive and proud Non-Aligned movement.[3] The West acknowledged Titoism as a special case of non-Soviet (or even anti-Soviet) Communism, and supported Yugoslavia as a strategically important buffer between the two blocs. Yugoslavs thrived on that in-between status which brought them, among other things, Western financial infusions and a higher standard of living through Tito's skillful brinkmanship between East and West.

People in Eastern Europe also acknowledged that, compared to them, Yugoslavia was "Western." But when, after the Wall fell, the East rushed to join the West, Yugoslavia ended up being pushed further to the South.

In 1997 Garton Ash reflected on this project:

> In the 1980s, when I and others popularized the notion of "Central Europe," it was directed due east against the Soviet Union, and against undifferentiated Western perceptions of a single Soviet bloc. The message was: Siberia does not begin at Checkpoint Charlie. In the early 1990s, I watched with some alarm as the cultural canon of "Central Europe" was turned to point south—to privilege the new Visegrad group of states (Poland, Hungary and what was then still Czechoslovakia) over Bulgaria, Romania and the rest. Now, the message was: If you had Western Christianity, the Austro-Hungarian empire and brown coffee with Schlagobers (Austrian-style whipped cream), then you were predestined for democracy. Orthodox, Ottoman Empire, Turkish coffee: Doomed to dictatorship! (Garton Ash 1997)

Viennese and Turkish coffee as metonymic markers distinguish two poles of a dichotomy that long predates the 1980s, a dichotomy that moreover tends to get recursively reproduced on both sides. The resulting map, where the decreasing Vienneseness shades into increasing Turkishness along the diagonal northwest-southeast gradient, although it is activated only intermittently, still exhibits a tenacious grip on European mutual stereotyping.[4] The question is how do those who are lower on this gradient of depreciation react to their stigma?

Goffman points out that it is possible for a group stigmatized by the larger society of which it is a part to have a separate system of honor, to be insulated by its alienation and protected by identity beliefs of its own and thus seem not to be impressed or repentant about failing to live up to what is demanded of it. This possibility, he writes, "is celebrated in exemplary tales about Mennonites, Gypsies, shameless scoundrels, and very orthodox Jews" (Goffman 1963:6–7). It is thus possible for a group, or only some of its members, not to internalize the scale of values of the wider community (in this case the dominant European values) that puts it near the bottom. It could be argued that, at least during the Cold War, most Yugoslavs were firm in their separate "identity beliefs" or "systems of honor" that hinged on self-definition as outside the West-East divide. Even before that, one could argue that Serbs, in particular, largely refused to judge themselves by Austro-Hungarian or later Central European standards. In fact, to this day the Sarajevo assassination is seen by Serbs within their "system of honor" as a supremely heroic act, a symbol of the just struggle for liberation. To the best of my knowledge, most Serbs are not at all concerned that from the Central European perspective this was seen, as my distant Jewish relatives in Prague saw it in the 1920s, as the supreme evidence of their Balkan violence.[5]

Yet the Austro-Hungarian Empire, or Central Europe in its many incarnations, has arguably been the most relevant European source of civilizational and cultural models for Serbia. At the crucial time of initial modernization and state building in Serbia in the mid-1800s, it was precisely the Serbs educated in the Austro-Hungarian Empire who laid down the foundations for education, the judiciary, and government in Serbia.

This means that we can expect to find both cases within Serbian society: those who do and those who do not internalize the Central European scale of values. A distinction has to be made between opposing or inverting these values (which still implies buying into them), on the one hand, and being indifferent or oblivious to them, on the other. The line is hard to draw, but the analytical distinction is perhaps useful to bear in mind.

I witnessed how both these attitudes can coexist when, in the summer of 1995, Hungarian writer György Konrád visited Belgrade. The hall in the venerable Kapetan Mišina Foundation building on the Student Square was overflowing; there were three professional TV camera crews present; and quite a bit of the intellectual elite of Belgrade was in evidence. Konrád was one of the main creators of the Central European idea, and on this occasion he magnanimously included Serbia in that imagined realm. After the talk, an ordinary-looking, middle-aged man stood up and asked:

> On what account do both you and I belong to Central Europe? I am from Serbia, you are from Hungary, but I never heard anybody here, neither teacher nor father or mother, neither a priest nor a politician, neither a writer nor a poet speak, think and write as you do. So what is that? Between you and me there is a huge difference.

As the question was being translated for Konrád, I overheard the following exchange between two women in the audience:

> FIRST FEMALE VOICE (IRONICALLY): "We are the *muddy* Balkans . . . Novi Sad [capital of the northern region of Vojvodina] is Central Europe and Belgrade is Balkans.

> SECOND FEMALE VOICE: Yes, yes, you are absolutely right, perhaps Zemun is still [Central Europe][6]

Konrád answered through his interpreter:

> A character from Molière didn't know that he was talking in prose and when he was told that he talks in prose, he was greatly surprised (laughter from the audience). Yes, just like that. I saw many couples from Cracow and Budapest and Novi Sad who seemed to me characteristically Central European although they themselves probably never uttered that word. In their way of life I see something in common. If we get a bit away from our home then we can better observe what is common. This gathering, for instance, so animated, and even a bit wild, is possible only in Central Europe (applause from audience).

Konrád, who is known to have excluded the Balkans from his beloved Central Europe in the past, was here extending this realm of culture to the Serbs. The year was 1995; Serbia was an international pariah. The Czech Republic, Poland, and Hungary were already seen as the formerly East European countries most likely to join NATO in the near future. What are we to make of this man, whose question could be interpreted as a declaration of cultural independence from Central Europe?

He seemed genuinely surprised that Serbia could be considered a part of Central Europe. Konrád's answer, on the other hand, sounded disingenuous. There was a taste of condescension in his claim to privileged knowledge of an objective observer from outside.

The audience sided with Konrád and applauded. In the comments I caught on my tape-recorder I could feel antagonism toward the man who asked the question, perhaps even shame and embarrassment one feels when a retarded family member who has been kept out of the way makes a show of his stupidity in front of honored guests. Those two Belgrade women were accepting the hierarchies of Central Europe, and, in what could be called the backstage attitude of self-recognition, they were admitting to each other, just between themselves, that whatever Konrád might have said, they knew Central Europe extends only as far as Novi Sad or at most Zemun—from Belgrade to the South it is "the Balkan *mud*."

CROATIA AND SERBIA, OR
MILK COFFEE AND TURKISH STAKES

Garton Ash used Turkish and Viennese coffee as diacritics or idioms of major symbolic geographical distinctions. Another substance, mud, was used by a member of Konrád's audience as a marker of Balkan backwardness. We will track these idioms as we go west to neighboring Croatia for, in this matter of symbolic geographies, Croat and Serbian narratives are not merely mirroring but co-constituting each other and thus are highly mutually illuminating.[7]

Croatia and Serbia could be seen as relating to each other analogously to the way Kundera's Central Europe relates to Solzhenitsyn's Russia. Some Serbs can sometimes admit that their Balkanness is, like Communism, a disease, and Croats can say they have it, too, but that *the disease is Serbs!* They can say that they have been "kidnapped" from the West by the Serbs, and that once they throw off that yoke they can return to "Europe," where, anyway, they have always belonged.

As could be expected, there are striking parallels between the end of the 1930s, when Croatia struggled for autonomy within Serb-dominated Yugoslavia, and the early 1990s, when they won complete independence. One indicator, among many, is that a book by Henri Pozzi, *Black Hand over Europe,* originally published in London in 1935, was reprinted in Zagreb in 1994.

What Pozzi (1879–1946) had to say in 1935 was music to some ears in 1990s Croatia:

> The Orient Express takes twenty hours to go from Milan to Zagreb in the heart of Croatia. It takes seven to go from Zagreb to Belgrade. Yet the difference, moral and material, is greater between Zagreb and Belgrade than it is between Milan and Zagreb.
>
> Therein lies the root of all the trouble between this Balkan Belgrade and this European Zagreb. Yugoslavia is the scene of a conflict between two mentalities and two civilizations . . .
>
> These two people are typified in their two chief cities. Zagreb by its atmosphere, the lay-out of its streets and homes, by its churches and stores and its cafes and hotels, is occidental. Belgrade, despite its transformation since the War, its modernism, and its tremendous growth in population, remains an oriental city. Centuries of barbarous domination, plus the Asiatic and Slavonic influences, have impregnated it with Balkanism.
>
> The Serbs are Balkan to the marrow.
>
> How different is Zagreb and the whole of the Croat lands! Their spacious and solid homes, orchards and prairies as well kept as gardens, are monuments to the method, harmony and intelligence applied everywhere!
>
> Think then of these two warring mentalities thrown together into this cockpit of a country. The Serb, filled with Slav mysticisms and Ottoman brutality; The Croat, emancipated by a long association with the Western world. Unity, under such conditions, is but an empty dream. (Pozzi 1994:9–10)

This is the kind of Balkanist discourse in the West to which official and dominant Croatian anti-Balkan discourses could appeal. The problem is that though grudgingly admitted to membership in the West, in the eyes of at least some of that "Europe" Croatia is still often seen as Balkan. Rasza (1997) puts it cogently:

> There are obvious reasons why Croatia should be sensitive to its classification as Eastern or Western. Croatia has fallen on both sides of the important historical divides of East and West, divided Christianity, Europe and the Balkans, the communist and the "free" world. Even Yugoslavia itself belonged to an ambiguous world where it was East to the West and West to the East. More importantly, Croatia is painfully aware that it is perceived as Eastern and Balkan in the only place where that judgment

ultimately counts, in the West. For example, when Tudjman, Milošević and Izetbegović meet, the Western headlines do not read "Two Balkan Leaders and a Central European Leader Meet," rather, they speak of "Balkan Leaders." (See also Lindstrom and Rasza 1998; and Jansen 2002)

An eminent Croatian ethnologist, Dunja Rihtman Auguštin analyzed some Croatian responses to this predicament. "The state media," she summarizes, "do not specify what the Balkans are, because, after all, we all know it!"

> They are the emblem of deceitful and treacherous political behavior of those *others*, and of backwardness and primitivity of those same (we know who). In all respects the very bottom of the pit, a black hole in the Southeast of Europe into which all those who conspire against Croatian independence and young democracy are trying to push it by force even though Croatia and Croats do not deserve it. (Rihtman Auguštin 1997:29)

Both the party in power and the opposition in Croatia seemed to agree that the Balkans were a black hole and a quagmire (*živo blato*), but the former saw it outside Croatia proper, whereas the latter saw it inside. What was a distinction between entity "Croatia" and entity "Serbia" got recursively reproduced inside entity Croatia. Going up the scale of inclusiveness, it is easy to show that this distinction is a local fractal inflection of a much more inclusive civilization-barbarity opposition that originated in Europe. A salient relationship could be reproduced (perhaps couched in different idioms and with peculiar twists) all the way down to a single individual who might find the opposition within his or her own self (see Irvine and Gal 2000:38). Although any relationship might be subject to recursiveness (or what is still referred to as Evans-Pritchard's "segmentary logic" among anthropologists), in practice we are most often dealing with binary oppositions. Recursive iteration of a salient dichotomy might resemble a "nesting" (matriushka dolls, Chinese boxes), or, if the dichotomy is spatialized, it might appear as a "gradient." Pragmatically what matters most often is whether your immediate neighbor is symbolically south or north of you, and compared to this situational dichotomizing, the gradients tend to be constructs of a more theoretical, or synoptic, view. This is not to say that gradients are never explicitly invoked in everyday conversations. A good example is the Yugoslav folk saying—*što južnije to tužnije* (lit., the more south, the sadder). This is explicitly a North-South gradient of "sadness," where "sad" most often oscillates ambiguously between sad as in "the songs get more melancholy" (as you go from Slovenia to Macedonia) to sad as in a sorry state of affairs in general. Nevertheless, fractal oppositions or gradients are, in my experience, much more often expressed in terms of concrete diacritics of identity such as coffee or mud viscosity (from ordinary to sticky mud, and all the way to quagmire). These indexes of group identity are notoriously prone to what Irvine and Gal called "iconization" (ibid.:37). From being an indicator of a group identity they become icons of mentality, and groups become like the brews they drink or like surfaces on which they walk. Such index/icons could then constitute (shifting and layered) maps of identity, and it is these maps I want to explore next.

To take up Rihtman Auguštin's advice, in tracing out the Balkan one-upmanship games (especially the Serb-Croat ones) we could do worse than to follow a great literary anthropologist, Miroslav Krleža.[8] In his four-volume novel, *Banners* (*Zastave*), for instance, Krleža chronicles the conflict between old Emerički, the Prime Minister of the Royal Croato-Slavonian-Dalmatian government, and his son Kamilo during the first decades of the twentieth century amid the complexities of Croatian politics vis-à-vis Vienna and Budapest.

Kamilo's great-aunt Amanda, born in Zagreb but living most of her life in Vienna, is dreaded by the Zagreb branch of the Emerički family. She is "a typical Austrophile snob," a strict arbiter of taste who mercilessly criticizes Zagreb's provincial manners: "You all dip your croissants into milk coffee like Balkan Gypsies," she admonishes her Zagreb family (Rihtman Auguštin 1997:33; Krleža 1982:235).

Viennese (milk) coffee is a prominent marker of Central European identity. Who drinks Viennese and who drinks Turkish coffee carries serious geopolitical consequences, as Timothy Garton Ash reminded us. Viennese coffee is associated with a bourgeois lifestyle and often stands metonymically for the whole region, just as Gypsies can stand for the Serbs or the Balkans as seen from the Austro-Hungarian perspective. The problem for Aunt Amanda, moreover, is not so much the coffee but the dipping. Keeping substances separate is a matter of the "civilizing process"—mixing itself is barbarous. And though Parisians can afford to dip their croissants, the Zagrebians dare not (at least not before those of them who made it to Vienna).

Viennese coffee reappears as a metonymic marker of mentality when old Emerički is contrasted with the Serb Stevan Mihailović Gruić, nicknamed Stevča, his student friend from Vienna where they both studied law. "All in all, my brother," Stevča tells old Emerički, "we who are coming out from under the Turkish stake are wiser than all of you who are living on Viennese milk coffee"[9] (Rihtman Auguštin 1997:33; Krleža 1982:338).

Viennese coffee here stands for being spoiled by civilization, and Stevča uses "Turkish stakes" and the horribly prolonged agony of dying impaled on them (favorite Ottoman punishment) in order to claim both a greater wisdom that supposedly comes from greater suffering and a high moral ground accorded to victimhood. Turkish stakes, of course, could be contrasted with Turkish coffee on the Serbian side of the Croat-Serbian comparison. Definitely an important marker of all the formerly Ottoman lands, Turkish coffee would in such an internal Serbian contrast stand for Oriental "sensuous pleasure" as a counterpoint to Oriental "cruelty,"[10] It is, however, conceivable that in another context Turkish coffee might be contrasted to Viennese coffee as, for instance, a stronger, darker, and more manly brew, in the manner in which Andalusian wine might be compared to Asturian cider in Spain. Comestibles, and especially such symbolically potent brews as coffee or wine, are among the richest idioms for creating what Fernandez (1988) calls "contrastive places."

When in his old age Stevča visits old Emerički he, however, lines up on his side defending the Austro-Hungarian status quo. As a Viennese student, old Stevča, now a retired Serbian minister, vehemently denounces the Balkan mentality of Serbs and upholds the virtues associated with Viennese milk coffee—Habsburg orderliness and cleanliness, their culture and civilization. Krleža manages to pack into several pages of Stevča's tirade a remarkably representative sample of abuse typically used by the Serbian elite educated in Central and Western Europe when they denounce their own people's character.

It was hard, Stevča reminisces, to return from Vienna as a doctor of law to "a primitive, backward Turkish *palanka* [meaning Belgrade][11] where one had to bow down to *čarsija*,[12] to *opanak*[13] and *gejak*,[14] that is to say, to *narod*,[15] as the holy of holies" (Krleža 1982:350). He describes the Serbian Army as "a crowd, a herd, a pack, a tribe, an amorphous heap of rams slouching in the mud" (ibid.:344), "the hands on the clock-tower of our history are turning back" (351), "all of our Serbian politics is eaten by the *memla*[16] of our Kurdistani mentality" (354), "*hajdučija*[17] is the leitmotif of our life, and those asses who make of it a romantic tradition are *buljuk*"[18] (371). Turkish loan words are packed with conspicuous density in this diatribe. Used among Serbs themselves, they are often cues to a register of pleasant, indulgent intimacy in the mode of "between ourselves" or what Herzfeld (1987) calls "self-recognition." In this case, however, they clearly index disparagement.

I find it useful to keep in mind this distinction between "self-display" and "self-knowledge" or "self-recognition," introduced by Herzfeld who understands it as "flexible representations of the dilemma, common to all societies, of balancing social knowledge against the exigencies of collective self-representation to more powerful outsiders" (Herzfeld 1987:123). These attitudes are analogous to what Goffman (1959) called "front region" and "back region" or "backstage" of a performance. It is the orientation to a specific type of audience, either present or imagined, that gives rise to both self-display and self-recognition as a pair of related and mutually constituted attitudes.

The tension between these two attitudes can be found at all levels of intergroup communication, from family and village to region and nation. When responses to stereotypes imposed on national groups by more powerful outsiders are considered, one problem is to determine which particular classes actively engage in responding. Attention is then mostly given to literate elites, partly because they offer readily analyzable texts. It is they, moreover, who are supposedly most aware of the stigma and most sensitive to it, who most often make it their business to respond in one way or another, and who, as members of the "cultural apparatus" (see Hannerz 1992:81–84), disseminate these responses to the public at large. The literate elites, then, are the logical place to look if one wants to find out the shared opinions on these matters in a given society. For these reasons it is important to focus on particular categories or groups of people as engaging in self-display and self-recognition on the national level, but if one thinks in terms of orientation to audience, the problem will be posed not in terms of particular groups of people but in terms of situations in which such orientation occurs. Literate or illiterate, elite or not, self-display and recognition will be a function of situations in which this particular orientation to a particular type of audience is called forth.

Mud, coffee, and Turkish stakes map out Central European hierarchies of taste, civilization, and culture. Nodes of this map are cities standing metonymically for nation-states, regions, and (past and present) empires—Prague, Budapest, Vienna, Zagreb, Zemun, and Belgrade. This map is organized by a combination of the East-West and North-South axes, the most prominent end points of which, at least for the purpose of situating Serbia on them, are Paris, Moscow, and Istanbul. Other maps, by no means independent of this one, rely on other idioms and nodes. One of them is organized not by particular prominent cities but by stereotypes of particular ethnic groups—Gypsies and Germans.

BETWEEN GERMANS AND GYPSIES

The Emerički family in Zagreb dipped their croissants into milk coffee, and, from her Viennese perspective, Aunt Amanda pronounced them Balkan Gypsies for that breach of good taste. It must have hurt badly, for we find those of Krleža's characters who represent various Austro-Hungarian and Croatian viewpoints repeatedly using Gypsy as a term of abuse when referring to Serbs. And yet it is still conceivable that Croats would in some sense identify both with the Balkans and the Gypsies.

The most popular Zagreb rock band of the early 1980s (and, arguably, one of the best Yugoslav bands of all times), "Azra," first started as the "Balkan Sevdah Band," and their first big hit, which came out in 1979, was titled "Balkan." "We are Gypsy people, cursed by fate" (*Mi smo ljudi Cigani, sudbinom prokleti*), sang Džoni Štulić, the leader of the band, and the refrain ran: "Balkans, Balkans, Balkans mine, be mighty [for me] and stand strong" (*Balkane, Balkane, Balkane moj, budi mi silan i dobro mi stoj*).

A word on *sevdah*. Sevdah comes from Turkish *sevda*—love, and Arabic *säwdâ*—black, black humor associated with melancholy. Most centrally associated with Bosnian Muslims, and embodied in the genre of *sevdalinke*, the love songs, it is considered key to the mentality of Serbs, Montenegrins, as well as Macedonians. The word came to denote a particular state of mind associated with unrequited love, certain types of

music usually performed in *kafana* (taverns) by Gypsies in all male company, and with not an insignificant element of irrational self-destruction
usually acted out in smashing glasses with bare hands. According to folk
belief, *sevdah* is a profound, unexplainable, tragic, yet sweetly painful
impossible yearning of the soul, while in the eyes of an outside observer
it is a ritual and a social institution (Simic 1979a; see also Simic 1976). The
word and all it stands for are Orientally tinged, and the northwesterners
of Yugoslavia—Croats and Slovenes—usually regarded it with certain
ambivalence. In the former Yugoslavia, the map of *sevdah* was oriented
along the northwest-southeast diagonal and corresponded closely to
the map of perceived "soulfullness" most prominently indicated by the
musical gradient of sadness. Slovenes had merry polkas, Macedonians
painfully sad, slow, slow laments. As folk sociology had it, the merrier
the music—the "shallower" the soul, and the higher per capita suicide
rate. As noted above, this notion that "sadness" increases to the South
is ambiguous. Those more to the North are more likely to see sadness as
a "sorry state of affairs" rather than an indicator of greater soulfulness.
To call a band in the relatively northern Zagreb "Balkan Sevdah Band"
with positive connotations is thus a stronger and more marked statement
than to do something like that in Belgrade, Skopje, or Sarajevo.

   Štulić was a poet of the "Balkan" side of Zagreb, the ugly, the de-
based, and the loathsome, the provincial and the primitive—the under-
side of its glittery European facade. His poetry could be seen as, among
other things, a rebellion against the self-display of the Zagreb *purger*
(burgher, bourgeois) decorum and "culture," and as a display of the intimate self-recognition that Zagreb is Balkan. The song was, of course,
also an expression of Yugoslav solidarity, a sincere identification with
Yugoslavia's Balkan fate, and many at that time throughout Yugoslavia,
especially among the young, shared Štulić's sentiments. It was only in
the late 1980s and early 1990s, when it became important for Croatia
to distance itself from the Balkans in its bid to "rejoin" the West, that
defiantly accepting Aunt Amanda's verdict—yes, we are indeed Balkan
Gypsies—would start sounding like a powerful statement if uttered by
a Zagreb band.

   And what about the Serbs? A Belgrade bank clerk[19] I met in the Budapest-Belgrade train in June 1996 told me why Serbs (and Slavs in general)
will never catch up with the West: "Look at the Gypsies," he said.

They work just enough to keep alive. A Gypsy doesn't work one bit over what is strictly necessary to keep body and soul together . . . And the Westerner, let's take Germans for whom it is said, and they say of themselves, that they are a superior race, and truth be said, they are (between ourselves). They live in order to work. That's why they have so much, and have saved so much, and made so much for themselves. Now, Serbs and Slavs are somewhere in-between: some are like Gypsies, some like Germans, but mostly they are somewhere half-way.

And a bit later, in another context, he mentioned that our ex-Yugoslav "brothers" (Croats, Slovenes) think we (Serbs) are Gypsies, and then with a slight pause, and in a slightly lowered tone of a confidential *between ourselves* aside, he said, "and we are."

The two most internationally recognized Yugoslav movies of all times happen to be Gypsy movies: Aleksandar Petrović's 1967 Oscar-winning *Skupljači perja* (*I Even Met Happy Gypsies*), and Kusturica's 1989 *Dom za vešanje* (*Time of the Gypsies*), the winner of the Best Director Award at the Cannes Film Festival. Mud and blood are visual dominants of these films, and even though there is singing and dancing in both, they are much more somber than the genre of highly romanticized Gypsy musicals best exemplified by Emil Lotianu's *Tabor ukhodit v nebo* (Lotianu 1975).

Skupljači perja is a film that acquired the status of cultural icon in the former Yugoslavia. Kusturica's *Time of the Gypsies,* despite its comic elements, presents a tragic tale based on a news item that provoked outrage in the former Yugoslavia by the end of the 1980s—the uncovering of a criminal chain that engaged in the buying and selling of (mostly Roma) children to be used for begging and petty thieving in Italy. Again, different audiences in Yugoslavia probably had different responses to the movie, but there is no doubt that its main musical theme—*Djurdjevdan* (St. George's Day)—became the unofficial anthem in Serbia in the 1990s.

The question is: Why should Gypsy movies be so popular domestically, and why should they be the most internationally recognized films? Is it a case of presenting oneself to oneself and to others as Gypsies?

As Dina Iordanova observed, Balkan films abound with Gypsies but they are not made *by* Gypsies or *for* Gypsies but *by* and *for* the dominant groups (Iordanova 2001:215). Gypsies are a kind of cipher, a polyvalent trope that the dominant group, in this case the Serbs, use to tell something to themselves and to others about themselves.[20]

Perceived by most (former) Yugoslavs as being at the very bottom of the hierarchy, Gypsies are often used to metonymically stand for the lower end of dichotomies at different levels of inclusion. This conforms to a general tendency in interethnic perception to cast both oneself and the other in terms of extreme contrasting elements. Thus Fernandez speaks about the demon of Andalusia that haunts Iberianists—"a place in Spain of such powerful and compelling character that it is hard to convince those foreign to the cultural complexity of Iberia that this part of Spain and its characteristic are not the whole of Spain" (Fernandez 1988:22). He finds that he has trouble convincing people that the part of Spain he works in, in contrast to the Andalusian part, "doesn't fight bulls, engage in the politics of patronage, have a large dispossessed rural proletariat, and so forth" (22). The demon is one of metonymic misrepresentation, "that is, the way one place, which is simply a part of a much larger place . . . comes to stand for a whole place" (22). But why Andalusia in particular? This demon, Fernandez argues, "jumps out of the tension between the north as a place and the south as a place" (22):

> If we take this North-South dynamic as real and usually insidious "definition of situation" in human affairs . . . we can understand why within that southern place, which from the perspective of northern Europe and North America Spain is seen to be, a southern part within that place should so often be taken to represent the whole. To take a northern part of a southern place, say Catalonia or Galicia, to stand for the whole would be to confuse the clear and simple identity-confirming sense of difference that stereotyping achieves. It would be to create cognitive dissonance. (Fernandez 1988:23)

Gypsies are exemplary pariahs, outcasts, the very bottom of internal hierarchies throughout Europe. If the Balkans are perceived as pariahs and at the bottom of European hierarchies, one can expect to see the demon of metonymic misrepresentation declare Balkanites to be the Gypsies of Europe. This logic is recursively reproduced on ever smaller scales. If the Balkans are the Gypsies of Europe, one can expect the Balkan countries to introduce intra-Balkan differentiation and try to pass that appellation to neighbors who are supposedly more Balkan than themselves. The Croats, for instance, who are to the west and north of Serbs, often pass this stigma to the Serbs—down the southeastern gradient of depreciation.

It is notable that the exemplary Westerner for that bank clerk who compared Serbs with Gypsies was the German. This is quite in keeping both with the historical importance of German culture for Serbs and the present day fact that Germany looms large in this part of the world, where hardly a family doesn't have somebody working there as a guest worker, and where the Deutsche Mark used to be the main currency for any serious transaction, far more respected than the American dollar, up until it was replaced with the Euro. What is unusual is the easy concession to German superiority when it is borne in mind that Germans are also perceived by Serbs to be their historic arch-enemies.

According to a cluster of images that has been around for more than a hundred years, the Germans are methodically machine-like, pedantic and humorlessly devoted to work.[21] They are cold, aloof, and in cafés they split their bills rather than treat each other (see Mitrović et al. 1996). Owing, however, to the importance of cultural and other links that Serbs had with Germany and Austria in the modern period—and many concur that they have been more important than links with France, England, or Russia[22]—this common notion of the superiority of our (Serbian, South Slav, or Balkan) soul could be seen as compensation for the feeling that we seriously lag on what we see as their scale of values. They really are a superior race, the bank clerk conceded, precisely because "they live to work." It is ironic, however, that it is those same Germans—considered soulless by those to the east (or south) of them—who originated the modern romantic notion of "soulfullness" in reaction to what they saw as imperialist Western rationalism coming from France. Irony is inherent in recursiveness—it is ironic that what from further down south/east (Serbia, Balkans) seemed as supremely Western (Germany, Austria) was itself east to those further up west (i.e., France).

EXTREMES AND THE LANDSCAPE OF SOULFULNESS

If we think of "Eastern Europe," for instance, as a continuum (in the mind of the West, as well as in Eastern Europe's own self-perception), that extends from the relatively most western Czechs, Poles, and Hungarians to the relatively most eastern Russians, then Kundera and Solzhenitsyn, respectively, will have different sets of options when they present their nations in relation to Europe or the West. The actual complexities and ironies of their respective histories are many, but the regularities of the semiotic process at work here are relatively simple. As the most extreme point of the continuum, Russia is taken by the West to stand for the whole of Eastern Europe just like Andalusia is made to stand for the whole of Spain. Kundera, however, whose nation is seen as closest to the West, has an option of repudiating the Russian stigma, or externalizing it as a "disease" and identifying that disease with Russians. Situated at the eastern pole of Europe, the Russians don't have the same option of transferring the stigma further eastward, at least not within the confines of European symbolic geography. They can and do transfer the eastern taint down to their own East, but in the eyes of Western Europe they remain tainted by it. As Wolff writes, "the most overwhelming eastern vector of influence upon Russia, viewed unequivocally as a force of barbarism, was that of Tartary and the Tartars":

> China, Persia, and Turkey could be recognized in the age of Enlightenment as possessing their own Oriental civilizations, but the Tartars received no such concession. If Russia belonged to the Tartar empire in the age of Batu Khan, Tartary belonged to the Russian empire in the age of Peter, but the relation, even reversed, still weighed in the balance between Europe and Asia, civilization and barbarism. (Wolff 1994:190–191)

If the stigma is that of Communism, Kundera has a relatively easy option of saying that it was the Russians who brought it to Czechs; Solzhenitsyn cannot blame it on anybody else (except perhaps the Jews).[23] The most he can do is to cast it as a disease, an unnatural growth on the Russian organism, and thus something that is curable.

Being at the extreme, however, can confer some discursive advantages not enjoyed by those closer to the referent other on the continuum. To Russia it was given to develop some of the German Romantic ideas formed in opposition to the rationalism and universalism of the Enlightenment to one of their most striking and extreme formulations—a notion, a discourse, in fact a whole institution, called the Russian, or Slavic, Soul.[24] Robert C. Williams traces the development of this notion in Russia from the seeds sown by German Romanticism to its full development in Dostoyevsky. Most interesting, however, is that Williams argues that this notion was then reappropriated in the West, especially in Germany where, in a sense, it first originated, as a more potent tool for criticizing the West's own internal discontents with modernity.

> German romanticism enabled the Russians to think of themselves as an individual nation with an historic purpose which was ultimately to triumph over that very Germany and Europe from which such an idea had initially sprung. European intellectuals critical of bourgeois society, in turn, found the Russian attack on the West a confirmation of their own malaise, and readjusted their social criticism with the help of anti-European sentiments expressed in Russian literature . . . "The German romantic rejection of the West," observes Hans Kohn, "was adopted, with similar arguments, by many Russians, who however included Germany in the rejected West." . . . The concept that the Russians had certain advantages over the West precisely because they were backward can be traced to the late eighteenth century . . . The other way in which European thought affected the concept was by reiterating it with enthusiasm later on, finding in it something peculiarly Russian with which to criticize the West . . . In the years before and after the First World War it became evident that those Europeans critical of their own societies would turn to countries on the margin of Europe in a search for a way out . . . Whereas the "Russian soul" to the Russians was utopian, identifying a historical potential to be realized in time, to Europeans it was arcadian, preserving a cosmos which was primitive and timeless. It was not only borrowed by Russians, but borrowed back by Europeans: the intellectual transfer was not one-way but cyclical. (Williams 1970:573, 575, 587–588)

Russia, of course, is exceptional in many ways, not least of which is that it is by far the largest country on the planet. It is a periphery to Western Europe as the (self-styled) Center of Civilization, and subject to problems of self-respect like other peripheries,[25] but it is also a place that can plausibly claim a civilization of its own. Nevertheless the stigma exists, and Russia is usually perceived as being both extremely cultured and extremely uncultured. Inhabiting a terminus of a particular West-East continuum in the global geopolitical imagination, the Russians have an option of using their reputation as a locus for the mysterious Slavic Soul that they claim in the current localization of the human condition (Appadurai 1986). Czechs are still Slavs, but that option is not particularly effective for them because of their position in this particular symbolic landscape. Kundera is indignant when Western critics see evidence of a deep Slavic Soul in his works. He disclaims that he has one. "Joseph Conrad was always irritated by the label "Slavic soul" that people loved to slap on him and his books because of his Polish origins," Kundera writes in his famous "Tragedy of Central Europe,"

> and about sixty years ago, he wrote that "nothing could be more alien to what is called in the literary world the 'Slavic spirit' than the Polish temperament with its chivalric devotion to moral constraints and its exaggerated respect for individual rights." (How well I understand him! I, too, know of nothing more ridiculous than this cult of obscure depths, this noisy and empty sentimentality of the "Slavic soul" that is attributed to me from time to time!). (Kundera 1991 [1984]:219)

On the other, more South-East vector of European symbolic geography that could be distinguished from the one extending to the east and which opposes Central Europe not to Russia but to the Balkans, one would expect analogous semiotic features of identity discourses oriented toward the West. Although the Balkans might be seen as beginning at the Masaryk train station in Prague, or the South Station in Vienna, it is a relatively easy option for Central Europeans to pass on the ethnic strife, violence, and backwardness to the Balkans proper. The Balkans cannot pass it further down, unless to Turks or Islam in general. The form this appeal usually takes is one of the nesting "Shields of Christianity." As Slavoj Žižek put it:

> For Serbs, the Balkans begin in Kosovo and they consider themselves as guardians of Christianity; for Croats the Balkans start in the Orthodox, despotic, and Byzantine Serbia, from which Croatia defends its values of western civilization; for Slovenians they start in Croatia, and we, Slovenians, are the paladins of peaceful central Europe; for Italians and Austrians the Balkans and the rule of Balkan throngs begin in Slovenia; for some Germans the Balkan Empire commences in Austria, which is stigmatized by Balkan corruption; an odd arrogant Frenchmen associates Germany with eastern Balkan wilderness; and this is how this story goes all the way to England where some of its extreme citizens consider the entire continental Europe as some kind of Balkan-Turkish Empire with Brussels as a new Constantinople—an authoritarian center of power and a threat to English freedom and sovereignty. (*Novi List*, July 1, 2001, 10)

SELF-EXOTICIZING AND "MINSTRELIZATION":
GYPSY MOVIES AND MAGICAL REALISM

The "Shields of Christianity" rhetoric doesn't seem to be very persuasive to those to whom it is addressed—the Civilized Europe—but can the Balkan peoples show to this Civilized Europe something analogous to the Slavic Soul? Do they have an option of reversing the valence of their particular taint by playing on Western discontents with modernity? Could they effectively claim "certain advantages over the West precisely because they were backward," as Russians did? If the Russians have staked their claim on the goods encompassed by the notion of the Slavic Soul, to what spiritual goods could the Balkan people lay their claim? Balkan Slavs, of course, also belong to the culture of "Slavic Soul" but are not usually perceived from the outside as its classical embodiments.

Maria Todorova has persuasively argued that "the Balkans have served as a repository of negative characteristics against which a positive and self-congratulatory image of the "European" and the "West" has been constructed" (Todorova 1997:188). What distinguishes the discourse of Balkanism from that of Orientalism, she claims, is that the former does not show the redeeming valences of the latter: however denigrated the Orient might have been, it was always also seen as possessing a resplendent civilization of its own, and in certain ways even superior to the Occident; the Balkans were nothing but Europe's "alter ego, the dark side within" with no redeeming characteristics whatsoever.

At least one significant exception does, exist, however—Rebecca West's monumental Yugoslav travelogue, *Black Lamb and Grey Falcon* (1969). Rebecca West consistently reverses the usual valences of Balkanist discourse by seeing something admirable in almost everything that from the viewpoint of the world she comes from is usually seen as despicable. This attitude is also seen in her reversal of the northwest-southeast "gradient of depreciation"—usually seen at work in Western representations of Yugoslavia as well as internal Yugoslav stereotyping—into a "gradient of admiration." Croatia, where she starts her Yugoslav journey, fares the worst. It is too tainted with Central Europe, with the Western decadence that Rebecca West is trying to escape. She certainly prefers Bosnia and Serbia to Croatia, but her heart really belongs to the southeast terminus of the gradient—Macedonia—the "Balkans of the Balkans" (see Irvine and Gal 2000:63; and Brown 2003).

Belgrade, then, appears in some of her reflections as the midpoint of that gradient. It used to be "a Balkan village" which "has its character, of resistance, of determined survival of martyred penury." But the modern Belgrade "has made the error of building streets that had already been built elsewhere much better." Serbia was liberated in 1815, she says, and "for a century it had been exposed to the peculiar poisons of the nineteenth century."

> But Macedonia had been under the Ottoman Empire until 1913; it had till then been stabilized by Turkish misgovernment in precisely those medieval conditions which had existed when it was isolated by its defeat at Kossovo in 1389. Macedonia should perhaps be looked on as a museum not typical of the life outside it. It had only twenty-five years of contact with the modern world. (West 1969:482–483)

Serbia stands to Macedonia as Croatia stands to Serbia and to some extent, recursively, as Central Europe stands to Yugoslavia as a whole. Serbia is positioned somewhere between the decadence of the West and pristine Balkan purity of Macedonia. For all its exposure to "poisons of the nineteenth century," however, this European degeneration that threatens Belgrade is "still a long way from consummation." Belgrade hotels might emulate those in London or Paris, but in "none of those great cities," writes West,

> have I seen hotel doors slowly swing open to admit, unhurried and at ease, a peasant holding a black lamb in his arms . . . His suit was in the Western fashion, but he wore also a sheepskin jacket, a round black cap, and leather sandals with upturned toes. (West 1969:483)

Western clothes and the three major diacritics of Serbian peasant *Volksgeist*—*gunjče* (sheepskin jacket), *šubara* (round black cap), and *opanak* (leather sandals with upturned toes)[26]—are finally complemented with the third essential element in this pregnant passage: the peasant with the black lamb "stood still as a Byzantine king in a fresco" (ibid.:483). The Serbian sense of identity does indeed significantly revolve around the various ways in which these three large themes—Byzantine heritage as a claim to High Culture, *gunjče* and *opanak* as egalitarian peasant *Volksgeist,* and more or less well-fitting Western clothes as uneasy membership in the Western civilization—are seen to complement or contradict one another. Even though she values them differently, Rebecca West here arrives at the same ingredients of Serbian identity that Velmar-Janković identified gazing from the Belgrade Kalemegdan Fortress.

Black Lamb and Grey Falcon could be seen as an ideal type of the position that discovers in the Balkans a vital something that the West has lost. According to this view, the more pristinely "Balkan," the more intense or pure that something is. The type ideally opposed to this evaluation—the one that shades the Balkans the more negatively, the more "Balkan" it is—has been amply documented by Todorova. Pozzi's *Black Hand over Europe,* for instance, written just two years before Rebecca West's Yugoslav journey, could be seen as a perfect geometric reversal of *Black Lamb and Grey Falcon* with its "gradient of depreciation" in place of Rebecca West's "gradient of appreciation." It is noteworthy, however, that although in many ways holding the views exactly opposite to those of Rebecca West, Pozzi at one point describes Belgrade in almost the same terms that betray a vestige of romanticizing the Balkans: "This new Belgrade," he wrote,

> is impersonal, cold and unoriginal. It is a caricature of other European capitals . . . The builders of the New Belgrade have killed the picturesque, warm-hearted inefficiency of the place. They have destroyed its past and killed its soul, and have inspired it with nothing but the spirit of Babylon. (Pozzi 1994:44)

Both the Serbian self-display and its "backstage" component, "self-recognition," are bound to be oriented, at least to some extent, toward these two opposed types of valuations. The Serbian responses to Western stereotyping could thus be usefully classified as ranging from the pole of the full acceptance of the negative valuation to maximal exploitation of the positive valuation, with all the intermediate shadings.

> The stigmatized individual exhibits a tendency to stratify his "own" according to the degree to which their stigma is apparent and obtrusive. He can then take up in regard to those who are more evidently stigmatized than himself the attitudes the normals take to him. Thus do the hard of hearing stoutly see themselves as anything but deaf persons, and those with defective vision, anything but blind. It is in his affiliation with, or

separation from, his more evidently stigmatized fellows, that the individual's oscillation of identification is most sharply marked. (Goffman 1963:107)

In the prevalent European symbolic geographies, Serbs are perceived as more "deaf" or "blind" than Slovenes and Croats. This is perhaps why they are more likely to accept the stigma and to oscillate between seeing themselves, as my informant in the train did, as being "between Germans and Gypsies" and being "Gypsies" pure and simple. In Goffman's terms, Serbs are affiliating themselves with those of their "own" who are even "blinder" than themselves, and presenting themselves to "normals" (Westerners) as more severely defective than they believe themselves to actually be.

Rueful introspection, as this mode of self-understanding could be called, is, however, only the "backstage" counterpart to the "front stage" of self-display. After all, the Gypsy movies mentioned above were also probably meant as a self-presentation before international audiences, and not only as self-criticism oriented exclusively toward domestic ones. Perhaps this is a case of "minstrelization"—"whereby the stigmatized person ingratiatingly acts out before normals the full dance of bad qualities imputed to his kind, thereby consolidating a life situation into a clownish role" (Goffman 1963:110). Dina Iordanova points out to a trend in recent films coming from the Balkans that involves such a mode of dealing with stigma:

> Based on the fact that their lands are geographically in Europe, and yet feeling that somehow they are not quite there, Balkan intellectuals believe that they need to make efforts toward "re-entering Europe." In order for this re-entering to take place, they feel obliged to be apologetic, and they are prepared to mirror stereotypes of themselves as part of the admission bargain which they believe they can re-negotiate. The projects of voluntary self-denigration take various shapes. (Iordanova 1996a)

"Minstrelization," or "voluntary self-denigration," however, are extreme modes of responding to stigma, and they are probably much more often tempered by what one could call self-exoticizing—a mode of response to stereotypes important others hold of oneself which, to a greater or lesser extent, plays on their positive valences. This is a mode in which we would expect the stigmatized, in this case, the Serbs, to play up to what they perceive as "spiritual goods" that Westerners like Rebecca West project into the Balkans as something they lack at home. Self-presentation is thus in a state of tension between mirroring the wholly negative image back to its originators and twisting it in ways conceived to appeal to their romantic fascinations and projections.

One such highly effective way of playing up to the Metropolis's thirst for the exotic is the genre of "magical realism." Kusturica's *Time of the Gypsies,* for instance, features many visual "quotes" from *Skupljači perja,* but it also introduces elements of "magical realism"—elements that would become even more prominent in his controversial *Underground* (Kusturica 1995).

A number of Balkan filmmakers use "intriguing images of magical realism" in their recent films, argues Dina Iordanova, and that makes their work "more easily accepted in this age of visualization." "They are conscious of the marginality of their own cultures," she says, and "know how to make this marginalization an asset" (Iordanova 1996:883, 888).

In the case of Serbia, one could distinguish two strategies used for self-exoticizing although in practice they are often amalgamated in various proportions. One strategy is to mine the Serbian Byzantine heritage for all the positively valued exoticism it can yield,[27] and the other relies on positive valuations of Balkan primitivity as something more vital and fundamentally "real" than overcivilized, "decadent," and "tired'" Europe. The first tries to resuscitate the splendor of a high culture, the second to offer the benefits of barbarity—splendidly expressed in the notion of the Balkan "barbarogenius."[28]

Self-presentation as Gypsies will then be an amalgam of these ideal-typical options in variable proportions:

(a) minstrelization: we know you think Gypsies are backward, thieving, shifty, obstinate in their otherness, and so on (as we also do), and that we are no better than Gypsies in your eyes—so here, we'll play out the worst Gypsies for you;

(b) self-exoticization: we know you sometimes think Gypsies are free, mysterious, and wild (and so do we), one of your ur-images of the romantic, noble/dangerous/exciting savage—compared to you, we are indeed like Gypsies, outside your iron cage of rationality, dirty, and poor but free, vital, mysterious, not a little dangerous, irrationally obstinate, and yes we'll play at being such Gypsies for you. Since Gypsies act as a conduit for soul for us (all that is irrational, incomprehensible and thus deep and precious about ourselves), we will act as a conduit for you, we will be your Gypsies;

(c) Or, by acting benevolently toward Gypsies by including them into our high art (film) we are emulating the West Europeans who show their superiority most not when they denigrate "lower races," but when they magnanimously exhibit their "primitive art" in their art museums.

The problem with any play on Civilization's enchantment with the primitive is that primitiveness has to be authentic, fresh, and extreme in order to sell. Serbs have only sporadically been able to exploit this niche, and that was usually at times when the Balkans rose to the attention of the "West" due to a crisis or violence. Vesna Goldsworthy points out how in those times, because of the "romance of war" they provide, the Balkans could attract the Westerner affected by the "civilized monotony" of the non-Balkan Europe (Goldsworthy 2002:30). Most of the time, however, the region more or less vaguely coincident with Serbia, even when it figures in the European exoticizing imaginary as a "mysterious and unhomelike Easter location for the unfolding of Western adventure," remains blank (ibid.:33). Agatha Christie's *Murder on the Orient Express* is a good example, and so is the fact that Serbia has been given a wide berth by James Bond throughout his long career. He only passes through by train once in *From Russia with Love*.[29]

Serbs seem mostly to inhabit the uncomfortable and unprofitable position of those neither properly civilized nor sufficiently primitive. They seem to hover around the midpoint of European gradients whether of appreciation or depreciation. Symbolic geographies seem to place them in the in-between position even within the Balkans as themselves an exemplary in-between place. And, indeed, the in-betweenness is perhaps the most ubiquitous self-understanding and self-designation in Serbia just as it is in the Balkans at large. Most famous of the clichés used to express this in-between status have certainly been the images of the Bridge and the Crossroads.[30] In the self-congratulatory mode the Bridge or a Crossroads imply a centrality and indispensability that should somehow be rewarded by the powers that be (they should build good roads there). Standing at the Crossroads or being a Bridge also implies the role of a broker or mediator. As Guardians of the Gates, or Shields of Christianity, various Balkan groups, Serbs among them, could also try to position themselves as guides, mediators, or watchdogs in the West's dealings with Islam. On the other hand, it could be a curse "to have your house built on the thoroughfare" where "the winds of history blow particularly hard," as the often-heard lament puts it, and we are, moreover, suffering the envy and covetousness of the powerful since we occupy such an important position in the world. This in-betweenness could then also be seen as a fatal flaw, the perennial neither-here-nor-there, neither fish-nor-fowl state of being expressed figuratively as twilight (not utter darkness), slumber (not deep sleep), adolescence (not early childhood), and a whole range of categorical abominations and images of liminality.

My hunch is that the in-betweenness could be derived from certain regularities in the semiotic logic of what could be called "self-definition through maximal contrast under the unequal distribution of power." Before I attempt a sketchy outline of such an argument, let me just layer my maps with some more amorphous substances.

AMORPHIA AND WAVERING FORM: THE VALENCES OF IN-BETWEENNESS

Živojin Pavlović (1933–1998), a prominent Serbian film director and writer, developed a whole theory of the two opposed civilizations: the crystalline and the amorphous. The crystalline civilization is the civilization of the West—the civilization of organization, competition, and progress, the civilization of the city and of individual pleasure. It is dominated by the straight line and sharp angle and characterized by the cult of eternity, health, and hygiene.[31] Amorphous civilization, on the other hand, is the civilization of the East—the civilization of ritual, irrationality, and patriarchal organization;

> horizontal civilization, the civilization of village, the civilization of necessity, the static civilization, the civilization of curved line, the civilization of circle. The civilization of all the faiths except Christianity (except Orthodoxy, which belongs to the amorphous civilization). The civilization

of generality, universality, universe (in opposition to the crystal civilization of detail, fragmentariness, specialization, individual virtuosity).
(Pavlović 1992:13–14)

The civilization of the crystal is characterized by "the centripetal
energy which concentrates everything towards the goal that has to be
clear, unconditional, and oriented towards eternity."

> In contrast to that, the amorphous civilization is put in motion by the cen-
> trifugal energy, which tosses everything around, scatters and disperses,
> so the world is in flux, in a mix, a turbulence, everything is in a seeming
> unrest. (Ibid.:16)

Thus "democracy cannot take root in amorphous civilizations.
Amorphous turbulence does not allow the forming of steady systems"
(ibid.:72). For us, he said, the longing for Europe is "a dream of a powerful tradition and a hierarchy of values, that is, the wish to walk more
comfortably, on a more pleasant but uniform asphalt surface, instead of
meadows, forests, gorges and mountain passes."

> For Europe is comfort as opposed to sweat and suffering; emptiness and
> sterility instead of spiritual wealth and the soul's enthusiasm. Europe is
> a synonym for culture; Balkan is an embodiment of freedom. That's why
> Europe recalls the beauty of tamed, that is to say, corrupted domestic
> animals, while the Balkans still dazzle with the unassailable, unfathom-
> ably wild beauty of the beast. (Ibid.:80)

"Members of crystalline civilizations have always talked about the
people of amorphia as 'uncultured,'" he said, but "not to be cultured is
the same as being vital!" (ibid.:106).

We can take Pavlović's opposition between the two civilizations to
be the exact counterpart of Rebecca West's musings on the decadence
of the West and the vitality of the Balkans. Moreover, by endorsing precisely amorphia as something good, creative, and vital, and, in a way,
superior to the orderliness of the crystalline West, Pavlović is reversing
the valence of one of the most prevalent characterizations not only of the
particular periphery that he belongs to but of peripheries in general.

Predicaments of each periphery are different and historically specific,
yet a certain semiotic logic could be seen to underlie all the processes of
"self-definition by maximal contrast under the unequal distribution of
power." Images of mixedness, unformedness, ambiguity, amorphous-

ness and miscegenation regularly appear both in the characterization of peripheries by those positioned at the center, the "Cores," and in self-characterization of the peripheries themselves as somehow in-between. That in-betweenness, expressed in the idiom of different local histories, could also be seen as a logical corollary of the process one can call mutual definition by maximally contrastive metonymic misrepresentation. Here are some of its characteristics:

· Each side will tend to represent the other in terms of those elements of the other's identity that are perceived as contrasting most sharply with the elements selected to form one's own self image.

· There will be a tendency to transform these elements from indexes into icons and thus naturalize the differences. (Irvine and Gal 2000; Herzfeld 1997:27).

· The dichotomies created in this dialectic of definition by contrast will tend to be reproduced recursively both inward onto intragroup relations and outward into intergroup relations (Irvine and Gal 2000).

· The process of defining self and other in terms of those selected segments of each other's identity that show the greatest mutual contrast will tend to create problems of what to do with those segments that are still perceived as part of one's identity but do not fit neatly into the essentialized contrasts. These elements are subject to various strategies of erasure,[32] ranging from inattention to active removal of "matter out of place." These areas tend to produce "cognitive dissonance" and an uneasy sense of "in-betweenness" that characterize both the way those more powerful represent those less powerful and the latter's self-representations.[33]

The "localization of the human condition," as Appadurai (1986) calls it, will thus tend to assume a form of a more or less consistent gradation along particular axes or continua. The most prominent of these are what I have called the North-South and East-West "gradients of depreciation" (Živković 1990). These gradients, like "the map of civilization on the mind of the Enlightenment" (Wolff 1994) are defined by their extremes—Paris on the one pole, the Far East on the other. The Metropolis is defining itself in opposition to the other extreme pole of the continuum, but, especially in the case of the East, that contrastive

Other is not perceived in purely negative terms, as Barbarity, but as an alien Civilization. The good case in point is the image of East Europe as a place that mediates between the extremes of Orient and Occident, a place identified neither with full civilization nor pure barbarity, but seen as an in-between place of backwardness. As Wolff argues, "Eastern Europe defined Western Europe by contrast, as the Orient defined the Occident, but was also made to mediate between Europe and the Orient" (Wolff 1994:7). The dichotomy between East and West is recursively projected inward onto Europe, but, in juxtaposing these two levels, the in-betweenness of Eastern Europe is generated. Todorova has similarly argued that the Balkan people have been perceived by the northwesterners not as full-fledged Orientals but as mongrels, cross-breeds, or a "wavering form." Setting out from Sweden in the 1920s and traversing the Balkans, Egypt, and the Holy Land in quest of "the soul of the East," Marcus Ehrenpreis thus characterized the race of people he encountered while crossing the "New Balkans":

> Oddish, incredible individuals appear on all sides—low foreheads, sodden eyes, protruding ears, thick underlips . . . The Levantine type in the areas between the Balkans and the Mediterranean is, psychologically and socially, truly a "wavering form," a composite of Easterner and Westerner, multilingual, cunning, superficial, unreliable, materialistic and, above all, without tradition . . . In a spiritual sense these creatures are homeless; they are no longer Orientals nor yet Europeans. They have not freed themselves from the vices of the East nor acquired any of the virtues of the West. (In Todorova 1997:125)

Živojin Pavlović could be seen as transforming this negatively valued "wavering form" into a largely positive one of "amorphous civilization." But even there, he sees his own society as being in-between—"at the borderland of both civilization blocks, with one part of our collective being firmly linked with amorphia while with another part we encountered and tasted charms of the civilization of the crystal" (Pavlović 1992:76).

The position a particular periphery inhabits on these gradients, continua, or hierarchies that are defined by the powerful centers will tend to constrain the repertory of responses at its disposal. Czechs and Russians, for instance, inhabit different positions on the Enlightenment map of civilization that is oriented along the West-East axis, and this gives them different options when it comes to dealing with the stigma of being "Eastern." Croats and Serbs, similarly, occupy different positions on the northwest—southeast gradient that characterizes the symbolic geography of the Balkans and they have different options when it comes to dealing with the stigma of the Balkans.

Having similar structural positions does not mean that the options will be the same, for each peripheral society has to deal with quite specific historical contingencies. Serbs, Greeks, and Romanians, for instance, have different response options even though they share both the Balkan peripherality and the Oriental taint.

Greek nation-building was based on European philhellenism, and Greek elites could (and still continue to) play on the theme of classical Greek heritage in their (ultimately successful) bid to gain admittance to a Europe which proclaimed ancient Hellas the cradle of its culture. It is thus understandable that the Greek elites would try to display the classical and hide the tainted Byzantine/Ottoman sides of Greek identity. No such option was ever available to Serbian elites who could never plausibly play on their classical heritage in a way analogous to the Greeks. For Serbs, the "classical heritage" could only be Byzantine—in the eyes of the West almost as Oriental as their Ottoman legacy—and precisely the heritage that modern Greece wanted to suppress in favor of a more ancient Hellenic one. As for the Romanians, they have an option of claiming Roman descent, and thus a direct link with another culture ancestral to the modern West—a tactic, however, that has not been politically successful (see Verdery 1991).

In laying out the repertories of responses to stigma, I tried to give examples that condense the ambivalences, ambiguities, paradoxes, and ironies. They were chosen in order to show as poignantly as possible how these responses vacillate between analytically distinguishable extreme positions that rarely, if at all, exist in their pure form. Wavering, ambivalence, and tension are possible between any of these positions. Furthermore, there is a tension between self-display and self-recognition that cuts across them. One could thus arrive at a complex grid of crosscutting tensions between ideal types of responses to predicaments of peripheries implicated in value hierarchies of the cores. Images, themes, and narratives that inform Serbian discourses on national identity and destiny are not always oriented toward these hierarchies. When they are, it is useful to keep in mind Serbia's specific position in the dominant geopolitical imaginings and the way this position constrains the range of responses to these imaginings.

Neither close to the West like the Czechs nor at the extreme end of easternness like Russians, neither affiliated with Central Europe like the Croats nor positioned as "the Balkans of the Balkans" like the Macedonians, Serbs find it hard both to pass the negative valuations further "down" and to exploit the exotic potential of the extremes. The stigma they bear combines the stigmas of the South and of the East, of Slavdom and Turkish Taint, of congenital Communism and Balkan violence. They do not have the option of claiming descent from one of the cultures that the West sees as ancestral to itself like Greeks and Romanians have. Accepting this stigma, their responses vacillate between playing it back in exaggerated form as "minstrelization" and various shades of ambivalent self-exoticization as, for instance, in "magical realism."

Magical realism is the periphery's self-exoticizing for the consumption of the Metropolis. The Metropolis is not interested in what is unexotic about the peripheries. Each periphery should ideally be an exemplary place, a perfect homogeneous embodiment of some exaggerated cultural difference—Spain has to be all passion, flamenco, wine, olives, and bull-fights; Russia has to be all soul, Balkans all ancient hatreds, ethnic strife, and slaughter. We Slavs are between Germans and Gypsies, says the bank clerk from Belgrade. But this is not interesting to the Metropolis, or so the Balkan author imagines. So if the Metropolis likes to see us as Gypsies, we'll give them Gypsies, and if they see us as wallowing in mud and blood, we'll give them mud and blood, while privately we sip our Turkish Coffee and Capucinos.

THREE

Highlanders and Lowlanders

In his 1994 *New York Times* article on the war in Bosnia, John Kifner (1994) draws our attention to "the rocky spine of the Dinaric Alps, for it is these mountains that have nurtured and shaped the most extreme, combative elements of each community: the western Herzegovinian Croats, the Sandžak Muslims, and, above all, the secessionist Serbs. Like mountaineer communities around the world, Kifner goes on, "these were wild, warlike, frequently lawless societies whose feuds and folklore have been passed on to the present day like the potent home-brewed plum brandy that the mountain men begin knocking back in the morning."

In his 1992 BBC documentary titled *Serbian Epics*, Paul Pawlikowski juxtaposed images of forbidding limestone peaks of the Bosnian Dinaric Alps with images of Bosnian Serbs listening to their epics performed on the *gusle* and their guns firing into besieged Sarajevo. "Bosnian Serbs are at the moment perhaps the most hated group of people in the Western world," runs the opening statement,

> Pictures of Muslims in concentration camps and stories of atrocities and murder have caused horror and indignation. What is not so widely known is that Radovan Karadžić, the Serbian leader, thinks of himself as a poet. Whatever one thinks of his poetry, or his political position, there is no doubt that the peasant tradition of epic verse which has survived since the middle ages in the mountains of Bosnia combined with an irrational view of history has helped fuel the horrific conflict in what was once Yugoslavia. (Pawlikowski 1992)

To connect the Dinaric Highlanders with epic poetry and barbarism is to echo a discourse that stretches back to the Venetian Enlightenment. The limestone peaks of the Dinaric Mountains in the Dalmatian hinterland were the home of the Morlacchi—the mountain folk made famous by Alberto Fortis's (1778) *Viaggio in Dalmazia* published in 1774, where they were admired for their "innocence and the natural liberty of the pastoral centuries" (ibid.:64) but, as it turned out, most famously for their Homeric prowess in heroic poetry. "The primitive Morlacchi, after Fortis's travels, became a fully European intellectual sensation, attracting the poetic attentions of both Goethe and Herder in faraway Weimar," writes Larry Wolff (2001:13). Fortis found living Homers in the Dinaric highlands in the early 1770s, as did Milman Perry in the early 1920s (Lord 2000), and in the 1930s Rebecca West still showed "intellectual traces of this sentimental "Morlacchismo" of the Enlightenment" in her *Black Lamb and Grey Falcon* (Wolff 2001:19). When they juxtaposed this particular mountain range with epic poetry, Pawlikowski and Kifner thus reconnected to more than two hundred years of Western writing about the region. In their rendering, as in much Western journalistic commentary on Yugoslavia's breakup, however, this connection of geography and character did not serve to romanticize highlander poets and their vanishing heroic way of life but rather to explain violence.

External observers were not the only ones who used geographically determined national character to explain Yugoslav violence or politics in general. Yugoslavs themselves often relied on oppositions between highland and lowland mentality in their internal apportioning of blame and their attempts to account for the violence of the breakup. Various idioms related to this "vertical" dimension marked group distinctions that exhibited the same recursive logic shown in the previous chapter to operate in the "horizontal" genre of symbolic geography. And again the Serbian-Croatian contrasts provide the paradigmatic case. The highlander/lowlander opposition was projected on the Serbian-Croatian opposition and then recursively reproduced on both sides as they discovered their own internal highlanders and lowlanders. The valuation of the terms was often Manichean. One was the epitome of good, the other of evil, and these valuations got reversed depending on the situation and political agendas.

There are several mountain ranges in the former Yugoslavia, but only the "rocky spine of Dinaric Alps," extending the length of Yugoslavia's Adriatic coast from Istria to Albania, bred the highlander type that carried the true symbolic charge. The association of these mountains with a particular heroic ethos and mentality goes back at least to Fortis, but it was the eminent Serbian ethnogeographer Jovan Cvijić (1865–1927) who firmly established and elaborated the Dinaric Highlander syndrome in Yugoslav political imaginary. The Dinaric Highlander is only one of his Balkan psychological "profiles" but it is by far the most influential. As Cathie Carmichael suggests, he constructed it initially out of a "desire to create a symbolic spine for any future South Slavic state" (Carmichael 2002:96) but not by "drawing entirely from his imagination," since he was a scrupulous scientist who "spent years undertaking a form of anthropological fieldwork in the region and had a detailed and intricate knowledge of his subject" (ibid.:96; see also Džadžić 1988:191).

Cvijić was by no means a geographical determinist. He believed that the direct influences of terrain or climate on human physiology and psychology are undeniable but extremely hard to specify and distinguish from a host of other non-geographical factors. Much easier to grasp are the indirect influences of environment—natural resources determine the material forms of human life such as types of dwellings, forms of economy, or food and clothing habits, and these in turn affect "a great number of psychological phenomena," yet their influence is intertwined with social factors and hard to distinguish from them. Most interesting for Cvijić, however, was the third group of geographical factors—those that influence the movements of human groups. Features of terrain facilitate or obstruct movements of people, and contacts between civilizations. They tend to channel the advances and retreats of conquering empires, and in the long run they tend to shape the zones of their civilizational influences. This is why Cvijić's ethnopsychological profiles largely coincide with cultural zones which in their turn tend to follow the geomorphology of the terrain.

Migrations dispersed and mixed populations of different ethnopsychological type, and for decades Cvijić advised his researchers to pay attention to the distinctions made by people in the villages they studied between old settlers and newcomers from other regions. It is partly from these folk distinctions that Cvijić arrived at his pan-Balkan synoptic map of ethnopsychological types. Once formulated, they percolated back to the popular level, if not directly through Cvijić's writings then from his numerous popularizers, and became firmly entrenched as basic terms of a genre of folk ethnopsychology. Since he established it, Cvijić was implicitly or explicitly invoked in most subsequent deployments of the Dinaric type even by his political opponents. The clearest example of such deployment of the Dinaric type in the Serbo-Croatian rivalries is offered by the way Dinko Tomašić used Cvijić against Cvijić.

BETWEEN SERBS AND CROATS: MOUNTAINS, HARDNESS, AND STATE-BUILDING CAPACITY

Dinko Tomašić was a Croatian sociologist who emigrated to the United States and taught sociology at Indiana University. His *Personality and Culture in Eastern European Politics* was published in 1948 but was resurrected again in the early 1990s in the work of another Croatian-American sociologist, Stjepan Meštrović (1993) and his collaborators. In *Habits of the Balkan Heart*, Meštrović et al. used canonical social theorists like Tocqueville, Veblen, and Bellah to promote an essentialist argument about the Serbian national character that served the Croatian war propaganda needs of the moment. Despite the trappings of the classical sociological theories, Tomašić's older arguments provide the backbone of the book, and it is more profitable to turn to the "original" because, in addition to providing a history of the adversarial use of this idiom, it will also lead us to its intellectual genealogy.

According to Tomašić, the mountaineers of the Dinaric region exhibit an "emotionally unstable, violent, and power-seeking personality" that is fully explainable by their social and family structure (1948:32). "The Dinaric child is born and reared in an atmosphere of rivalry and antagonism," says Tomašić. "Deep feelings of insecurity in such a family environment create a strong need for self-assertion, with the resultant overcompensation in boastfulness and illusions of grandeur" (ibid.:32–33).

Tomašić relies quite heavily on Cvijić whom he obviously respects as the foremost authority on the Dinaric mentality but whom he casts as a geographical determinist, in contrast to his own "Culture and Personality School" emphasis on the family upbringing. The Dinarics show a "ceaseless concern with their own importance and reputation," and "can hate with a consuming passion and a violence that reaches a white heat," writes Tomašić quoting Cvijić. In the Dinaric regions, again quoting Cvijić, one can find "excessively fierce, wild and narrow-minded men who are goaded beyond endurance by the smallest insult" (ibid.:35). In a word, Tomašić concludes, the Dinarics are characterized by

> a malevolent, deceitful and disorderly view of the universe, and an emotionally unbalanced, violent, rebellious and power-seeking personality, together with tense interpersonal and cultural relationships, and extreme political instability. This herdsman-brigand-warrior-police ideal furnished a program for the conquerors of urban centers and of the surrounding peasantry. (Ibid.:12)

Opposed to the Dinarics stand the peaceful, stable, and tolerant peasants from the regions between the Drava and Sava Rivers who, at least in the past, have been organized in large communal households called *zadruga*. In his account of the *zadruga* family structure and resulting personality type, Tomašić relies heavily on the data provided by the premier Croatian ethnologist Antun Radić (1868–1919), who was the ideologue of the Croatian Peasant Party that dominated Croatian politics in the Kingdom of Yugoslavia. In contrast to the power-hungry, violent, and unstable personality of the Dinarics, according to Tomašić, the personality formation of *zadruga* society "accentuated the humanistic values."

> The wide diffusion of political power, personal freedom and economic security, combined with exposure to happy family life and a mild, but reasonable, just and firm family discipline, favored an optimistic, peaceful, just and well-ordered conception of the world, an emotionally well-balanced, non-violent and power-indifferent personality, and smooth and harmonious interpersonal and intellectual relations. (Ibid.:12)

The main conflict in Yugoslavia, according to Tomašić, "was essentially a struggle of the *zadruga* peasantry against the Dinaric warriors who had imposed themselves upon Croatia as Serbian military" (ibid.:204).

What is noteworthy here is that, with minor exceptions, the equivalence is established between the *zadruga* society and Croats, on the one hand, and the Dinaric society and Serbs, on the other. However, the *zadruga* type of socioeconomic organization was widespread among both Croats and Serbs. The patriarchal Dinaric social organization was also significantly present among Croats and not only Serbs.[1] Both Croats and Serbs have their own internal highlanders and lowlanders, and this master dichotomy tends to be reproduced on ever smaller scales on both sides, whereby supposedly homogeneous highlander and lowlander communities further divide themselves into internal highlanders and lowlanders, and so on, even to the level of a single person. But before I pursue this recursiveness on the Serbian side, I want to show yet another feature of this type of dichotomizing discourse—the way that valences of the opposite poles get reversed.

Obviously Tomašić has an agenda—he is arguing in favor of the idealized *zadruga* type identified with the Croats against the maligned and negatively slanted Dinaric type that is ascribed to Serbs. When he talks about *zadruga*, he is quite clearly promoting the ideology of the Croatian Peasant Party. When he discusses Dinarics, however, Tomašić is relying on Cvijić who, in his view, was "the outstanding theorist of Serbian imperialism," and thus his direct political enemy. He is therefore using Cvijić's observations on Dinarics against Cvijić's own alleged political agenda. That in doing so Tomašić only moderately resorts to quoting Cvijić out of context could be seen as giving his political enemy some credit for objectivity by this very practice—meaning that Cvijić himself was critical enough about Dinarics that he could be used against them without too much distortion. In any case, there is no doubt that, by and large, Cvijić's valuation of the Dinaric character was the opposite of Tomašić's, and it may help to present Cvijić through Tomašić's characterization because that will put the valence reversal in the sharpest possible relief.

Tomašić writes that, according to Cvijić, there are "four main types of man among the southern Slavs: the Dinaric, the Central, the East-Balkan, and the Panonian. Each of these is subdivided into a few subtypes. Superior to all types is Dinaric man, and of his five subtypes the Šumadija variety is the best" (Tomašić 1941:54). Šumadija is the heartland of Serbia, the cradle of the Serbian uprisings against the Turks at the beginning of the nineteenth century and the core from which the modern Serbian state expanded. If the Šumadians were the best type for Cvijić, Tomašić writes, "the most inferior of all seems to have been the Panonian type to which the majority of Croatian and some Serbs of the Panonian plains belong" (ibid.:55). I would argue, however, that, for Cvijić, the main contrast is between the pride and heroism of those who retreated into the Dinaric "mountain fortress" before the Turkish invaders, on the one hand, and the *rayah* mentality and moral mimicry of the groups who remained in close proximity to Turks in valleys and alongside main communications.

Literally "cattle," or "flock," *rayah* was the term used by the Ottomans to denote the non-Muslim subjects of their empire. "Rayah mentality," according to Cvijić, is a cluster of character traits acquired by the subject populations as a result of centuries of Turkish oppression. It includes the worship of authorities, pragmatism, egoism, submissiveness, servility, resentment, and "moral mimicry" (his gloss for "identification with the aggressor"). The worst odium in Cvijić's characterology therefore falls not to the Panonian (as Tomašić claims) but to the Central and East-Balkan types, and particularly to Bulgarians (the Easternmost group) who are depicted as totally unimaginative yet insidiously cunning, as neither remembering nor honoring their ancestors and past glories, and as generally crude, callow, and coarse.

The qualities of Dinaric man, as defined by Cvijić, continues Tomašić, "are live spirit, sharp intelligence, deep feelings, rich fantasy, impulsiveness provoked by nonmaterial motives, national pride, and the ideas of honor, justice and freedom. Dinaric man is a born statesman, and his main urge is to create a powerful state, to resurrect the 'Czardom of Dušan,' the medieval Serb political community abolished by the Turks in the battle of Kosovo" (ibid.:54–55).

If, for Tomašić, highlanders are negative and lowlanders positive, for Cvijić, to put it somewhat schematically, it is exactly the opposite— the higher the altitude, the nobler the character. One of the keys to understanding these valuations lies in the phrase "a born statesman." State-building capacity was a matter of great importance at the time Cvijić was doing his major research. As one of six senior experts at the Paris Peace Conference, Cvijić was closely involved in the formal creation of Yugoslavia. It is certainly not a matter of chance, Halpern and Hammel note, "that his monumental work, *The Balkan Peninsula,* was published first in French in 1918, and only later in Serbo-Croatian" (1969:20).

Cvijić was obviously concerned about presenting a little-known population to "civilized" Europe in the most favorable light, and most important was to present it as inherently capable of state-building.[2] To understand this concern one has to bear in mind the prevalent characterizations of Slavs in the "civilized" Europe of that time as being of the "dovish disposition"—peaceful, passive, and non–state-building (*nedržavotvorni*), as Dvorniković, a very important student of Cvijić, notes in his huge *Characterology of Yugoslavs* (Dvorniković 1939:141). According to the famous Slavicist Alexander Brückner, Dvorniković reports, Slavs are:

> good-natured and hospitable, carefree and joyful . . . without initiative and energy, indolent and superficial . . . they retreat before every attack, avoid all authority . . . In addition, they are inordinately humble, seek after nothing, and that's why despite their courage, large numbers, and physical endurance, they were not made for conquerors or founders of states. (Dvorniković 1939:141–142)

Dvorniković's *Characterology* can be read as a 1,060-page-long refutation of the above view. Tomašić relates *zadruga* culture, and, by extension, Croats, to the culture that existed among the Slav farming folk in the marshy plains of Polesia at the beginning of the Christian era. For Tomašić, this ancestry is something positive, especially contrasted to the "Ural-Altaic" or even Tartar origins he ascribes to Dinarics. For Dvorniković, however, that same ancestral Slav population is tainted by its passivity and inability to build states. He is at great pains to establish at least some high altitude pedigree for that portion of Slavdom that migrated to the Balkans and to thus differentiate them from their passive, amorphous Slavic brothers.[3] For Dvorniković, even more than for Cvijić, the state-building capacity is related to higher altitudes that breed the necessary backbone, initiative, and hardness. Perhaps this is why so much of this thick volume is devoted to various plays on the hard-soft and active-passive continuum.

On the most inclusive scale, the mountain-hardened South Slavs are contrasted to the soft Russians and Poles with their "lack of highland energy," "soft languages," and love of diminutives (Dvorniković 1939:283). The same dichotomy is then refracted recursively among the South Slavs themselves, and could be seen, for instance, reflected in the dialects of Serbo-Croatian. "Štokavian is a 'hardened' Slavic speech," Dvorniković writes,

> Kajkavian is, like Russian, a soft language of the lowlanders . . . Particularly sharp is the opposition between the masculine *što* and feminine *kaj* . . . which was not without influence on the tribal-political relationships between Serbs and Croats, between the Štokavian Belgrade and mostly Kajkavian Zagreb. (Dvorniković 1939:635, 642)

Hardness is evident in the montagnard physiognomies as well. Their faces are "sharp, angular, accented: [This is] the type that does not bend, does not retreat before the clash, ready to thrust and parry. No, this is not the old Slav of Prokopios and Herder . . . who 'retreats before every pressure!'" (ibid.:197).

For Tomašić, mountains correlate with violence and with the whole syndrome of factionalism, power seeking, and what Banfield (1958) will later call "amoral familism." Though he realizes that the bearers of that syndrome played an important role in the state formation, even more important for Tomašić is the instability they bring to the whole region. Opposed to turmoil brought by the highlander element, and its congenitally undemocratic personality, *zadruga* mentality, Tomašić argues, offers a factor of stability and democracy.

Here we have seen how the opposite poles of the same highland-lowland dichotomy can reverse valence depending on who is talking to whom and for what purpose. This dichotomy, furthermore, is reproduced within both of its poles—namely, both Croats, supposedly on the lowlander side of the scale, and Serbs, supposedly at the highlander end, divide themselves further into internal lowlanders and highlanders.

HIGHLANDERS AND LOWLANDERS AMONG THE SERBS

It was not very hard for Tomašić to use Cvijić in emphasizing the negative traits of the Dinarics.[4] Alongside his romanticizing and extolling, Cvijić also criticized the Dinaric ethnopsychological type. Yet, by and large, wittingly or unwittingly, he was the originator of what historian Slobodan Jovanović called "the Dinaric psychosis."

> What was an ethnological finding for Cvijić was transformed into a national ideal in Serbia at the turn of the century . . . and in that trans-

formation, the Dinaric type was significantly simplified . . . What was emphasized was his dynamism, his impetuosity and heroism, and his reckless bravery that asks not what is and what is not possible. (Jovanović 1991:83)

For Cvijić, the most strongly opposed to Dinaric pride and impetuosity was the *rayah* mentality of the valley folk in those regions where the population was exposed to centuries of Turkish oppression. How strong the positive image of Dinarics was in Serbia could, for instance, be discerned in the attempts by certain followers of Cvijić to claim more Dinaric traits for some of these populations. Thus Dušan Nedeljković tries to prove, in 1929, that the South Serbians—very much a *rayah* tainted population in Cvijić's account—were, in fact, "typically Dinaric in their basic psychic traits" (in Jovanović 1992:102).

Yet there are internal divisions among the Serbs that use the idiom of the opposition between mountaineers and valley folk where the valuations are reversed—the mountaineers are seen negatively and the valley folk positively, often in terms identical to those used by Tomašić and Meštrović on a larger scale. Appeals to this ethnopsychological idiom became very prominent at the time when the Yugoslav crisis was rapidly devolving into a civil war.

A well-known Belgrade psychiatrist, Vladimir Adamović, wrote in January 1991, on the eve of the war in Croatia, that he was afraid of the conflict between the Serbian and the Croatian Dinarics in Croatia. Of different faith, they are nevertheless of the same psychological constitution—fanatics and capable of boundless hate—and that's why the conflict between them, Adamović concluded, was bound to bring so many casualties. This is a footnote to an essay in which he contrasts the Serbs of the Morava region with the classical Dinaric Highlanders. Cvijić considered the population of this heartland of Serbia to have been predominantly Dinaric, but Adamović, contrary to Dušan Nedeljković mentioned above, argues that the Morava Serbs are *less* Dinaric than Cvijić thought. They are less narcissistic and vengeful, more rational and pragmatic, and more inclined toward compromises. After the war in 1945, however, the Dinarics swept into Serbia, Adamović says, especially cities, and became dominant in party, state, military, and police institutions. This is a type, he says, inclined to extremism, disproportional aggressiveness, rigidity, and fanaticism with elements of messianism.

Dinarics are good for a short war, an uprising or a revolution, the Morava Serbs for periods of peace, negotiation, and dialogue. On the eve of the war, however, the predominance of Dinarics in Serbia can spell disaster, Adamović thinks, so he pleads for "more Morava types wherever the fate of the nation is being decided" (Adamović 1991:93).

"On the Morava rivers," writes Danko Popović (1994:80), "they fear that the warmongers could drag Serbia in the new bloodlettings." An author of the immensely popular *Book of Milutin,* an ode to the Serbian Šumadija peasant that was reprinted in seventeen editions by 1986, Danko Popović was certainly one of the most influential promoters of the thesis that pits the impetuosity, irrational extremism, and nationalistic fanaticism of the Dinaric Highlanders against the sobriety, wisdom, pragmatism, and peacefulness of Morava peasants. "Is it normal that Serbia is ruled by the Serbs from outside of Serbia, as if it were a colony populated by primitive tribes?" Popović asks. No, he replies, "it is exactly the opposite—they are the ones who are forcing the tribal spirit and habits on an area which is legally organized as a state" (ibid.:93).

Echoes of Tomašić! Here is Danko Popović, a prominent Serbian nationalist, claiming, as Tomašić did fifty years before, that it is the peaceful lowlanders who are the state-builders while their mountaineer Dinaric brethren are warmongers and state-destroyers.

The highlanders are often collectively referred to as "Serbs" (Srbi) in opposition to "Serbians" (Srbijanci)—meaning the Serbs from Serbia proper. The "Serbs" are also called "prečani," meaning "those across the river," in this case, the Drina River that forms the natural boundary between Serbia and Bosnia.[5]

If the sober, peace-loving lowlander Serbians are lamenting what they see as domination by their megalomaniacal, impetuous highlander brethren, it is only to be expected that the latter might have a different view of the situation. In 1991 the influential Belgrade weekly *NIN* was running a series of essays titled: "The Dinarics and the Serbians." The fifth installment featured Nikola Koljević, a professor of English literature at the University of Sarajevo, and later one of the top leaders of Republika Srpska (he committed suicide in 1997). He accused *NIN* of abusing its newly won freedom from communist control by conducting an "anthropogeographical" survey of "who is who" among the Serbs in which "the so-called Dinarics got the worst deal." He goes on to sarcastically enumerate their supposed sins in the eyes of the Belgrade weekly: they are guilty for refusing "to be cast in chains preferring instead to be in a centuries long mountain hideaway," and for "taking over many respectable and influential positions" through their connections in Belgrade. This is not "civilizationally" correct, Koljević notes with heavy irony—"How could it be when, since the times of Cvijić, it is well known that those are one and all violent types who are poisoning the agrarian tender souls with their aggressive visions of Serbian unity and concern for the brothers in other Serbian regions" (Koljević 1991). It should be noted that Koljević puts the "agrarian tender souls" in the same category with the "decadent" Belgrade elite luxuriating in fine distinctions, overly sophisticated democratic principles, and neurotic individualism at the time when the great danger to the nation as a whole necessitates the highlanders' superior mettle and sense of national mission.

The Belgrade cosmopolitan intellectuals, of course, strike back. In an essay titled "Murder of the City," for instance, Bogdan Bogdanović, an architect-philosopher, a former mayor of Belgrade (1982–1986), and an impeccably sophisticated urbanite, posits an "eternal Manichaean battle" between "city lovers" and "city haters," or "city destroyers" (Bogdanović 1993). The immediate context is the Serbian shelling of Vukovar, Dubrovnik, and Sarajevo, and one can easily discern the dichotomy of mountain vs. urban folk, or the Dinaric Savage vs. Sarajevo Urban Cosmopolitan underlying his argument. Bogdanović was perhaps the most outspoken representative of the opposition intelligentsia in Serbia that condemns the montagnard mentality as the antithesis to civility, modernity, and Europeanness (Veselinov 1992; Vasiljević 1992).

As for the "agrarian tender souls," here is a very characteristic response to highlanders in the extremely lowland northern Vojvodina coming from Nikola J. Novaković, a lawyer from Novi Sad, and secretary of the local Rotary Club:

> Our peasants lean on the Fruška gora[6] with their feet in the Danube and they see to the ends of Europe. Those others [highlander newcomers] do not have the breadth [of view] and do not know how to look. They see nothing but the mountains up to their noses, only the sky, vertically . . . Some hard and harsh people. They holler and snarl, swallow vowels or twist them.[7] They proclaimed force and power as justice, deception and corruption as morality, malice and envy as custom, Asiatic howling as

music, and pistols and revolvers as the national costume . . . Comrades,[8]
here we celebrate others' successes and we pay for our own drink. This is
the essential difference between the comrades and the gentlemen (gos-
poda). I am not losing hope that you will understand the importance of
good manners and good domestic upbringing. (Novaković 1994)

Not having mountains to block his view, the Vojvodina lowlander peasant can see to the ends of Europe and is thus allied with
it. In Novaković's view, he is a kind of peasant-cosmopolitan.[9] And for
all the bitterness the natives feel for the newcomers, according to the
saying, "came the wild, and kicked out the tame" (došli divlji, isterali
pitome), Novaković believes that the "wild" will eventually get tamed
themselves.

We see how somebody like the Rotarian Novaković—obviously an
urbanite intellectual—extols the virtues of peasants over the vices of
highlander newcomers. In that he is allied with the influential writer
Danko Popović with his idealized Morava peasants. Cosmopolitans like
Bogdanović, however, are contrasting idealized urbanites rather than
idealized peasants to the violent highlanders. The highlander urbanite
Koljević pits his proud Dinarics against both the "agrarian tender souls"
and the Belgrade decadent urbanites who somehow coalesce into a single
group.

These oppositions could also be expressed in the idiom of lowland
mud vs. highland limestone (with urbanites represented by either asphalt or cobblestone). Thus ecologist Dragan Jovanović meditates, in
1995, on how a Piroćanac (inhabitant of the South Serbian town of Pirot),
"nurtured by the limestone of Stara Planina" (Old Mountain) shares
more with the distant Herzegovinian, nurtured in the harsh limestone
(ljuti kras) than the Herzegovinian shares with his neighboring "lead"
Bosnian. On the other hand, the Danube-Morava lowlanders, with "centuries of river mud in their genes," have much in common with their
brethren nurtured on the mud, sludge, and mire of the Northern Vojvodina plains (Jovanović 1995).

Depending on who is talking to whom, when, under what circumstances, and for what purpose, the permutations and combinations of
these ethnopsychological distinctions, sometimes seemingly logically
inconsistent, can assume dizzying complexity, not least because the
highland/lowland dichotomy sometimes aligns with, and sometimes

cuts across, the urban-peasant one. The tokens of highlander or low-lander mentality could be pinned on different regions and different groups of people in order to "exalt or debase identities" in the "quality space" (Fernandez 1986). Both could be given a whole spectrum of variously shaded valuations: lowlanders could be seen as rational, pragmatic, cultivated, on the one hand, or degenerate, soft, and submissive, on the other; the highlanders, as brave, proud, of superior mettle or, obversely, as violent, primitive, and arrogant.

SERBIAN EPICS: BALLADS AND BULLETS IN BOSNIA

Cvijić, Dvorniković, and Tomašić worked within disciplines that were ancestral to modern-day social/cultural anthropology: Ratzel's human geography, Volkerpsychologie of Lazarus and Steinthal, characterology of Ludwig Clages, or national and social character studies. These disciplines are now consigned to the museum of sciences, and we are inclined to relegate the notions of ethnopsychological type or national character to the status of tokens of identity or rhetorical devices. Who would dare say today that the Dinaric type accurately describes the actual character of a whole people? Yet Halpern and Hammel, American anthropologists who spent decades studying Yugoslavs, say in their overview of the intellectual history of ethnology and other social sciences in Yugoslavia that

> these theories about "folk mentality," as the Yugoslavs call it, are now a firm part of folk social science, encapsulated in a series of ethnic stereotypes. Interestingly enough, they are fairly accurate; whether because they originally summarized behavior in an adequate way or because people live up to role models, or both, is hard to say. (Halpern and Hammel 1969:21)

It is this "folk mentality"—seen as a sediment of centuries and almost biological in its resistance to change—that was seen not only by outside observers but also by many local actors to lie at the root of the Yugoslav disaster.

Different types of mentality were invoked to explain different predicaments, but when it comes to explaining the Yugoslav wars of succession, it was usually the violent Dinaric character that was seen as the root of all evil by outsiders and local actors alike. The Dinaric type is, of course, associated with mountains, and mountains were often invoked as if the highland pedigree is sufficient to explain the mentality.[10] But mountains are just one metonymic marker standing for a whole cluster of traits that is consistent with the typical Mediterranean "honor and shame" complex, including semi-nomadic pastoralism, absence of state-imposed order, agnatic descent groups, blood feuds, and the whole "game of honor" pattern. In the case of Yugoslav highlanders, another prominent feature enters into the mentality equation—epic poetry.

Jovan Cvijić based his influential study of the violent Dinaric character on the analysis of one epic poem in which irrational violence plays a major role. For him, just like for his Croatian counterpart, Dinko Tomašić, epic poetry of the Dinaric Highlander was an expression of his underlying mentality and a good diagnostic tool.[11]

For the German Slavicist Reinhard Lauer, however, the Serbian epics were more than mere expressions. They were not just models of but, more significant, models for—they were prescriptions for violence. For Lauer, violence in poetry spelled violence in actual behavior. Evil myths lead to evil acts. In an article published in the *Frankfurter Allgemeine Zeitung* of March 6, 1993, under the title "From Murderers to Heroes: On the Heroic Poetry of Serbs," he argues that in turbulent times national myths can bring to the fore potential militancy, brutality, intolerance, and inhumanity—thus "turning humans into the beasts."[12] These characteristics are supposedly inherent in the "Serbian myth" which is different from, and more malignant than, myths of other nations.

It is easy to demonstrate that oral epics as a genre, wherever they are found, are full of cruelty and bloodshed of truly "epic" proportions. In the sheer hyperbolae of gratuitous slaughter Serbian epic poetry is quite mild in comparison with the *Mahabharata*, for instance. But this is poetic, not real, violence. Epic battles and rivers of blood are tropes of a metaphysical argument. If there is a connection between violence in myths and oral poetry and actual violence of war, than that connection must be more complex than Lauer's argument would grant.

For one, Lauer admits that the myth of the wolf, of *hajduci* (brigands), and the epic songs celebrating Prince Marko (his main evidence) are to be found in other South Slavic and Balkan traditions, yet somehow it is only the Serbs who are "turned into beasts" by them. What is a fund of motifs common to a number of related groups slips into not only the index but an icon of only one—the Serbs. In reality, all three communities that were involved in the war in Bosnia have their mountain, as well as valley and urban folk, all of them have used the *gusle*,[13] and have a long tradition of heroic or epic oral poetry. After all, Milman Parry's famous collection of oral poetry is mostly drawn from Bosnian Muslim bards, not from the Serbs (see Lord 2000). With the advent of war a boundary reinforcement occurred, and each community selected only some out of the general pool of largely shared traits as markers of their identity, so that epic poetry accompanied by the *gusle* became firmly associated with the Serbian community only.

Together with this segregation of traits goes the tendency to convert them from diacritics, or badges of identity into essences, or from indexes into icons in the process of "iconization" (Irvine and Gal 2000:37). Thus the *gusle* and epic ballads somehow display the "inherent nature or essence" of a group—in this case the Bosnian Serbs. One can find this assertion on the part of Bosnian Serbs themselves. After all they willingly posed for the BBC filmmaker Pawlikowski, and Radovan Karadžić himself, in what has now become a famous scene, played the *gusle* and sang an epic song in the house where Vuk Karadžić, the Romantic language reformer and collector of epic songs—the true father of the modern Serbian nation—was born. And not only did Radovan Karadžić choose to play the *gusle* in Vuk Karadžić's house (now a museum), but he also claimed direct descent from this ancestral figure by pointing before Pawlikowski's camera to a dimple in Vuk's chin and a similar one in his own as proof.

Let us now turn to another prominent German Slavicist—Gerhard Gesemann (1968), who studied the heroic ethos of the most exemplary group of Dinaric Highlanders, the traditional Montenegrins.[14] His primary source were the short heroic stories, particularly those collected by one of the last authentic embodiments of Montenegrin "heroic lifeform," Marko Miljanov (1833–1901). Those stories were not just expressions of the underlying ethos; they had a central role in actually sustaining it (see Miljanov 1967).

Within the moral economy of a traditional Montenegrin or Albanian society, epic songs fulfill a function similar to that of short heroic stories. Here is how Marko Miljanov expresses it when he talks about the Albanians and their songs:[15]

But what out of all their customs most strictly binds them to their law and teaches them to embrace the beautiful and spurn the ugly—are their folk songs that crown their death and life. The one who deserves that folk songs disgrace him, that one has no life among them, neither he, nor his progeny, but the curse spreads also to those who would intermarry with them or have other friendship with them. And the one who deserves to be sung in the heroic songs . . . those they respect and even glorify, and ask to intermarry with the blood of such as him, if only, as they say, in the ninth remove . . . In a word, with them the rise and fall are by the song, for other damage to honor could be repaired so as not to be suffered forever, and what is ugly could be caught and washed away with the beautiful. But the songs, once they are let loose among the people, they will not be caught, nor washed, but the stain of darkness will stay on him and his lineage forever. Under this whip of severity is the honor of Albanians bound (Gesemann 1968:36–7).[16]

Heroic short stories and epic songs were a major part of its moral economy. They were not explicitly formulated rules of honor but examples of its practice. Marko Miljanov was among the last people who belonged to this heroic world. His writing down of stories coincided with the disintegration of the very society that gave birth to them. The game of honor, as Bourdieu (1966) would call it, had to die as lived practice in order to be reincarnated as literature.

In the 1830s Vuk Karadžić published his collections of Serbian epic poetry. Serbian oral tradition became fixed once and forever in writing. From their embeddedness in the heroic societies of patriarchal mountaineers, the epics migrated into school textbooks to become the backbone of Serbian national ideology and state-building. A century later, in the 1930s, Milman Parry stayed away from Serbian epic singers precisely because they were mostly literate and were simply reproducing the fixed songs from Vuk Karadžić's canonical collections verbatim, whereas he was interested in how illiterate bards rapidly compose in performance without the notion of a fixed text to be memorized (Lord 2000).

By playing the *gusle* in the birthplace of Vuk Karadžić, Radovan Karadžić was engaging in what the Belgrade ethnologist Ivan Čolović calls the "war propaganda folklorism." Politicians, he says, "garnish their militant speeches with quotations from epic poems and popular proverbs and references to personalities who symbolize national identity . . . The aim of this strategy is to suggest that whatever is sought, desired or offered in these messages reflects the deepest feelings of the nation and represents the voice of the people, *vox populi,* and not the master's voice" (Čolović 1993:116–117).

Briggs and Bauman refer to this strategy in terms of what they call the "intertextual gap." The fit between a particular text and its generic model, they argue, is never perfect. The process of linking particular utterances to generic models—here Serbian epic songs—thus necessarily produces an intertextual gap. Given the gap, however, one could pursue the strategy of either minimizing or maximizing it (Briggs and Bauman 1992:149). Radovan Karadžić is certainly trying to minimize the gap between what epic poetry used to be in the old heroic times and the present moment where he is performing for Pawlikowski's camera.

It is important to note that Pawlikowski is himself also trying to minimize the intertextual gap, and so is Reinhard Lauer—only they do it with an opposite aim. They agree with Karadžić that Serbs are people moved by epics; for Karadžić, however, the epics are heroic, whereas for Lauer and Pawlikowski the epics are evil. They are erasing the gap between traditional genres and a complex event such as the war in Bosnia—between rhetoric and action. In effect, they are colluding with Radovan Karadžić in short-circuiting the twisting path that links the ballads and the bullets in Bosnia.

It is actually not very hard to expose the fallacies inherent in the kind of argument Lauer or Pawlikowski advances.[17] On the other hand, this is not to say that mountains and upbringing, myths and epic ballads, as well as the modern poetry and political rhetoric that draw on them have nothing to do with war and violence. The path that connects them, however, is neither short nor straight.[18]

FOUR

Tender-hearted Criminals and the Reverse Pygmalion

Stone, mud, and asphalt are substances that figuratively distinguish groups and exalt or debase identities. In their various oppositions and alignments they stand for highlanders vs. lowlanders, urbanites vs. peasants, the civilized vs. the barbarous. Dvorniković showed how these recursive distinctions and metaphoric continua could easily get gendered—the highlanders hard and edged like limestone that nurtured them, their faces angular and accented, their language sharp and strong on augmentatives, are opposed to the soft dialects of lowlanders, and their meek, dovish dispositions born of the mire and mud of their marshes. It is very easy to translate this hard-soft distinction into the male-female one. Asphalt, on the other hand, stands for civilization/ urbanity, softer than stone but harder than mud. These substances are used as tropes in everyday speech as well as in literature and social commentary, but they are also embedded in scripts, plots, and narratives. People of stone and people of mud are actors in historical dramas that pit them against each other, and variously align them with, or oppose them to, the people of asphalt. They conquer and colonize each other only to be corrupted by, or converted into, the element of the conquered in a kind of rock-paper-scissors game. Hard Dinarics become softer in the Vojvodina lowlands, and asphalt, though perennially muddied by rural newcomers, transforms peasants into urbanites. But these oppositions are also gendered, and one could expect them to play themselves out in that most popular of genres—romantic plots. Conquest, corruption, conversion—what better arena for their dramatization than that of romantic entanglement. Not all possible combinations, however, equally attracted the imagination of people in Serbia and the former Yugoslavia, as evidenced in preferences for particular pairings and the near absence of others. As I will show through feature films and popular literature, in the rock-paper-scissors game played by men and women of stone, mud, and asphalt, it was practically always the female who represented the higher civilizational position at whatever level of inclusion.

THE TENDER-HEARTED CRIMINAL

In the 1970s and 1980s, in Belgrade, a definite stereotype was formed as a part of urban folklore—the stereotype of the Noble Criminal. Its crystallization probably owes a great deal to the figure of Ljubomir Magaš, popularly known as Ljuba Zemunac, who became a "legend" during his lifetime, and whose death in Frankfurt at the hands of another Belgrade criminal, in 1986, finally enthroned him as the embodiment of the type. Since then the tough boys of Belgrade figured prominently in Belgrade sensationalist press and aspired for the status of the "urban legend" approximating that of Ljuba Zemunac. And, indeed, as folklore has it, when they wanted to show respect, they would hail each other with: Hi, legend! (*De si legendo!*)

In *Pretty Village, Pretty Flame* (*Lepa sela lepo gore*), a 1996 Serbian film based on a true story, seven Serbian soldiers find themselves besieged by their Muslim foes in an abandoned tunnel in Eastern Bosnia.[1] The Belgrade director Srdjan Dragojević made each of them a distinct type instantly recognizable by the local audience—a retired Yugoslav army officer, a provincial grade school teacher, a Belgrade junkie, and two simpleminded peasant Chetniks.[2] Flashbacks offer character summaries and provide the reasons why each one of them ended up fighting in the war. The story revolves around two prewar friends from Bosnia, both perfectly ordinary and likable guys, one Muslim the other Serb, who find themselves on the opposite sides. The film is powerful and rich, brimming with allusions, citations, and vignettes, the unpacking of which could illuminate much of the background to the Bosnian war, but in this chapter I focus on only one of the instantly recognizable social types, that of Velja, the Belgrade criminal.

As a dramatic and visual medium, film, among other things, offers the advantage of packing a huge amount of character clues in the very demeanor of the actor. In addition, skillful casting can take advantage of a wealth of associations particular actors bring from roles they played in other movies, TV shows, and theater plays that are well known to the domestic audience. Dragojević was especially lauded for casting Velimir Bata Živojinović as a Yugoslav army officer, for as the hero of countless patriotic Partisan movies Živojinović's face alone, in the context of *Pretty Village,* brings a devastating critique of a whole era of which he may well have been the most visible and famous popular embodiment.[3]

The actor Nikola Kojo who plays Velja the criminal in *Pretty Village* continued to be cast in practically identical roles in several subsequent Serbian films. With the help of these other films I propose to reconstruct a more detailed portrait of the Belgrade Noble Criminal.

Characters imply stories. They are fashioned by stories, they encapsulate them, and they generate them. In one of the flashbacks in the *Pretty Village,* we see Velja flamboyantly arriving home from Germany in a brand new BMW full of stolen booty. "Don't look at me like that," he says to his mother, "I honestly bought all of this, only I lost the receipts, hee hee." Military police appear at the door asking for Velja's younger brother—a promising archaeology student. They are going to draft him and send him to Bosnia to fight a war in which Serbia is officially not involved. The majority of young men in Serbia, especially in Belgrade, developed elaborate draft-dodging strategies in 1992, but Velja's brother is obviously about to be caught. Before anyone can react, Velja coolly steps in and presents himself as his brother. "Here are the car keys," he tells his brother as the Military Police take him away, "the seats you pull down from the side, and the legs you put on your shoulders, pardon me mom."

The Noble Criminal is extravagantly magnanimous and generous. He is an archetypal protector of the weak. In his brilliant study of the myth of Ljuba Zemunac, Ivan Čolović (1994) analyzes what he calls "the paradox of the protector." Ljuba is not only the noble protector of the weak, extravagantly generous and tender, he is at the same time extremely ruthless, violent, and cruel.

Čolović's primary sources are numerous articles and serials published in Belgrade newspapers after Ljuba was killed, as well as more than a hundred obituaries and the poem carved on his tombstone in the Zemun cemetery (figure 4.1). Here is the text of the poem:

His heart was warm for the little people	Toplo je srce imao za male
He carried a sword into the unjust world	U svet nepravde nosio je mač ljuti
He punished insatiable ogres	Kažnjavao je nezasite ale
His path led to Robin Hood.	Robinu Hudu vodili ga puti.
He saved those down and out	Spasavao je kome beše teško
Gave away lots of his blood	Razdelio je mnogo svoje krvi
Everything became noble with him	Sve je kod njega postalo viteško
Born to lead, he remained the first.	Rodjen za vodju, ostao je prvi.
Cowards he despised strongly	Kukavice je tvrdo prezirao
He knew the secret that binds people	Znao je tajnu koja ljude veže
In the German trap he fell bullet-ridden	Nemačkom zamkom izrešetan pao
In his soil with dignity he rests.	U svoju zemlju dostojanstven leže.

Some of these motifs are echoed in a song about a tender-hearted criminal, "Žika the Nerve (*Žika Živac*)" by one of the most popular Yugoslav rock bands, Fish Soup (*Riblja Čorba*) which is much better known than Ljuba's epitaph.

Žika the Nerve is utterly benign	Žika Živac je dobar k'o panja
if you leave him alone.	Ako ga mnogo ne diraju.
In principle, he stays out of trouble	On, u principu, izbegava sranja
but he's easy to provoke.	Ali ga lako iznerviraju.
Žika was born with a miraculous gift:	Žika je rodjen sa čudesnim darom:
his right will send you to the grave.	Sa'rani kad potegne desnicu.
That's why he only slapped,	Zato je tuk'o samo šamarom,
he never used his fist.	Nije koristio pesnicu.
Žika the Nerve is the usual suspect,	Žika Živac je dežurni krivac
he is a bad guy by definition.	One je obeleženi negativac.
When kids rob a bank	Dripci kad banku obiju
Žika goes to jail.	Žika zaglavi robiju

FIGURE 4.1.

The bronze statue of Ljuba Zemunac on his grave in Zemun.

When in Germany once	Kad su u Švapskoj 'apsili Žiku
terrible German cops arrested Žika	Grozni nemački policajci
He faced them, spit and said:	Žika se okrete, pljunu i reče:
—Hey cops up yours!	—Ej, policajci, steram vam ga majci!
His hands are like shovels	On ima ruke k'o lopate
but his heart is bigger than Russia.	A srce od Rusije veće
That's why he and his wife are miserable	Zato se on i žena mu zlopate
for he has no luck, no luck at all.	Jer nema sreće, nema sreće.

The war in the former Yugoslavia with its violence, poverty, and the breakdown of moral standards brought the "tough boys of the Belgrade asphalt" to a new prominence. A fascinating documentary titled *See You in the Obituary: The Crime That Changed Serbia* (*Vidimo se u čitulji*) appeared in 1995 showing some of these self-proclaimed "legends" talking openly about themselves.[4] Some of them were quite eloquent, especially one by the name of Christian, who provided a sophisticated social critique of the circumstances obtaining in the present-day Serbia that gave rise to the upsurge in petty gang wars and the promotion of small-time criminals into national heroes.

As testified by a retired officer of the State Security Service (SDB) in the documentary, the Yugoslav government at one time issued fake passports to criminals that allowed them to return repeatedly to Western Europe and engage in criminal activities so they would have no reason to do so at home. At the same time the Service used some of them as hit men against the militantly anticommunist circles of Yugoslav emigration in the West. The criminals were thus under the control of, and protected by, the police and could claim the status of patriots. A faked passport was considered a badge of honor.

The conflict between generations emerges as one of the main themes in the documentary. Old "legends," in their forties and fifties at the time of filming, constantly express their dismay over the supposed lack of honor and decorum among the new kids. They consider themselves noble knights, quite in keeping with the Ljuba Zemunac heritage, while they accuse the younger generation of gratuitous violence, the indiscriminate use of massive firepower, and a total lack of "business" sense. "They'd rather have ten thousand Deutsche Marks if they can get them now," one of the "sober businessman" types said, "than work steadily for a year in order to get a million." The young, for their part, emphasize the superiority of their "fast lane" lifestyle over that of the downtrodden, meek masses of mere "mortals." "What I experience in a day, they don't get to experience during their whole lives," declares one of the youngsters in the documentary. Expensive cars, beautiful girls, gambling in the most exclusive casinos, risk and adventure, massive golden chains around their necks—this is the kind of glamour everyone dreams about, the same character says, only they are too cowardly to take a plunge. The young "knights of asphalt" (*vitezovi asfalta*) parade their bravado and expect to die young. They settle their accounts with Hecklers, not with fists, and greet one another with "see you in the obituary."

Two films produced in Serbia at the end of the 1990s have this generational conflict as their main story. The first, *Rage* (*Do koske*), released in 1997, tells about a seventeen-year-old Belgrade tough boy who in a fit of rage abducts his older criminal mentor and boss, and together with his youthful gang tortures him throughout the film in an abandoned steel mill. The older gangster, played by Lazar Ristovski (who also plays Blacky in Kusturica's *Underground,*[5] is a complete stereotype: He is enormously virile and vital, seemingly indestructible. He sees himself as an honorable criminal, a rational businessman, and a patriot who helped the government fight its secret war with radical emigrants in the seventies and who took part in the recent war (as many of his class actually did).[6] The young toughs, on the other hand, engage in nothing but totally blind rage and gratuitous violence. Even their quite eloquent leader never really expresses anything but unfocused anger at everything. The film ends with a shootout between the Old Guard and kids in which everybody but the old boss gets killed.

Finally, the director of *Pretty Village, Pretty Flame* Srdjan Dragojević in his 1998 film, *Wounds* (*Rane*), takes up a very similar plot. Born after Tito's death in 1980, the two main protagonists of *Wounds* grow up in the bleak disoriented world of Milošević's Serbia. They become apprentices of the local petty gangster, Crazy Kure,[7] who aspires to the status of an "urban legend." He drives a BMW but lives in a shack with his cheap tavern singer girlfriend. He bosses it over the locals but backs down before the bigger cats. His ambition is to appear on the (imaginary) TV show

The Pulse of the Asphalt (*Puls asfalta*), in which an attractive hostess invites prominent Belgrade criminals to talk about themselves. Mostly in the character of Crazy Kure, the director undermines the romanticism of the Noble Criminal. While, for instance, he brags about robbing a bank in Germany, we are shown Crazy Kure actually robbing a small drugstore with a plastic gun, and so on.

The actor who played Velja, the Noble Criminal of *Pretty Village*, Nikola Kojo, appears in both movies. In *Rage* he is the old boss's right hand and one of the Old Guard. In *Wounds* he is one of the urban legends, nicknamed Biberče. We see him appearing briefly in *The Pulse of the Asphalt* talking about his preference for brains over guns and showing his school grade report with straight A's. "We were gentlemen in Germany," he says about his fellow Belgrade criminals, "everybody respected us." Early in the movie he humiliates Crazy Kure, and one of the boys kills him later with hardly a flinch. Unlike Velja in *Pretty Village,* there is nothing romantic about Biberče in *Wounds.* He is just a criminal and a war profiteer whose only motive is money.

One of our heroes, Pinki, serves as the narrator in the film. He is highly articulate like the real-life Christian in *See You in the Obituary* or like Alex in Anthony Burgess's *Clockwork Orange,* but he is not providing any coherent social critique, and he couldn't care less about high culture. Nothing really interests him, not even money. After they kill Biberče, our heroes suddenly find themselves addressed as "legends" among aspiring members of the Belgrade underground. They have achieved the coveted status, but they couldn't care less even about that. When they appear on *The Pulse of the Asphalt,* and when the hostess asks if they have any wounds to show like her other, older guests, the inarticulate one, Švaba, takes that as an insult and shoots himself in the thigh, so as to have a wound to show. As the audience scrambles out of the studio in panic, Švaba forces the cameraman to continue shooting. He limps to the camera lens waving his gun and, as his face fills the TV screens, he shouts at the multitudes watching in their homes: "Hah, you shat in your pants, didn't you, you miserable mice!"

Pinki and Švaba, as well as the kids in the movie *Rage,* are particular ciphers, or incarnations, of the inchoate misery of Milošević's Serbia. They are not even attempting to offer any ideological rationalization for their behavior. They are pure rage born of the particular Serbian anomie, and that rage is inarticulate, directionless, and blind. As a critic has put it:

> Kids who take guns and in between two cocaine hits start shooting at anything that moves are just the oblivious, inarticulate Avengers who don't have a clue about anything except that it should be somehow Different, or otherwise life is not worth living. But there is no easy and cheap exit from this gutter [of Milošević's Serbia] and that's why all that they accomplish is to kill each other cross-wise like those types from Tarantino's *Reservoir Dogs*. (Pančić 1998:37)

It is wrong, however, to make too much of the analogy between *Wounds* and either Kubrick's *Clockwork Orange* or Tarantino's movies. The anomie, or moral breakdown, that produced their characters was of a different hue, if not of a different order, than that of Milošević's Serbia.

There is no catharsis at the end of *Wounds,* and Dragojević (1998:38) explicitly stated that he didn't want to provide it. After the two protagonists shoot each other, "Tarantino style," Pinki as the narrator addresses the audience from beyond the grave: "If you are hot on being cool, then I must be your idol, hah mice? I do sometimes regret that I haven't seen that Abroad, but fuck it, you cannot do everything in your life. Stinkers here stinkers there, who cares anyway. Only, it is too bad I haven't screwed a black girl. As for that Eiffel Tower Kure talked about, well my cousins, I don't give a shit about it. This is the End, cousins. And I must say it seems to me in the end that I fared better than you."

Wounds presents a savage critique of the romanticism surrounding the Noble Criminal in Serbia. In *Pretty Village, Pretty Flame,* however, Velja is still presented as a noble, self-sacrificing hero. His portrayal in the film is caricatural and thus tongue-in-cheek, and yet it emerges as essentially sympathetic. Part of his appeal as a character comes from the role he plays as a "knight of Belgrade asphalt" in a short romantic subplot that involves a foreign woman. I take this romantic plot as a starting point in describing a scenario I call the Reverse Pygmalion.

THE REVERSE PYGMALION

An American women journalist joins the ensemble of characters as a stowaway on the truck that the Belgrade junkie drives into the abandoned tunnel. The junkie is the only one in this small band of Serbian paramilitaries who speaks English, and as an urban cosmopolitan he is her only ally. The others are initially hostile, and she serves as a cardboard figure representing the (anti-Serb biased) Western media in the situation. It is, however, Velja the criminal with whom she enters into a special relationship. He inspects her bag and fiddles with her video camera, and as she reaches for it, he slaps her brutally and sends her flying into a corner. "Oh how they loooove it when you beat them," he comments. As the film goes on, however, the relationship between them changes. Driven crazy by the song of his youth which the Muslim fighters play for them, Velja asks the journalist if she would dance with him. "My legs are killing me," she jokingly refuses, whereupon Velja starts dancing alone in the full view of their Muslim besiegers, taunting them to shoot at him in a fit of irrational, suicidal bravado. "You disappoint me," he says, looking at the bullet wounds to his legs but still standing: "These legs jumped from the second floor of the Volks bank." When he later decides to kill himself (so as not to encumber his comrades should they dash for freedom), before pulling the trigger he asks the American who stares at him: "One kiss for a dead man?" and while the junkie is filming with her video camera, she gives him a long passionate kiss. "A true Hollywood slobbering," Velja says impressed, "that's worth living for, at least for a little while longer," and then, after a second, "I am joking, you go on!" and he blows his head off.

There exists a logic, I would argue, that makes Velja the criminal the only male in this cast of characters with whom the American woman will have a romantic relationship. As she is quite obviously representing the eye of the West in the movie, we can well expect to see reflected in the way other characters relate to her that tension between the self-presentation and intimate self-recognition that Michael Herzfeld showed in the Greek case (see Herzfeld 1985, 1987). And just as his Cretan highlander animal thieves, even though a marginal group considered "barbaric" in their own nation-state can, under certain circumstances, stand for the whole of Greece, so can a Belgrade criminal stand for the Serbian male in general. His nobility and the way his violence is supposedly irrational and at the same time obeying the strictest rules of (the game of) honor (Bourdieu 1966) make him—both in reality and in narrative—a practitioner of what Herzfeld (1985) calls the "poetics of manhood."[8]

The logic of self-presentation is recursive. The oppositions tend to get reproduced at ascending or descending levels of inclusiveness. Let us then explore this logic which brings together a Belgrade criminal and an American woman in *Pretty Village* by amplifying it with a set of Yugoslav movies that recursively reproduce this opposition on ever smaller scales.

Actually two quite popular Yugoslav movies portray a romantic relationship between an American woman and a Serbian man as their central theme. The first, *Something In-Between* (*Nešto izmedju*) by the Prague-film-school–educated Srdjan Karanović (1983), tells a Jules and Jim story of two Belgrade friends and an American journalist in-between them. The film plays on the theme of in-betweenness so often experienced by peripheries exposed to the gaze of centers. We are a little bit of Vienna, a little bit of Venice, a little bit of Turkey and of Germany, neither here nor there, neither East nor West, neither North nor South, the two friends explain to the naive American. Both friends are actually sophisticated urbanites, not barbarians or criminals, and yet their charm for the pragmatic, rational American journalist comes from their Balkan otherness. One (played by Miki Manojlović) is moody and indecisive, a complex soul torn by inner conflicts; the other (Dragan Nikolić) is an extroverted happy-go-lucky playboy but, at least initially, the American journalist finds this departure from her own sober pragmatism inherently sexy. A much weaker Serbian film, *Better Than Escape* (*Bolje od bekstva*), mirrors this relationship (Lekić 1993). In both movies the Serbian male is abandoned in the end by the pragmatic American female who realizes that the moody, indecisive, even self-destructive Serbian male is not worth the trouble.

Opposing a woman from a civilizationally higher position with a male from the civilizationally lower position is being reproduced internally in a number of Yugoslav movies. I would further argue that the opposite situation is conspicuously absent both in films and in literature. It seems that collective imaginary in Serbia has no place for a script involving a male from the higher position and a female from the lower one. I am thus tempted to frame this situation as the Reverse Pygmalion and to try to show why, in the Balkans, Henry Higgins tends to be a woman and Eliza Doolitle a man.

The two movies explicitly dealing with the American woman versus the Serbian man, however, do not display what could be seen as essential to a Pygmalion-like relationship. The Serbian males are more or less equals to their American female counterparts in terms of class and education, and the women do not actually try to polish their manners or in general cultivate them. But if we extend this relationship to include its recursively related versions, I would argue that such a composite narrative will, in fact, be a Reverse Pygmalion and, in a circuitous way, return us to the tunnel in *Pretty Village, Pretty Flame.*

In Rajko Grlić's 1981 film, *Melody Haunts My Reverie* (*Samo jednom se ljubi*), a ballerina from a bourgeois family teaches a communist commissar from an unspecified Croatian hinterland how to eat properly. She is "the remnant of the class enemy," he a powerful officer of Tito's victorious Partisans. In some small town in Croatia, right after World War II, these two class enemies fall in love and it ends tragically. Not only does the commissar, played by Miki Manojlović, belong to a lower class, most probably peasant, the domestic audience is also likely to classify him as a "highlander" because of the actor's features and manners, as well as other more explicitly "highlander" roles that he played in other movies.

The movie is mostly about the purity of revolutionary resolve being corrupted over time by bourgeois mentality, and about how revolutions end up eating their own children. This is even more bluntly presented in the *Officer with a Rose* (*Oficir s ružom*) which is, artistically, a much weaker twin of *The Melody* (Sorak 1987).[9] Here, however, I am interested only in the fact that this clash of classes and cultures is presented in the idiom of the male-female relationship in which the female is from the culturally and civilizationally higher position than the male, and in which she undertakes to cultivate him.

Finally, the *Premeditated Murder* (*Ubistvo s predumišljajem*) offers a purely intra-Serbian version of the Reverse Pygmalion (Stojanović 1995). There are two parallel stories. One is happening in 1992 during a student protest in Belgrade, where an urban girl gets involved with a Serb from Krajina, a highlander, albeit meek and chaste, as he recuperates from wounds received fighting in Croatia. This story is juxtaposed with the story of the girl's grandmother, an upper-class Belgrade girl who fell for a Partisan commissar right after World War II. The Belgrade student girl and the Krajina boy are not class enemies, but they do belong to two different worlds. As a cosmopolitan urbanite, the girl treats him, at least initially, as a likable but provincial, uncultured pet. "And don't you leave your hair on the soap!" she shouts after she lets him use her bathroom for the first time.[10] The Pygmalion relationship, however, is more pronounced in the grandmother's love story, which is more or less the mirror image of both *Melody* and *Officer with the Rose*.

This repetition of a pattern over generations is a powerful expression of a lament so often heard from the urbanite class in Serbia: as soon as a thin middle-class layer is formed in this peasant society, so the narrative goes, a war or revolution brings forth a new deluge of barbarians (usually the highlanders) that wipes it out. Thus the solid, burgher virtues of rationality and hard work necessary for civic society, as well as cosmopolitanism, never manage to establish themselves as dominant, and this is the main reason for Serbia's predicaments.

It is true that, especially in Serbia, victorious Communists literally decimated the urban middle class—that is to say, mostly its male component. Thus it was statistically quite likely that the male conquerors would claim the remaining middle-class women as a war booty. The Partisan general–fragile ballerina pairing that became a commonplace piece of folklore could then probably claim some statistical basis in reality.[11] According to the popular ideology, she fell for the brutal and manly vitality of the barbarian, and he fell for her culture. And even though, as both a male in a patriarchal culture and a victor in a class war, the male was dominant, it was the burgher woman who, in the end, "tamed" and civilized him. The stories of such pairings tend to end tragically with the suicide or utter ruin of the male, signaling the incompatibility of the two worlds, but the product of this ill-fated union remains in the woman's womb—a new generation that will grow up cultivated by their mothers only to perish in another Balkan apocalypse and repeat the same pattern.

The cultivated, civilized males, at all levels of opposition, if they play any role in these narratives, are universally shown as effete, decadent, and impotent. There is no place for a virile Westerner who sweeps the Balkan woman off her feet in the Serbian imaginary, or at least such a script has not, to the best of my knowledge, appeared yet. Similarly, there is not a trace of a supremely self-confident Serbian Higgins to raise a Serbian Eliza Doolitle from her low status.[12] It is always the reverse.

Here is my stab at an explanation. I have posited certain regularities in the semiotic logic by which a periphery usually tries to manage its "spoilt identity" or stigma, to use Goffman's (1963) terminology. In the symbolic geography of Europe, it is an adult, male Frenchman or Englishman who stands at the apex. To the East and South, there extend the gradients of civilizational depreciation that obey a recursive logic. The civilizational hierarchy, however, produces its counter-hierarchy even within the centers themselves. Thus a metropolitan Romantic reaction to Enlightenment equates civilization with decadence and sterility while extolling the vitality of barbarism. One move open to a periphery denigrated as uncivilized, then, is to play on that countercurrent within the metropolis by reversing the valence of primitivity. The more primitive the more vital. The Yugoslav variant even has an appropriate label for this strategy—the claim of being a "Balkan Barbarogenius" who brings life and vitality to the decadent and tired Europe.[13]

If civilizational, cultural, or racial difference could be coded as class or gender difference (without prejudging which one is more fundamental or generative of others), then Higgins would be to Eliza as the British Empire is to its colonies, and English higher classes to English working classes. An adult Serbian male, however, no matter how dominant his patriarchal status at home, and no matter how high his class position might be within his own society, is still a part of a larger hierarchy in which his society (and he as its dominant, unmarked representative) is inferior—and thus structurally female and lower class in relation to the West. But for a Serbian male it is rather unpalatable to express a sense of inferiority to the West, even when it is conceded, in the idiom of his male subjection (or that of his womenfolk) to the Western male, for this would put the Serbian male in the position of a woman and undermine his male pride.[14] If, however, the civilizational superiority is made to bear the feminine guise, then the Balkan male can assert his superior virility, and thus at least conquer on that plane. In the mode of self-presentation then (as a film director, for instance, and all of them are male in this case), he will thus tend to choose as his representative (or champion) those who are the most virile—in this case, the Violent Highlander, or the Noble Criminal. The other face of this self-presentation is, however, a rueful self-recognition that can undermine male bravado with severe self-criticism and an intimate admission of inferiority in matters of culture, rationality, and civilization.

Left by their American girlfriends, the Serbian males despondently sink back into the nauseating in-betweenness of their Yugoslav (or Serbian) reality. The Krajina boy gets killed in *Premeditated Murder,* as does the communist commissar two generations before him. In the tunnel Velja puts the gun in his mouth and shoots his head off. So does Miki Manojlović in *Melody Hunts My Reverie.* The Old Guard and the young toughs kill themselves off, Peckinpah or Tarantino style, at the end of *Rage* and *Wounds.* Almost never do we see the kind of "moral transformation" that Anthony Burgess made his Alex go through in the last chapter of *Clockwork Orange,* even less is there a happy end to a love story that audiences so adamantly demanded of George Bernard Shaw. There is no resolution, no closure, and no catharsis in these stories, and this, in a sense, makes them cinematographic laments, or what I will subsequently analyze as "Serbian Jeremiads."

POSTSCRIPT: THE "FEMALE GAZE" OF THE INTERNATIONAL COMMUNITY

Here I shall briefly analyze a more recent film, Goran Marković's 2002 *The Cordon,* where I claim to detect the Female Gaze—a thesis I developed as a corollary of the Reverse Pygmalion in discussing a collection of papers on ex-Yugoslav masculinities (see Živković 2006, 2007).

The director, Goran Marković, the author of cult films such as *Special Education* (1977), *National Class* (1979), *Variola Vera* (1981), and *Tito and Me* (1992) was among the several hundred thousand citizens who walked the streets of Belgrade every day for more than two months in bitter cold to protest Milošević's election theft in the winter of 1996–97. Known as the "Yellow" or "Egg Revolution," since egg pelting of regime institutions was one of its weapons of choice, the protest was a clash of demonstrators' carnivalesque spirit and increasing police brutality.[15] Marković first used the voluminous footage made by the protesting side in a documentary titled *Poludeli ljudi* (1997), before exploring the police side in *The Cordon.* The film, however, is neither about condemning or humanizing the "enemy," nor is it intended primarily as a portrayal of a particular historic event; rather, it is an exploration of more persisting Serbian predicaments that takes the 1996–97 protests as a stage.

Just as Dragojević did in *Pretty Village, Pretty Flame,* Marković, too, puts a handful of characters under extreme pressure by locating them in a confined space that acts as a crucible—in this case a bus that shuttles a group of tired policemen led by an elderly major on random errands—chasing, blockading, and beating up the protesters.[16] The bus slips in and out of documentary footage seamlessly. It sometimes plows through a sea of protesters in the city center, sometimes roams deserted suburban streets of the dilapidated socialist kind (a stage fitting for *Clockwork Orange*) in an aimless trajectory that resembles those nightmares where a familiar city becomes a collage of half-recognized places in unrecognizable juxtapositions.

This spatial indeterminacy and directionlessness is mirrored by the film's temporal shape. There is something resembling a main plot—involving the elderly major and his daughter—but the film meanders through little episodes without the clean structure of buildup and climax. The characters clash but do not pass through unidirectional moral transformations, and there is no catharsis at the end.[17]

The Cordon could be seen as a meditation on violence as a convulsive propping up of threatened borders. The bus is a protective cocoon, a shell or perhaps a bubble, and as it nightmarishly roams the rioting city, its membrane is constantly breached.

One of the boundaries that the policemen are desperately trying to preserve is between themselves and their fellow citizens. They call them "jerks" and "traitors," and try to convince themselves that they deserve to be brutally beaten, even killed. The desperation comes from the fearful recognition that the "traitors" are their neighbors, wives, and daughters.

Perhaps even more fundamental, however, is the anxiety about gender boundaries. In the bus the policemen are propping up the bubble of typical Balkan machismo by enacting tough maleness before one another. Their posturing, however, is constantly undermined by the women who take them out of the bus and their all-important man's work. They are the strong ones, and the Balkan macho knows that. This is why he desperately and often pathetically tries to show, not so much to the women but to his pals, that he is in charge.

Early on in the film a wife summons one of the policemen out of the bus to demand that he come with her to the hospital for artificial insemination. For a moment she succeeds in dissolving the all-importance of his macho world of police work while they lovingly argue over the sex of the future child—he would like a girl, she a boy. The bus, however, soon pulls him back inside to the lewd comments of his colleagues in a typical display of Balkan machismo.

A neighbor calls Blacky, a policeman constantly on the verge of going berserk, to tell him that he just drove his wife and son to the doctor and that the son has been diagnosed with leukemia. Blacky accuses the neighbor of sleeping with his wife and beats him. He eventually does get to the hospital, where the neighbor and the wife stoically endure his violent abuse and in the end, after a great display of macho posturing, he finally concedes to see his son.

The daughter of the old major brings him his medicine but resolutely refuses to step over the line that separates the protesters from the police cordon her father is commanding. After the unit brutally beats her boyfriend and brings him to the hospital without an eye, the major suffers a stroke. The daughter he brought up single-handedly (he lovingly recounts how he carried her twenty-five kilometers to the hospital when she ruptured her appendix) refuses to see him ever again, but in the concluding scene she takes him home from the hospital in a wheelchair. She will take care of him despite everything we are led to believe, in a role reversal Andrei Simic (1983) called "cryptomatriarchy"—where the Balkan macho becomes a child to his spouse (or daughter in this case) as he grows older.

Framing the whole police-protester battle is the imminent arrival of the observers from the European Union. The major reveals the ultimate reason why the protesters have to be removed from the streets—if Europe witnesses this, he tells his unit, we (Serbs) won't be able to show that we can manage our own affairs. In effect, we'll become wardens— no longer bosses in our own house. And the protesters outside the bus are Europe's allies. They are, on a more local scale, what (Civilized) Europe is to Serbia imagined as a patriarchal household—bearers of a gaze that undermines the authority of the male household head already made hollow by modernization and the degradation to the peripheral pariah status. To be a periphery is to feel powerless, and when power is coded as masculine dominance, the threat to it tends to assume the hues of emasculation. Our women are trying to get us out of the bus; the neighbors who help them to take our kids to the hospital are effeminized, urbanite types; and the civilized Europe, when it arrives on the scene, will take their side. The outside gaze recursively reinforces the local one in undermining the masculine bubble. And that gaze is female.

This is the same Female Gaze that I developed as a somewhat provocative thesis when commenting on a collection of papers that explored gender regimes in the former Yugoslav states in 2005.[18] Through an ethnographically nuanced approach to micro-practices of masculinity, these papers showed how much of the crucial dynamics in the ex-Yugoslav societies—rule of law, viability of states, international recognition, and travails, if not tragedies, of transition—tended to be gauged by and, even more significant, mediated through gender idioms and practices. All these post-Yugoslav states seemed to share certain common ingredients such as an ethnonationalist re-traditionalizing rhetoric of return to some sort of idealized masculinity of bygone eras coupled with "economic emasculation."

The ethnonationalist imagination seems to be ruled by a fantasy of the sexless reproduction of the nation through males. However, this fantasy is spoiled by the necessity of women as double reproducers—as necessary wombs, but also as socializers, that is, conveyers of culture as tradition and *Volksgeist*. In that latter role, women then tend to be bearers of "civilization" among the relatively "uncivilized." They tend to have this affinity with the civilized—they care more about hygiene and good manners, they don't curse, they dislike all kinds of vulgarities, they seem to enjoy accouterments of civilized life, and, worst, they tend to conspire with the More Civilized Enemy to civilize their own males (make him spit less, curse less, drink less, abstain from beating his wife, gays, or from going to war). This predilection to recognize women's civilizational superiority is a part of what I call the Reverse Pygmalion.

Another crucial ingredient in the situation is the "economic emasculation" in post-Yugoslav societies. The road to the kind of masculinity that comes from the male's ability to provide, to act confidently as a breadwinner, is now cut off for a sizable portion of the population. This precipitates a "crisis of masculinity" that offers a fertile ground for nationalist re-traditionalizers to advocate a return to "real manhood" and denounce all the sissies, fags, and other emasculated men. Most ominously, such an economic emasculation means that other traditional venues for regaining masculinity gain in appeal—going to war and engaging in criminal violence.

When the old order crumbles (in this case, that of Tito's Yugoslavia), women in general seem to be the more resilient ones. Even popular culture has produced striking images of men, their familiar roles disrupted, becoming useless, depressed wrecks while the women adapt and survive. There is a scene in Tone Bringa's 1992 documentary, *We Are All Neighbors,* where a young Bosnian man who lost his job embarrassingly accepts his wife's dishwashing instructions in front of a Western female anthropologist's camera gaze. A Serbian feature film that documented travails of UN sanctions and hyperinflation, *Dnevnik uvreda '93* (*A Diary of Insults*) is, among other things, a story of male fragility born of rigidity counterposed to female pragmatic flexibility. While he sinks into depression when his stable world crashes down, she starts knitting caps and selling them on the street (something he, as an intellectual, would never stoop to). Like Andersen's Matchbox Girl, however, she freezes to death (Šotra 1993).

And finally, to come back to the Female Gaze, these internal dynamics are significantly framed and influenced by the scrutiny of the so-called International Community that is felt strongly if not by all, then by a significant number of constituencies throughout the region. And that International Gaze is definitely gendered. Civilizational superiority is conceded to the International Community, but the ex-Yugoslav male likes to imagine this civilizational superiority being compensated by the masculine deficiency of civilized males. Feminizing the civilizationally superior males, however, may not be as important in this case as the other side of the Reverse Pygmalion pattern—the ambivalent relation to the civilizationally superior female and the feminization of the International Gaze.

The International Gaze crucially focuses on gender relations as a gauge of modernity, democratization, and all these qualities that count toward eligibility for inclusion in the (civilized) family of nations. As Dimova notes, "Since the Western Enlightenment, Westerners have commonly used the "status" of a group's women to judge a group's "modernity." Ignorant, oppressed, and backward women are the hallmark of a "backward" group—at least according to commonly accepted Western stereotypes" (Dimova 2006:309).

This poses an irresolvable dilemma for national re-traditionalizers that Dimova casts as "the dilemma experienced by men from ethnic minorities who must educate their women in order to be accepted as "modern," but whose experiences in seducing the educated women of dominant groups lead them to believe that educated women are likely to betray them" (ibid., 309).

At all levels of inclusion, recursively, the more "civilized" side tends to be seen as effeminate, feminist, and feminizing all at once. Its males are emasculated, its women dangerously emancipated and in charge, its scrutiny explicitly aimed at gender inequalities and critical of patriarchal, masculinist values. I am thus tempted to suggest that the Civilized Gaze may in certain situations assume the qualities of a Female Gaze. If the civilizationally superior males could be effeminized in fantasy, the civilizationally superior female might be fantasized as vulnerable to the superior virility of the uncivilized, but that only belies a very real sense of her power. In other words, the International Gaze, as well as its local representatives, seems to appear as a Female Gaze—penetrating, stern, and demanding.

Imagine in the end these ex-Yugoslav states as a communal apartment building in the process of subdivision—another confined space analogous to the bus in *The Cordon* and the tunnel in *Pretty Village*. Now this whole disintegrating communal apartment building is under close scrutiny. The powerful outsiders are conditioning their help in reassigning rooms and apartments, as well as refurbishing and redecorating the damaged ones, on certain proprieties being observed that often strike the dwellers as strange, demeaning, and well . . . emasculating. Women are becoming unruly, especially since men lost their jobs, but beating them up, for instance, is a grave sin in the eyes of the powerful outsiders. The whole building is falling apart and is full of gaping holes from the recent settling of accounts (as well as general negligence). It is thus made semi-transparent, so it is hard to keep your daughter from going to school, to abuse your wife unobserved, or to beat the gay person next door without reprimand. It seems that in those unstable times, with the building crumbling and with resentful, perhaps still vengeful, neighbors all around, that muscle-bound, real masculinity is more in demand than ever, and yet the pesky foreigners insist precisely on emasculating proprieties, as do their representatives in the building itself.

So many of these foreigners, or their representatives, who come to scrutinize the dwellers are women. The male dwellers may try their macho charms on them (foreign women are supposed to be vulnerable to barbarian virility) but they are also chaffing uneasily before their gaze, painfully aware of the power and legitimacy behind that scrutiny. After all, a lot of the masculinity in the building is a public performance for other men, while in the privacy of one's own little room it is often the mother or the wife who really rules. What to do in this crisis of masculinity? While the war lasted, one could escape the Female Gaze at home by volunteering and joining the boys. Or by becoming a "knight of asphalt," living dangerously, buying the company of beautiful women, and dying young.

FIVE

Serbian Jeremiads

Too Much Character, Too Little *Kultur*

Culture without character is, no doubt, something frivolous,
vain, and weak; but character without culture is, on the
other hand, something raw, blind, and dangerous.

—MATTHEW ARNOLD, "Democracy," 1861

At the televised July 1994 session of the Serbian Parliament debating
the issue of control over the regime-run television channels, a respected
singer of Medieval Serbian spiritual music, Pavle Aksentijević, acting
as a member of the largest opposition coalition (DEPOS), brought a
tape recorder to the podium and played a recording of a contemporary
Iranian popular song. Without uttering a word, he then played a song
by Dragana Mirković—one of the most popular female singers of the
so-called turbo-folk genre in Serbia at the time. The tunes were practically identical. Aksentijević didn't feel the need to explain. The near
identity of the two musical pieces was taken to speak for itself. Before
leaving the podium he uttered only one sentence: "As Dedijer [1914–1990;
a prominent Yugoslav historian] would say, we Serbs sometimes behave
as if we were made [in the sense of "begotten"] by drunken Turks." (*Kao
što je rekao Dedijer, mi Srbi se nekada ponašamo kao da su nas pravili
pijani Turci*).

At one level Aksentijević was accusing Milošević's regime of promoting kitsch, primitivity, and unculturedness epitomized by the musical genre of turbo-folk. Born in the early 1990s turbo-folk, among intellectual circles in Serbia, was seen by many as the ultimate abomination of taste, culture, and civilization, and as a cunning plot that "they" (Milošević, the Socialist Party, and the authorities) had devised to reduce the population to "utter idiocy" by relentlessly unleashing it through the regime-controlled media. Aksentijević's performance, moreover, added an Oriental theme or, more specifically, a Turkish Taint to the implied disgust for a musical genre. He accused the ruling party of deliberately polluting the Serbs with Oriental tunes, at the same time positioning himself and his party as defenders of a certain kind of pristine Serbian culture. Given that he was a well-known singer of Medieval Serbian spiritual music, the type of pristine Serbian culture thus opposed to the kitschy, Oriental tunes was clear, a culture derived from the supposedly unbroken continuity with the Golden Age of Byzantine High Culture.

Finally, one could also detect a note of deep anguish in that statement—indeed, it might be construed as saying that all of us [Serbs], the present speaker and his opposition party included, have some serious character flaws in their blood traceable to "the drunken Turks." Aksentijević may or may not have intended such self-inclusion, but this kind of anguished meditation on national character flaws that implicitly includes the speaker was widespread in Serbia during this entire period. I call this way of talking "Serbian Jeremiads"—an enduring speech genre akin to the Russian laments analyzed by Ries (1997)—and contrast it to the genre of the everyday "sifting of politics" (*bistriti politiku*) that is usually laced with conspiracy theorizing. Rather than in local or global conspiracies, typical Jeremiads seek the reasons for the present Serbian predicaments in "deeper" causes having to do with fatal flaws in the Serbian character. Turkish Taint is then simply one of the most potent idioms in which all these accusations and self-recriminations could be expressed.

Turkish Taint was, especially at the time of Aksentijević's little performance, often rhetorically linked to the corruption of communism in laments over Serbian predicaments that contrasted the surfeit of (negative) character traits with the fateful lack of culture. Culture was an important stake in the rhetorical wars waged during this period between variously positioned oppositional intellectuals and the Milošević regime. Culture's most visible opponent was seen to be turbo-folk and the mentality of those who listened to it—the peasant-urbanites cast as the "riders of the cultural apocalypse."

INTERNAL TURKS AND RAYAH:
TURKISH TAINT AS A RHETORICAL WEAPON

Paradoxically, just at the moment when he was turning from a warmonger to a "peace-monger" (as the opposition sarcastically labeled it), Milošević's despotism started to assume explicit Turkish hues in public discourses. Right at the time of the parliamentary episode with Iranian music in August 1994, the Bosnian drama was reaching yet another peak. When Bosnian Serbs refused to accept the Contact Group Peace Plan, the Federal Republic of Yugoslavia (Serbia and Montenegro) accused them of "the greatest treason of the Serbian national interest that has ever occurred" and imposed what then seemed a total blockade upon their brothers across the Drina River. A major client of the Milošević regime—Radovan Karadžić—was thus cut loose, and the media campaign was unleashed with the aim of transforming him from a hero to a villain, from a noble fighter for the just cause of Serbs in Bosnia to a gambler, war profiteer, even a war criminal. Overnight the state-run TV changed its tune completely. "Peace has no alternative" was the new slogan, and for weeks an endless procession of people, from passers-by on the streets to company directors and politicians, parroted it on the TV screen in complete contradiction to what they had been saying only a day before. The "Proud People Who Would Stand Up to The Whole World" did not riot, and did not topple the "traitor" Milošević. Instead they went about their business as usual, and the social commentators, even those who were against the war from the outset, and who should have applauded the latest peace turn even if it came from Milošević himself, increasingly turned to Turkish Taint in trying to account for such "incredible docility and malleability of the masses."

A term rich with historical and literary associations was available—the *rayah mentality*.[1] "Until yesterday," writes Žarko Trebješanin in the daily *Politika* of August 13, 1994, "the authorities, with the help of their television channels, have been enthusiastically promoting national identity based on the *hajduk* [brigand, outlaw; pl., *hajduci*], warrior character dominated by defiance and courage, whose highest ideals are freedom, honor, and justice. Today, however, it promotes the *rayah* mentality characterized by pragmatism, readiness for compromise, selfishness, hedonism, cunning, and fawning servility."

Blaming the proverbial "centuries of Turkish yoke" for all kinds of flaws in national character or political culture is a widespread rhetorical topos among all the former Ottoman subjects in the Balkans, anthropologically perhaps best documented by Herzfeld for Greece (i.e., 1985, 1987, 1997). The flavor of this topos, however, varies across the region and according to the context and the need of the day. During the war in Bosnia, for instance, there was a strong tendency for Serbs to refer to the Bosnian Muslims as "Turks"—thus seemingly transporting themselves into a (mythical) past, as many foreign commentators noticed. Rhetorically they were also trying to transfer the Turkish Taint onto the Muslims who were, ironically, because of their avowed commitment to multiculturalism, often perceived by Westerners as more "European" than the Bosnian Serbs.[2]

On the ground, the militants on the Bosnian Serb side were doing their best to effect a complete cultural cleansing in addition to the ethnic one—obliterating any and all traces of Islamic culture from mosques to toponyms. In Serbia proper, however, no matter how frequently cited (especially to foreigners), the invocation of the "500 years under the Turks," despite all the Kosovo battle folklore, remained somewhat abstract. Nobody, for instance, waged language purification campaigns. As the author of the *Dictionary of Turkisms,* Abdulah Škaljić wrote in his introduction, "It is an interesting fact that in the process of purifying Serbo-Croatian language from foreign, borrowed words, the Turkisms were always treated with more indulgence than the words taken from other non-Slavic languages" (1989: 14). It is the intimate words of everyday life, of food and character traits considered most uniquely Serbian that tend to be Turkisms. Very often they are not even perceived as being of Turkish origin. There was little urge to cleanse oneself from the Turkish Taint in Serbia, at least not in the realm of language, or food and drink.[3] Nobody wanted to purge the most intimately Serbian ethnic cuisine from *sarma* (rolled cabbage), *ćevapčići* (kebabs), or *baklava,* while the half-hearted official attempts to re-label "Turkish coffee" as "Serbian" on some restaurant menus had no influence on everyday usage. However, with the advent of turbo-folk as perhaps the most contentious arena in the culture wars of the 1990s, previously largely un-remarked oriental hues in certain genres of folk music suddenly became notable. Aksentijević relied on a widespread current discourse on Oriental pollution in music for the effectiveness of his performance. He didn't have to put it in so many words—the message of his demonstration of "Teheran tunes" in the song of one of the most popular turbo-folk Queens, was immediately understandable to his audience.

A professor at the Musical Academy in Belgrade, Zorislava Vasiljević, gave one of the clearest examples of this discourse when she appeared on the *Impression of the Week* (*Utisak nedelje*) TV show of April 2, 1995.[4] "We have a problem now" she said,

> of how to cure our people . . . it is this music which is not *šund* (kitschy garbage); it is just not Serbian, it should rather be sung in Arabic. It was given to people here, just like when you want to put a chicken to sleep [to slaughter it easier], you put its head under your arm and swing, and it falls asleep [demonstrates]. To put our nation to sleep [is the aim of that music], so that the people would lose interest in their own true musical tradition, and lose their, their *very existence,* not only their identity. A nation that starts to lose the characteristic and recognizable sound, song, music is doomed to vanish without a trace. So . . . you have this phenomenon of implanted Teheran music which is seductive. You cannot go to a children's party anymore without hearing that music of Dragana Mirković, Ceca Veličković, and that Sneki who dances [with expression signaling disgust]. She would be very good for the Turkish harem. This is an epidemic, a plague. (emphasis and parenthetical explanations mine)

Just like Trebješanin, Vasiljević implies that someone (the regime) is purposefully encouraging subservience and docility whether by promoting values characteristic of the "rayah mentality" or by hypnotizing people with Oriental tunes. Note that she therefore positions herself as both a healer and an awakener of the nation.

The other way that Turkish Taint got activated as a rhetorical topos in Serbia at that time was in defaming political opponents. Or, put differently and more to the point, a long tradition of referring to domestic despots as "Internal Turks" was reactivated. In 1874 Svetozar Miletić wrote: "In order to liberate ourselves not only from the Turks without, but from the Turks within (referring to the regime of Mihailo Obrenović), we have to fight to the death even at the risk of exposing national unification to total danger, for the unification alone would be worth nothing under [internal] slavery" (in Čanak 1994).

This kind of idiom was resurrected in the mid-1990s. In June 1995, for instance, the ultranationalistic Serbian Radical Party leader Vojislav Šešelj was stripped of his parliamentary immunity and incarcerated. The occasion was trivial and was probably provoked by the police. The deeper reason was that, after August 1994, Šešelj was transformed from Milošević's trusted ally to his most vociferous enemy in one of the many flip-flops of the regime.[5] The statement issued at one of the Radical Party's protest meetings prophesied the imminent fall of the "last dictatorship of the proletariat led by the *dahia* [pl., *dahije*] from Dedinje." The statement offers an excellent example of how a Turkish Taint idiom could be used in internal political fights. The *dahije* were the renegade Ottoman authorities who ruled the Belgrade region with extreme terror and violence which prompted the First Serbian Uprising in 1804—a momentous event immortalized in epic poetry. Dedinje is the part of Belgrade where the villas of politicians, and diplomats, are situated, where Tito used to live, and where Milošević, the "*dahia* from Dedinje," resided.

Turning the tables, Mira Marković, Milošević's influential wife, called Šešelj a *dahia* in a clear call to the people to rise up and dispose of him, according to the lines of the famous epic song "The First Uprising against the Dahije" which everybody in Serbia knows by heart. Danica Drašković, the influential wife of Vuk Drašković, responded with a famous line from the same epic song: "Each kill your own *dahia*."[6] She agreed with Mira Marković that Mira's *dahia*, Šešelj, should be disposed of, but she added that her own, [Danica's] *dahia* is Milošević himself. So she called upon Mira to kill her own *dahia*—Šešelj, Danica will kill Milošević, and everybody else will kill their own *dahije,* so that "finally Serbia will be clean and they can all rejoice" (Drašković 1994).

Calling one another Janissaries is another interesting example of how the idiom of the Ottoman legacy was used in political struggles. In a 1995 media campaign against the Soros Fund, for instance, Dragoš Kalajić called the young people who accepted Soros Fund fellowships for study abroad the "Janissaries of the New World Order" (Kalajić 1995).[7]

A peace activist from Vojvodina, Nenad Čanak, on the other hand, had an entirely different take on who the Janissaries were. "We learned in school," he wrote, "that Turks used to take the "boy tribute."[8] Forcibly removed from their homes and brought up in the capital, these boys made the most savage soldiers of the Ottoman Empire. Rootless, without a past, without a future, blindly loyal. Totalitarian organizations, he continues, "send their officers far away from their homes so that the unwritten local obligations will not stand in the way of ruthlessly performing their duty." He goes on to list such uprooted persons, in most cases the refugees from Bosnia and Croatia—the highlander types who have been given important positions in Serbia by the regime which trusts them to be more loyal and ruthless than the locals. "Comrades Janissaries!" he asks them in the end, "what will become of you when your Red Sultan [Milošević] starts to send you the silk cords [to hang yourself] in order to save his own neck?" (Čanak 1994).

Labeling your political opponent as a *dahia,* Janissary, or Sultan, that is to say, an "internal Turk," flared up as a rhetorical weapon in 1994 and 1995, but I find that the laments about the "docility" of the ordinary people in terms of "rayah mentality" were a much more important component of the whole Turkish Taint topos during that period. Moreover, these laments about the character flaws of the Serbian people often juxtaposed the five centuries under Turks with the fifty years under communism. Just as Milošević was called the "Red Sultan," the docility and other character traits of his subjects were supposed to be a product of some combination of communist and Ottoman legacies. A brief detour into what could be called the "communist taint" is thus in order.

COMMUNIST LEGACY AND THE MORAL
BREAKDOWN OF THE SERBIAN PEOPLE

On August 21, 1994, right after Milošević's turn from warmongering to peace-mongering, the *Impression of the week* had Dragutin Gostuški, a renowned musicologist and highly respected culture-critic, as one of the three guests in the studio. Asked by the hostess what he remembered as the strongest impression of the previous week, he launched into a classical Jeremiad underlined by the look of deep depression on his face, and the leaden tone of his voice punctuated with long sighs and silences of a deeply troubled man (marked by ellipses in my transcription):

> You know, the impression that I am carrying from this week, from these last weeks, unfortunately is the same impression that I have been carrying for exactly fifty years . . . And that is a heavy impression . . . bad . . . the moral breakdown of the Serbian people.

Gostuški's deep anguish is obviously occasioned by the latest evidence of how his people easily bend under the pressure of an authoritarian regime, and change overnight what should have been deep convictions. For him it bespoke a tragic lack of moral fiber, of integrity and backbone.

> For, you see, the moral breakdown is something terrible . . . heavy . . . something with huge consequences. You could change the political system, you could regain lost territories, but a loss of morality, that is a thing which affects the human soul so deeply, that it could not be rectified even in a hundred years.

And he immediately associated this most recent event with the situation in 1945, after the communist takeover.

> I was surprised . . . by the extent to which our people suddenly changed their opinion, under various pressures, to be sure, but also often without any need. How treason, cowardice, sycophancy, falsehood, and deceit started to appear, mass joining of the Communist Party by people who never thought they would turn into Communists, and who calculated it to be a good move bringing some social privileges and a better life.

Such lack of backbone does not agree with the entrenched self-image of Serbs as heroic, independent, and proud people, and Gostuški now starts to doubt even the most hallowed instances of Serbian heroism.

> I wondered how could a people who makes so much of its heroism, its courage and honor, who proved through history . . . I started to doubt, I am telling you sincerely, I started to doubt even the Kosovo battle, even the Salonika front,[9] and all these heroic and honorable deeds of the Serbian people and I asked myself how could something like this happen.

And, in explanation, he offers a wide-ranging thesis:

I pretty much tend towards a thesis, supported in particular by our writer Danko Popović, that the Serbian people has not, in fact, recovered . . . biologically . . . from its losses in wars. Terrible losses in the First World War and in the Balkan War . . . and then it was (sigh) . . . finished in this war . . . when it happened that . . . as everybody knows, in the war only the bravest, that is to say, also the most honorable men get killed . . . So that, it is not too far-fetched to conclude that with this damage we have become, in the majority, a genetic trash heap, because those who remained were mostly deserters and dodgers, and people of bad character, and that, of course, through generations has been reproduced.

If the fifty years of communism had broken the Serbian moral backbone, a further question can be asked of why the Serbs succumbed to communism in the first place, and why were they still supporting another neo-communist regime—Milošević's. While Gostuški and Danko Popović adhered to the popular thesis of the "genetic thinning out," especially after the turn of 1994, the answer to that question came to be increasingly sought in the proverbial five centuries of Ottoman rule. As one aphorism put it: "The Communists didn't pick the Serbs for nothing. Five centuries under the Turks were our best recommendation" (Rade Jovanović in *NIN,* June 2, 1995).

There was, however, another, more nuanced theory about the effects of Yugoslav communism on the Serbian psyche. This theory argued that Tito's special brand of communism, with its anti-Soviet rhetoric, open borders, apparent freedoms and higher living standard, might have corrupted the Yugoslavs in a way even more devious and sinister than the Soviet type of real socialism. I came to call this the Bearable Evil thesis. The expression comes from a prominent Serbian writer, Milovan Danojlić, who provided perhaps the clearest version of this widespread argument.

LIVING IN BEARABLE EVIL

Socialist regimes often seemed to breed a particularly strong sense of living in "parallel worlds." On the one hand, a world of official dogma, slogans, and parades; on the other, the intimate, private world of kitchen talk, dachas, and the meandering of everyday life. The daily reality often starkly contradicted the official dogma, yet the majority of people living in such systems managed to adjust and even consider their lives quite "normal." Depending on the country and period, the world of official communist ideology was more or less rigid, and it tended to encroach upon the private world of everyday life to a lesser or greater extent. Yugoslav socialism migrated from a typical Stalinist model in its earlier stages (1940s and 1950s) to a system in which the encroachment of ideology into everyday life was arguably felt less than in any other "people's democracy." Moreover, in the Yugoslav case, the blame for half a century of communist rule could not be shifted to the "Evil Soviet Empire" to the extent that was possible in other Soviet bloc countries. If we were corrupted by communism, as many domestic critics were saying, then, in all honesty, we have only ourselves to blame.

A prominent domestic writer, a one-time dissident (of sorts), and a social critic, Milovan Danojlić wrote penetrating analyses of Yugoslav communism that invite comparison with Havel, Konrad, and Michnik.[10] "The moment some notions are put beyond the reach of free debate," he wrote in his *Trouble With Words* (first published in 1977),

> other relationships are also disturbed, the perspectives become skewed. That which is passed over in silence throws its shadow upon that which is spoken openly, the lie swallows up the remaining truth. Thinking about public matters turns into a farce: people talk and write as if freely, wisely and responsibly, yet everyone knows what is forbidden and could not be uttered. (Danojlić 1990:79)

Writing in late-1970s Yugoslavia, Danojlić was up against a much stronger popular feeling that "nothing is wrong with our way of life" than was presumably the case in Soviet-dominated "people's democracies" at that time. Havel, on the other hand, set up an absolute auto-totalitarian world of *living in lie,* against which *living in truth* shone with the complementary brilliance of absolute morality (see Havel 1986).

And it was exactly this relative lack of the Soviet-type total control in Yugoslavia, this relatively larger "room for the genuine aims of life," as Havel would put it, yet itself "shadowed" and ultimately "swallowed by the lie," that Danojlić saw as morally, mentally, and spiritually more damaging than the absolutely totalitarian system. "We lived in Bearable

Evil," he wrote, "it devastates the soul worse than tyranny" (*Politika*, March 11, 1995).

Laments about our corruption, lack of moral backbone, or "devastated souls" were about fatal shortcomings of the national character. Such laments were, moreover, often combined with another kind of lament—about "our lack of culture." By shuttling back and forth between "culture" and "character," the Serbian Jeremiahs also staked their claims to cultural supremacy in the culture wars that raged in that period.

BETWEEN CHARACTER AND CULTURE

Labels like "culture" could be likened to empty thrones, wrote Edward Sapir, "The rival pretenders war to death; the thrones to which they aspire remain splendid in gold" (Sapir 1924:402). In his performance in the Parliament, Aksentijević was advancing the claims of a particular pretender to the empty throne of culture, and implicit in this move was a claim to cultural supremacy over the ruling Socialist Party. His performance was perhaps most significantly a claim to authentic nationalism of his own party as opposed to the cynical nationalism of Milošević. Far more than just an argument over the musical taste, this constituted a claim to power.

Aksentijević was, as noted, a well-known singer of Medieval Serbian spiritual music. He belonged to those who looked for authentic roots of Serbian culture in its Byzantine legacy. Such claims, however, are problematic, since even if one could reestablish the broken continuity with High Byzantine culture, the fact remains that it is itself considered Oriental and inferior by the "West." In order to claim it as the core of one's cultural identity, it had to be seen as at least equal, if not superior, to the cultural roots of the Western Christian world. And this is precisely what Aksentijević stood for. As he stated in an interview,

> Our ancient folk music is autochthonous, authentic, unadaptable to and impossible to capture in the trap of European clichés. This is a music with miraculous, microinterval scales the world cannot grasp and which the limited pentatonic system is not able to record. (Aksentijević 1994)

Aksentijević was thus positioning his party as a defender of a pristine Serbian culture defined in a particular way.[11] In some other context this might have been a powerful rhetorical move, but not in the totally marginalized Serbian Parliament that people almost universally considered a "circus." The ruling party held it up to the international community as proof of its "democracy," and the domestic public was deliberately treated to a televised spectacle of the opposition's utter futility. And just like in the circus, the audience was laughing at the clowns: While Aksentijević was playing his tapes, the (in)famous Dobrivoje Budimirović-Bidža of the ruling Socialist Party—a local despot of the Svilajnac municipality whose fat, bald, boar-like figure signaled a self-satisfied vulgarity to those with pretensions to cultural refinement—was mocking his efforts by making a show of swaying to the music in the Oriental fashion and clapping his hands with a beatific expression on his face as if to say—yes, this is exactly the music we, "the people," like the most—thus sending the populist message to the TV audience: Let the pretentious intellectuals rant and rave, we (the Socialists) are not ashamed of the music that the people obviously love.

One social commentator observed how behavior like Bidža's serves to impress the people with the power of the ruling party. The contempt toward the opposition and arrogance thus shown, he argued, "press the right buttons with the people accustomed to docility due to the proverbial five centuries of the Turkish Yoke" (Stanojčić 1995). But, more important, it was the "uncultured" who were arrogantly showing their contempt toward the "cultured" and thus, in the perception of the "cultured," they were turning the normal scale of values upside down.

I have shown how the discussions of national character in Serbia significantly revolved around the dichotomy between "highlanders" and "lowlanders." Lowlanders could be seen as rational, pragmatic, cultivated, on the one hand, or degenerate, soft, submissive—the embodiment of *rayah* mentality—on the other. Similarly the highlanders could be seen as brave, proud, and of superior mettle or, obversely, as violent, primitive, and arrogant. These character types, however, are often used without geographic localization in order to talk about the general Serbian character. In that sense the Dinaric character and *rayah* mentality could be seen not as characterizing different populations but as being two sides of the same coin, or two phases of the same character structure, in a way, for instance, that mania and depression could be just different phases of the bipolar psychosis. The analogy is not spurious, for psychiatric diagnoses of the national character became a prominent type of story Serbs told themselves about themselves in the 1990s. A good case in point is the analysis of national character performed by Vladeta Jerotić,[12] an eminent Jungian psychiatrist and cultural critic, at a panel of very distinguished culture critics that assembled in June 1995 in Belgrade to discuss the literary critic Petar Džadžić's two-volume work on ethnopsychological themes, *Homo Balcanicus, Homo Heroicus* (Džadžić 1994).

Jerotić enumerates the important traits of Balkan Dinarics: violence, *rayah* psychology and moral mimicry, sudden alterations between active and passive periods, giftedness of what Dvorniković called, "sparrow's intensity," resentment, revengefulness, envy, insufficiently developed conscience and sense of responsibility, binary opposition in thinking, the warrior-patriarchal archaic mentality, or conversion to Islam out of spite (*turčenje iz inata*). And then he proceeds to compare these traits to those of an average adolescent:

> Inclined to strong imagination, his emotional life at odds with thinking, at times omnipotent . . . at times dejected, as if he's lost everything, the Balkan Dinaric does not judge reality well precisely because of these traits of temperament and character. It is impossible not to notice a similarity between the behavior of the Serbian Dinaric and the behavior of an average adolescent.

Here the national character embraces both *rayah* moral mimicry and megalomaniacal Dinaric heroism united in a Balkan "homo duplex." To liken national character to that of an adolescent is like comparing those lacking culture or civilization with children, lunatics, women, and with nature. In that sense Jerotić would situate the Serbs somewhere in-between—as an adolescent is halfway between the child and the adult, so is the Balkan man halfway between barbarity and civilization, nature and culture, tradition and modernity, raw and cooked. Indeed, one might say, he is half-baked, neither here nor there, and he needs finishing, polishing, refinement, maturing—in a word, cultivation.

In his famous article, "What the Serbs Can/Should Learn from the English," Bogdan Popović, another "pillar" of Serbian culture,[13] wrote that the Serbian people, "since their resurrection, are a race just a little bit older than a hundred years—a nice age for an individual, but hardly adolescence (*mladićko doba*) in the life of a nation" (Popović 1929:255), and that therefore it didn't have enough time to properly learn how to control, put in order, and cultivate its too passionate feelings. The Serbs, as a "young nation," have to learn self-control from the English, and it is the elite native intellectual, Bogdan Popović, who will teach them how to do it. The relationship between "cultured" and "uncultured" nations thus gets recursively reproduced within the "uncultured" nations themselves in the distinction between domestic "cultured" elites and "uncultured" masses.

All the panelists in various ways lamented the many faults of the Serbian national character, some, like Jerotić, by comparing it to adolescence, some, like Zoran Gluščević, by concentrating on the Serbian megalomania. There was a general feeling at that book promotion, certainly reinforced by the current events, that something essential and very important was lacking from the national character. It was Ratko Božović, a sociologist of culture and a prominent culture-critic, who explicitly talked about that lack, as the lack of a "cultural model" *(kulturni obrazac)*, by invoking a famous 1964 essay on Serbian national character by Slobodan Jovanović, one of the most influential intellectual and political figures in recent Serbian history (Jovanović, S. 1992).

Serbs have developed both the political and the national models, Jovanović was saying, but they lack a cultural one. He was talking about culture in the sense of self-perfection of the individual, the harmonious and comprehensive development of the person, that is to say, in the sense of German *bildung*. What he had in mind was a cultural model concerned not with "perfecting the social institutions, but with cultivating the individual, such as, for example, the model built by the old humanists on the basis of ancient philosophy, the English "gentleman," or the German "cultured man" (Jovanović, S. 1992:230).

"Culture"—that refinement that we need in order to rectify our half-baked character—has to be imported from places that have already developed it, and models are, as Liah Greenfeld (1992) would say, by definition superior to model imitators. Emulation can bring resentment, and resentment can prompt various strategies of reversing the values coming from the powerful model-giving nations by somehow transforming one's faults into virtues, and others' virtues into vices. Thus our (German)

Kultur, or our (Russian) *Soul* is superior to your (French) *civilization,* or your (Anglo-Saxon) soulless money-grabbing.

Some among the Serbian elites, like Slobodan Jovanović, whole-heartedly embraced imported Western models. Those, however, who resented them have shown two types of analytically distinguishable responses: one lays claim to the Byzantine High Culture heritage of the Serbs, presented, of course, in its positive valence as a civilization and culture superior to that of the West; the other extols the native "barbarogenius"—the innate superiority over the West of the Serbian peasant *Volksgeist.* In practice, the two are mostly amalgamated and mixed in various proportions and permutations, but sometimes they come to be distinguished and even opposed to each other.

Both Božović and Jovanović, constantly conflated several important senses of the term "culture." One is "culture" as *bildung*—personal refinement and perfection. Another is "culture" as a marker of social "distinction," in Bourdieu's sense. In yet another, "culture" stands for the collective, national genius in its various guises. The story of how *Kultur* as a weapon of interclass distinction in Germany had been transformed into the international distinction between French civilization and German *Kultur* is one of the founding stories of modernity (Elias 1994, 1996; Greenfeld 1992), and the term "culture," as Raymond Williams (1993:87–93) has famously shown, has been oscillating around all these disparate meanings ever since.

Once nationalized, culture became democratized, then massified, and mechanically reproduced, thus causing the cultural angst of a new breed of cultural critics from Simmel through Benjamin to Sapir and Adorno. Through all these historical accretions, the notion of "culture" became supercharged with a kind of Bakhtinian "internal dialogism." As it accumulated the "taste" of numerous past and present contexts in which particular social groups imbued it with their "socially significant world views" (Bakhtin 1994:290, 293), the term "culture" became an extremely potent multipurpose weapon in all kinds of social struggles. It became heavily contentious and emotion-laden. When I approached Ratko Božović after the book promotion and asked him what exactly did he mean by "cultural model," he became highly agitated and almost shouted at me: "What do I mean? What do you mean I mean by culture?—sensibility, intellectuality, morality . . . sense of responsibility!

That's what we lack!" And then with a pained expression of revulsion mixed with indulgence toward the character flaws of his own people he abruptly turned and left.

We might lack culture as something that would tame, polish, and complete our unruly character, the panelists were all saying, but they probably didn't mean that the whole of the nation equally suffers from "too much character and too little *Kultur*"—not all Serbs lack culture, and those who actually do have it should reform, educate, and cultivate, that is to say, lead those who do not. The "cultured," however, were not leading the "uncultured" in Milošević's Serbia. As another, anonymous Jeremiah had put it, "the wise got silenced, the fools climbed into the saddle, and the rabble got rich." The Serbian Jeremiads of the mid-1990s were coming from marginalized intellectual elites, ignored, or at most used as disposable mouthpieces by the regime.

When culture is used as a multipurpose weapon in the struggle for social supremacy, it is always wise to look at who in particular the proponents of culture are writing against because the enemy position gives one a clue as to what the promoters of culture mean by that fuzzy word in each concrete case. Who, then, were the "Riders of the Cultural Apocalypse" in 1990s Serbia, as Ratko Božović himself had dramatically put it at the two-day conference where the cream of oppositional intelligentsia gathered to discuss "Culture as Self-Defense of Society and Personality" (FIGURE 5.1).

THE RIDERS OF THE CULTURAL APOCALYPSE

Some three months before that book promotion, the marginalized and besieged oppositional intelligentsia gathered for a conference titled "Culture as Self-Defense of Society and Personality,"[14] where for two days they engaged in agonized denunciations of what Ratko Božović, who again was one of the participants, termed "The Riders of the Cultural Apocalypse":

> From the *half-world* of the [criminal] underground, from the provincial suburbs, from the *twilight* of metropolis, from the hell of war—there emerged *the riders of the cultural apocalypse*. More precisely: the white-collar criminals, the hard currency rentiers, the war profiteers and the dangerous, criminal types—the mafiosi.

DEMOKRATSKI CENTAR
organizuje dvodnevni skup pod nazivom:
KULTURA KAO SAMOODBRANA DRUŠTVA I LIČNOSTI

FIGURE 5.1.

Flyer for the "Culture as Self-Defense of
Society and Personality" conference.

More or less everything that was objectionable in spiritual and moral terms appeared at the very center of the degraded reality. Like some formless and terrifying shadows, the new primitives accompany the times of crisis, anxiety, fear, and emptiness. There, one can begin the story of their spiritual poverty, of the nature of their raw strength which is far from either culture or cultivation, removed both from emancipation and education . . . Our aesthetician Dragutin Gostuški was surprised by the extent to which the scale of values had been degraded, and especially by the tendency of the urban youth to fall into the embrace of primitive and Islamicized music and abandon the "international pop sphere." . . . The nouveau riche take all that life offers, all they can grab . . . These fishers in troubled water (*mutnolovci*)—foreigners to intellectuality, sensibility and morality, and very close to the aesthetic of kitsch— achieved the strategy of winning important positions in the society. . . . Immoderation, bad taste, grandomania, and arrogance are marks of their lifestyle. A style without style. The refinement of the newly composed rich is laughable and caricatural. Full pockets, empty souls.

Clearly, in Bourdieuian terms, Božović is engaging here in a classification struggle, a game of cultural one-upmanship predisposed, like all talk of art and cultural consumption, "to fulfill a social function of legitimating social difference" (Bourdieu 1984:7). He is certainly trying to put himself in the place of "cultural nobility" by denouncing the "undifferentiated hordes indifferent to difference" (469).

The impression one gets from reading Bourdieu's *Distinction* is of an almost crystalline structure of minute distinctions within which is waged a lively but highly ordered "classification struggle." No sense there that every so often some catastrophe totally erases these distinctions and the very classes engaged in the struggle. Serbian intellectuals, however, often viewed the very structuration, that is, the differentiation and hierarchization of their society as something very recent, undeveloped, and precarious. It is, moreover, subject to tragically frequent disasters that level the painstakingly built differentiation or completely reverse it.

To summarize brutally, Serbian society, at the time of its "birth" in the uprisings against the Ottoman rule in the early 1800s, starts out as a remarkably "flat," undifferentiated society composed predominantly of peasants, and in the next two hundred years whatever social differentiation develops gets repeatedly "flattened" again in a series of wars and other catastrophes. This, according to Latinka Perović, was the social foundation for what she claimed had been the most enduring and influential Serbian ideology, summarized in the saying: "I don't care how little I have as long as my neighbor doesn't have too much more"—that is, the ideology of the lowest common denominator, egalitarianism in poverty, anti-liberalism, anti-capitalism, in a word, anti-differentiation.[15]

Those who aspire to cultural nobility have always denounced the parvenus, the nouveau riche, or the philistines in more or less the same terms Božović uses—for their "raw strength," lack of "culture or cultivation," for their "spiritual poverty," their "immoderation," "bad taste," "arrogance," or "empty souls." What makes a Jeremiad like his, and the chorus of Jeremiahs heard at the conference, so rich and revealing were the particular local twists on these generic themes.

It is essential to notice that in the Serbian version it is not the "peasants" who are the "Riders of the Cultural Apocalypse." If the urban elite, which in Serbia overwhelmingly descended directly from the peasantry, acquired "culture" in the sense of urbanity, education, refinement, and *bildung*, the peasants were supposed to embody "culture" in the sense of the repository of the national genius, as *Volksgeist*. It was thus extremely difficult for the elite to denounce the peasantry as lacking culture because that would contradict the elite's traditional position as spokesmen, if not wholesale inventors, of the *Volksgeist* embodied by that same peasantry.

In a "flat" society based on the ideology of egalitarianism, moreover, elitism that would stray too much from the common run was always suspect, resented, and frequently even forcibly suppressed. "Even in the most elite institutions," wrote Stojan Cerović, "there was always squatting in some corner a feeling of inauthenticity, the guilt for raising above the people and for emulating the outside world. That's why a powerful category of domestic intellectuals loves to invoke the authority of their peasants and to remind everybody to heed that source of wisdom" (Cerović 1994).

If, then, the authentic "peasant" is idealized and beyond critique, the odium falls on the *inauthentic* peasant, the one who had abandoned that pristine condition and lost *Volksgeist* authenticity without acquiring the "cultural model" of the urbanite cosmopolitan instead. This inauthentic peasant, the "half-breed" or "halfling" (*polutan*) deserves a whole sociological treatise. As a socioeconomic category, the peasant-urbanite appears in all rapidly urbanizing and modernizing societies. Andrei Simić (1973) did a classical anthropological study of the way Serbian peasants urbanized in the 1960s and 1970s, and how their familial networks and kinship ideology helped them avoid many of the problems such rapid change tended to cause elsewhere. Here I am more interested in the peasant-urbanite as cultural token, icon, or cipher—as the negative hero of Serbian Jeremiads. And it is at this point that the puzzle of turbo-folk, posed at the beginning of this chapter, could finally be addressed.

In the words of Eric Gordy, the term "turbo-folk" was coined by Antonije Pušić, better known as Rambo Amadeus, to describe his "satiric co-optation of neofolk forms and imagery" (Gordy 1999:114). A music academy graduate who styled himself as an idiot-savant peasant rapper, Pušić carved for himself a unique role in 1990s Serbia. "Incorporating the madness, paranoia, kitsch, and inauthenticity of the neofolk ascendancy into his antimusic," as Gordy observes, "Rambo Amadeus presented a detailed ironic reading of the cultural moment, with the capacity of reaching broad audiences . . . However, commercial neofolk performers who lacked Rambo's irony adopted the term [turbo-folk] for themselves, and it came to refer less critically to an amplified and synthesized dance kitsch form, which received tremendous commercial promotion" (114, 119).[16]

Turbo-folk was a mutation of the so-called "newly composed" as opposed to "original" folk music (*novokomponovana vs. izvorna narodna muzika*), a neofolk genre that boomed in the 1960s in Yugoslavia and appealed to recently urbanized peasants as well as those who were working in Germany and other European countries as guest workers (*gastarbeiter*). Its lyrics were mostly about family and romantic relationships, and often played on nostalgia for the countryside (see Simic 1976, 1979; and Gordy 1999). In terms of sound, neofolk introduced Western pop into a matrix locally recognizable as folk. From its inception, however, neofolk was radically opposed to the so-called authentic folk music (*izvorna narodna muzika*). "Authentic folk," as Gordy observes, "is a minority music on a level with symphonic music, its performance most often restricted to professional ensembles of trained musicians, while "neofolk," like most other commercial forms, is performed principally by self-educated performers" (Gordy 1999:129).

In the 1970s neofolk was the prime target of the socialist-style "culture campaigns" aimed at exorcising it as kitsch and garbage (*šund*) which, of course, never hurt its enormous popularity. As a musical marker of peasant-urbanites and *gastarbeiters,* neofolk was denounced and even viscerally despised by three overlapping yet distinguishable groups—the young urbanites who listened to rock and jazz, the classical music lovers and the guardians of the authentic (*izvorna*) folk music.

Turbo-folk introduced Western pop and rock elements much more aggressively than neofolk had before. "Although turbo-folk's radical extension of the influence of western commercial pop styles did represent a continuation of a process of change that had been occurring in the neofolk genre for at least two decades," Gordy says, "it can hardly be thought of as an "organic" development" (1999:133).

> The trend continued as turbo-folk developed, with more folk elements falling out of the mix. Finally, only two musical elements identified with "folk" would remain in the music: the sound of accordions . . . and the tremor in the voice characteristic of some types of traditional duophonic singing, generally described by the derogatory term *zavijanje* (howling). (Ibid.:134)

Turbo-folk was no longer about predicaments of urban migrants and nostalgia for the lost idyll of the countryside. It aggressively promoted "images of glamour, luxury, and the good life" as imagined by the peasant urbanites—a world populated by young women in miniskirts who drive luxury automobiles, live in fantastically spacious homes and spend their time in fashionable hotel bars" (Gordy 1999:134–135). In contrast to the old neofolk, furthermore, turbo-folk was widely seen not as a grass-roots phenomenon but as something imposed by the authorities from above through the state-run television channels, radio, and music production companies. Finally, it was definitely identified as a music not only of peasant-urbanites but of the new criminal class that was becoming indistinguishable from the regime itself. Nothing epitomized this association better than the much celebrated wedding, in 1995, of the state-sponsored criminal warlord turned businessman Željko Ražnjatović-Arkan and the turbo-folk queen Svetlana Veličković-Ceca.

Turbo-folk was thus a lightning rod attracting wrath and disgust from several directions at once, and this is what made it such a valuable diagnostic tool in Serbia's "culture wars" of the 1990s. It was viscerally repugnant to young, urbanite "rockers" of various shades and hues as a musical identity badge of their enemies—provincial, halfling *narodnjaci* (*folkniks*).[17] For guardians of folk purity, like Aksentijević and Zorislava Vasiljević, it was detestable both as inauthentic folk (as opposed to "authentic" Serbian music) and as polluted by Oriental tunes ("howling"). It was seen as an abominable mix of things that should not be mixed— namely, folk elements and Western music. It was despised as the ultimate kitsch, and resented as a conspiracy of the regime to drive the population into "utter idiocy" or prepare it for slaughter by putting it to sleep.

Practically all Serbian Jeremiads abound with images that suggest the state of being somehow half-, semi-, unfinished, neither here nor there, in transition, in-between, and so on. Božović talks about the "half-world" (*polusvet*) of the criminal underground, about "suburbs" (*predgradje;* suggests a zone of neither country nor city proper, thus a liminal, in-between, transitional zone of peasant-urbanites), and about the "twilight" of the metropolis. And when he mentioned the "fishermen in troubled water (*mutnolovci*)," Božović invoked an influential 1938 essay by Vladimir Velmar-Janković (1992) on the "Belgrade man," quoted extensively in chapter 2, that centered precisely on the phenomenon of "transitionality" (*prelazničarstvo*), thus establishing a link of this type of lamentation with one of its prominent pre–World War II incarnations.

In one or another of its guises, it is obvious that the peasant urbanite is the "rider of cultural apocalypse" denounced in the Jeremiads. As an in-between figure, however, he often comes to stand for a number of other in-between, half-baked, neither-here-nor-there positions: between *bildung* and *Volksgeist,* between tradition and modernity, provincialism and cosmopolitanism, between Turkey and Germany, the Balkans and Europe, East and West. The peasant urbanite thus comes to stand for the whole of the Serbian society rather than just for its uncultured stratum.

In this respect, the peasant urbanite is not just a sociological or demographic category but almost a mythical creature, a cipher for the predicament of being stuck halfway toward modernity lamented by Serbian Jeremiahs. This image of being stuck halfway between tradition and modernity has found its most complex philosophical elaboration in Radomir Konstantinović's (1991) *Filosofija palanke* (Small-town philosophy)—arguably the ur-text of this whole genre of discourse. The organizing metaphor of Konstantinović's treatise is *palanka* (a small town)—neither village nor city.

Konstantinović sees the spirit of *palanka* underlying the whole of Serbian mentality and culture, as a spirit of a "tribe in agony." No longer a "tribe" with its a-historical mentality but a spirit (to use Konstantinović's German philosophical terminology) already "infected" with history, already "conscious" of tribe as tribe, thus irreparably distanced from it, *palanka* is

> a consciousness rebelling against itself, a consciousness of particularity (individuality) which, on its way towards the freely-open world of the world spirit, as a spirit of infinite possibilities, a spirit of the stylistic multivocality, got stuck, which did not go over from the particularity (or individualism) to the attitude of creative subjectivity, but is a consciousness which, precisely for that reason, seeks self-cancellation of its own self as cancellation of its own particularity, as a consciousness of the tribe in agony, a tribe which has taken leave of itself and tries to come back. (Konstantinović 1991:18, 19)

This rather densely written book is one of the most powerful statements, or rather indictments, of the national character and its half-bakedness. Konstantinović's *Palanka* is some sort of abysmal Purgatory-like twilight zone between the village (tradition) and the city (modernity) where Serbs as a whole seem to have gotten stuck for good.

IT'S NICER WITH CULTURE

Whatever their position was, however, with Milošević's great turn in August 1994, the oppositional Jeremiahs suddenly found their own agendas and rhetoric appropriated by the very regime they accused of promoting the various "Riders of the Cultural Apocalypse." "Battle against newly-composed kitsch and chaos in culture," reports *Naša Borba* on September 22, 1994, "this is the motto upon which the program and the future endeavors of the Serbian Ministry of Culture are based, announced by the minister of culture Nada Popović-Perišić yesterday at the press conference in Hyatt Hotel." The Ministry of Culture mounted an offensive against the "tide of all that is ugly and low, present not only on the radio and television waves, but in everyday life, behavior, speech, morals and the appearance of the city" (cited in Glišić 1995), that was couched in the rhetoric hardly any different from that of the oppositional Jeremiahs. With that move, the regime, through its Ministry of Culture, colonized the initiatives of the marginalized oppositionary culture critics and simulated their crusade against the very phenomena these critics strongly associated with the regime itself.

The whole campaign was seen by most oppositional intellectuals as insincere and vacuous, if not outright cynical: "How could she, poor soul," writes Milivoje Glišić about Nada Popović-Perišić, "how could she strangle turbo-folk, when the PMs from her own party are singing to these very tunes in the Serbian Parliament!" (Glišić 1995) And we know who that Socialist Party PM was—none other than Bidža of Svilajnac.

The opposition might have protested the insincerity and vacuity of the campaign, but it couldn't prevent their own rhetoric from being stolen by the center which called all the shots, just as the peace initiatives and rhetoric of several parties and groups vehemently opposed to the war from the start were stolen by Milošević's "peace has no alternative" campaign.

The Ministry of Culture next moved from simulating the critique of unculturedness to a wholesale colonization of "what kind of a good thing culture is" discourse by proclaiming the year 1995 a "Year of Culture," and launching an ostentatious PR campaign under the motto: "It's nicer with culture (*Lepše je sa kulturom*)." The Belgrade affiliate of Saatchi & Saatchi was paid a large undisclosed sum to produce posters, videos, flags, stickers, and badges in the glittery Western marketing style. Thus an endeavor clearly reminiscent of old communist campaigns to "culturally uplift the masses" (*kulturno uzdizanje masa*) ended up couched in a form that suggested the opposite—free-market capitalism. "Culture" was treated like any other product to be advertised: "when we work on coffee, a cream, or cookies, it's the same procedure," a member of the Saatchi & Saatchi creative team explained in a televised documentary, "we decided not to talk *against* kitsch, but *for* culture . . . to try to make culture more interesting . . . more familiar to our audience, so that in the market competition between the one and the other [kitsch and culture] we somehow win." (see Dragičević-Šešić 1995).

The campaign covered just about every possible meaning of the term "culture": the emblem of the campaign was a well-known Mesolithic figurine from Lepenski Vir (FIGURE 5.2)—therefore culture in this area is thousands of years old;[18] the figurine wears a tie—hence the culture of dressing; holds a spoon and knife—hence the culture of eating, that is to say, good manners; and so on. The customary objects and institutions of high culture were heavily represented in their most generic form, but so were the objects of the established pop culture such as Levi's jeans or Coca-Cola. Nor were the emblems of national culture neglected. There is a video clip showing almost all the icons of national culture in their chronological order, starting with archeological finds of Neolithic, Celtic, and Roman times, through the medieval Serbian monasteries, images associated with nineteenth-century romantic nationalism, and ending with fashionable Paris-based Serbian painters. Practically all the senses of the term "culture" were covered: culture as manners, culture as tolerance, culture as objects of high culture, culture as long-standing tradition, culture as expressions of national genius in all its forms, the High Byzantine embodied in a famous fresco, as well as the populist, Romantic *Volksgeist* type embodied in the familiar portrait of Vuk Karadžić.

In the culture wars of the 1990s in Serbia, various groups that were kept away from the center of power were trying to promote their pretenders to the throne of culture and themselves as a legitimate cultured class entitled to its share of power. They all had to come out and say what kind of a good thing they consider culture to be, and what kind of a bad thing "unculture" (*nekultura*) was. The center of power, however, didn't need to define anything. The regime just proclaimed that "It's nicer with culture," something nobody could disagree with. Completely empty of content as it was, that slogan was for this very reason all the more powerful. By avoiding all content, the regime was showing that it is indeed the center, for only the center doesn't need to name itself—everyone knows it is where it should be (*tamo gde treba*) and that it is doing what should be done (*šta treba*). In that sense, the Ministry of Culture's slogan was just an extension of the slogan the Socialist Party used in the 1992 elections: *Tako treba*—a deictic masterpiece if there ever was one.

FIGURE 5.2.

Poster for the Serbian Ministry of Culture's
"It's nicer with culture" campaign.

Tako treba could be translated as "This is how it should be" or "As it should be" or "In this way" or simply "Thus!" Instead of a certain definable goal or quality of action, the utterance brazenly proclaimed that the setting of goals or the quality of action, whatever they may be at any moment, is dependent on the point of view of the one actor whose identity everyone knew. The phrase also carried with it an echo of a whole genre of expressions widespread in communist regimes that named the unutterable center of power with precisely such shifters. The slogan immediately became a part of everyday talk easily establishing the intertextual link with the already familiar usage of such shifters during Tito's era: "He phoned where he should" (*telefonirao je tamo gde treba*), "it was decided where it should" (*odlučeno je tamo gde treba*), "he told whom he should" (*rekao je kome treba*), and so on.

A passage from Vladimir Voinovich's *The Life and Extraordinary Adventures of Private Ivan Chonkin,* gives a brilliant example. The translation from the Russian original (Voinovich 1975) was done by Dale Pesmen, who tried to make the untranslatable wordplay understandable in English. Unlike English, the Serbian translation retains the same wordplay that exists in the original Russian.

> To readers from distant galaxies, unfamiliar with our earthly customs, a legitimate question might occur—what does the Place Where You Belong mean? Where You Belong for whom and for what? In this connection, the author offers the following explanation: In the bygone times described by the author, there existed everywhere a certain Institution, which was not so much military as militant . . . This Institution acquired the reputation of seeing everything, hearing everything, knowing everything, and, if something was out of line, the Institution would be there in a flash. For this reason people would say, if you are too smart, you'll end up Where You Belong; if you blab too much you'll end up Where You Belong . . . One person blabs What he Should, and another, What he Shouldn't. If you blab What you Should, you'll have everything you Should and even a little more. If you blab what you Shouldn't, you'll end up Where You Belong, that is, in the above mentioned Institution.[19]

The slogan was a masterpiece of cynicism. It took the whole inchoate experience of that period, with all its misery, trauma, and impoverishment, and brazenly declared that even all that was As It Should Be. In everyday usage the slogan was commonly given all kinds of ironic twists ranging from "*Tako* nam i *treba*" (it serves us right)—a rueful recognition of our own responsibility for the miserable condition of our lives, to sardonic counter-slogans such as those used in the massive protests in the winter of 1996 which countered, one by one, all the slogans the Socialist Party of Serbia used in previous elections (from *Naša Borba*, November 25, 1996, Internet edition): "With us there's no uncertainty—war" (*Sa nama nema neizvesnosti—rat*); "As It Should Be—sanctions" (*Tako treba—sankcije*); "Serbia will not bow down—Dayton" (*Srbija se saginjati neće—Dejton*); "Let's go on—The Hague" (*Idemo dalje—Hag*). A popular song by the rock band Fish Soup (*Riblja čorba*) capitalized on the fact that "bread" in the genitive case (*hleba*) rhymes with "should" (*treba*) and produced these lines that were echoed in many less successful versions:

Today, there's no milk, today there's no bread,	*Danas nema mleka, danas nema hleba,*
So eat shit—perhaps it "Should be That Way"	*zato jedi govna—možda tako treba.*

All these ironic twists, however, only rebounded on the one who uttered them because, no matter how you twisted it, by the very act of alluding to the slogan you were still forced to acknowledge that you know very well who was behind it, who the real boss was—which was exactly what its whole point was.

So with culture—the Center spoke the word and thus claimed the throne. If the Ministry said what kind of a good thing culture was, it would have been open to argument. Instead, the slogan preempted all argument, debate, and negation, for culture is simply whatever is associated at any given moment with the throne—proximity to the throne is the only criterion of value.

This latest appropriation, notwithstanding the apparent ease with which the campaign came to be ridiculed by the cultured opposition in 1995, added yet another moral/cognitive warp to an already benumbingly warped world of Serbia, and it made this latest round of Jeremiads sound a tone of deeper, more desperate anguish than their illustrious ancestors like Slobodan Jovanović, Bogdan Popović, or Vladimir Velmar-Janković some sixty to eighty years ago. Even though they talked about the same phenomena, and used the same phrases, these ancestors belonged to a generation of Serbian intelligentsia that essentially *was* in charge. The Jeremiahs of 1994 and 1995 were used and discarded, marginalized and ridiculed, co-opted and silenced, and then finally robbed of their agendas and rhetoric by a chameleon regime wearing the face of Bidža and his likes one day and that of a smiling Mesolithic figurine the other.

SIX

Glorious Pasts and Imagined Continuities

The Most Ancient People

"It was in the early autumn of 1985 when by some Ostap-Benderesque[1] diplomatic swindle a charlatan from Mexico came to Yugoslavia and proclaimed the mouth of river Neretva to be the location of the ancient Troy," wrote Svetlana Slapšak in her essay "How It All Started." She recounts how the domestic experts at the presentation the charlatan gave in a large Belgrade University auditorium "did their best not to say anything clearly critical and to suppress any intervention from the audience" (Slapšak 1994:57). Sitting in the audience and unable to publicly intervene, Slapšak passed the time making fun of the presentation with her two friends until threatened with physical violence by those sitting near her who wanted them to shut up. She realized then that this was no longer a laughing matter:

> Most of those present yearned to discover that they actually belong to an ancient and glorious lineage, repeating the European mythology of ancestors of Romans but older than Greeks, which is the essential ideological and state-building text of the myth of Trojans. (Ibid.:58)

All the essential elements of what was to come were present at this event, Slapšak claimed. Even before various Yugoslav nationalisms tore the country apart, this event showed a vague but strong need to define a dangerous enemy. "Someone mysterious stole our ancient identity, and now we had a chance to denounce the culprit and get back what right-fully belongs to us. That mysterious enemy could only, in an autistic reversal, be those," Slapšak says, "who wouldn't accept the ravings of the Mexican charlatan" (1994:58).[2] This failure of qualified critics to do their critical duty, the result of a combination of cowardice and the "idea of the utility of lying for the collective," was seen by Slapšak as one of the main causes of Yugoslavia's slide into nationalism and war. Finally, this event presaged how a yearning for a positive identity can become co-opted into the "colonization of the past as a magical operation of colonizing the actual space" where the past serves as "a source of the right of the *first*" (58).

A very good way of sorting out the range of political positionings taken in Serbia starting with the national mobilization in the mid-1980s is to note the kind of past a speaker would implicitly or explicitly "co-opt" or "colonize." In practice, several desirable pasts would often be combined (sometimes in ways that must strike an outside observer as logically incompatible), and yet it is possible to analytically separate the main prototypical narratives that connect a particular desirable past with the present. We have seen how Byzantine legacy, idealized peasant *Volksgeist*, and Western civilization figure as identity options in politi-cal positionings. To put it most schematically, as a mainstream Serbian nationalist you could embrace either the Byzantine elitist or the populist (peasant) position, try to combine the two, or even present yourself as a Western democrat of Serbian nationalist persuasion. As an anti-nation-alist you had to wholeheartedly embrace European or Western ideals and present them as idealized universal cosmopolitanism opposed to what you see as the oxymoron of the Serbian "national democrat." In addition to these positionings, the nationalist neo-fascist fringe that occasion-ally commanded center stage in Milošević's Serbia would mostly opt for Byzantine glory or even more remote phantasmic pasts. Conversely, imputing Turkish Taint or communist legacy to your opponents was to saddle them with (what you cast as) undesirable pasts. These were the prototypical positionings that fractured Serbian intellectuals but that, in their popularized versions, provided templates for everyone who cared to debate Serbian identity and destiny. Now is the time to connect these identity options to their underlying origin stories and trace out several strategies for appropriating or rejecting different pasts that people in

Serbia used since the Mexican charlatan paid them a visit in 1985.[3] In practice, these strategies come mixed in all conceivable ways but, for analytical purposes, I treat them as separable ideal types. I will proceed by unpacking a series of "revelatory incidents" (see Fernandez 1986:xi) where these ideal types of response come together in a particularly condensed and poignant way. The first scene is a farmer's market—the famous *Kalenić pijaca*—in the part of Belgrade called Čubura.

SANSKRIT IN THE FARMER'S MARKET

One June morning in 1995, trailing an empty two-wheeled cart behind, my mother and I walked uphill on the narrow street leading to the unfinished giant edifice of the St. Sava temple and entered the familiar maze of even narrower streets in Čubura. Shabby little houses were interspersed with dilapidated villas, inner courtyards with the a water tap in the middle, where Čuburians gather for coffee, gossip, even to give each other a haircut in the open. Gardens managed to be both neat and weedy. Like many other parts of Belgrade, Čubura bears a Turkish name. The mosques and Turkish baths almost all disappeared from the city more than a century ago, together with other, visible (and easily removable) signs of Ottoman rule, but the names stayed and still carry that rough, yet intimate aura of things Turkish.

In the farmer's market you may pretend to be the most highly polished urbanite but most likely you are just barely a generation removed from the peasant across the stall, and that gives the market an egalitarian feel. Here one glimpses the barrel-chested, bearded figure of a well-known National Opera baritone buying onions, over there an actress who sang gypsy songs in an Academy Award–winning Gypsy film of thirty years ago.[4] The tenor is dressed in worn out, nondescript clothes, the actress in something cheaply garish.

That morning we bumped into a an old acquaintance of my mother's—a sculptor and the widow of a prominent literary critic.

"What are you doing here?" she asked me.

"I am studying the stories Serbs tell themselves and others about themselves," I gave my one-sentence answer.

"Oh, everybody is studying us these days," she said. "There was this American psychiatrist poking around who's studying human aggression. But no matter how hard they try, they will never understand us. They can put us in a computer and still they won't understand."

And then with a conspiratorial wink toward a fellow native: "Take for instance, our *inat*."

Oh, how well I knew this turn. *Inat* is supposed to be one of those ineffable essences of being a Serb, thus by definition untranslatable. We may bewail the foolishness of doing completely irrational, often self-destructive things "just in spite" (as *inat* translates, actually quite well), but we also think of it as unfathomably noble and would like others to take it as such. Popping out of the fellow-native confidante role, I took a stab with my little test:

"It is a Turkish word."

"Oh no," she said with the air of indulgent superiority as to a cub who has strayed, "many of those words we thought were from Turkish in fact come from Sanskrit."

"They might be Persian or Arabic in origin," I persisted, "but they came through Turkish."[5]

"No," she would not budge, "you must surely know that Serbian is practically identical with Sanskrit, and besides, you would be well advised to look into the Hittites as well."

Several things were done in this exchange. An identity supposedly unfathomable to rational Westerners was encapsulated in a Turkish loan word. The Turkish Taint was then rejected, but in her retreat from identity tainted by Turkishness my mother's acquaintance didn't claim the Serbian Byzantine legacy—the usual move in such situations. Instead of the glorious Byzantine past she co-opted an alternative and much more ancient heritage, first with Serbian's supposed affinity with Sanskrit, and then with their supposed Hittite descent. The Byzantine gambit is indeed a major one, but before embarking on Serbian problems with their Byzantine legacy, let me first explore this more ancient connection.

THE MOST ANCIENT PEOPLE

There is a mantra every schoolboy in Yugoslavia could repeat in his sleep: "Slavs came to the Balkan Peninsula in the sixth and seventh centuries." I was hardly aware that there were alternative theories until 1990, when a man I met at a party told me a story of a Serbian woman who, despite all odds, defended a controversial dissertation at the Sorbonne in the 1960s, and of a powerful conspiracy of silence that prevented the publication of her manuscript. Only later did I learn that the book in question was *Serbs . . . the Most Ancient People* (*Srbi . . . narod najstariji*) by Olga Luković-Pjanović, first published by the *Glas Srba* (*Voice of Serbs*) from Indianapolis in 1988, and subsequently reissued in Belgrade in 1990, 1993, 1994, and 2003 (Luković-Pjanović 1988). The book became a best seller in the 1990s and was followed by a deluge of magazine articles, serialized digests in the dailies and weeklies, as well as entire books devoted to the thesis that Serbs are the most ancient of peoples.

If the Mexican charlatan was the first to provoke a vague yearning for ancient identity in 1985, the publication of *Serbs . . . the Most Ancient People,* in 1990, was a fulfillment of that yearning. The theories about ancient Serbian origins offered in this hefty two-volume work were not new. Olga Luković-Pjanović was actually revamping the work of a group of nineteenth-century Romantic Slavophiles. A Montenegrin writer, Draško Šćekić, offers a compendium of practically all these theories in his book, *Sorabi* (*Sorabs*), published by a private Belgrade publisher in 1994. I will try to summarize the main tenets of this odd mixture, although a summary may impose a misleading semblance of order and logic on the kind of free-associating that characterizes the whole genre.

According to most of these theories, the ancient homeland of Serbs or "Sorabs" (one of their faux-archaic names) was in India. From India they migrated around 4500 BC to Mesopotamia, where they took part in the building of the Tower of Babel. Some stayed but the majority migrated further to Africa, where they ruled Egypt for some time. Two more waves of migration from India dispersed ancient Serbs throughout Asia from China to the Urals, and from the Caspian Sea to Siberia or Sirbiria or Sirbidia, that is to say, Serbia. Migrations to Europe followed, centuries before Christ, and the historical map Šćekić provides shows how these migrations covered a great deal of Central, East, and Southeast Europe with Serb states. The evidence for such claims is sought in writings of Herodotus, Strabo, Tacitus, Pliny, and Ptolemy, who supposedly documented the existence of ancient Serbs and their states all over the world of classical antiquity. However, the theories that see Serbs everywhere most often neglect to mention that these classical historians and geographers were talking about Sarmatians and Scythians, Venets and Getae, Thracians and Dacians, Etruscans and Trojans, Illyrians and Pelazgians, but not Serbs. When this potentially damaging discrepancy is noted, the following explanation is offered. For one, says Šćekić, the foreigners couldn't pronounce the word Srb so, often for nefarious purposes, they distorted it beyond recognition. "Fortunately," he writes,

> these [false] attributions usually cannot mislead the erudite and objective searchers after the autochthonous Slavic origins. Even if doubt does appear, they can rely on the deeply rooted Serbian memory of their own most ancient existence and name. This precious evidence is preserved by the *Serbian language*—the primordial words, names, myths, wise sayings, traditions, legends and poetry. (Šćekić 1994:75)

"Linguistic" evidence is central to this genre, and it is mostly toponyms combined with fantastic etymologies that provide the main "proofs" of Serbian ancient origin. The Serbian language as it is spoken today, this literature claims, is the closest to the proto-Indo-European among existing European languages. Serbs lived in India since times immemorial, as attested by various place names, and they were most likely the precursors of Vedic poets, as attested by the mention of names like "Srbinda" in the most ancient Rg-Vedas. Srbinda, of course, corresponds to the modern Serbian *srbenda*.[6] "SRBINDA is not the only ancient Serbian word in the VEDAS," writes Šćekić, referring to unnamed Slavic Sanskritologists of repute. "Our native tongue has preserved more than three thousand words from the times of the most ancient Vedic hymns, and these words have changed neither their form nor their meaning to this very day" (1994:103). My mother's acquaintance in the farmer's market used this theory to bypass the uncomfortable Turkish Taint and claim a more ancient and more noble lineage.

For all their nebulous quality, there is a systematicity to these theories if we analyze them as a series of moves to "out-ancient" all the competitors. If Illyrians are actually Serbs, then Albanian claims to be descendants of Illyrians, and thus to predate Serbs in the territories they now inhabit, is invalidated. If the Pelazgians were actually a Serbian tribe, then Serbs can out-ancient the Greeks who claim to be the direct descendants of ancient Hellenes; similarly with Etruscans and Venets with respect to Rome and Venice, and Dacians with respect to Romania. It is interesting also that this literature makes a strong move to establish

Serbian preeminence with respect to Slavs by arguing that all the Slavs were originally Serbs. One can easily see the politics of this move which reverses the intra-Slavic hierarchy, especially the older brother claim of Russians. If all the Slavs were originally Serbs, than Russians, too, are our "younger brothers."

This whole literature rests on a fundamental conspiracy theory. The enemy is the Nordic or Berlin-Viennese School of History—a powerful cabal bent on suppressing the findings of what is often called the Serbian Autochthonistic School. While the Autochthonistic School claims that the Serbs are the autochthonous inhabitants of the Balkans, the Danubian Basin, and even wider areas in Europe and Asia since times immemorial, the Nordic School pushes the theory that we all learned in school as the Holy Writ, namely, that Serbs came to the Balkans only in the seventh century.

To claim pre-Vedic India as the homeland and the status of proto-Aryans is, of course, quite sufficient to out-ancient all these powerful historic deniers of Serbian antiquity. There is, however, another theory that puts the origins of Serbs even further back into prehistory.

In the late sixties (1965–68) archaeological excavations on the banks of the Danube near the Djerdap straits led by Dragoslav Srejović exposed the culture that came to be known as Lepenski Vir which dated back to about 6000 BC (Srejović 1972). Remains of buildings, tombs evincing strange burial rituals, sophisticated stone, bone and horn weapons, and various jewelry were found, making it one of the most important Mesolithic finds in Europe. Most striking were the monumental sandstone figurines (probably of deities and demons), with their characteristic down-turned mouths and fish-like eyes. The oldest Lepenski Vir sites belonged to hunter–fisher–gatherers. Later dwellings built over the same site and elsewhere in Eastern Serbia (middle Danubian region) belonged to early Neolithic agriculturalists and pastoralists (5000–4500 BC) of what is called the Starčevo culture. For Srejović, these archaeological discoveries suggested the possibility that the impetus for the great cultural takeoff did not have to come to Europe from the Near East, but that one of its possible originating points was the autochthonous culture of Lepenski Vir. The leap that Srejović never made, however, was, predictably, easily made by searchers after Serbian immemorial antiquity. Lepenski Vir culture was patriarchal; it venerated fire, the hearth, and the dead.

The pagan Serbian religion, as reconstructed by the noted historian of religion Veselin Čajkanović, was also centered around an ancestor cult. This was enough for Sčekić and others like him to conclude that "the cradle of the Slavs is in the Danubian Basin," and that "the Serbs, since their embryonic stage inhabited they same ground they inhabit now." Lepenski Vir reveals the truth, he says, "the truth about ourselves, that has been attacked by Germans, the Vatican and the Turks for centuries" (112). Sčekić does notice, uncharacteristically for this genre, that there is a logical inconsistency between the Mesolithic Danubian and pre-Vedic Indian origin of the Serbs. He resolves it in a footnote. The discovery of Lepenski Vir, he says, "suggested another theory according to which the Sorabs, or the ancient Serbs, originated not in India but in the Danubian region, from which they then migrated to India, taking their culture with them and bringing it to fruition with Vedic religious hymns and the Laws of Manu" (112).[7]

SERBIAN ARCHAEOLOGY'S RESPONSE
TO THEORIES OF SERB ANTIQUITY

How did official Serbian archaeology respond to all these theories of Serbian antiquity? I knew that Serbian archaeology tended to focus on either prehistory or the Roman presence on present-day Serbian territory rather than the Slavic or Serbian past. In July 1996 I had the honor of spending two days with Professor Dragoslav Srejović at the Gamzigrad excavation site in Eastern Serbia.[8] As a discoverer of both Lepenski Vir and the late-Roman-era Imperial palaces in Gamzigrad and Šarkamen, Srejović was the premier authority on these traditional foci of Serbian archaeology.

"Serbs have this megalomaniacal trait," Srejović told me, "the Piedmont complex, which makes them play patrons to their unwilling neighbors. So, as long as everything is fine, the Serbs don't think they have anything to prove to anybody about their greatness." That is one of the reasons, he said, why Serbian archaeology neglected the period from the settling of Slavs in the Balkans to their Christianization (sixth to tenth centuries), and why we have so little data about that period of our past:

> When this last (nationalist) euphoria started it was too late to make up for the lost time. There were no real specialists in this area. Then there appeared that assistant professor who took it over

and he claimed that he found Slavs as early as the Roman period
... At that moment this kind of research was lucrative but it was
done unprofessionally, to say the least, and was often quite bizarre
(*sumanuto*). There is an example, for instance, of that guy who
presented himself as an expert on Etruscans [Svetislav Bilbija] and
who bragged that he had deciphered their inscriptions by using
Cyrillic?! and Olga Luković-Pjanović [in her book *Serbs . . .
the Most Ancient People*] cites him totally uncritically. Now it's reversed again into the other extreme and now anything that smells
of Serbs [in archaeology or history] is suspicious and made odious
by the previous period's excesses.

Even though it was not his specialty, Srejović told me that he'd like to
see more research on our national past, even if it is fueled by nationalist
motives. More facts will be accumulated, and in time, after the nationalistic excesses blow over, the data will remain, on which a solid edifice
of reliable knowledge could be painstakingly built.

Srejović took a public stance, in a 1994 interview, against all kinds
of crackpot theories in the 1990s, calling them "euphoric delusions of lunatics" and "totally fraudulent claims about Serbian prehistory" (*Vreme*,
no. 198, August 8, 1994). "Instead of endeavoring to make our people feel
truly proud," he said in that interview, "knowing what great things were
created on the territory of Serbia, the great spiritual creations of various
populations and peoples, and instead of that being the pride and hope
of the citizens of Serbia, it is in some people's interest to build our hope
on deceptions and to confound us with lies."

"The books by various painters and amateurs who claim that the
Serbs are the most ancient people do not worry me," Srejović told me,
"but it is terrible if a scientist joins such mindless and uncontrolled
behavior. This is then to be severely condemned." I assume that at least
one of the scientists Srejović was talking about was Djordje Janković—
that same "assistant professor" who "took over" Slavic archaeology and
did "unprofessional" but lucrative research in Republika Srpska that
he mentioned in the quote above. I learned more about Janković from
one of his colleagues in Belgrade University's archaeology department
with whom I talked in July 1995, exactly a year before my pilgrimage to
Gamzigrad.

Janković's colleague was particularly incensed at him and "those like him" precisely because he thought that Serbian archaeology has always been unusually free of nationalistic bias. Since its beginnings in the 1840s, Serbian archaeology focused on prehistory and non-Serbian themes, he said. This is in contrast to practically all our neighbors whose archaeology is thoroughly imbued by the national element—Romanians, Bulgarians, even Hungarians, not to mention Greeks and Macedonians. His thesis was that one of the possible explanations for this state of affairs is that, in Serbia, there are well-preserved monasteries with frescoes. "Frescoes are political statements. The way the rulers are depicted in them signifies a lot and sends a definitive message," he said, "just like television does today. This, alongside coins with the ruler's image, was what presented the ruler to the illiterate people." Therefore, he said, "there isn't much pressure on archaeology in Serbia to dig out the history of the nation. Croats, for instance, had to dig out artifacts that pointed to their kings." In a word, he insisted that Serbian archaeology, from its inception, was almost completely free of the obsession with the nation, that this is a big advantage over practically all our neighbors where this is not the case, and that we should preserve that advantage so that we can look the world in the eye.

MILIĆ OF MAČVA, THE "MAD PAINTER": PEASANTS AND THE INVERTED PERSPECTIVE

As a scientist and scholar, Srejović said that he worried more about people with scientific credentials promoting "euphoric delusions" than about, as he put it, "various painters and amateurs who claim that the Serbs are the most ancient people." It was quite obvious which particular painter Srejović meant—the self-proclaimed "mad painter" Milić of Mačva who, since the early 1960s, had made a career out of Salvador Dali–like eccentricity and extravagant public boasting.[9] In the late 1980s and particularly the early 1990s, he became one of the main disseminators of the various theories of Serbs as the most ancient people. For years he was taken as an amusing eccentric whose excesses were indulged as artistic liberties, and whose outspoken Serbian nationalism, being packaged as ravings of a "mad painter," was more or less tolerated even by Tito. Then in the mid-1980s, when the genres began to blur (as evidenced by Slapšak's analysis of the Mexican charlatan episode), it was suddenly not entirely clear whether Milić was just an "eccentric artist" or whether he was for real. When he was commissioned to paint the walls of the Orthodox Church in Voždovac (part of Belgrade), there was a public outcry. Orthodoxy has very strict rules about who can paint churches and a very strict canon of how to do it, and, by even the most relaxed criteria, allowing Milić to paint the walls of a church in his eccentric surrealist style was blasphemous.[10] In 1991 another Serbian cultural institution broke its tacit gate-keeping rules. Milić was the first living Serbian painter to have a retrospective exhibition in the National Museum.[11] This was the occasion for his long interview in *Duga* (no. 463, November 23, 1991), when Milić managed to present practically all the tenets of the "Serbs as the Most Ancient People" theories prompted by the seemingly serious questions of the interviewer, Ljiljana Habjanović Djurović.

In March 1995 Milić had another exhibition, this time in the Belgrade Ethnographic Museum, pompously titled: "My Farewell to Alberti's False, Narrowing Renaissance Perspective." This event showed what I call the "Byzantine revival" in 1990s Serbia in a very "graphic" way. Moreover, it was a particularly striking example of how the tokens of the Byzantine great tradition could easily get mixed with the emblems of the little tradition of Serbian peasant culture.[12]

The opening was announced by the sound of church bells, the choir sang an Orthodox liturgical song, and the central theme of the exhibit was the "inverted perspective" of Byzantine religious art. The museum was completely packed for the opening, and Milić staged one of his typical performances. He read his long "Manifesto" dressed first all in black—to symbolize the evil Western "narrowing" perspective to which he was saying farewell, reappearing later decked all in white to show his conversion to the Byzantine "inverted" or expanding perspective (figure 6.1).

It is notable that the event took place in the Ethnographic Museum—a typical Central European temple of the Romantic *Volksgeist*, amid relics of peasant life. Here is how the art critic Djordje Kadijević reconciled the two elements in his speech (printed in the exhibition catalog):

> Milić of Mačva found a model of a similar understanding of space, often identical to the Byzantine one, in the treasure house of our ethnographic heritage, in our folk art. This folklore element deeply infuses Milić's artistic imagination . . . In the creations of these folk artists, so close and dear

FIGURE 6.1.

Milić of Mačva reading his "Manifesto"
at the Belgrade Ethnographic Museum.

to Milić of Mačva, there is not a trace of Latin, Renaissance understanding of space. Those anonymous creators of masterpieces sheltered under
the roof of the Ethnographic Museum were under the influence of our
Church art, they revered frescoes on the wall of Nemanjić's monasteries, were awed by the carvings on their iconostases. By returning to the
Orthodox Byzantine "expanding" perspective he encountered in their
creations, Milić of Mačva returns in a symbolic way to the roots of our
national art tradition.

The image of illiterate peasants staring in awe at the frescoes of
medieval Serbian monasteries throughout the dark centuries of Ottoman rule is an iconic presentation of a problem in constructing Serbian
identity. The problem is how to account for the unbroken transmission
of a High Culture, or great tradition, through the typical carriers of
little tradition—the illiterate peasants? We will return to this key image
after an excursion through some other manifestations of the "Byzantine
Revival" in 1990s Serbia.

THE SPIRITUAL VERTICAL OF THE
EURASIAN INTERNATIONALE

In July 1994, as part of its Summer Festival (Beogradski letnji festival, or BELEF), Belgrade hosted a "Gathering of the Cultures of Spiritually Kindred, Eastern Orthodox Peoples" (*Sabor kultura duhovno bliskih, istočnohrišćanskih naroda*) attended by representatives from Armenia, Bulgaria, Greece, Georgia, South and North Ossetia, the Crimean Republic, Cyprus, Nagorno Karabakh, Republika Srpska, Republika Srpska Krajina, Rumania, Russia, Ukraine, and Byelorussia. The Gathering was accompanied by musical performances and art exhibitions, but the central event was a roundtable discussion on the "Eastern Orthodox World and the Challenges of the New World Order." Disparagingly or admiringly, the Gathering was variously labeled in the Belgrade press as "The Eurasian Internationale" or "The Byzantine Commonwealth." It was opened by the then vice president of the Yugoslav federal government Željko Simić and was attended by a number of prominent Serbian intellectuals (among them linguist Pavle Ivić, historians Milorad Ekmedžić and Veselin Djuretić, writer Dobrica Ćosić, and our "mad painter" Milić of Mačva), but its real grey eminence was Dragoš Kalajić, a painter, art critic, essayist, and publisher and editor of the popular magazine *Duga*.

Tall, handsome, and dandyish, Kalajić was filling a small niche in Belgrade cultural life in the 1970s and 1980s with his diatribes against modern art and all kinds of Western decadence. Full of obscure, hermetic references, and the kind of erudition that dazzles the half-educated, he combined the views of the Western elitist right (appropriating the likes of Julius Evola, Ortega y Gasset, and Ernest Jünger) and of the Russian "Euroasianists" (such as P. Savitsky, Valentin Rasputin, Aleksander Dugin, and Igor Shafarevich). His essays and books were a compendium of conspiracy theories in which Freemasonry, the Tri-Lateral Commission, the Vatican, and, most important, the "usurers' international" (*lihvarska internacionala*) led by the "high priests of supra-national capital" (*žreci nad-nacionalnog kapitala*), helped by the fifth column of domestic "mondialists" and "deracinated, decadent cosmopolitans," try to undermine the "spiritual vertical" of the Serbian and other Orthodox cultures of the Byzantine Commonwealth. Like many previously marginal phenomena,

Kalajić and his little coterie suddenly gained in public prominence with the general blurring of criteria that started in the late 1980s and was in full swing in the early 1990s. They formed the "New Serbian Right" (*Nova srpska desnica*) and started publishing a glossy journal titled *Our Ideas* (*Naše ideje*).

The phrase that perhaps best characterizes the agenda of the Eurasian Internationale is the "third way." In the words of one of the participants, Natalia Narochnitskaya:

> In the Orthodox world the awareness has ripened of the necessity to formulate and undertake what A. I. Solzhenitsyn called "the third way" of the Orthodox. More than anybody else we have personally experienced the evil and degeneration of communism. Thank God, there's no return to it. We shouldn't, however, repeat the tragic mistakes of the equally degenerate Western liberalism and its corresponding economy (in his writings Dragoš Kalajić illuminated that better and with greater tenacity than I could). That does not mean that we shouldn't take over the good elements, the positive experiences of both sides. In that way we will find crystallized before us a "cross-like order." The Horizontal [axis] will be made of the undoubtedly positive heritage of the Left: social justice, social concern, equal starting positions for all . . . The Vertical will be embodied in the spiritual-ethical and god-aspiring hierarchy of the classical European Right, in the aristocracy of spirit and virtues.

These appeals to hierarchy and the "aristocracy of the spirit" could find hardly any resonance with anything in Serbian history and experience relevant to the present situation, and in their extreme misalignment with arguably the core Serbian sentiment of egalitarianism they often bordered on the comic.[13] What did resonate well with the Serbian public at that time and acted as a salve for the spoiled identity of a pariah people (at least on the international stage at that time) was disparagement of the West combined with the affirmation of one's own cultural or "spiritual" superiority.

Tracing that cultural superiority back to the Byzantine heritage, however, poses a number of problems. One is that the West, to say the least, does not recognize the superiority of Byzantine culture. On the contrary, it traces its cultural and civilizational superiority to Greek Antiquity, Roman Law, the Italian Renaissance, the German Reformation, the French Enlightenment, English Parliamentarism, and the American

Revolution all bound in a seamlessly continuous story of triumphant evolution. Whoever has not passed through this idealized sequence is deemed civilizationally inferior. Another problem is whether there is any justification in claiming continuity between modern Serbian culture and the Byzantine great tradition. There is something dreamlike in claiming such a continuity, as was noted in a daily *Politika* article of April 27, 1996, devoted to Ivan Lalić (1931–1996), hailed as "A Poet of Serbian Byzantium." Here is an excerpt from his poem "Raška" (my translation):

> Stars over Raška are not like other stars:
> Short fuse, the powder wet, the flash unclear,
> The Big Cart[14] in blood and mud mired,
> And the hills werewolfishly red at dawn—
>
> Then why does the angel agree to pause
> On the wall of the new church, to light this place
> By dubious glory marked?

In Lalić's poetry, the critic Aleksandar Jovanović writes in the *Politika* article cited above, "Byzantium is truly an open, polysemic symbol and could be understood in a multiplicity of ways: as a homeland and extended memory of a culture, as a search for the cultural and civilizational identity, and as a dream of continuity which tells us that there was little continuity in actuality." I am not qualified to present a comprehensive history of Byzantine influences on Serbian culture that alone could provide a full answer to the question of whether and to what extent modern Serbian culture can claim continuity with its past Byzantine heritage. Yet, through a few vignettes, I will endeavor to show a few glimpses of what that heritage could represent to present-day people in Serbia.

CONTINUITY OR DISCONTINUITY: THE SPIRITUAL ACADEMY IN THE STUDENICA MONASTERY

In July 1996 I visited the Studenica Monastery some 200 kilometers south of Belgrade. It was built by Grand Prince Stefan Nemanja (1113–1199), the ruler of the Serbian state of Raška (the same Raška of Lalić's poem) and the founder of the Serbian Nemanjići dynasty.[15] At the time of my visit Studenica was hosting the "Spiritual Academy," a kind of summer camp for Orthodox liturgical singing led by the Academician Dimitrije

Stefanović, a great authority on Serbian medieval church music. For eight days young people, already members of various amateur choirs from Serbia, assembled there to learn the art of complex liturgical singing. I arrived the day before the last and attended the evening talk given by Dimitrije Stefanović in the large refectory.

Rather than lecturing, Stefanović was showing slides of Serbian monasteries, frescoes, and medieval manuscripts, and improvising around them. With enormous erudition and contagious enthusiasm, he was weaving a fascinating web of associations spanning centuries of Serbian history. He would, for instance, go from a particular manuscript to the monastery in which it is kept to a famous fresco in that monastery to the holy relics of a saint kept there and then launch into the story of how these relics were carried from one monastery to another over the centuries of exile and return prompted by the ebbs and flows of conquering empires. He recounted an experience he and his students had before an icon brought to Szentendre (Sent Andreja) in Hungary by the largest such wave of migration from Ottoman-occupied Serbia—the great migration under the Patriarch Arsenije Čarnojević in the seventeenth century. "When we looked at that icon," Stefanović said, "and when we tried to analyze it, we understood how that art, painting and music, and text and the liturgy, how all of that is assembled together and of a piece so that it could not be set apart." It was that coherent unity that I glimpsed emerging from Stefanović's thick web of associations linking monasteries, frescoes, and manuscripts, migrating relics and icons, architecture, music, and liturgy—the unity of what used to be the Byzantine-derived great tradition of Orthodoxy in the Serbian lands.

As he was showing his slides, Stefanović would quiz the audience about what this fresco depicted or where that icon was kept or what was the most famous three-word expression in this manuscript. In itself, this quiz format was nothing extraordinary, but the way Stefanović intoned these questions was quite distinctive. Over and over again he would plead: "I am asking only for that *minimum* that everyone should know ... You *have* to know this, I mean, you don't *have to,* but you should, you really should. I repeat, this is ours, we are a part of this, and please, don't let it be that we cannot recognize these, as they say, at first glance." "All Greeks know these things," he said, "since early childhood, so to say."

Stefanović's tone of an exasperated educator who nevertheless cannot blame his wards for what he considers criminal ignorance reminded me vividly of the tone our instructors at Jewish summer camp used as they tried to instill some elementary knowledge of Judaism in totally assimilated Jewish children—their "you should at least know what Hanukah is," is the exact equivalent of Stefanović's anguished pleas. In both cases a handful of experts were trying to re-instill at least the rudiments of a great tradition into younger generations who had completely lost touch with it.

At some point Stefanović showed a slide of an old manuscript. "Who is the youngest here?" he shouted. "Quick, quick, give me the youngest, let the youngest, what is it, sixteen, anyone sixteen, seventeen, come over quick, don't be afraid." While the search for the youngest was going on, Stefanović boomed: "Children, the issue here is whether we have any continuity and whether we are able to read something that was written in the fourteenth century." Finally, a seventeen-year-old girl came before the screen and, with some help from Stefanović, managed to decipher the line: "Hvalite jego psaltiri i gusli" (Praise Him psalteries and gusle). "Therefore," Stefanović concluded, "we can more or less say that the alphabet (*azbuka*) has in essence remained"[16] "Only ten minutes ago," he said, "the monks finished the evening liturgy (*bdenie*) ending it with those very same lines which are sung to this day."

Yes, Studenica monks were singing the same lines as they did in the fourteenth century, and a high school student could be made to decipher a fourteenth-century text, but it was obvious that, save for a few experts like Stefanović, who made it their lifelong calling, the majority of the younger generation in Serbia did not have access to what could be called the Great Byzantine Tradition, at least not in the way their Greek counterparts do—instilled in them from early childhood as a matter of general education. But this discontinuity was not just a matter of communism suppressing religious education for half a century. The rift between the great tradition symbolized by Byzantine-style frescoes in Serbian monasteries and the little tradition symbolized by illiterate peasants staring at them through the centuries of Ottoman rule has a much longer history.

After the fall of the medieval Serbian states and the effective elimination of the local aristocracy, the Orthodox clergy remained the only bearer of the High Byzantine–derived culture. The question of exactly how much was preserved, and to what extent the Orthodox Church managed to keep alive some of that heritage for the illiterate *rayah* in the intervening centuries, is a question that demands detailed historical investigation. More relevant here is that the two traditions did emerge as distinctly configured ideological positions in the nineteenth century, and that, because of particular political and ideological circumstances, they came to a head-on clash known as "The War for Serbian Language and Orthography." In that "war" the illiterate peasants, led by the language reformer Vuk Karadžić, won a total victory over the custodians of the Byzantine-derived High Culture—the conservative clergy and educated Serbian higher classes from Austrian Vojvodina and Slavonia. Even though the victory for one side was total, the arguments of the vanquished periodically resurfaced in the form of laments over the broken continuity with the only High Culture to which Serbs can lay claim. Before going to the most recent echoes of that battle, let me first sketch out what the war was about and who the main protagonists were.

VUK'S WAR FOR THE SERBIAN LANGUAGE AND ORTHOGRAPHY

After taking part in the First Serbian Uprising in 1804, Vuk Karadžić found himself in Vienna in 1813 as a protégé of Jernej Kopitar—the powerful censor for all Slavic, Romanian, Greek, and Albanian books published in the Austro-Hungarian Empire. A student of Schlegel, von Humboldt, and Herder, Kopitar was a "notoriously zealous advocate of national languages, and believed that Slavic movements inside Austria would eventually fulfill his dream of Austria being a *Slavic* nation-state" (Greer 1997).

The point of origin for such a language was to be in the speech of the "folk," and in a world that resonated strongly with the ideas of Herder and the Grimm brothers, Vuk was a heaven-sent prodigy—a speaker of a pristine vernacular and imbued with precisely the kind of oral epic poetry and folk-tale tradition that was all the craze in the Europe of that time. It was then Vuk's own speech that became the "the ideal, authoritative, pure standard of Serbian speech and hence the Serbian language" (Greer 1997). The main opponents of Vuk's radical language standardization projects were the Austrian Serbs who were the only representatives of Serbian literate culture. Greer outlines three alternatives that existed at that time:

> The most radically "Orthodox" approach to the Serbian language would be one in which the existing written tradition would continue, undisturbed by and separate from any Serbian speech whatsoever. This camp, which controlled all Serbian presses until Vuk's debut, in effect advocated a strong linguistic tie to the traditions of Orthodox Christianity.

> A moderate reformist view of standardization, advocated by the majority of productive Serbian writers of the time, would keep much of the abstract lexicon of Church Slavic, while attempting to replace most of the everyday written language with material based upon speech.

> Finally, Vuk's idea of Serbian had no place whatsoever for literary tradition or the authority of literary production. The current written language, viewed as corrupt and unwieldy, was to die out in favor of one based exclusively on speech. (Ibid.)

Language and orthography were an important political issue for Austrian Serbs. To stubbornly preserve the hybrid language and Church orthography, marked by heavy Russian influence, thus became a traditional national policy of the Austrian Serbs as a bulwark against the threat that Austro-Hungarian expansionism posed for Serbian national and religious identity within the Empire. On the other hand, Vuk's radical project was at least initially in alignment with Kopitar's national language policies whose explicit aim was precisely to make Vienna, not Moscow, the center of Slavdom. The Serbian Orthodox clergy could thus attack Vuk's reform as an Austrian Catholic plot to undermine the Serbian Church and thus the Serbian national cause in Austria (see Selimović 1970:82–83, 95–97; and Skerlić 1925:260).

The political context surrounding this "language war" became irrelevant in time, but the direction Serbian literature, as well as cultural life in general, took was decisively set by the fact that it was Vuk's alternative that won the day. As history is written by the winners, Vuk's opponents are now remembered as little more than simpletons destined to oblivion. Yet, as the great Bosnian writer Meša Selimović put it in his *For and Against Vuk*, some of their arguments were not without merit and kept reappearing in different guises, especially at times when "something important was changing in our orientations" (Selimović 1970:105).

One of the arguments was that Vuk's "language of peasants and herders" lacked the abstract vocabulary, the means for expressing subtle, inner, psychological states, or matters spiritual that transcend everyday pragmatic reality—all already existing in Church Slavonic or the hybrid literary language based on it. The influential critic Jovan Skerlić raised this issue at the turn of the century by reporting the following dialogue that took place between Vuk and the other pillar of Serbian culture, the Montenegrin Archbishop and poet of the *Mountain Wreath* Petar Petrović Njegoš:

> Verily, Mr. Vuk, the archbishop said, this language of ours is very impoverished. It doesn't have the word for "idea" or for "era," and so many other concepts.
>
> Master, Vuk replied, if the people (*narod*) could find a name for each part, each tiny piece, each screw and bolt on the cart, they could have found the names for these concepts as well, had there been a need for them. When they are needed, the people will find them. (Skerlić 1925:272)

The last chapter of Selimović's *For and Against Vuk* is devoted to Gavril Stefan Venclović, a Serbian monk who lived in South Hungary at the end of seventeenth century and whose poetry was completely forgotten until a young scholar edited and published his manuscripts in 1966. Selimović stands in awe before the "wondrous" Venclović. Here was a language full of vernacular vitality yet able to express the inner, the subtle, the transcendent. "Is it possible that a poetic Serbian language imbued with such marvelous expressive potential already existed more than two centuries ago?" Selimović asks. "The missing link has been found, the continuity has been reestablished," he exults, but we are confused, for it is too late. Serbian literature *did not* flow from this obscure and forgotten monk. He disappeared without leaving a trace, and after him, starting in the mid-eighteenth century, owing to Russian influence, "a strange, static, supposedly pan-Slavic language incomprehensible to the ordinary people starts to dominate," resulting in a

> serious stagnation in culture, in language, and in literature, in a great step back in comparison to Venclović. That Slavic Esperanto had no chance, and the national uprising had to put its liquidation on its list of priorities. Thus everything had to start from the beginning, from the eternal popular basis, from popular songs and fables, from hard laborer's speech. (Selimović 1970:153–154)

BETWEEN THE BYZANTINE COMMONWEALTH,
THE MYTH OF KOSOVO, AND THE UN

Vuk was resurrected yet again in the mid-1980s in Serbia, and that "resurrection" could be seen as yet another point "where it all started." "The power elite took its first steps towards instrumentalizing popular tradition for political uses at the bi-centennial celebration of Vuk Karadžić's birth (in 1987)," Slobodan Naumović suggested. "Vuk Karadžić, the man who formed most key symbols of Serbdom, himself became one of its symbols, and the pomp with which he was celebrated symbolized a change of attitude towards the Serbian nation and tradition" (Naumović 1994:103).[17] Vuk's image was used as an emblem to signal (or feign) an ideological change—from communism to a fuzzily defined Serbian nationalism. Both the regime that preempted the Serbian nationalist-populist position and the opposition parties that were striving to regain that position by outdoing Milošević tended to indiscriminately mix together a whole array of decontextualized emblems of Serbian identity. Thus mixed with Vuk, and those emblems of Serbdom associated with him, the public space became glutted in the 1990s with images taken from what was, strictly speaking, the Byzantine-derived great tradition. The *White Angel* (the most famous Serbian fresco from the Mileševa monastery), for instance, was spreading its wings everywhere—behind prison bars on a poster protesting UN sanctions, in tourist agencies' windows, and on the ceramic-point pens imported from Korea![18]

The argument which sharply opposes Vuk's Romantic populist legacy to the Byzantine-derived High Culture, however, resurfaced again forcefully in 1996 in an acrimonious literary polemic initiated by the Belgrade writer Svetislav Basara.[19] Basara was by no means the first to take Vuk to task as directly responsible for the backward-looking cultural isolationism based on an idealization of the peasantry and disdain for the "decadent West" (*truli zapad*). At the turn of the century Jovan Skerlić leveled the same accusation against Vuk and contrasted him with the Enlightenment rationalism and cosmopolitanism of Vuk's older contemporary, Dositej Obradović. Basara's case is noteworthy, however, because the utopia that emerges from his criticism of Vuk is not the rationalist Enlightenment one but the utopia of unbroken conti-

nuity with Byzantium. As Belgrade ethnologist Ivan Čolović (1996) presented it in his brilliant analysis, Basara's argument runs as follows.

If a language has weak expressive potential, if it is imprecise, crude,
and full of loan words, such as the Serbian language has been after Vuk's
reforms, then the nation speaking it is condemned to endure at the margins of history. That language—peasant, pragmatic, concrete, vulgar,
and earthy—made "Serbian thinking" hopelessly mundane and provincial. Because Vuk profaned the language, Serbs cannot reach God.
Another road, however, could have been taken—the imperial, sacred,
Byzantine one—had not Vuk forcibly separated the Serbian language
from the linguistic treasure house of the older literature.

Basara's argument, based on so-called sacral or mystical geopoli-
tics, Čolović says, "developed in the ranks of the European extreme
right, which arrived on our shores owing to a group of authors gathered
around the journal *Our Ideas* (*Naše ideje*)." Basara is against the aggressive Serbian nationalism because that nationalism is too folksy and
vulgar. "Serbian culture and politics, founded on folklore and folk myth
making," Čolović summarizes Basara's argument, "should give way to a
sacral order founded on the myths of the medieval Serbian elite, Slavic
being and Byzantine civilization. In other words, Basara is rejecting
rightist populism in the name of rightist elitism" (Čolović 1996).

Those, who like Basara, "are disappointed by the return to the epic
Kosovo," Čolović concludes his analysis, "are recommending a return to
Byzantium. Nobody, including Basara, suggests a return to the United
Nations, but many, and he is among them, rather expect that, as of tomorrow, Serbia will again gain membership in the alternative international organization of the spiritually gigantic and spiritually kindred
nations called, as we all know, the Byzantine Commonwealth" (Čolović
1996).

VAGARIES OF IMAGINED (OR INVENTED) CONTINUITY

When people in the peripheries engage in inventing continuities, the
desirable pasts they create are usually not entirely imagined. What will
be selected is usually a period or an aspect of actual history that is seen
to serve a number of purposes—from staking territorial claims to mend-
ing a spoiled identity. If that identity is seen by significant others as

corrupted by a long Turkish rule, for instance, then recourse can be had in emphasizing some kind of a Golden Age predating the Ottomans. Whereas Greeks and Romanians have the option of claiming continuity with ancient Hellenes and Romans, respectively, the Serbs have no ancestor that the West would accept as their own illustrious predecessor. The only pre-Ottoman Golden Age that Serbs can claim with some justification is their Medieval Byzantine–derived High Culture. The problem is that even though monuments of that culture were well preserved, the continuity was not. The illiterate peasants could stare in awe at the very finest Byzantine frescoes in their monasteries through centuries of Ottoman rule, but they were not inheritors of the full splendor of that great tradition. The other problem is that if the Serbs want to claim that they are heirs of that culture in order to escape their spoiled identity, they have to undertake an additional operation. Because in the eyes of the West the Byzantine civilization is denigrated as Oriental, despotic, petrified, and, in any case, inferior, and because the adjective "Byzantine" came to connote a world of devious, crooked, infinitely dense webs of intrigue, the Byzantine heritage has to be revalued. It has to be shown that it was superior, not inferior, to the civilization of the West with its roots in the Italian Renaissance. This move is graphically exhibited by Milić's embrace of the "Inverted Perspective." At the crudest level of pure buffoonery, his "Manifesto" was actually invoking a much subtler argument of Father Pavel Florensky—a Russian theologian, Orthodox priest, mathematician, scientist, and art critic who perished in Siberia in 1937—who in his "Inverted Perspective"[20] and *Iconostasis*[21] opposes the Orthodox metaphysics of the icon to Renaissance and Protestant religious art, concluding that the latter are spiritually inferior (Florensky 1996).

Another option is to skip the Byzantine ancestry entirely and look for continuity with something much older. In Serbia this takes the form of often quite fantastic escapes into pre-Vedic India or even Mesolithic cultures. To claim Indo-European roots as a lineage conferring prestige today feels anachronistic in addition to being fantastic. The reason is probably that these theories were first formed in the nineteenth century in opposition to German scholarship, which at the time was obsessed with Indo-European philology and Aryan roots. The theories claiming the Lepenski Vir or Starčevo culture as proto-Serbian, on the other hand, are more recent and were probably partly encouraged by the iconic prominence of Lepenski Vir figurines.

Oriented as much to domestic discourses as toward significant others, the varied historical lineages Serbs have been claiming since the Mexican charlatan discovered Troy in Herzegovina in 1985 often got mixed and combined in contradictory ways according to a dreamlike logic. The "mad" painter Milić offered perhaps the most extravagant but certainly not the only example. In the Serbian national dreamwork, the Lepenski Vir figurines could morph into Byzantine White Angels and grow the long mustaches of Vuk Karadžić.

SEVEN

Narrative Cycles

From Kosovo to Jadovno

To praise highlanders or to denounce their violence and arrogance in favor of lowlander peacefulness and rationality meant to position oneself at different ends of a particular dimension in the quality space of Serbian politics. Along other dimensions, both highlanders and lowlanders could be collectively opposed to cosmopolitan urbanites. Similarly, to claim High Byzantine heritage or Serbian peasant culture could signal different ideological and political alignments, although the tokens of both were usually mixed up in populist discourses and opposed to the pro-Western civic position.

My discussion of these idioms, oppositions, and themes up to this point has had something structuralist about it—I mostly dealt with reversals and permutations of a few recursive dichotomies and only gradually introduced some elements of narrative. This chapter is about novels and poetry turned into slogans, and will cross into the realm of full-blown national narratives. I focus more explicitly, moreover, on the period in which the national ideology that would dominate the late 1980s and the entire 1990s in Serbia, bring Milošević to power, and play such an important part in the dissolution of Yugoslavia crystallized.

MILOŠEVIĆ'S RISE: MOUNTING THE HORSE
SADDLED BY THE SERBIAN INTELLIGENTSIA

The starting point for what might be called the Serbian and Yugoslav disaster is often traced back to the fateful day of April 24, 1987, when, during his visit to Kosovo, Slobodan Milošević, at that time the president of the Serbian Communist Party (more precisely, the Serbian League of Communists), in Budding's words, "experienced the political power of national feeling first-hand, and began his conversion from Communist apparatchik to national leader" (1998:354).[1]

The story of Milošević's rise to power involved at least two separate "tracks." On one track Milošević was climbing through the Serbian Communist Party ranks on the coattails of his mentor, the then president of Serbia Ivan Stambolić.[2] Commonly seen as a typical apparatchik of a decidedly hard-line bent, Milošević initially pleased Serbian Party conservatives by being tough on "dissident intellectuals, all demands for liberalization, and any manifestation of Serbian nationalism" (Djilas 1993:86).

On the other track, an important segment of Serbian intelligentsia, gathered around the Serbian Academy of Arts and Sciences and the Serbian Writers' Association, was at the same time—mid- to late 1980s— increasingly engaging in the rhetoric of Serbian national grievances. At that point the major grievance had to do with the problems of Kosovo Serbs, whose voices were suppressed by the Serbian Communist Party for fear they would stir up Serbian nationalism. The Academy and the Writer's Association were the first Serbian institutions that made this problem public by promoting petitions and organizing protest gatherings in support of Kosovo Serbs.

Since the Yugoslav federal constitution of 1974, the two autonomous provinces within the Republic of Serbia, Kosovo and Vojvodina, had all the elements of a full statehood except the right to secession granted only to the six Yugoslav republics—Slovenia, Croatia, Bosnia and Herzegovina, Montenegro, Serbia, and Macedonia (see Hayden 1999). Kosovo and Vojvodina were made to be constituent members of the Yugoslav Federation, and each had a seat in the Yugoslav presidency that succeeded Tito. Provinces sent their delegates both to the Serbian and the Federal Yugoslav assembly thus creating in effect a confusion of levels akin to a Russelian paradox: Serbia as a whole could not decide anything internally without the consent of its autonomous provinces, and the same autonomous provinces could (and often did) vote against Serbia (of which they were constituent parts) in the Federal Yugoslav presidency. This arrangement was applied only to Serbia, thus significantly reducing its relative power.

Serbian Communist leadership, led by Stambolić, was troubled by this awkward position and was already working to bring about constitutional changes that would address the issue. However, they were doing that behind the scenes, and taking great care not to disrupt the delicate balance of power that existed between Yugoslav republics.

In 1981, a year after Tito died, ethnic Albanians in Kosovo took to the streets to demand their own republic. Though the demonstrations were repressed, the Kosovo Albanian campaign for republican status (with its clear secessionist implications) only increased. On the other hand, the Serbian public was made increasingly aware of the protests of the Serbian and Montenegrin minorities over their treatment by the Albanian majority. Kosovo Serbs and Montenegrins were claiming that the Albanian majority was pressuring them to leave using all kinds of means ranging from covert threats to overt acts of violence. This was a drive, so the complaint went, to make Kosovo "ethnically clean," and the Serbian minority in Kosovo had no redress within the province.

The two tracks merged when Stambolić dispatched Milošević to Kosovo in April 1987 to quell the frustrations of Kosovo Serbs and Montenegrins. While Milošević was meeting with various local functionaries and representatives of Kosovo Serbs, some fifteen thousand Serbian and Montenegrin protesters gathered around the building throwing rocks. As police moved to stop the crowd from storming the building, beating people with their truncheons, Milošević stepped outside and uttered the sentence that miraculously transformed him from a gray apparatchik to a Serbian nationalist icon: "No one should dare to beat you."[3] Whether he was genuinely moved by the plight of Kosovo Serbs, or whether he cynically recognized the potential of nationalism, from then on Milošević used his new status as a "tsar of Serbs" to oust his mentor, Ivan Stambolić, and rise to be the ultimate power in Serbia.

Practically all accounts stress the way Milošević preempted, appropriated, colonized, simulated, or, as Aleksa Djilas put it, "cannibalized"[4] nationalist discourses. These discourses were being developed by a significant segment of most influential Serbian intellectuals quite independently of Milošević's rise through the party hierarchy, indeed initially in a fierce opposition to the Serbian Communist Party's anti-nationalist policies. When the two tracks met, it was not so much Milošević who tried to attract the national intelligentsia but rather the intelligentsia who eagerly embraced Milošević. Some of those who supported Milošević at the crucial time when he was rising to power soon sobered up, but it was too late. They were no longer important once the reins of power were firmly in his hands. As one of the major opposition figures, Vuk Drašković said four years after the event: "With his speech in Kosovo Milošević mounted the horse that the Serbian intelligentsia had saddled long ago" (in Djukić 1992:130).

This "saddling of Milošević's horse" involved political rhetoric that drew its power from entrenched national narratives comprising an already existing fund of ethnonationalist mythology—a sort of "Serbian Dreamtime." But who were the people who shaped these stories? Members of the Serbian Academy of Arts and Sciences (SANU) were certainly among the most prominent. Certain eloquent archbishops of the Serbian Orthodox Church were another important group. Journalists, pundits, and various TV personages played a central role in disseminating this kind of discourse. It was, however, a group of poets who provided the most extreme, condensed, and persuasive forms of the new mythicized speech in the mid-1980s. They were the prophets of the reawakened nation, professional wordsmiths whose poetic hyperbolae were so extreme as to overpower rational discussion. They turned Serbian grievances, imagined and real, into a poetically exaggerated metaphysics of national victimhood.

POETS AS MASTER SLOGAN MAKERS

Preeminent among these eloquent poets, enjoying near divine status as both an academician and president of the Serbian Writers' Association, was Matija Bećković, a distinguished looking, white-haired Montenegrin whose poetry was steeped in regional dialect and "Montenegrin metaphysics."

The Serbian Writers' Association (Udruženje književnika Srbije—UKS) was the most prominent stage for the new prophet-poets of Serbdom. In 1982, prompted by the case of Gojko Djogo, a poet whose book *Woolen Times* (*Vunena vremena*) was banned while he himself was sentenced to prison, the Committee for the Defense of Artistic Freedom (Odbor za zaštitu umetničke slobode) was established at the UKS. In the early 1980s the Association (through the Committee) openly and publicly confronted the Yugoslav regime over book bans and the political persecution of writers and dissident intellectuals in general. It was the first Yugoslav institution to do such a thing in an organized and overt manner, and during the early 1980s it intervened in cases of Adem Demaći (one of the leaders of the Kosovo Albanians), Vojislav Šešelj (an ultranationalist Serbian leader), Vladimir Šeks (a Croatian nationalist, later a minister in Tudjman's government), and Alija Izetbegović (later the president of the Bosnia-Herzegovina Federation). At that stage, the democratic credentials of the Committee and the Association were impeccable as they vigorously defended and helped dissidents of all nationalities, including some who will soon end up in various enemy camps.

In 1987, a year after the first petition of Kosovo Serbs and Montenegrins who sought redress for their persecution at the hands of the Albanian majority in the province, a series of "protest evenings" in their support started at the UKS Belgrade headquarters. But, by 1987, Milošević was already firmly set on his way to power on the promise to solve the Kosovo problem and restore Serbia's jurisdiction over the autonomous province. The Association was then essentially in agreement with the emerging Serbian regime, and it became one of its main "surrogates."[5] Its discourse was no longer about freedom of speech and democracy but exclusively concerned Serbian victimhood, not only in Kosovo but in Yugoslavia as a whole. And, indeed, it was these intellectuals who accomplished what Budding argued was the most crucial thing for Milošević—they "generalized Kosovo, spreading the belief that not just Kosovo Serbs, but *all* Serbs, were deprived of their national rights, and urgently in need of a savior" (Budding 1998:358).

Poets were the leading firebrands who turned the thesis of victimhood into a poetically exaggerated vision of national metaphysics, and it is their pronouncements that offer the purest and most extreme version of what Ivan Čolović called the "Serbian ethnonationalist myth."

Nearly as prominent as Matija Bećković was another poet hailing from the highlands, the Herzegovinian Rajko Petrov Nogo. A selection from both their oeuvres should provide a good introduction not only to the content but to the language and the style of this nationalist discourse.

In an interview given in August 1991 (*Duga,* no. 455, August 2–16, 1991), Nogo recounts how he rediscovered the authentic language of his youth:

> I had the gusle and the decasyllabic, the Herzegovinian speech for the first ten years of my life while I was growing up in a patriarchal family in which the forms of life hadn't changed since the arrival of Slavs to these mountains (*gudure*). Then I tumbled (*strmeknuo*) into an orphanage, lost and forgot (*poboravio*) that language and, as a guinea pig and Janissary of the bright future, I learned that provincial, Balkan variant of the real-socialist newspeak. The June rebellion of 1968 finally destroyed that big lie and together with Gavrilo Princip and the Young Bosnians (Mlado-bosanci), on a St. George's Day morning vigil we washed our faces in the mountain spring of language. And as we were watching our reflection in the spring water we were growing the mustaches of Starina Novak.

Here is a succinct, poetic account of personal reawakening intended as a metaphor for a larger national reawakening. Nogo explicitly establishes his early childhood and his natal family as a primordial, unchanging patriarchal idyll and names the main markers of the genre he will resurrect—the gusle, the decasyllabic meter, and the Herzegovinian speech of Serbian epic poetry.[6] The word he uses for mountains is *gudure* a term connoting rough, almost impenetrable, wild terrain, and immediately brings to the mind of a native reader one of the major topoi of Serbian imaginary—the mettle, valor, and toughness of highlanders. The fall into the orphanage is the fall from the primordial linguistic and patriarchal idyll. Nogo uses a neologism *poboraviti* (instead of the standard *zaboraviti*, to forget) that clearly indicates a poetic affectation and produces an effect of making him an expert in an authentic regional dialect (even though the word most likely doesn't exist there either). The term "Janissary" implies that he has been converted to the enemy faith (communism) and its perverted language (newspeak) and that he thus became a soldier in the shock troops that persecuted the pristine folk he hailed from (Herzegovinian highlanders). He then suddenly invokes, as his contemporaries and peers, the long dead assassin of Archduke Ferdinand (Gavrilo Princip) and the organization (Young Bosnians) of which Princip was a member in a move that makes the washing of his face an archetypal act removed from ordinary time—a move characteristic of this whole genre of speech. As they (it is not specified who, Serbian poets? the awakened avant-garde of Serbdom?) get rejuvenated in the mountain spring of authentic language, they are magically transformed into a legendary hero (Starina Novak) of Serbian epic songs.

Speaking about his years in Bosnia as a popular anchor of a TV youth show, Nogo meditates on how lucky he was as a poet that this established, cozy position was taken away from him. Poets, he implies, have to be martyrs or they are unworthy of their name. In an exemplary style of nationalist poets he uses an extreme metaphor to describe the process:

> I exchanged the microphone, to put it metaphorically, for the stake. Blaspheming (cursing) echoes further and strong[er from the stake than from the state microphone. Our ancestors—expertly impaled in order to survive longer in death agony—blasphemed from the stake at the Turkish faith hoping Turks would finish them off sooner. That's why it is said: "He curses like the Vlach[7] from the stake!" Poetry in our Eastern Despoties—that's singing from the stake. And I know that three hundred disgraces would be mine had I not been among the victims.

This is a perfect example of the kind of bloodcurdling exaggeration that was the stock-in-trade of nationalist poets. A nauseatingly detailed account of prolonged death at the stake was familiar to every schoolchild in Yugoslavia from the required reading of Nobel Laureate Ivo Andrić's *Bridge on the Drina* (*Na Drini ćuprija*). It was the starkest possible image of the proverbial five centuries of slavery under the Turks, the ultimate evil in the Serbian worldview. Being a Serbian poet in the socialist republic of Bosnia and Herzegovina during the 1970s under Tito, a place Nogo calls "Eastern Despoty," might have been hard, especially if the poet insisted on his Serbian identity.[8] To call it singing from the stake carries the poetic license in the direction of extremely inflammatory speech. What do you do with people who impale patriotic poets?

"Every man becomes enamored of his own suffering," says the Prince of Serbian Poetry Matija Bećković, "and becomes that for which he suffered. Perhaps in the moment of humiliation we can recognize the instant in which a poet is born, for the poet is born from his own bruises, and to him his own skin is the map of the world" (1989:27).

This Romantic/Dostoyevskian apotheosis of suffering gives a clue to the kind of world Bećković and his peers inhabit. It is a closed, solipsistic universe focused on one's own suffering. The Poet's identification with the nation is implicit in Bećković's statement. A leading nationalistic historian Veselin Djuretić, however, makes explicit this predication of wounded skin onto the national identity as he extends Bećković's metaphor into the realm of politics. The ethnic map of Bosnia and Herzegovina was often likened to leopard skin, and this image was usually invoked to argue that it was impossible to divide it cleanly into ethnically homogeneous parts. Djuretić, however, twisted this metaphor by saying that the spots on the leopard skin of Bosnia and Herzegovina are "actually wounds on the body of Serbian ethnic being" (in Čolović 1997:37, 2002:35).

National poets like Nogo and Bećković did most of their work not through poems but through slogans that relied on powerful images, allusions, and paradoxes. These slogans were sound bites that drew their power from invoking certain larger narrative units, and ultimately what Čolović calls a "constellation of narratives." The whole, he says, "stays latent as a matrix to which the dispersed parts of the myth refer. They function as synecdoches of the whole, both as its small-scale incarnations, and ciphers for connecting to a particular communication program (in the computer sense), for entering a mental space of ethnonational identification and participation" (Čolović 1997:15). And these synecdoches, of which Bećković's sound bites are the best example, most often, in a more or less direct way, point to the mythicized Battle of Kosovo.

> That synecdochical function is often relegated to fragmentary actualizations of the Kosovo myth . . . The very mention of Kosovo has become established as the clearest sign that the discourse on nation and politics is seeking its fulcrum in an arsenal of stories that are sacred and taken for granted for Serbs as an ethnonational community. That's why it could be said that the Kosovo myth, as a reference to that mythical fulcrum, has become a myth about myth, and that the so-called Kosovo Choice is in fact a choice of myth. But that does not mean that all these stories, that is to say, Serbian myths about nation and national state in general are merely variations of one central myth, the myth of Kosovo. The Kosovo themes, as well as other themes, both older and more recent, that make up the matrix of ethnonationalist mythology are gathered in a constellation the center of which is occupied by none of them. Rather the center

is occupied by . . . a phantasm of political power based on the supposedly natural and divine right of ethnic community to consider itself the sole measure of all things. (Ibid.:16)

When Čolović here collapses the Serbian "constellation of narratives" into their "latent matrix," and when that matrix is in turn collapsed into its empty center, the navel of the Serbian national dream, or a kind of black hole (to keep with Čolović's astronomical metaphor), where the "phantasm of political power" resides, he is not doing that prematurely. Starting in the 1980s, he has produced the most comprehensive collection, and the most detailed analysis, of various genres and subgenres of Serbian ethnonationalist mythology that exist in any language (Čolović 1985, 1993, 1994, 1994a, 1996, 1997, 2002).[9]

Here I cannot possibly go into all the details of the Kosovo mythology. I will just show how the hyperbolic rhetoric of poets linked Kosovo, as the central mystery of Serbian national identity, to narratives of Serbian victimhood in Croatia and Bosnia, thus generalizing Kosovo to all Serbs perceived as threatened. One narrative strategy of this generalizing is the Kosovo-Jadovno axis.

FROM KOSOVO TO JADOVNO

My first guide will be the poet Rajko Petrov Nogo, whose neat spatial summary of eternal Serbian victimhood describes the three parallel migrations of the Serbian people—to the heavens, into foreign lands, and to the depths, into the pits. These three "migrations" correspond to particular clusters of Serbian ethnonationalist mythology. We will start with downward migration—into the pits.

Numerous deep pits are a prominent feature of the limestone landscape of that area of Bosnia, Herzegovina, and Croatia which was populated by the Serbs of the so-called Krajinas (Military Borderlands) and which belonged to the Independent State of Croatia during World War II. It was in these pits that slaughtered Serbs were thrown by the Croatian Ustaše as part of their campaign to get rid of all the Serbs in their territory (see Denich 1994; Hayden 1994, 1996; and Carmichael 2002:55–59). One of the most notorious pits was called "Jadovno," and just as Auschwitz came to stand for all concentration camps and the

Holocaust in general, so Jadovno came to stand for all the pits and for the genocide itself.

One could object that it is not Jadovno but the concentration camp Jasenovac run by the Croatian Ustaše that provides the closest Yugoslav analogy to Auschwitz. Jasenovac was by far the largest concentration and extermination camp in Yugoslavia. It was run by the Croatian Ustaše from 1941 to 1945 and the number of those killed there, often in the most horrible ways that appalled even the visiting Germans, went into hundreds of thousands—mostly Serbs, Roma, Jews, and political opponents of the Ustaša regime. The numbers of people who perished at Jasenovac (and the percentages of various ethnic groups therein) were hotly disputed in the late 1980s—with the Serbian side exaggerating and the Croatian side minimizing (Croatian president Franjo Tudjman's role in this minimization was notorious). Jasenovac had visibility, even during Tito's rule when such disputes were suppressed. A Memorial Park was built on the site in the 1960s featuring a museum and a monument in the shape of a stylized stone flower designed by the architect Bogdan Bogdanović (the mayor of Belgrade from 1982 to 1986). Jadovno was one of the very first concentration camps in Croatia, but it operated only for a few months in 1941. The victims were thrown into a limestone pit, many reportedly still alive. Their number is estimated at around thirty-five thousand. The appeal of Jadovno for the nationalist poets in the 1980s lay more likely in its character of suppressed memory than in the sheer number of victims—obviously dwarfed by Jasenovac. Poetic pilgrimages and homages to Jadovno thus had an additional appeal of bringing the forbidden to light. This is not to say that Jasenovac was absent from the poetic slogans. One of the most bloodcurdling of Bećković's metaphors, for instance, proclaimed Jasenovac "the largest Serbian underground city."

Archbishop Atanasije Jevtić of the Serbian Orthodox Church made a pilgrimage, in 1983, from Kosovo to Jadovno and published his travel diary under the same title in 1987. In the introduction, his colleague, Archbishop Amfilohije Radović, wrote:

> Kosovo is the beginning and measure of Serbian Jadovno, and Jadovno is a continuation of Kosovo. Between them, the cross-bearing path of a people, a path of the Cross which, like an arch, as if by a heavenly rainbow,

conjoins our old and our new torments . . . In Jadovno, Kosovo culminates; the word and reality of Jadovno is the full revelation of the secret of Kosovo and confirmation of the Kosovo Choice and Kosovo Covenant. Up until then Serbian fate unfolded under the sign of Kosovo; from then on it would unfold between these two poles, Kosovo and Jadovno, the base and the peak of [our] Golgotha. (Jevtić 1987:5)

"Kosovo is the most expensive Serbian word," proclaimed Matija Bećković in the speech he gave in Canberra, Australia, in 1989, as part of the celebration of the six hundredth anniversary of the Kosovo Battle. This became one of his most famous slogans. It worked powerfully as a magic incantation, a code word that would transport those who utter it or hear it to the realm of metaphysical Serbian victimhood. It is worth quoting Bećković at some length in order to get a sense of this kind of discourse:

Six centuries ago, nothing more significant on the globe than the Battle of Kosovo took place. And today, after 600 St. Vitus's days,[10] there is nothing more fateful for the destiny of Serbian people than the battle that is taking place in Kosovo and for Kosovo. The outcome of the Kosovo Battle is still unknown, both of that previous and of this present one. Since the beginning, two truths endure and neither gives in to the other. As time goes by we know less and less whether we will be heavenized[11] or whether the Kosovo wound will swallow us . . . The Kosovo Battle has never ended. As if the Serbian people fights only one battle—enlarges the Kosovo bone yard, adds weeping upon weeping, joins new martyrs to the Kosovo martyrs. Kosovo has long since reached Jadovno and it is a miracle that the whole Serbian land hasn't assumed the name of Kosovo.

Kosovo is the most expensive Serbian word. It has been paid for with the blood of the whole people. With that price in blood it became enthroned on the throne of the Serbian language. Without blood it couldn't have been bought, without blood it couldn't be sold.

Kosovo is the equator of the Serbian planet. The roof of the lower and the foundation of the upper world. This is where the consciousness of the Serbian people split into what came before and what came after Kosovo. Kosovo is a Serbianized story of the flood: the Serbian New Testament.

Kosovo is a hearth that assembles, a pillar that congregates the Serbian people. Kosovo is the crossroads on which the Serbs found themselves and found their path. Kosovo is the deepest wound, the longest remembrance, the most vivid memory, the most beloved ash—the spiritual cradle of the Serbian people. (Bećković 1989:19, 23)

Another famous Bećković slogan is that the Serbs in Croatia are "the remains of a slaughtered people" (*ostaci zaklanog naroda*). He uttered it at the protest evening organized at the Serbian Writers' Association in the summer of 1989, in support of the leader of the Serbian cultural society Zora (Dawn) who had been arrested by the Croatian authorities for statements made at a celebration of the six hundredth anniversary of the battle of Kosovo. This was, as Budding says, when the "Kosovo and Croatian themes converged, and the Association's protests reached their climax" (1998:394).

On the mystical body of Serbdom, the Archbishop Atanasije Jeftić inscribed the Cross of Serbian suffering by making a pilgrimage from Kosovo to Jadovno and back. It was a journey both in time and in space, both horizontal and vertical. Kosovo is the bottom, the base of the Serbian Golgotha, but also the peak, the ascension of the whole people to the Heavenly Kingdom—the migration heavenward that Nogo talks about. Bećković's juxtaposition of pillars and wounds, equators and hearths, crossroads and cradles induces the same kind of motion sickness. Kosovo is both above and below, it is in the past, in the present, and in the future, it is the alpha and the omega of the Serbian national being, and it is fundamentally identical to Jadovno. Let me then "dig up" some of the underlying premises of the Kosovo-Jadovno link.

ANCESTRAL BONES, MARTYRS' BLOOD, AND TERRITORIAL BORDERS

The greatest Serbian historian of religion, Veselin Čajkanović, argued that the pre-Christian Serbian religion (which he believed still underlies the more or less superficially Christianized popular practices) was, in essence, predicated on a highly developed body of beliefs about the world of the dead. In a word, it was primarily an ancestor cult (see Čajkanović 1973, 1985). In *The Political Lives of Dead Bodies,* Verdery devotes an entire chapter to the former Yugoslavia. One of the specificities of Yugoslavia, she remarks, is what could be called its "very intense burial regime," meaning, among other things, that "people hold strong ideas about proper burial and about continuing relations with dead kin" (1999:97). And these ideas, Verdery argues, "even if no longer held in a form identical to ideas from the past, enter into the penumbra of meanings that politicians and others can draw upon, alter, and intensify" (46).

One of the major premises that underlies the Kosovo and Jadovno narratives is the premise that links bones, graveyards, and spilled blood with soil, borders, and territory. Bećković, as ever, succeeds in giving one of the most succinct formulations:

> According to our popular belief, the land where there are graves is not for sale. Householders without progeny, or those who feared that their descendants might sell the land, would prevent this possibility by bury-ing their dead in the yard. Both the buyer and the seller would balk at the grave. In the Kosovo graveyard the whole Serbian people have been buried and that's why Serbs can neither sell nor trade that land. (Bećković 1989:28)

Bećković first gives us what seems to be sober ethnological informa-tion about Serbian beliefs regarding the relationship between the graves and soil, and then, in his trademark fashion, he shocks us with his meta-physical paradox: if the *whole* of Serbian people were buried in the "Ko-sovo graveyard," who is then left (to sell or not to sell the land)? This is a brilliant example of yet another code phrase that jolts the listener into entering the dreamworld of the nation. What we cannot grasp with our ordinary logic must therefore pertain to some greater mystery. The nation can obviously perish completely and yet continue to exist. It dies only to be resurrected. And the native soil, drenched with blood and strewn with the bones of ancestors or martyrs, obviously plays an important medi-ating role in this resurrection process. All of this, the meta-message of Bećković's paradox tells us, we should grasp not with our ordinary logic but absorb as a higher, mystical truth of the nation's being.

Nations are imagined in ways that defy ordinary logic. Ivan Čolović, for instance, neatly encapsulated the paradoxical logic that links soil, blood, and the nation in the image of the "double bloodstream." The nation, he says, reproduces itself mythically through a "double vascular system." One transmits the "blood" through the wombs of individual biological mothers; the other, more important one, through the blood of successive generations of fallen heroes whose sacrificial blood soaks the native soil. "The soil fertilized by the blood of those who fell for the native land is given the role of the ethnic uterus, while the wombs of individual biological mothers are reduced to the role of relaying the embryos that come *ex terra*" (Čolović 1997:23).

> That's why the places of that spilled blood—battlefields, pits and killing fields, graveyards and graves—have an extraordinary symbolic value. They are germs of national revival which implies prior sacrificing and death, as well as roots that bind the people to the ancestral land. Graves are thus the real natural borders of Serbia. (Ibid.:14)

Denich (1994), Hayden (1994), and, drawing on both, Verdery (1999) have written extensively about how, in the late 1980s and early 1990s, exhumation and reburial of those slain in World War II helped symbolically revive the genocide and played an important part in the nationalist mobilization that led to the dismemberment of Yugoslavia.

Atanasije Jevtić made a pilgrimage that connected Kosovo to Jadovno in 1983 and published his account. In 1988 and 1989, as part of the comprehensive preparations for the commemoration of the six hundredth anniversary of the Kosovo Battle, the holy relics of Prince Lazar, the leader of the Serbian Army at Kosovo, were carried from the Patriarchate in Belgrade through parts of Croatia and Bosnia, back to Serbia, and finally returned to the monastery Gračanica in Kosovo.[12] The relics were passing through the same areas in which the pits were being excavated and the bones of those who perished in the World War II genocide reburied. The Serbian Orthodox Church organized both. It was beyond doubt that these rituals marked the extent of what was seen as the maximal potential range of Serbian territory.

It was Vuk Drašković, the one who ruefully admitted to "saddling Milošević's horse," who formulated the relationship between graves and territory most clearly in the speech he gave at the Serbian Writers' Association in 1989. Author of *The Knife* (*Nož*) (1982) and *The Prayer* (*Molitva*) (1985)—bloodcurdlingly detailed literary accounts of the World War II slaughter of Serbs in Herzegovina that both presaged and reinforced the actual digging up of the bones—and later the leader of the Serbian Renewal Movement (SPO), the largest Serbian opposition party of the early 1990s, Drašković famously stated that in the case of Yugoslavia's breakup, the Western borders of Serbia will actually extend as far as the Serbian pits and graves in Croatia. If Yugoslavia disintegrates, he said in a typical poetic exaggeration, "the right of vote will be extended to Jasenovac and

Jadovno, to all our pits" (Drašković 1990:111). In this ghoulish metaphor, then, the dead will vote under the ground and will claim the part of Croatia framed by their pits and graves for a new, enlarged Serbia.[13]

In September 1988, discussing borders, Drašković quoted his fellow writer, poet, and party member, Milan Komnenić, who had said that "the borders of the Serbian people are marked on the east by sacred places that must not become pits, and on the west by pits that must become sacred places" (in Drašković 1990:89). Here was the most succinct formulation of the Kosovo-Jadovno axis: The Albanian other is threatening to turn the sacred places of Kosovo (medieval Serbian monasteries) into Jadovno-like pits and that must be prevented. The Croats had already filled the pits with Serbian martyrs (in World War II) and thus consecrated them as sacred Serbian territory.

Kosovo and Jadovno were connected by means of ritual performances and pilgrimages. In public discourses nationalist poets like Nogo, Bećković, and Komnenić connected them in pithy, paradoxical formulas. One of the powerful idioms they used relied on ancient associations between ancestral bones, martyrs' blood, and soil. Battlefields soaked in blood of medieval heroes and limestone pits filled with slaughtered Serbs both became claims to territory. The underlying message of these discourses was that Serbs are eternal innocent victims. "Innocent victims are the greatest spiritual treasure of a people," Bećković said in his Canberra speech.

> Just like the greatness of a people is measured by the number of innocent victims, innocent victims are a measure of how highly a people value their ideals . . . Innocent victims are the only motif of art. The only thing worthy of remembrance that distinguishes the human brain, the only concern of mind and of speech, the only topic for any serious reasoning. (Bećković 1989:27)

Drašković also seized on the Jews as champions of victimhood when he asserted that the Serbs are "the thirteenth, lost and the most ill-fated tribe of Israel." Thus the Kosovo-Jadovno axis was intertextually "thickened" by assimilating it to the archetypal narrative of Jewish suffering. Under the ground, Jews and Serbs establish their eternal kinship of victimhood; on the horizontal plane, they are subject to cycles of exile and return. One of the three migrations Nogo spoke about was the migration into foreign lands, and the main template for this kind of talk about Serbian migrations to foreign lands in the late 1980s and early 1990s was the story of the Jewish Exodus.

Another obsessively repeated theme in this kind of discourse was that of fratricide. "Most ferocious punitive expeditions were made up of people of our own kin, blood, and language—Albanicized, Islamicized, Uniaticized Serbs," Nogo said in the *Duga* interview, and he then provided this stunning psychological explanation for the hate "our brothers" harbor against us: "[Our enemies] killed us, slaughtered us, they threw us into the pits, finished us off with maces. They cannot forgive us the crimes they committed against us!"

Victimhood in its archetypal, metaphysical, eternal power was the main message of this discourse. Launched by poets, multiplied and disseminated massively through regime media, the story of how "they" slaughtered "us" bombarded Serbian citizens incessantly at least since 1988 (for the media's dissemination of this discourse, see Milinković 1994; Thompson 1994; Nenadović 2000; Matić 1996; and Marković 1996). Needless to say, such "monumental evil" done to "innocent victims" cried out for revenge. Yet the poets usually did not overtly advocate hate toward Serbia's enemies (mostly "our own brothers"—Croats and Bosnian Muslims)—and yet the secret message of their poetics of victimhood was revenge and reconquest.

For Vuk Drašković, for instance, the dilemma of revenge versus Christian forgiveness became a major obsession, perhaps because he was so often accused of fomenting hate. "No, no, no! I never advocated hate as a response to hate," he responded to such an accusation in an interview:

> What I advocate is the duty of defense against hate and knife. And because there are situations in which prayers and books don't work against hate and death, then you have to defend yourself with different means ... That question has been answered in two totally different heavenly ways. On the one pole, there is Tolstoy with his Ivan the Fool, and on the other is our Bishop Njegoš. Ivan the Fool preaches necessary suffering as a response to evil, our bishop preaches something quite different. Njegoš never denies Christ's words about the other cheek, but he doesn't forget that that same Jesus could also erupt in anger and use a whip in the Jerusalem temple ... My hero in *The Prayer,* an old man from Herzegovina,

says: "If somebody commits evil against you once and you are innocent—may God slay him. If he commits evil against you for the second time and you are innocent—then let God kill you both. And if he commits evil against you for the third time, then let God kill only you and not him." (*Duga,* no. 422, April 28, 1990)

Drašković's most influential novel, *Nož* (*The Knife*), could be seen as primarily about fratricide and the dilemma of revenge. After all the evil we (Serbs) suffered at the hands of our brothers (Muslims and Croats), are we right to seek revenge? In her analysis of *Nož,* Budding concludes that it "preaches reconciliation rather than revenge," with the proviso that the reconciliation be "based on Muslims' recognition that they are "really" Serbs" (1998:390). My reading of *Nož,* however, is different. Just as in the above quote, I would argue, Drašković in the end *does* justify revenge and does foment hate despite all his protestations to the contrary.[14] Pious insistence on Christian forgiveness as an inherent trait of Serbian character—a prominent topos of nationalist mythology—only serves to cast Serbs as incurably naive and to reinforce the real underlying message of all these texts—that it is finally time for the Serbs to stop "turning the other cheek."

Those who were elaborating on the Kosovo-Jadovno axis and performing major work for Milošević by extending Kosovo martyrology to Serbs residing in Croatia and Bosnia-Herzegovina were most often highlanders, that is, they hailed from Montenegro (Bećković) or Herzegovina (Drašković and Nogo). They were energized by the trauma of World War II and the current predicaments of the Serbs who live outside the Serbian heartland. It is perhaps no surprise that the major figures among them happened to be poets, rather than novelists (Drašković is a novelist, but his speeches belong to the same genre of extreme poetic hyperbolae practiced by Bećković, Nogo, and Komnenić). It is also no surprise that they were the major enunciators of the reawakened Kosovo myth—the highlanders had the reputation of more zealously preserving the "heroic epic mentality" and the Kosovo tradition than their lowlander brothers in the heartland of Serbia. It is thus fitting that they were at the forefront of bringing together the Kosovo and the World War II cycle of the Serbian national narrative. There exists, however, yet another major cycle—the one centered on the First World War—and it happens to be the preserve of lowlander novelists.

THE DILEMMA OF THE LAST STAND: KOSOVO
AND THE WORLD WAR I NARRATIVE CYCLE

There is now a wide scholarly consensus that several novels played a key role in the reawakening of Serbian nationalism in the 1980s (see Popov 1993; Djordjević 1995; Vujačić 1995; Budding 1998; and Wachtel 1999). Among them, three novels figure as central in all analyses: Drašković's 1982 *The Knife* (*Nož*), Ćosić's 1978 *A Time of Death* (*Vreme smrti*), and Popović's 1985 *The Book of Milutin* (*Knjiga o Milutinu*). I have already classified *The Knife* as belonging to the highlander-dominated cycle of World War II. The other two, however, were the work of authors who hailed from the peasant heartland of Serbia and whose preoccupations were different from, and sometimes directly at odds with, those of national bards hailing from the highlander regions.

Politically the most important message of both novels was that Yugoslavism was a wrong historical choice for Serbs. These novels were therefore instrumental in effecting a move from Yugoslavism to Serbian particularism extensively documented by Budding (see also Vujačić 1995; and Wachtel 1999). They did so by implanting, through the mouths of their heroes, the main tenets of the new Serbian national discourse—most important, the idea that "Serbia had somehow lost out by joining the other Yugoslav nations in a common state" (Vujačić 1995:232). According to this "stab-in-the-back" thesis, the "ungrateful" Western brothers (Slovenes and Croats), heroically liberated by the Serbs from the Austrian yoke, "repaid" that magnanimous sacrifice by resenting Serbian hegemony, undermining Yugoslav unity, and finally by dismantling the common state. "The Serbs win in wars and lose in peace" was Ćosić's famous dictum that summarized this thesis. And the crucial war that ushered in this historical mistake was the First World War in which Serbian leaders chose Yugoslavia, not enlarged Serbia, as the spoils of their victory.

The narratives clustering around what was popularly known as the "Golgotha and Resurrection of Serbia" in World War I form an analytically separable cycle of Serbian national narrative. The songs from this cycle, for instance, *March to the Drina River* (*Marš na Drinu*) or *Over There, Far Away* (*Tamo daleko*), vie for the status of the unofficial Serbian anthem. The heroes of that war, such as Vojvoda Mišić and Radomir

Putnik, are national icons equal in stature to Vuk Karadžić or to the leader of the First Uprising against the Turks, Karadjordje. They occupy the place in Serbian national imaginary comparable to the place occupied by Kutuzov or Suvorov in the Russian. The Tolstoyan parallels are indeed appropriate here, for the main source of this imagery in its latest incarnation is Ćosić's *A Time of Death,* a novel intended to be, and hailed by critics, as the "Serbian *War and Peace.*"

A literary analysis of these two novels (such as that done by Djordjević 1995 and Wachtel 1999) could be very illuminating, particularly in pointing out the narrative means by which they convey their central political message. By contrast, I concentrate on how they resonate with what is arguably the mystery at the core of the Kosovo myth—the theme of the Kosovo Covenant or the Kosovo Choice (*Kosovski zavet or Kosovski izbor*).

Telling the story of Kosovo poses a formidable problem, in fact the same problem faced by Bruner and Gorfain (1984) when they attempted to tell the story of Masada. Both stories are of the kind that became "so prominent in the consciousness of an entire society that [their] recurrent tellings not only define and empower storytellers but also help to constitute and reshape the society" (Bruner and Gorfain 1984:56). The Kosovo myth is indeed a national story for Serbs, even more than Masada is for Israel. It is used to "integrate the society, encapsulate ideology, and create social order." It is also "replete with ambiguity and paradox," it "allows for conflicting readings and dissident, challenging voices," and it "creates an arena for ideologies at war" (65). Bruner and Gorfain call this process of various tellings and interpretations "dialogic narration," and this conception recognizes that "no story is 'a' story or 'the' story but rather a dialogic process of many historically situated particular tellings" (57).

I begin with the barest historical facts that could be more or less reliably distinguished from the later mythopoetic elaborations. According to the Belgrade historian Olga Zirojević,

> The date of the battle is indisputable, it was the St. Vitus's Day, 15 June (28 June according to the new calendar) of 1389. On the Serbian side, along with Prince Lazar Hrebeljanović, fought his son-in-law Vuk Branković (who would, in a legend which arose much later, be accused of treachery) and the Bosnian Duke Vlatko Vuković. The Turkish side was led by Sultan

(Emir) Murad, with his sons Bayezid and Yakub Celebi. If Murad's *turbeh* [tomb; still standing today] was indeed built on the exact spot where the Turkish Sultan lost his life, then the battle must have taken place on that part of the Kosovo plain at the confluence of the rivers Lab and Sitnica, in the vicinity of Priština. It is also certain that both rulers lost their lives on the battlefield. Murad was knifed to death by a Serbian feudal lord, identified in later sources as the Prince's son-in-law, Miloš Obilić [or Kobilić]. Such are the data that contemporary historical science have at its disposal. Despite the efforts of numerous researchers, we still do not know the number of either the Serbian or the Turkish troops, the time of death of either ruler, the number of casualties on each side, or even the outcome of the battle. (Zirojević 2000:189)

Very soon after the battle, the process of mythopoesis began. The two main lines in the development of the legend could be traced to the oral tradition of epic poetry (codified in the nineteenth century by Vuk Karadžić as the "Kosovo cycle"), on the one hand, and the written sources largely inspired by the Serbian Orthodox Church. The epic tradition and the Church hagiographies sometimes converged and sometimes diverged over the following centuries, the former generally insisting more on the archetypal motifs of Miloš Obilić's heroism, and Vuk Branković's treason, and the latter on the Christified Lazar through the New Testament themes of the Last Supper and the Choice of the Heavenly Kingdom.[15]

The cult of Miloš Obilić as the ancestral hero developed especially strongly in Montenegro. The phrase, "The faith of Obilić (*vera Obilića*)," for instance, came to stand for the whole amalgam of Serbian Orthodoxy and Kosovo-inspired epic ethos, especially as it was transformed into the Serbian state ideology in the nineteenth and early twentieth century. The motif of Vuk Branković's treason is also endlessly invoked in inter-Serbian political struggles. It is enough to allude to a few lines from the famous poem "The Prince's Supper" (*Kneževa večera*), for example, to brand your political opponent as a new Vuk Branković—the eponymous, archetypal traitor.

The Kosovo Battle came to be seen as a glorious defeat and the end of the medieval Serbian state, although the outcome of the actual battle was most likely a draw, and it took the Ottomans another seventy years to completely conquer Serbia (Serbian lands finally lost their independence with the fall of Smederevo in 1459). One way to look at the myth of

Kosovo, then, is to see it as an attempt to come to grips with this fateful event. And the myth indeed offers several mutually contradictory causes or justifications for the Serbian defeat. On the one hand, the defeat was blamed on the disunity of Serbian feudal lords, and Vuk Branković's treason came to stand as its epitome. According to theologians, the defeat came as a divine punishment for the sins of the medieval ruling classes (Tomashevich 1991:208–209). And, finally, and perhaps most important, the defeat was an outcome of the conscious choice made by Prince Lazar on the eve of the battle. As told in the poem "The Fall of the Serbian Empire" (*Propast carstva srpskoga*), the prophet Elijah, the Thunderer, in the form of a falcon brings the message to Lazar from the Mother of God. She offers him a choice: Should he choose the Earthly Kingdom, he will win the battle, but if he chooses the Heavenly Kingdom, he should build the church at the field of Kosovo, give communion to his soldiers, and they will all die. Lazar chooses the Heavenly Kingdom, for:

> an earthly kingdom is but fleeting
> But God's kingdom shall endure for ever!
> (Translated by Helen Rootham; in Tomashevich 1991:210)

He builds the church, gives communion to his soldiers, and they are all slain at the field of Kosovo. The final lines of "The Fall of the Serbian Empire" give the paradox of this defeat in a nutshell. The Serbian Army is winning, but Vuk Branković switches sides at the last moment and turns the tide of the battle. Then,

> And the Turks o'erwhelmed Lazar the Glorious,
> And the Tsar fell on the field of battle;
> And with him did perish all his army,
> Seven and seventy thousand chosen warriors.
> (Ibid.)

And yet, as the last two lines of the poem proclaim: "All was done with honor, all was holy, / God's will was fulfilled upon Kosovo."

There is hardly a man (or woman) of letters in the history of Serbian literature who hasn't penned a poem, a meditation, or a philosophical exegesis about Kosovo and the meaning of the Kosovo Choice. One of the compilations of such works lists 104 authors, starting from Patriarch Danilo, a contemporary of the battle (fourteenth century) and ending with a poet born in 1954 (Djurić 1990). The Kosovo Choice, or Kosovo

Covenant, is perceived as the wellspring of Serbian history, the secret of Serbian ethos, the holy of holies, and the *mysterium tremendum*. There is always something that escapes our ability to understand it, and it is this opaqueness that fascinates. "The whole of Serbian history cannot explain the secret of Kosovo," said Milan Komnenić, "In the huge whirlpool of our obsession there is always something opaque blurring" (Komnenić 1989:35).

From its very inception the myth of Kosovo and its poetic, literary, religious, and philosophical exegesis was intertwined with political agendas and ideologies. In the fourteenth century it might have been the interest of the Serbian Church in sanctifying Lazar; at the beginning of the nineteenth, it might have been Vuk Karadžić's conscious effort to infuse the First Uprising against the Turks with Kosovo spirit (Delić 1990); it might have been the establishment of St. Vitus's day (*Vidovdan*) as a state holiday in 1889 (Durković-Jakšić 1989) and the incorporation of the myth into Serbian state ideology (Djordjević 1991); and, finally, as the above analysis has shown, the Kosovo myth played a central role in the violent destruction of Yugoslavia in the 1990s. All of this means that the Kosovo myth has always been hopelessly tainted with political instrumentalization. There is, however, something powerful at the core of the Kosovo myth that fascinates no matter how much we acknowledge its repeated crass instrumentalization in Serbian history. I know that even to speak in such terms is perhaps to make an unwarranted distinction between what might be called the "pristine myth" and its political instrumentalization, and yet I feel a need to acknowledge the position according to which there indeed exists an authentic core to the myth that could be saved from the banality of everyday politics. Such was an attempt made by Zoran Mišić, a renowned Serbian literary critic (d. 1976) in his 1961 essay, "What Is the Kosovo Choice."

Mišić starts by lamenting the fact that we (Serbs in 1960s Socialist Yugoslavia) accept foreign gods, mythologies, and mythical heroes without a problem, but that any mention of our own myth of Kosovo, of Lazar or Miloš raises accusations of religious obscurantism, reactionary traditionalism and, what's worst, Serbian romantic nationalism. And we shouldn't be surprised, he says, "for we know how much misunderstanding has accumulated around our traditions. There aren't many who can approach our past with love and understanding and separate the authentic rhythms from fairground jigs, real poetics from high school stutterings, the mythical consciousness from the didactic consciousness."

> Kosovo became a warrior myth of a warrior tribe, and in its most degraded forms it was transformed into battle cries of warmongering tribal chiefs. It became a state-building myth of a state-building nation, and became an imperial and hegemonic program of one class.
>
> The Kosovo Choice is not a war slogan, although warriors engraved it on their flags; it is not a weapon of revenge, although wars were waged to avenge Kosovo. The Kosovo Choice is not the same as the oath to avenge Kosovo.
>
> To make a Kosovo Choice means to renounce all that is deceptive gain and covetous fame, to relinquish what is attainable for the sake of the unattainable, to will, like Njegoš, that which could not be. It means to accept the game of winning by losing, to grab victory by dying, to bet on the impossible, the only eternal trump card. (Mišić 1990:196–197)

If, at least for the sake of an argument, we agree that the "pristine" Kosovo myth possesses some sort of authentic power, there is little doubt that, in the mouths of Serbian national bards like Bećković, Komnenić, Drašković, or Nogo, that power was usurped for "war slogans" and "battle cries of warmongering tribal chiefs." Or, at the very least, it is hard to discern where in their words genuine inspiration with the "authentic core of the myth" shades into warmongering slogans. Like the *Mahabharata,* for instance, the Kosovo myth could be seen as expressing a profound metaphysical and religious message in the idiom of an epic tale about a great battle (see Bakić-Hayden 1997). But what happens if that message, summarized in the words, "let us die in order to live eternally," turns into a call for young people to sacrifice their lives for territory? In terms of national history, this message amounts to a repeated call for suicidal acts and fosters a Last Stand mentality. And, indeed, it is a beloved motif in nationalist discourse to enumerate the famous Last Stands of Serbian history, all taking their template from the Kosovo Choice. As ever, we can rely on Bećković to supply a classical statement:

> From the words of Patriarch Danilo, a Kosovo contemporary—let us die in order to live eternally, spoken by Lazar, to djakon Avakum; from djakon Avakum to Nikac of Rovine; from Nikac to Tanasko Rajić; from Tanasko Rajić to major Gavrilović[16]—exultation with death does not end and the resolve to die does not falter. (Bećković 1989:21)

Serbia's experience in World War I is one of the most important instances of a Last Stand scenario assimilated to the Kosovo Choice, and Major Gavrilović's suicidal defense of Belgrade in 1915 is but an episode in what is, in effect, a whole narrative cycle.[17] And just as Jadovno was one of the code names for the World War II narrative cycle, so is the "Albanian Golgotha" probably the most often used code name for the World War I cycle.

The Albanian Golgotha refers to the retreat of the Serbian Army together with the government, the King, and a large number of civilians through the mountains of Albania in the winter of 1915–16.[18] The army was decimated by cold, hunger, and the depredations of Albanians along the road, as well as with the outbreak of typhoid fever. It recuperated on the island of Corfu and returned to fight at the Salonika front in 1917.

It is important to note that the decisions of Serbian leaders in World War I could very easily be interpreted as suicidal. This was a country that, although small and exhausted from two Balkan wars, fought with two of the major powers of the day, the Austro-Hungarian Empire and Germany. And to retreat with the army and leave the country altogether rather than capitulate could indeed be seen as a suicidal gamble. One could see how these events of epic proportions indeed resemble the "Golgotha and Resurrection," and how easy it would be to exalt them as one of the most powerful instances of the Serbian Kosovo Choice.

Yet it seems that something else is happening in the two novels that form the classical loci of the narrative cycle, Ćosić's *A Time of Death* and, more succinctly, Popović's *The Book of Milutin*. It seems that the suicidal Last Stand scenario is, in fact, strongly challenged. In opposition to the hot-headed, highlander exaltation of total sacrifice, the two novels seem to embrace its opposite—the pragmatic, down-to-earth judgment of the Serbian peasant (the lowlander from the heartland of Serbia in my classification) that such epic suicidal choices should have been avoided and lives, that is to say, the living substance of the nation, preserved rather than sacrificed.[19] If the Kosovo myth seemed to reign supreme in the Serbian imaginary, perhaps this is an alternative telling that challenges the dominant narrative, in a word, the evidence of what Bruner and Gorfain (1984) would call the inherent dialogism of great national narratives. Let me then pursue their method and compare the Kosovo Last Stand story to that of Masada.

In both the Kosovo and Masada stories, it could be argued, the underlying logic is one of exchanging life for remembrance. In the guide to the Israeli TV series on Masada, the Jewish leader Eleazar presents the alternatives to his followers, "The choice is yours. You can choose to fight them in the morning. They'll kill you or enslave you. You can choose to hide from them. They'll find you. Or you can choose to take their victory from them. They will remember you" (Bruner and Gorfain 1984:62). Eleazar is, according to Bruner and Gorfain, in effect asking his compatriots to exchange life for memory, for the construction of a story.

Ralph Bogert makes the same argument about the Kosovo legend:

> For the Serbs . . . their defeat (was) the method of sacrifice whereby they will be assured a promise of future freedom; and their glory, the elevation of their prince to the status of savior of the nation's soul. For the Turks, therefore, Kosovo is primarily historical—from this point on they are on the map of peoples. For the Serbs, however, Kosovo is primarily national myth, the death of an epoch and the birth of an epic. Thus, a fictional process supersedes the historiographic one as the dominant mode of accounting for the national fate. History as source is supplanted by legend as resource. As the Serbian people loses the basis for its material existence it acquired a prime means for sustaining its spiritual existence—myth. (Bogert 1991:176, 178–179)

As Bećković put it,

> Kosovo is not the field where the Kosovo battle took place, neither is it the stage of treachery and treason, it is not the grave of two emperors but a point from which the Serbs looked up and showed an ability to believe in something greater and more important than themselves. A field on which poetry defeated history. (Bećković 1989:23)

The Kosovo and Masada stories could be seen as a coil, a steel spring wound up with the tremendous power of martyrdom that uncoils and releases that bound-up energy through the ages of slavery by energizing the powerful notions of death and resurrection of the nation. "Heavenly Kingdom is a brilliant poetic trick with which to justify defeat," stated Nogo in the *Duga* interview cited above. "We survived and lived to see the Sun at the end of a long winter, warmed exactly by that metaphor." To die for the sake of a powerful story is to create an obligation never to forget. The Covenant with future generations has to be sealed in blood.

Bruner and Gorfain argued that, even though it is a powerful national narrative, the story of Masada is challenged by equally powerful alternative stories. A Last Stand story is challenged by the story of accommodation, the leader of the Zealots, Eleazar, is balanced by Johanan ben Zakkai, who established an academy of learning at Yavneh, and the image of the scholar can be counterposed to the image of the warrior. It is impossible to find comparable alternative stories that stand in a "dialogic" relationship with the Kosovo narrative in Serbian self-understanding. I see no alternative story of equal persuasiveness comparable to the Jewish story of Diaspora and survival through learning—by means of prayer, study, accommodation and retreat. The only alternative stories in Serbia seem to be the Enlightenment stories told by cosmopolitan intellectuals which simply reject the Kosovo mythology as so much irrational national romanticism. But if there are no powerful stories that can challenge the Kosovo myth "from the outside," as it were, is the Kosovo narrative itself allowing for conflicting readings and dissident voices? Is it "internally dialogic," that is, open to alternative readings?

In 1915, retreating in disarray before the Austro-Hungarian Army, Serbia desperately needs military help from its Allies. But the Allies condition that help on Serbia's ceding Macedonia to Bulgaria so that the Bulgarians will enter the war on the side of the Allies. The Last Stand script reasserts itself and, in *A Time of Death*, Ćosić has the Serbian Prime Minister Nikola Pašić say this at the fateful meeting of the government, the opposition, and army commanders:

> But we must be clear about one thing, gentlemen. We can resist the Allies' ultimatum only if we wage the war with our maximum effort. Whatever the cost. Do you agree that the government should inform the Allies that Serbia is ready to fight side by side with them to victory, provided they withdraw their demand that we surrender Macedonia to Bulgaria? (Ćosić 1978)

Pašić here makes the Covenant (Bargain) with the Allies—sacrifice of life in exchange for moral power that will make the Allies grant Serbia what it wants after the war. We will be martyrs, fight to the last on your side, and our moral argument will thus be irresistible—after the war our heroism and sacrifice will demand to be honored. We are exchanging lives for a morality story so compelling that you, Allies, would have to honor our demands and give us what we deserved—in this case Yugoslavia, where finally all the Serbs will be living in one country.

Ćosić makes this a painful dilemma by making the argument of his main character, a leading opposition politician, Vukašin Katić, very powerful and persuasive. Compromise, yield territory, submit to superior force, argues Katić, but save lives, or our "victory" will be futile.

At the meeting General Mišić demands that the student battalion (the legendary thirteen hundred sergeants) be sent immediately to the front lines to boost morale. Katić is appalled:

> If any nation loses its intelligentsia, then it loses the war, no matter what the result on the battlefield . . . No one has the right to sacrifice a nation's future, its children, for any cause whatsoever . . . What kind of future can justify such a sacrifice? (Ćosić 1978)

Ralph Bogert talks about the interrelation between the eternal recurrence of the Kosovo defeat paradigm in all subsequent battles of the Serbs and the ongoing depletion of those worthy of perishing in conflicts crucial to the national existence. The intellectual response to this is to conclude that the only ones ever left after such struggles are those unworthy souls still living, souls who are nevertheless caught up in the endless process of reviving their ethnic sense of moral worth only to repeat the whole thing over again (see Bogert 1991:184).

> The choice to sacrifice oneself for a Heavenly Kingdom implies an immediate earthly defeat, even as it signals a moral victory and opens the way for national liberation in the future. Such a covenant necessitates that the struggle continue *at all costs*. And the greatest contradiction it presents, one that obsesses the characters of Ćosić's novel, is seen when the question is asked: What good is the promise of continuing the struggle, if in fact all those worthy of carrying it on—its elite leaders—perish in the first instance? (Ibid.:186)

Ćosić seems to challenge the motif of glorious defeat by having his main character ask: Was it necessary? Yet, paradoxically, he enhances the irrational appeal and pathos of the tragic choice precisely by questioning it. Wasn't it totally irrational to sacrifice so much? asks his main character. But we did, the novel seems to say, and this is our recurring and tragic fate. The apparently strong voice of reason that calls for accommodation in order to preserve life might in the end only make the suicidal Last Stand seem more glorious.

Not bowing down and making choices that lead to national destruction seem to have been entrenched as the very core of Serbian identity by the fevered nationalist discourses since the 1980s. To bow down and preserve life is to be like cowardly Czechs, as the popular stereotype would have it, not heroic Serbs.[20] And yet again, it was Matija Bećković who, as early as 1978, expressed this idea of what constitutes true Serbian identity most forcefully. In a few lines that may well be the best (and most frightening) summary of this whole ethos he says:

> Had there been no battles
> There would have been more of us, but more of who?
> And it would have been better, but for whom?[21]

Without decimations Serbs would not be Serbs—their whole identity, Bećković says, is inextricably bound with an endless cycle of suicidal battles.

A Time of Death, however, did powerfully enunciate an alternative to the Last Stand mentality championed most strongly by the highlander poets, and it has certainly been read that way in Serbia. A middle-aged bank clerk, P., whom I met on the Budapest-Belgrade train in 1996 (see chapter 2) repeatedly insisted that we needn't have died at Kosovo, and that it would have been much better if Lazar had become a Turkish vassal just like the most famous hero of epic poetry, Prince Marko. "So what if Marko was a vassal?" P. asked. "It only meant he had to provide a certain number of troops for the Turks when they called upon him. Otherwise, he retained a great deal of freedom, he wasn't a slave." P. similarly argued against another suicidal Serbian decision—to break the pact with Hitler in 1941. "The pact was not about joining the Axis powers, just a nonaggression pact to allow German troops passage to the south," P. said. It was the prevaricating Brits who instigated the coup and the demonstrations that broke the pact, he argued. It was fascinating to see P. assert what, strictly speaking, were highly incongruous, if not incompatible, views. Perhaps a bit more eloquent than average (he kept on for almost seven solid hours), P. seemed to be fairly representative of the array of views circulating in Serbia at that time. The Last Stand scenario in its many incarnations was "in the air" but so were numerous variants of its opposite—a pragmatic view that stressed survival and denounced needless loss of life. P. was expounding a version of Serbian nationalism different from that of Bećković and highlander poets. In that version, contrary to the Kosovo Choice, the preservation of the "national being" was more important than the attainment of the Heavenly Kingdom. P. did not cease being a Serbian nationalist when he exploded the myths of Kosovo or the breaking of the pact with Hitler. He did mention that Ćosić was his favorite Serbian novelist, and clearly much of his "philoso-phy" was derived from the opus of the "Serbian Tolstoy." Ćosić himself, as Vujačić (1995) has brilliantly shown, espoused seemingly disparate, even contradictory positions both in his novels and in his numerous public pronouncements. The fuzzy logic of his position, which embraced both liberalism and nationalism, vacillated between Yugoslavism and Serbian particularism, and straddled the divide between highlanders and lowlanders, was certainly in tune with the general fuzziness of Ser-bia's political and intellectual life in the 1980s and 1990s.

In one of his poems, Branko Miljković once asked: "How can I jab a tender word into a hard ear?" The poet was despairing of his subtle messages ever penetrating the crass sensibilities of ordinary people. Miljković's suicide in 1961, at the age of twenty-seven, surrounded him with a Romantic aura and made him a favorite poet among adolescent rebels and dreamers. The poets of the 1980s and 1990s, led by Bećković and Nogo, however, were, on the contrary, jabbing hard words into ears made "tender" by their eagerness to receive the message of victimized Serbdom.

This avalanche of extreme words did not necessarily make ordi-nary people in Serbia into rabid nationalists ready to fight for Greater Serbia, as evidenced, for instance, by widespread draft dodging in most Serbian cities. Most people under most circumstances in most places hold onto views that, under close inspection, are heterogeneous and often outright contradictory. A great variety of often logically incompat-ible ideas about Milošević, Yugoslavia, Serbia, communism, or Kosovo have circulated among the citizens of Serbia during these decades, and were often held by one and the same person without any clear sense of inconsistency. Even if, in general, one can say that the avalanche of hard words coming from the poets of Serbdom had indeed effected a turn from widespread Yugoslavism to Serbian particularism, that turn was slow, tortuous, hesitant, incoherent, and subject to reversals. After all, the ideological work of building Yugoslavism was immense and of longer duration. The slogan of Yugoslav brotherhood and unity was driven into tender ears for more than forty years before the message of Serbdom got its turn.

EIGHT

"The Wish to Be a Jew"; or, The Power of the Jewish Trope

In their quest for the most powerful metaphor, the most extreme analogy, the allegory that would top any other allegory, the Serbian mythmakers, spearheaded by Vuk Drašković, embraced a rhetorical strategy in the 1980s that I call the Jewish Trope. Serbian narratives of martyrdom and suffering, of exile and return, and of death and resurrection were in this strategy linked, both metonymically and metaphorically, to their Jewish equivalents in an attempt to appropriate for the Serbs what is, at least in the West, the most powerful of all morality stories—that of the Holocaust. This rhetorical strategy, together with the martyr bones and "double bloodstream of the nation" played a role in the dreamlike logic that connected Kosovo and Jadovno as two nodes in the Serbian ethnonationalist myth constellation.

Recall the spatial summary of eternal Serbian victimhood offered by the highlander poet Rajko Petrov and his imagery of downward migration into the limestone pits. This time, the pit is a mine shaft in Kosovo. In the late winter of 1989 the tension in Kosovo reached a peak with the hunger strike of thirteen hundred Albanian miners who vowed to stay underground until their demand for the resignation of the pro-Milošević leadership of the province was met. On February 27, 1990, while the strike was still going on, in the Slovenian capital of Ljubljana a meeting was held in a prestigious concert hall (Cankarjev dom) to express Slovenian support for the Albanians. The Slovenian youth organization—

one of the organizers of the meeting—distributed to the participants traditional Albanian white felt caps with a Star of David affixed on them. The intended message was clear—Albanians are the Jews, a persecuted minority, and, by implication, the Serbs are the Nazis. Underlying this was also the identification of Slovenes, as a minority in Yugoslavia, supposedly dominated by the majority Serbs, with Albanians in Kosovo, so that the link could also be read as Slovenes equal Albanians equal Jews. The meeting, which was televised live throughout Yugoslavia, caused a burst of outrage in Serbia, a big rally in Belgrade, and a barrage of harsh denunciations of Slovenes in the regime media.[1] And this time, too, it was Matija Bećković who came up with the most extreme formulation. Here is what he said about the whole event after the strike was over:

> The first Albanians thrown into pits were volunteers who came out of it hale and happy. In Ljubljana they were proclaimed Jews thrown into pits by Serbs. They forgot that the pits are the only ethnically clean Serbian habitations and that somewhere under the ground the kinship of Jews and Serbs has been forever sealed. (Bećković 1989a:436)

So, according to the Slovenes, Bećković implies, the Serbs are Nazis. And they are "throwing" (that is to say, forcing) poor Albanians into a pit (the mine). In the pit Albanians are starving in protest against Serbian oppression. But it is all staged, Bećković implies, and the "starving" miners emerged healthy in the light of day at the end of the strike, whereas the Serbs never returned from their pits. He invokes the World War II Independent State of Croatia in which the Serbs, thrown in pits only because they were Serbs, and the Jews, exterminated in Ustaša concentration camps only because they were Jews, cohabitate in a joint, "ethnically clean" underground realm.

This is probably the most powerful and succinct statement of the thesis for which the *locus classicus* could be found in the "Letter to the Writers of Israel" written in 1985 by Vuk Drašković, where he proclaimed that "it was by the hands of the same executioners that both Serbs and Jews have been exterminated at the same concentration camps, slaughtered at the same bridges, burned alive in the same ovens, thrown together in the same pits."

> It is as if we Serbs are the thirteenth, lost and the most ill-fated tribe of Israel . . . I hail you (the Israeli writers) as our brothers and with the same

oath that our ancestors heard from the Jews, the meaning of which is carried in the heart of every Serb expelled from Kosovo: "If I forget thee, O Jerusalem, let my right hand wither." (Drašković 1987:71–75)

After this proclamation, the following set of correspondences gained currency in Serbia:

- Both Serbs and Jews are the "chosen peoples"—slaughtered, sacrificed, denied expression, yet always righteous, always defending themselves, never attacking.
- The Kosovo Albanians stand to the Serbs as the Palestinians stand to the Israelis.
- Serbs are the ones who should say "never again" like Israel and rely on their military power to defend their brethren wherever they happen to be living in Yugoslavia, and bring them together in a unitary state which alone can guarantee them safety in a hostile world.

The discourse set in motion by Drašković's letter in 1985 came to be embodied in the Serbian-Jewish Friendship Society (Društvo srpsko-jevrejskog prijateljstva) established in 1988 by a number of prominent Serbian writers and intellectuals together with a smaller number of Jews. The majority of Serbian Jews did not join the Society feeling that it had become mainly a political organization openly backing the Serbian regime (see Gordiejew 1999:389–396).

The Society immediately set upon improving the ties between Israel and Serbia (the Federal Yugoslav authorities, or what was left of them, were still refusing to reestablish diplomatic relations with Israel at that time). It organized a delegation of 440 businessmen, politicians, and intellectuals who went to Israel in 1990, and helped establish sister-city relations between fifteen Serbian and Israeli cities. During the Gulf War a delegation of twelve city mayors from Serbia went to Israel to demonstrate Serbian solidarity with Israel's plight. Underlying these activities was a naive hope of eliciting Israel's support for the Serbian cause, and even obtaining Israeli weapons for the "reconquest of Kosovo"—the Serbian Jerusalem. There were also attempts to enlist the American Jewish lobby, imagined to wield immense, mythical power, to help in the "Serbian cause."

In Tito's Yugoslavia the Jewish community, numbering no more that six thousand (largely assimilated) members, kept a low profile and was mostly left in peace.[2] With the imminent breakdown of the country, the Yugoslav Jews found themselves stranded in mutually hostile republics. Owing to their small numbers and relative inconspicuousness, the issue of loyalty to the new regimes turned out, however, to be less pressing than the dilemma posed by the symbolic charge of Jewish symbols that their respective republics sought to appropriate for their own political ends. Perhaps more than with anti-Semitism, those Jewish communities had to cope with the efforts that their Croatian, Serbian, or Slovenian compatriots were making to woo them, identify with them, or co-opt them for the media struggle against the hated enemy. Responses were varied—some Yugoslav Jews allowed themselves to be co-opted by their new regimes, some even enthusiastically offered their services, but the majority tried to walk the tightrope of politely refusing to lend their heritage of suffering and its attendant symbolic power to political uses while still affirming their loyalty to their new states. The power of the Jewish Trope, however, was largely out of the hands of the Yugoslav Jews themselves. The various republican regimes fighting to secure the most advantageous media image in the West could not resist exploiting it. What follows are brief analyses of the ways the imagery of Jewish suffering, or what I call here the "Jewish Trope" was used in Croatia and Bosnia.

CROATIA

Croatia has been largely successful in presenting itself as a Westernized, democratic, and free-market–oriented republic oppressed by the Byzantine, totalitarian, Bolshevik Serbs. Yet there were a few blemishes on that image—most important was the atrocious record of the Independent State of Croatia during the Second World War, when Croatian fascists committed the wholesale slaughter of Jewish, Roma, and Serbian populations. The other, more current problem was the anti-Semitic statements of their president, Franjo Tudjman.

The media in Serbia tried their best to exploit these weak spots both on the domestic and international fronts. On the domestic front, harping on World War II genocide was largely successful, if not in the wholesale mobilizing of the Serb population for war, then at least in insuring its passive acceptance of events like the Yugoslav Army's shelling of Dubrovnik and Vukovar. On the international scene, however, it is my sense that this strategy achieved much less. Predisposed to let bygones be bygones, and charging Serbs of being obsessed with history, the Western media did not, with some exceptions, unduly pester Croatia with its unsavory past. Tudjman's anti-Semitic statements, on the other hand, especially in his book *Wastelands of Historic Reality* (published in Zagreb in 1989), earned him the opprobrium of international Jewish organizations, the ire of such influential figures as Simon Wiesenthal, and criticism from the Croatian Jewish community; Israel, for its part, stalled in establishing full diplomatic relations with Croatia for years after recognizing Croatia's independence.

On the Croatian side, officials protested, of course, that the English translation (provided by Serbs) was misleading or that the quotes were out of context, and Tudjman himself publicly apologized in 1994, revising the controversial parts of the book for the new edition. This damage control, however, was apparently not particularly successful. Croatia's atrocious World War II record, whatever the successes or failures of Serbian propaganda in exploiting it, was perceived in Croatia as a dangerous threat to its media image. To simplify what was often a convoluted struggle over numbers of victims and historic interpretations, the Croatian media essentially pursued a two-track strategy in dealing with this issue. The main defensive strategy has been to present anti-Semitism in the Independent State of Croatia as purely a Nazi import and to depict the Croatian population at large as strongly opposed to the Ustaša regime, as exhibiting solidarity with their Jewish compatriots, and as perishing alongside them in the anti-fascist struggle.[3] Yet, though this strategy might have worked well domestically to calm any lingering sense of guilt, the record of who did what during the war was far too well established for this strategy to really work on international Jewish organizations, Wiesenthal, or Israel. The second track, therefore, relied on the maxim that taking the offensive is the best defense, so that rather than minimizing one's own responsibility, the attempt was made to show that the Serbs were actually no better, and possibly worse, than Croats when it came to genocide against Serbian Jews during the war.

By the end of 1990 the official Catholic newsletter (*Glas Koncila*) in Zagreb published a series of books titled The Jewish Question in Serbia during the Second World War. The author, Tomislav Vuković, tried to show that anti-Semitism was firmly entrenched in the Serbian mentality and that it was the Serbian quisling authorities under German occupation who were largely responsible for the Holocaust in Serbia—thus transferring the blame from the Wermacht, the SS, and the Gestapo to the Serbs themselves. The same author published a two-hundred-page book on Serbian anti-Semitism in 1992, with some four hundred footnotes and more than a hundred references (see Vuković and Bojović 1992). For the international media campaign, however, the Croatian Ministry of Information relied mainly on a few simple points like the report to Hitler in 1942 proudly proclaiming Serbia as the first *judenfrei* country in occupied Europe—that is to say, completely cleansed of the Jews. The trick consisted in not mentioning that the report was sent by Harald Thurner, the Head of the Wermacht Military Administration in Serbia, to Lieutenant General Alexander Löhr, Commander for South East Europe, thus implying that it was the Serbian authorities who did the dirty job.

The culmination of this strategy was a book by Philip Cohen, *Serbia's Secret War: Propaganda and the Deceit of History* (1996). The strategy was simple and effective: assemble all the manifestations of Serbian anti-Semitism during the last 150 years, and the thesis easily emerges that anti-Semitism is a deeply rooted, institutionalized, and all-pervasive tenet of the Serbian mentality and national ideology. Most sophisticated about this argument is that there is no need to lie or distort the sources (as far as I was able to check, Cohen did neither). It suffices to neglect weighing that evidence. The reader gets no inkling of the actual societal impact these manifestations of anti-Semitism had in Serbia, and no sense of whether they were marginal or dominant (I return to this question in the last section of the chapter).

The Jewish Community in Serbia again faced a delicate situation—the historical facts were well established for that period in Serbia[4] and it was relatively easy to refute the gross distortions in Vuković's thesis, but the Serbian record in the Second World War, though definitely better than the Croatian, was nevertheless far from spotless. If the Jews in Serbia had taken it upon themselves to refute the Croatian claims, this could easily have been construed as the rehabilitation of Serbian quisling authorities and paramilitary units who did, in fact, help the Germans to exterminate Jews in Serbia. Such absolution, because it would come from the Jews themselves, would indeed carry much weight. The dilemma, then, was how to counter the abuses of history and the instrumentalization of Jewish suffering coming from the Croatian side, while at the same time avoiding the corresponding instrumentalization by the Serbian side. Although the majority of Jews in Serbia and the leaders of the Federation of Jewish Communities of Yugoslavia tried to hold to this precarious line, some members of the Serbian Jewish community argued that Serbian Jews should side more strongly with the Serbs and defend them more actively against the demonization carried out in the former Yugoslav republics and in the international media.[5]

BOSNIA

The jockeying for position on the "Jewish issue" in the former Yugoslavia was from the beginning heavily influenced by the surrounding "symbolic landscape" of the Western media which all the participants rightly perceived as highly sensitive to the history and legacy of Jewish suffering. It was, however, only with the start of the war in Bosnia, that the Holocaust, and more generally the Second World War, definitively emerged as the dominant metaphor, particularly in the American media. Milošević was cast as Hitler; a number of Western leaders seen as appeasing him were likened to Chamberlain in Munich; the International Criminal Tribunal for the former Yugoslavia was seen as the Court in Nuremberg; and Bosnian Muslims were presented as Jews facing another Holocaust at the hands of Serbs.

Here are a few characteristic headlines appearing in the leading American daily newspapers over a period of several months in 1992 and early 1993: "What Do We Say When 'Never Again' Happens?" (Stuart Goldstein, *USA Today,* August 5, 1993); "The Holocaust Analogy Is Too True" (Henry Siegman, President of the American Jewish Council, *Los Angeles Times,* July 11, 1993); "'Never Again'—Except for Bosnia" (Zbigniew Brzezinski, *New York Times,* April 22, 1993); "Make 'Never' Mean Never" (*USA Today,* April 22, 1993); "Are Comparisons to Bosnia Valid?" (interview with Patrick Glynn, *USA Today,* April 20, 1993); "Stopping Holocaust" (Abraham Foxman, *Atlanta Constitution,* August 6, 1992); "'This Is a Holocaust': Surrounded by Death, Sarajevo Resolves to Live" (Storer Rowley, *Chicago Tribune,* August 30, 1992); and "It's Not a Holocaust: Rhetoric and Reality in Bosnia" (Richard Cohen, *Washington Post,* February 28, 1993).

The rhetorical strategy of presenting Bosnia as a Holocaust reached its crescendo with the two powerful symbolic events of April 1993—the fiftieth anniversary of the Warsaw Ghetto Uprising, and the opening of the Holocaust Memorial Museum in Washington, D.C. The war in Bosnia haunted both occasions, and hardly a dignitary in attendance failed to draw a parallel to it. The Holocaust Museum in Washington, in particular, was seen as a reminder to the civilized world never to let the Holocaust happen again.[6] Situated so prominently on the Washington Mall, in the center of American memory and power, the Holocaust Museum emerged as perhaps the most important nodal point in the emotionally charged debate over Western policy in the Balkans. In the light of all this, it is quite understandable that the Muslim-led Bosnian government did its best to present the plight of Bosnian Muslims as another Holocaust. Less easy to understand is the speed and zeal with which American Jewish organizations and a number of prominent Jewish intellectuals embraced this position. While the Jewish community in Yugoslavia mostly tried hard not to get involved and to remain neutral in the ongoing conflict, their American counterparts seemed only too eager to join the Balkan game of the political instrumentalization of the Holocaust.

THE JEWISH TROPE AND ANTI-SEMITISM IN
SERBIA AFTER THE NATO BOMBING

If we take Drašković's 1985 "Letter to Jewish Writers" as the starting point, over the next fifteen years the Jewish Trope only intermittently claimed the spotlight of Serbian national identity discourses. It played a prominent role in the "saddling of Milošević's horse" in the late 1980s, and it was present whenever Kosovo was compared to the Serbian Jerusalem, but the strong philo-Semitism and identification with the Jews were more of a continuous undercurrent to Serbian narratives of victimhood than a dominant "story."

The Kosovo crisis of the late 1990s, which led to the NATO intervention, once again reawakened the Kosovo theme with its Jewish associations, but it was the bombing itself that made even those Serbs who up to that point had been immune to the state-disseminated paranoia, see themselves as innocent victims. As the *Chicago Tribune* reported on September 27, 1999, in the wake of the bombing, Serbs were claiming: "We are the new Jews of Europe." "The analogy with the Jews may be breathtakingly inappropriate," wrote Tom Hundley, "but most Serbs truly feel they are the wronged party in this drama."

The Holocaust analogy was again at the very center of justifying the NATO bombing of Serbia in the spring of 1999. In an interview for Radio Free Europe on May 18, 1999, the famous Yugoslav film director Dušan Makavejev invoked a *New York Times* article[7] on General Wesley Clark (Commander-in-Chief of the 1999 NATO operation in Serbia), published a few days earlier:

> Our national morbid identification with the bones of slaughtered ancestors has been transposed onto the planetary level. We are now learning that Clark's ancestors perished in the Holocaust and that he is resolved to "go all the way." Raša Karadžić shot at Turks in Sarajevo, while Clark thinks that Belgrade is inhabited by Germans who killed his grandfather.

Makavejev was obviously drawing from his memory when referring to the *New York Times* article and got it wrong. Clark's grandfather was not a victim of the Holocaust but, according to the article, "was a Russian Jew who fled his country to escape the pogroms there a century ago." But, when we distort our memories, it is usually along the lines of dominant narrative patterns, and Makavejev's mistake is very telling. Two weeks after he read the article, the story in his mind had migrated from Russian pogroms to the truly central story of the Holocaust. I venture to say that this was exactly what was intended by the *New York Times* article.

The centrality of the Holocaust for the ideology of "humanitarian intervention" as a newly forged global interventionist policy of the U.S. and its allies deserves further study. It would, however, be a study of "Stories Americans tell,"[8] whereas I am mentioning American uses of the Jewish Trope here only to point out that it conditions some of the stories Serbs (as well as Slovenes, Albanians, Croats or Bosnian Muslims) tell themselves and others.

As a Jew in Serbia I never personally experienced anti-Semitism. Moreover, in all my personal interactions with Jews in Serbia, I have never found even one who complained of Serbian anti-Semitism. The opinions of the Jews I talked to ranged only from neutral to highly pro-

Serb (see Mihailović 1996 and Sekelj 1997 for anti-Semitism in Serbia in the 1990s). And even though I was aware of occasional anti-Semitic incidents (documented by the Jewish Community in their *Bulletin* and other publications), I tended to agree with what a prominent Jewish intellectual, sociologist Laslo Sekelj,[9] said in *Naša Borba:*

> In Serbia anti-Semitism is a peripheral phenomenon. Not because of some special tolerance, but because there are a lot of minorities here, so that Jews don't stick out. The main channel of hate is oriented toward nations with which you are in conflict, the Croats, Muslims, Albanians . . . The South Slav brothers hate each other so badly they don't need Jews to have someone to hate. (In Biševac 1997)

Another prominent Jew from Serbia, writer Filip David, however, remarked that as Serbia kept losing its wars, "the list of 'enemies' became exhausted. In the end, only the 'domestic traitors' and 'world conspirators' remained. And while it is already known who the 'domestic traitors' are, the role of 'conspirators' is traditionally easiest to hang onto Jews" (David 2000).

Innumerable variations on the theme of world conspiracy against Serbs have been highly prominent features of everyday life in Serbia during the last fifteen years or so. Most of them feature the usual cast of Serbian enemies—Germany, the Communist International, the Vatican, and, of course, the "New World Order." As these theories conveniently transfer responsibility for the whole series of the last decade's disasters (four lost wars, one of the world's highest hyperinflations, Serbia's pariah status, and so on) from Milošević's regime to outside enemies, they have been actively promoted by the regime itself. An important node in this dissemination of conspiracy theories was the so-called New Serbian Right—a small group of neo-fascist intellectuals led by the Belgrade art critic Dragoš Kalajić. Their quasi-erudite theories often featured the Freemasons, or the "Usurers' International" as the secret enemy of Serbdom (or Orthodox Slavdom in general), and quite clearly they were using the classical World Jewish Conspiracy as their template. Yet even there, it was very hard to find any overt negative reference to Jews. I would argue that the power of the Jewish Trope in Serbian discourses on identity acted to counteract overt manifestations of anti-Semitism, and led even the likes of Dragoš Kalajić and the New Serbian Right, whose neo-fascist ideology predisposed them to virulent anti-Semitism, to sometimes pay lip service to the prevalent philo-Semitism.

This however, seemed to be changing as conspiracy theories, which gripped Serbia during and after the bombing, began increasingly to display openly anti-Semitic tones. Grabbing at any support they could get, some diaspora Serbs disseminated anti-Semitic articles written by American extreme right-wingers over the Internet during the NATO bombing. The bombing itself was officially justified by Holocaust analogies, and endorsements of the "humanitarian intervention" coming from Jews were given a lot of attention in the American media. President Bill Clinton's team featured several Jews (i.e., Defense Secretary William Cohen, State Department Spokesman James P. Rubin), and Madeleine Albright and Wesley Clark both conveniently discovered their forgotten Jewish roots around that time. It is no surprise, then, that the "conspiracy of the whole world" or "the New World Order" against Serbs was often presented as a Jewish conspiracy in Serbia.

More important, however, the hyperbolic philo-Semitism inaugurated by Drašković, and later, in the early 1990s, by the Serbian-Jewish Friendship Society, fueled unrealistic and naive hopes that both the "powerful Jewish lobby" in America and the state of Israel would leap to the defense of Serbia in the international media arena as well as in terms of military hardware. What happened instead was that Israel (understandably) remained neutral, and many prominent Jewish figures in the West (i.e., Alain Finkielkraut, Susan Sontag, and Bernard Henry-Levy) stepped to the forefront of denouncing Serbian savagery in Croatia and Bosnia. This provoked resentment and a sense of betrayal among the Serbian public which culminated when, on September 1, 1993, more than a hundred prominent individuals (including such well-known Jewish figures as Elie Wiesel, Josef Brodsky, George Soros, Susan Sontag, the director of the American Jewish Congress Henry Siegman, etc.) signed an open letter to President Clinton asking that, among other things, NATO warplanes bomb the Bosnian Serbs and even military targets in Serbia proper. Some members of the Serbian Jewish community, including the chief rabbi Cadik Danon, publicly denounced the Jewish signatories of the open letter, and a message was sent to international Jewish organizations asking them to refrain from passing judgment and taking sides in the Yugoslav civil war "because they don't understand its historical roots." Ordinary citizens wrote letters to editors of the type "we (Serbs) sacrificed ourselves for Jews in World War II, we offered them our friendship, but see how the Jews pay us back—by leading the demonization campaign in the West against us and by calling on Clinton to bomb us."

The final twist came with the conspiracy theory that circulated in Belgrade in the wake of the NATO bombing. As Filip David reports, the Belgrade TV channel *Palma* started promoting theories about Jews as "killers and criminals," responsible for all the catastrophes of modern history, from the October Revolution and both world wars to the recent bombing of Yugoslavia.

> A long-held "secret" is unveiled that the modern (Ashkenazi) Jews are actually not true, but "false" Jews—the descendants of the Khazars, a Turkic tribe that converted to Judaism and then miraculously disappeared. This is (according to these theories), a great deception, for the Judaized Khazars actually assimilated the (true) Jews. Now these "false Jews" or Khazars fill the highest positions in the U.S. and Russia, are heads of leading European states, receive instructions from secret conspiratorial cabals, and pull the strings of world politics aiming to rule the entire world and destroy Serbia in the process. (David 2000)[10]

I see this latest conspiracy theory as a kind of "compromise" formation between two opposing narrative forces at work in contemporary Serbia. On the one hand, the xenophobia and paranoia actively fostered by the regime, and finally driven home by the NATO bombing, seemed to bring classical Jewish World Conspiracy theories to the fore in a way seldom seen before in Serbia. On the other hand, it seemed that among national intelligentsia there was still a large investment in portraying Serbian victimhood as analogous to Jewish victimhood, and of keeping alive the story of that special Serbian-Jewish friendship, forged in common suffering. The "Khazar theory" thus found a "happy" resolution to this contradiction by splitting the Jews into the evil ones, who are false, and the "real Jews," who could still supposedly be our "friends."

The link that came to be established between the Holocaust and the state of Israel helped promote the perception that to be a victim of a genocide is to be entitled to a state. Thus the narrative strategy of identifying with Jews as archetypal victims of an archetypal genocide is a high-stake game in that part of the world in which the Holocaust had come to assume the place of the central morality story. It pays to be a Jew (symbolically)—thence the "Wish to be a Jew" or, as some have called it, "Holocaust Envy." The war of words that accompanied and even fueled the Yugoslav wars in the 1990s has shown how such a powerful morality story as that of Jewish suffering could be misused—precisely because it was perceived as powerful. In the southeast corner of Europe it was misused by Serbs and Slovenes, Albanians and Bosnian Muslims, as they strove to position themselves as victims, but these local misuses were contingent on and sometimes fatally interlocked with misuses of the Jewish Trope in the global media space dominated by the U.S. and Western Europe. It is hard to steer between the strong ethical messages that the Jewish narrative of suffering can impart and the dangers of its misuse in international relations. In my personal efforts to find a "moral gyroscope" in this situation, I find best guidance in the gut feelings of those Serbian Jews who were as uneasy with the outburst of philo-Semitism in the late 1980s and early 1990s as they were uneasy with the anti-Semitic conspiracy theories propagated by Belgrade TV in the wake of the 1999 NATO bombing.

NINE

Garbled Genres

Conspiracy Theories, Everyday Life, and the Poetics of Opacity

In the winter of 1993 Serbia and Montenegro were under the strictest sanctions ever imposed by the United Nations and undergoing one of the highest hyperinflations in the world's economic history. Belgrade journalist Nenad Stefanović described the seemingly endless line of people waiting for food being distributed by a welfare organization.

> At Republika Square, a scene from a concentration camp. Such a long, stooped, miserable and silent line of Serbs I saw only once in an Ustaša documentary "Sentry on the Drina River," where along the [river] Sava dam the Ustaše are taking an endless column of docile and quiet Serbs into the Jasenovac concentration camp. (Stefanović 1993:14)[1]

This is a harsh comparison indeed—equating the Milošević regime with the Croatian fascist regime responsible for the World War II genocide against Serbs. It is the docility of his fellow citizens, however, that especially enrages Stefanović. "I wonder," he writes, "how many people from this line will vote for those who put them in it." Stefanović then reports how a member of the welfare organization that distributed food on the square (affiliated to an opposition party) said to an old woman who was putting a frozen head of cabbage in her basket: "Now Granny, think carefully about who you will vote for." He was assuming (or hoping?) that she will blame the current regime for her misery and vote for the opposition coalition he represented. The old woman shook her head: "Eh Son, the Germans are to blame for this" (Stefanović 1993:14).

This old woman epitomized what many oppositional social commentators like Stefanović saw as the central paradox of Serbia in the 1990s, and what Belgrade political scientist Srbobran Branković named the "phenomenon of support for failed authorities" (Branković 1995). How was one to explain that Milošević had repeatedly won in multiparty elections despite the disastrous effects of his rule—a drastic drop in living standards, the reduction of the country to pariah status, one of the highest hyperinflations in world history, and a score of lost wars? In a word, a shrinking, instead of a promised Greater Serbia, and poverty instead of a promised "Swiss standard of living." This is not so much a question of the crude coercive instruments of his authoritarian rule but of the continuous willing support given to the regime by precisely those most adversely affected by its policies. Was conspiracy theorizing playing a part in this phenomenon, perhaps by shifting the blame to Germans?

The old woman in the line made sense of her experience in terms of a conspiracy theory; social commentators like Stefanović often engaged in a mixture of analysis and anguished laments; and social scientists such as Srbobran Branković developed models that accounted for the "phenomenon of support for failed authorities" in terms of macro- and micro-sociological factors. These ways of comprehending the reality of Milošević's Serbia could be usefully divided into distinguishable genres.

First, there were social scientific analyses, often of great systematicity and high sophistication that were generated in numerous Belgrade social science institutes whose sizable research and publishing activities did not cease even during the harshest times.

Second, the 1990s in Serbia have brought to the fore a number of brilliant social commentators who published their short columns in oppositional newspapers and magazines. These commentators often had a solid social science background, and their insights were as penetrating as any coming from social science institutes, but they conveyed them in witty vignettes rather than in social science jargon. They were superb "native ethnographers"—immersed in everyday life but also managing to survey the social landscape from a "higher altitude." They were the anatomists who dissected and analyzed, and their own political positioning came out as a sophisticated irony. This relatively distanced, dispassionate stance is what distinguished them from the third ideal-typical genre—the lament or the Jeremiad.

A typical Jeremiad sought the reasons for the current predicaments in the abiding flaws of the Serbian character, expounded on the perceived misery in the set idioms such as the Turkish Taint and communist corruption, or simply lamented the situation in more or less ornate metaphors that most often elaborated the themes of in-betweenness.

Finally, there were conspiracy theories, a genre of speech recognized both at vernacular and scholarly levels. It was mostly nested within the larger genre of "sifting politics" (*bistriti politku*), archetypically associated with coffee shop debates, where it intermixed with laments and lay sociological analysis. Conspiracy theorizing must be a universal phenomenon, if not of humankind as a whole then certainly of modern mass societies. In that sense, it is a normal genre that will always be present as a way of coming to terms with the social reality that is ineradicably impenetrable to individual minds and thus perceived as veiled, alien, and generally opaque. In Serbia, during the 1990s, conspiracy theorizing intruded on my attention as unusually ubiquitous. It may be that my mind, trained in rigorous social theory, was simply stunned by its prevalence in everyday conversations with people I considered "rational."

It is tempting for a social scientist to order these genres in terms of their epistemological sophistication. Perhaps, following Jameson, one can talk about them as various types of "that mental map of the social and global totality we all carry around in our heads in variously garbled forms" (1988: 353). The old woman's conspiracy theory would then be the most garbled, followed by the Jeremiads, while the perceptive social commentators and sociologists would come out as the least garbled. This hierarchy rests on several assumptions. One is that the more sophisticated view is more "elevated" than the others, that is, it is synoptic, theoretical, detached, or decontextualized. The other assumption is that the more sophisticated explanation involves impersonal agencies rather than personalized plots. The third attributes some sort of superior rationality and logic to accounts that approximate the social scientific ideal, whereas conspiracy theories are seen as pathological thinking, infantile, or pre-logical. All these genres, however, could be seen as examples of what Martin Parker, following Alasdair Spark (2001), suggested we call "dietrologia" or "behindology"—a generalized project of looking behind things, of assuming there is a behind to things" (Parker 2001:203). What the old woman, Stefanović, Branković, and the present author all share is then "a form of explanation which is capable of pulling apart the fabric of what appears to be real in order to uncover the pattern behind the order of things" (ibid.:201). A move from conspiracy theory to theory *about* conspiracy theory is then just to "displace one form of explanation by another" that social scientists deem superior (ibid.:198). I am less interested in establishing or dismantling such hierarchies of garbledness than in assessing what these various genres can tell us about living in Milošević's Serbia. In this I am led by a hunch that "by connecting disparate dots from across our far-flung universe into often bizarre constellations . . . conspiracy theorists may capture strange, startling truths" (Comaroff and Comaroff 2003:297).

Even though I don't have any hard numerical evidence, I am starting from the premise that conspiracy theories did indeed proliferate in Serbia in the 1990s and 2000s well beyond some sort of (hard to gauge) "normal" level. And not only do I think they proliferated in everyday talk, but I also claim that they moved from the fringes to the very center of mass media presentation during this period. My claim parallels that of Peter Knight (1999), who argued that conspiracy theories were far more widespread in 1990s America than was the case at the time of Richard Hofstadter's classic 1964 book, *The Paranoid Style in American Politics*, and that they were no longer confined to just "a small percentage of Americans on the political fringe," as Hofstadter believed. If this was also the case in Serbia, then the phenomenon presents us with important questions: Could such proliferation and centrality be seen as a symptom, and, if so, of what? If conspiracy theorizing is related to the perceived opacity of society, could increased conspiracy theorizing come from increased opacity, and, if yes, how can we account for such an increase? What was the nature of that opacity, and how much of it could be attributed to Milošević's technology of rule, for instance, and how much to the confusions of Serbia's transition amid the Yugoslav wars or hyperinflation?

Second, conspiracy theories are a social and political fact. They are not only a symptom to be interpreted but also a part of the political equation. Their "garbledness" may not only be a sign of the incomprehensibility of the social world but also a causal factor in fostering that incomprehensibility, which in turn contributes to the "phenomenon of support for failed authorities." The question, then, is what part did the proliferation of conspiracy theories play in Serbia during the period under consideration. Apart from the supposed increased opacity of the social world, how much of this proliferation may be attributed to the regime's cynical manipulation? Finally, can we find something particularly illuminating about the Serbian situation in the content of the conspiracy theories, in their form and pragmatics as a genre? I believe there was something ineradicable about the lived experience of social opacity in Milošević's Serbia that even the most sophisticated scientific accounts failed to exhaust. The "garbled" genres, then, exhibited not just more or less deficient cognitive mappings but also something we might call the "poetics of opacity." Finally, their supposed cognitive deficiency combined with their alleged potential for instructive allegory may point to a fruitful view of conspiracy theorizing as akin to collective dreaming.

CLOUDING OF RESPONSIBILITY: CONSPIRACY THEORIES AS CYNICAL MANIPULATION

One of the best examples of conspiracy theories in Serbia that moved to the center stage in the early 1990s was a group loosely gathered around "The New Serbian Right" and their main ideologue, the Euroasianist/ Fascist dandy Dragoš Kalajić, a group we already encountered as a major disseminator of the Serbs as the Most Ancient People theories. Here was a group that, under normal circumstances, would be on the far-out fringes but in the early 1990s was given exposure in the mainstream media and thus moved to center stage. It could still be argued that even though one of their main outlets, the Belgrade bi-weekly *Duga,* boasted high circulation, Kalajić and his acolytes remained a marginal group whose pompous show of obscure erudition could reach only a minority audience with higher educational aspirations. A much larger audience at a lower educational level, however, was reached by a whole host of "mouthpieces," most notably by a number of soothsayers and astrologists who flooded not only the tabloid press and independent TV channels but also the regime-controlled "serious" newspapers and state television in the early 1990s. Perhaps the most influential of these was Milja

Vujanović, a former actress and model turned astrologer who was given a full hour show during the peak time on the Third Channel of state television. Acting as a popularizer and broadcaster of Kalajić's geo-political theories, Milja used astrology, numerology, fantastic etymology, and toponymy, as well as other hermetic arts to expound on the endless variations of the satanic Western plan to punish Serbia as the epicenter of Culture, Civilization, and Spirituality.

Because access to the TV channel that broadcast Milja's show, and a host of other media outlets, was directly regulated by the government, clearly it was the Milošević regime that actively encouraged the dissemination of conspiracy theories. And the regime's interest in doing so is also clear. By sowing conspiracy theories that most often featured the "old enemies of Serbdom"—Germany, the Vatican, and Turkey—the regime could successfully obscure its own responsibility for the disastrous situation in Serbia by shifting it onto Evil Others.

One must bear in mind, however, that the actual policies of the U.S. and its European allies toward Serbia made Milošević's task of shifting the blame to "foreign conspiracy" relatively easy. It is easy to demonstrate that the Western policies toward Serbia—from the UN sanctions to the NATO bombing of Bosnian Serbs in 1995, and of Serbia itself in 1999—worked to confirm Serbian paranoia and thus strengthened Milošević. As a corollary of this, it was also relatively easy for the regime to denounce various pro-Western opposition and antiwar groups in Serbia as traitors and collaborators, and thus neutralize their challenge to its power.

Leaving the question of Western (one would hope unintended) "help" aside, political scientists like Srbobran Branković were justified in arguing that the deliberate fostering of conspiracy theories and a paranoid atmosphere constituted a major tool of Milošević's regime. This argument posited that the authorities were "not in the grip of a pathological delusion, but ruthlessly rational in their manipulation of public sentiment" (Knight 1999:33). In that sense one could talk of a conscious and cynical conspiracy to promote conspiracy theories. We do not know, of course, what was in the minds of the regime decision makers, but both the motive (maintaining power by, among other things, shifting or "clouding" one's own responsibility) and the means (controlling state TV and other major mass media) are quite discernible. A psychology

professor from Belgrade University, Dragan Popadić, in his analysis
of the "Nation's Mental Health," asked, in the oppositional *Republika:*
"Are we making ourselves crazy or are we made to be crazy?" (Popadić
2000:21). Those who promote conspiracy theories in order to maintain
power might also believe in some of them, as Popadić argued. These two
possibilities, however, do not exclude each other, and it is hard to say,
Popadić wrote, which one is more frightening.

CONSPIRACY THEORIES AS ATTEMPTS
TO DEAL WITH OPACITY

The proliferation of conspiracy theories could be attributed to deliberate manipulation by those in power, or it could be seen as a normal
response to the increased opacity of the social environment. These two
perspectives, of course, are not mutually exclusive. I have come to see
this increased or abnormal opacity of the social world in Serbia as a
compounded effect of a series of "moral/epistemological warps." Our
social universe is always warped in the sense of being vastly more convoluted than any individual map can chart. It is as if our two-dimensional
maps were curved and folded in upon themselves beyond our capacity to
straighten them out. In that sense warping is analogous to our inability
to think of extra dimensions in our multiply folded social space. Here,
however, by "warps" I mean something that goes beyond the normal distortions of our social universe, mostly the major instances of massive and
deliberate deception, obfuscation, and, perhaps most important, various
simulations that the regime engaged in after Milošević came to power.

For simplicity's sake, one can take Tito's Yugoslavia as the baseline
distortion. As a socialist society, Tito's Yugoslavia was subject to the
warps characteristic of real socialism elsewhere—of the type described,
for instance, by Havel (1986) as "living a lie." This kind of distortion is
felt as going beyond normal, prompting citizens of people's democracies to refer to their country as a "land of miracles" (see Pesmen 2000).
Moreover, the Bearable Evil theory, held by many in Serbia, argued that
Tito's "operatic communism," precisely because of its (seeming) liberties,
constituted a situation more warped than the already warped experience of other Soviet bloc countries and, according to one of the main
proponents of the thesis, writer Milovan Danojlić, "corrupted the soul

worse than tyranny." The fall of communism brought with it further bewildering warps by now widely documented in the literature on the predicaments of "transition." And the transition in Serbia was probably more distorted than elsewhere in East Europe, since it was, simultaneously, retarded and obfuscated by the nationalist mobilization and the subsequent wars.

The Serbian populist "anti-bureaucratic revolution," which brought Milošević to power several years before the fall of communism in Eastern Europe, moreover, also contained a major simulation. This (highly orchestrated) movement, Branković argued, "at once absorbed and discharged opposition to the old regime: the people saw it as the eradication of the worst aspects of the old order (bureaucracy and the repression of national feeling). The Serbs as a nation, therefore, enjoyed the charms of opposition long before the rest [of the communist bloc], but in an absurd way by supporting the authorities" (Branković 1995:201).

Milošević preempted, cannibalized, or simulated the nationalist discourse of Serbian opposition, which thereafter resorted to self-defeating attempts to beat Milošević at his own game by appearing even more nationalistic than he was. As the opposition journal *Vreme* put it, "The nationalists believed that he was only pretending to be a Communist, and the Communists that he was only pretending to be a nationalist" (in Budding 1998:355).

The problem with describing all these warps is that they necessitate very detailed accounts of the Byzantine intricacies of Serbian politics— a daunting task I cannot attempt here. And even if one did assemble such an account, it would be impossible to re-create in the reader what I think is the dimension of moral warps most responsible for creating social opacity and a sense of bewilderment among those who lived them, namely, the effect of their relentless compounding over a long period of time. It is as if you could keep track when you are told that black is white, and even when that white (which is really black) is called black again, but after that you lose count. This is precisely the experience of bewilderment that I am interested in. Before delving into conspiracy theorizing as a response to the increased opacity of the social environment, let us first explore some of the idioms in which that opacity was expressed in Serbia in the 1990s.

DESCRIBING OPACITY: FROM RUBIK CUBES AND
MUSICAL CHAIRS TO MIST, SLUSH, AND GELATIN

One of the best social commentators in the 1990s, Stojan Cerović, expressed his sense of bewilderment in his commentary on the July 1995 UN hostage crisis:[2]

> Sometimes it is of great advantage to be a foreign correspondent. When you don't understand something, you think that it is because you are not from here and not initiated into the mysterious customs of this exotic country. But how could we, who are from here [that is, *natives*], how could we confess that we don't understand what is happening here any better than if we suddenly found ourselves in the midst of Kazakhstan? (Cerović 1995)

The ability of almost everyone in Serbia at that time to figure out the social landscape was severely impaired. That landscape was populated by government ministers, central bank governors, directors of big firms, regional bosses, Socialist Party functionaries, generals, prophets and pundits, influential writers, opposition leaders, police chiefs, criminal/warlord/"businessmen," and the mysterious State Security Service. How much power, influence, and autonomy all these actors and institutions actually had was far from clear and yet was important to figure out in a world where nothing seemed to be stable, rational, or what it was supposed to be. The regime largely succeeded in transferring the responsibility for the disastrous results of its rule onto either foreign powers or a cast of internal enemies, and yet, paradoxically, the conviction that "the Germans are to blame" coexisted with a widespread understanding that, ultimately, all power indeed flowed from Milošević, that he was the only one who "shuffled the deck" of Serbian politics.

Eric Gordy, for instance, used the image of "musical chairs." "By rotating its cast of ideological surrogates through the musical chairs of power," he observed, "the regime protects itself from its own positions and actions. Rarely speaking or otherwise appearing in public, Slobodan Milošević can rightly claim that he never advocated nationalist or any other positions. In fact, every major political move of his regime has been announced, defended, and removed from the agenda by surrogates" (Gordy 1999:17).

One of Cerović's colleagues from the oppositional *Vreme* (August 22, 1994) likened the situation to a Rubik's Cube. Seemingly autonomous political actors seemed powerful one day only to disappear from the scene the next day and reappear a few months later. The analysts of the Serbian political scene had to rely on hints. Thus if a politician entered the presidency building and emerged two hours later his rating increased (whereas that of his opponents diminished), because he might have talked with Milošević. The process was popularly known as "building" (as in "bodybuilding").

To talk about musical chairs or a Rubik's Cube is to build potentially useful tools for thinking about a complex situation. Both social scientists and commentators were engaged in model building. Yet such models might be seen as too simple and thus inadequate to describe the full extent of the experiential confusion. Sober analysis is then apt to slip into metaphoric predications that serve not to clarify the situation but to express exasperation. A striking example of such talk that vacillates between social analysis and Jeremiad is again offered by Nenad Stefanović (1994) in another of his articles published in *Duga*.

The article, titled "Red Mists Are Dawning" (*Sviću crvene magle*), argued that "communism is returning to Serbia riding on the corpse of tarnished (*okaljani*) nationalism" (Stefanović 1994:14). Although it might have appeared that nationalism could be differentiated into the authentic (*izvorni*)—supposedly operating among the people—and the cynical, operating at the level of leadership, Stefanović argued that the distinction had become hopelessly blurred in Serbia, where "mimicry is an octopus which intertwines sincere with useful feelings" (15). Milošević's (cynical) nationalism, which he used as a lever in his internal party showdown in 1987, was popularly interpreted as anti-Yugoslavism, anticommunism, and, even more surprising (given that Milošević never even bothered to feign any religious sentiment), as a call for the revival of Serbian Orthodoxy. A line from a neofolk ode to Milošević, which Stefanović quotes, encapsulates the confusion: "Slobo, you are a Communist, we love you like Jesus Christ" (*Ti si Slobo komunista, volimo te k'o Isusa Hrista*).

Stefanović was trying to disentangle a nauseatingly muddled situation in which the authentic could not be distinguished from the cynical, in which supposed political opponents readily exchanged ideological hats overnight, in which simulations were themselves simulated and nothing seemed to be straightforward or what one expected it to be. Even an octopus with its eight tentacles impossibly entwined seemed like a model of clarity in this situation, where successive simulations of simulations blurred the reality beyond the power of metaphors such as mimicry or façade to convey it. The reality Stefanović tried to comprehend was beyond even "hopelessly entangled," which would suggest that at least ropes were there that might be picked out; rather, it was an amorphous mass, a colloid whose basic ingredients were impossible to sort out:

> In Serbia all politics turned into gelatin. Our consciousness is slush, and the situation in which we seem to be mired appears infantile. Here we can neither fight it out nor sit down together like human beings. Corrupted and neglected for decades, we are living through a morally provisory period. (Stefanović 1994:16)

Images of mud are ubiquitous in the self-representation and self-understanding in Serbia. Mud tends to metonymically stand for "our backwardness" or "peasant origin" with positive or negative valuations depending on who is talking to whom. Mud is a code for a complex of traits associated with countryside and peasants, and a way of indicating the primitiveness of oneself or one's neighbor in the Balkans. And, as beautifully exemplified by Živojin Pavlović's disquisition on the "amorphous and crystalline civilizations," at the most general level mud could be seen as belonging to a whole family of idioms in which a periphery expresses its sense of in-betweenness by resorting to images of mixedness, unformedness, ambiguity, amorphousness and miscegenation. Stefanović's article shows that amorphous substances like mud, slush, gelatin, or mists were also used to describe the lived experience of the failure to penetrate the opacity of the social, and to cognitively map out its totality (see Živković 2001).

To complain about being mired in slush and gelatin, enveloped in red mists, or reduced to a bewildered child are idioms characteristic of Jeremiads. The Rubik's Cube, on the other hand, is a model that hints at tesseracts, Hinton's cubes, and other models for imagining hyperspace.[3] Conspiracy theories lie somewhere between poetic laments and scientific modeling. The "grammar of these theories," as Parker observes, "is not insane speculation—or a romantic poetic wildness—but a form of detective work that uses the tools of the hypothetico-deductive method" (2001:192). In that sense conspiracy theories are a species of "behindology" that, similar to Morelli, Freud, and Sherlock Holmes (not to mention anthropology), relies on clues; indeed, they could be seen, in Ginzburg's (1979, 1984) words, as "conjectural sciences." Still the grammar or logic of conspiracy theories' conjecture is specific, and its peculiarity may be related to the contradictory situation of the conspiracy theorist who urgently needs to connect the unconnected into a grand theory and yet is mired in the immediacy of everyday life—the very opposite of the elevation needed for any theoretical attitude.

LOGICAL PROPERTIES OF CONSPIRACY THEORIES

Conspiracy theories, contrary to Jeremiads, project a strong sense of transparency onto the inchoateness of the social world. This presumption of transparency, however, is full of contradictions. The presumably most secret dealings of the powerful shady masters are exposed for all to see on TV, in newspapers, and in widely read books, even though we are at the same time given to believe that the secret movers are prepared to kill in order to hide their identities.

Writings of Kalajić, his acolytes, and mouthpieces like Milja Vujanović exhibit a peculiar logic or a lack of logic that can induce a kind of cognitive vertigo. It is precisely these qualities—connecting the most unrelated phenomena, the veiled insinuation and innuendo, and the very fuzziness and ambiguity—that can create a sense of great and terrible truths on the brink of revelation, for "if we are not quite getting it, it must be something very deep indeed." Conspiracy theorists dazzle not only with the massive evidence they marshal but even more with intimations of ever greater secrets about to be revealed. They seduce with seemingly rigorous logic but then commit the most incredible leaps of imagination. As Hofstadter put it, "What distinguished the paranoid style is not, then, the absence of verifiable facts . . . but rather the curious leap in imagination that is always made at some critical point in the recital of events" (1965:37).

This associative looseness which nevertheless gives an impression of logical rigor makes conspiracy theories very flexible. One can easily substitute one element for another and respond to challenges of the skeptic by creative permutations. It has been noted that conspiracy theories exhibit what could be called "self-sealing" properties. Watzlawick (1977:48–50), for instance, describes an ingenious experiment carried out by Alex Bavelas in which two subjects without any medical training are separately shown medical slides and asked to distinguish between sick and healthy cells. Subject A is given accurate feedback about his or her responses from experimenters and in time guesses with a fair degree of accuracy. Subject B, however, receives noncontingent reinforcement— his or her feedback has nothing to do with the actual performance. B is searching for an order that does not exist in relation to his or her own theorizations. A and B are eventually asked to discuss what they have come to consider the rules for distinguishing between healthy and sick cells. A's explanations are simple and concrete; B's are, of necessity, subtle and complex—after all, B had to form his or her hypothesis on the basis of tenuous and contradictory hunches. Most amazing, Watzlawick notes, is that A does not simply shrug off B's explanations as unnecessarily complicated or even absurd but is impressed by their sophisticated brilliance. A tends to feel inferior and vulnerable because of the pedestrian simplicity of his or her own assumptions, and the more complicated B's "delusions," the more likely they are to convince A. Indeed, Watzlawick continues, their very baroqueness may itself be self-fulfilling, as further evidence to the contrary tends to produce even more elaboration rather than correction (48–50).

Other authors have analyzed different ways in which symbolic systems or idioms of belief resist the impact of adverse evidence. Michael Polanyi, for instance, uses Evans-Pritchard's classical study of Azande witchcraft to discuss three aspects of stability that such idioms of belief exhibit (Polanyi 1958:288–292). His discussion is primarily aimed at illuminating certain properties of scientific theories, anticipating (and surpassing in scope and sophistication) Thomas Kuhn's analysis of incommensurability of scientific paradigms. Self-sealing and circularity, baroqueness and paranoid dispositions, have, of course, been repeatedly noted in relation to such comprehensive theories as Marxism and psychoanalysis. Conspiracy theories that are rife in Serbia certainly share some properties with an entrenched cultural belief system such as Azande witchcraft, or with Marxism and classical psychoanalysis, even with all social theory, but they should not be glibly equated to them. Conspiracy theories exhibit a peculiar dissociation coupled with seemingly rigorous logic that is all their own.

Vygotsky offers a clue to this logic in his account of children's "thinking in complexes." He studied the preconceptual thought of children by means of a simple but ingenious experiment with wooden blocks of different shapes, sizes, and colors that children were instructed to classify. The bonds that create the resulting "complexes" lack logical unity—"*Any factually present* connection may lead to the inclusion of a given element into a complex" (Vygotsky 1986:113). In building an *associative* complex, the child may add one block to the nuclear object because it is of the same color, another because it is similar to the nucleus in shape or in size or in any other attribute that happens to strike the child. Any bond between the nucleus and another object suffices to make the child include that object in the group and to designate it by the common "family name." In the *chain* complex, the structural center of the formation may be absent altogether. Two objects included in the complex may have nothing in common, and yet remain as parts of one and the same chain on the strength of sharing an attribute with still another of its elements.

> It is well known that the child is capable of surprising transitions, of star-tling associations and generalizations, when his thought ventures beyond the boundaries of the small tangible world of his experience. Outside it he often constructs limitless complexes amazing in the universality of the bonds they encompass. (Vygotsky 1986:114, 117–118)

Everyday awareness normally tolerates a certain amount of contra-diction and inconsistency. Most people don't exhibit Milja's extremely disassociated thinking, and are capable of adult conceptual thought, but they often resort to preconceptual thinking characteristic of children. "The adult constantly shifts from conceptual to concrete, complex think-ing," Vygotsky observed. "The transitional, pseudoconceptual form of thought is not confined to child's thinking; we too resort to it very often in our daily lives" (1986:134). Is there, then, something about the qual-ity of our daily life that makes resorting to pseudoconceptual thinking, or in Jameson's terms, to more garbled genres, more likely and more prevalent?

THE INCONSISTENCY OF EVERYDAY LIFE
AND CONSPIRACY THEORIES

The everyday awareness of ordinary people in Milošević's Serbia combined seemingly mutually exclusive senses of opacity and transparency.
Bewilderment existed side by side with an assumption of perfect knowledge. On the one hand, as Cerović put it, the ordinary people couldn't
understand what was happening there, as if they were in the midst of
Kazakhstan. On the other hand, nobody who has spent even a very short
time in Serbia could mistake the peculiar all-knowing look of a native
about to impart some piece of wisdom about "how things really are
here." That supposedly perfect knowledge, however, exhibited glaring
contradictions and inconsistencies—slippages through which bewilderment seeped into seemingly watertight certainty.

Alfred Schutz asserted that "the knowledge of the man who acts
and thinks within the world of his daily life is not homogeneous; it is (1)
incoherent, (2) only partially clear, and (3) not at all free from contradictions." An ordinary person is not usually interested in explicit, clear, and
coherent knowledge of his everyday life. He does not quest for absolute
certainty—"that the subway will run tomorrow as usual is for him almost
of the same order of likelihood as that the sun will rise" (Schutz 1970:75).
The ordinary citizen of Serbia, however, had learned that whatever functions today may not function tomorrow, and that public transportation
as well as other everyday utilities that Schutz's citizen takes for granted
are highly erratic and indeed subject to catastrophic collapse.

If problems with cognitive mapping of the social world have something to do with the immersion in everyday life, then the quality of that
everyday life and of the immersion in it might affect the mapping. After
all, mapping implies some sort of "elevation," an ability to assume a synoptic viewpoint as if from above, a kind of aerial reconnaissance. To be
immersed in the everyday is then the opposite of this elevation and will
degrade our cognitive mapping. And what makes immersion in the everyday life more imperative is its instability and consequent unpredict-
ability. Instability, of all these things Schutz's citizen takes for granted,
made the citizens of Milošević's Serbia much more preoccupied with
the everyday tactics of survival. This preoccupation, in its turn, made
people lose sight of their total social system and thus arguably impaired

their ability to act politically. There may have been a direct link between the inordinate and forcible immersion in the everyday and the ability of Milošević's regime to diffuse discontent and stay in power. Nowhere was this link more evident than during the hyperinflation of 1992–93.

INFLATION, BEWILDERMENT, AND CONSPIRACY

Yugoslavs were already accustomed to inflation, which steadily rose from about 40 percent in 1980—the year Tito died—to 251 percent in 1988. In 1989, the year of Milošević's triumph in Serbia, the annual inflation rate was alarming—2,733 percent. It was cut down in 1990, under the last Yugoslav federal prime minister Ante Marković. This was the year of high salaries and well-stocked stores—a golden year before the plunge.

People were still believing in that erratic stability of major social institutions they had known in Tito's Yugoslavia. With all its faults and inconsistencies, the system was a familiar one and stable enough to allow for predictable coping tactics. Even high inflation was something one could get used to, but when, in February 1992, hyperinflation set in, the rate of change even started outstripping ordinary people's capacity to adapt.

In 1995 a young assistant professor at the faculty of Economics in Belgrade, Mladjan Dinkić, published a book, *The Economics of Destruction: The Great Robbery of the People,* where, in non-technical language, he laid bare the mechanisms by which the hyperinflation of 1992–93 was produced and manipulated by what he called the "Serbian and Montenegrin political oligarchy."[4] The book reads like a first-class thriller, a whodunit in which the true culprits for the untold misery of these years were revealed. Absolutely stunning is that the vast majority of ordinary people caught in the everyday ravages of living under hyperinflation tended to blame anything and everything—from street dealers and the Serbian opposition to UN sanctions and the international community— except the ones who actually produced it, the very authorities they kept in power by their continuing support.

When hyperinflation started in February 1992 people would wait for days to get their salaries and pensions and would spend them in seconds just trying to buy whatever was available at the moment. In mid-November 1993, Dinkić writes, "you needed two average monthly salaries to buy the simplest electric plug, while a baby carriage cost 97 average salaries ... In December 1993, the highest pension (to which only 300 persons in Serbia were entitled) could buy one bar of soap or ⅓ of a toothpaste tube ... An average pension could buy only two pounds of carrots!" (Dinkić 1995:243).

In order to survive people were forced to take whatever hard currency they still kept "under the mattress" and sell it to the street dealer. "Nobody in their right mind would sell currency to the state bank" (where the exchange rates were as much as fifteen times lower than on the street)," Dinkić writes. "Although seemingly paradoxical, this was what the state wanted, because formally at least it absolved itself from responsibility for the monetary chaos that had to follow the permanent rise in the street exchange rate" (Dinkić 1995:87).

Street dealers were everywhere but they particularly congregated in the center of the city and at farmer's markets. Their conspiratorial hissing of "*devize, devize*" (hard currency) under their breath came out as dzzz, dzzz—the sound that marked the period. Usually young unshaven people in leather jackets or track suits, they seemed to belong to a shady world that most ordinary citizens would otherwise shun. Yet during the period of hyperinflation, practically everyone had to deal with them every day. Despite their unreliable looks, the dealers actually proved to be very reliable—if they didn't follow the rule that honesty is the best policy they would lose customers.

So the people accepted them as a necessary evil, Dinkić said, but "they always unconsciously blamed them for the inflation, believing that only the dealers were profiting from their misery."

> But had the street dealers kept all the currency they bought for themselves—would there be a single one who after a certain time wouldn't exchange endless hours of standing on dirty streets for Hawaii, the Bahamas or the Caribbean? ... Hardly anybody asked themselves how the dealers got all these incredible amounts of dinars that formed the basis of the exchange rate." (Ibid.:87–88)

The answer was simply through the unofficial issuance of money channeled to a few trusted banks, which in turn gave it to their street dealers. "As they sold their currency to street dealers," Dinkić says, "many citizens were not aware that they were selling them to none other than the state banks" (ibid.:91).

From January 1993 to January 1994 the inflation rate was 5.5×10^{20} percent while the rate of exchange rose 6.6×10^{20} percent. During the period of hyperinflation the Federal Bank of Yugoslavia issued thirty-three new banknotes, twenty-four of which were issued in 1993 alone.[5]

The inflation stopped on January 24, 1994, when new economic measures were pompously inaugurated under the leadership of the new Federal Bank Governor Dragan Avramović, the "Super Grandpa" (*super deka*) as he was to be called. The exchange rate was fixed at 1 dinar for 1 Deutsche Mark, and the prices started to drop. It seemed like a miracle. A savior finally arrived in the guise of the personable, extremely homey-looking Grandpa Avram, an old hand with extensive experience with the World Bank, wearing shabby sweaters even at state occasions, and constantly invoking the wise counsel of his wife. People believed that it was his miraculous powers that stopped the inflation when it was just a matter of the puppet masters deciding to end it, at least for a while. State authorities blamed the inflation on the war, the embargo, the enmity of the New World Order, but all these circumstances still obtained and yet the inflation was miraculously cut down overnight. The majority of people never reached the logical conclusion that perhaps these conditions were not to blame for the inflation at all, and that, in fact, those who were able to abruptly stop the inflation must have been the same ones who produced it in the first place.

According to the regime media, everything was in perfect order. Rump Yugoslavia was a respected state with all the accoutrements of statehood but unjustly punished by the evil West led overtly or covertly by Serbia's traditional enemies: the Vatican, a revived Habsburg Empire, Germany, and Freemasonry. Harvesters were harvesting abundant crops filmed in a way that recalled already half-forgotten communist imagery, factories were producing more and more, and if anything was not functioning as it should, it was invariably the nefarious doing of internal enemies—the opposition in cahoots with external enemies of Serbdom, unions in cahoots with both opposition and external enemies, and so on.

The society and its institutions were in a flux—there was no law in courts and no money in the bank. Yet people were clinging to any semblance of solidity and normalcy they could find or somehow sustain for themselves. And somehow things functioned. Public transportation was terrible but still running, offices opened, life went on despite the chaos. It was not as rosy as the regime media portrayed it, but neither was it a total disaster as depicted in the opposition media. Perusing the former you'd think you were in Switzerland, while the latter made you wonder how anything at all could still be functioning.

The society was at once totally opaque and totally transparent. Everyone knew who the real Boss was, yet many laid the responsibility for their misery not at his door but at the feet of his various surrogates and proxies. As Dragan Popadić put it, it was a "dream atmosphere in which impossible and illogical things are following one another with incomprehensible speed—everything is simultaneously absurd and possible— it is possible to buy an apartment for 50 Deutsche Marks and have no bread to eat . . . people cease to wonder, to be surprised . . . One shrugs off even quite outrageous things" (Dragan Popadić in *Vreme,* August 22, 1994, 27).

Under these extreme circumstances the everyday struggle for survival became frantic and tended to blot out everything else. Like a hamster in a wheel, all you saw was the next rung in front of your nose. You kept your eyes close to the ground searching feverishly for elementary necessities, lacking the ability to stop, take a breath, look around, or form a coherent strategy. Tactics of survival impaired one's ability to rise above the everyday scuttling, to survey possibilities, make informed choices. When running from one empty store to another holding onto money that turns into worthless paper within minutes, you forgot what normal life was like, you lost a vantage point from which to judge your present situation in a comprehensive way. Branković compared the predicament of the "little man" "terrified by . . . this vortex of events occurring at breakneck speed which he could neither understand nor influence" to "the state of mind of a bad driver who clearly sees that he has lost control of the vehicle and is heading for trouble, but is terrified of making any sudden moves . . . Let it all end up in the ditch, just as long as there are no sudden changes and that the actual plunge may be postponed as long as possible" (Branković 1995:208).

Speaking about the "etatization of time" in Ceausescu's Romania, Verdery refers to Zerubavel's suggestion that one "effect of temporal regularity is to create the background expectancies upon which our sense of the 'normal' is erected" (Verdery 1996: 54). If this is so, then "a possible consequence of socialism's arrhythmia," Verdery concludes, "would have been to keep people permanently off balance, to undermine the sense of a 'normal' order and to institute *uncertainty* as the rule." Ceausescu's Romania seized its citizens' time in such a way as to make "all planning by average citizens impossible." Such seizures of time expropriated initiative and produced subjects who no longer saw themselves as independent agents. "The time that might have gone to counterhegemonic purposes had been expropriated" (ibid.:49).

The "etatization of time" was much milder in Tito's Yugoslavia than in Ceausescu's Romania, and the Yugoslav socialist "economy of favors" (see Ledeneva 1988) was arguably a relatively stable one, thus affording the majority of citizens a sense of "cognitive well-being" that comes from temporal and other kinds of regularity (Zerubavel 1981:12). It is this cognitive well-being, in my view, that constitutes the main ingredient in the deeply felt, all-embracing notion of "normalcy" so often (longingly) invoked by the citizens of "transitional" societies. Hyperinflation was only the most extreme dislocation of normalcy experienced by citizens under Milošević's rule and its effects were similar to those brought on by Ceausescu's seizure of time in Romania.

Michel de Certeau (1988) celebrated the practices of everyday life as poetic meandering, unorthodox poaching, and inspired improvisation within the confines of the iron cage of a modern-day technological order and its panopticon-like institutions. Citizens of people's democracies were acknowledged adepts of poaching and creative improvisation as they practiced their "economy of favors" (Ledeneva 1988). They could at times be jubilant about a particular coup, a clever ruse that got them some coveted good by unorthodox means, but such everyday tactics were often accompanied by a rueful recognition that one was forced to go through all these contortions in order to survive in an irrational and unpredictable system. When even this relatively stable economy of favors was disrupted by the collapse of socialism (see Pesmen 2000 and Shevchenko 2008) or, more specifically, by Yugoslav wars and hyperinflation in Serbia, the panoptic order of Western democracies such as that which de Certeau decried in France could become an object of idealization and longing. It is as if the citizens of societies in which nothing seems to be functioning are crying, "Give us the grid!"[6]

Lacking a view of the whole, everyday tactics, de Certeau says, "are limited by the blindness resulting from combat at close quarters" (1988:38). Far from resisting some panoptic order, the "combat at close quarters" that citizens engaged in during the everyday madness of 1990s Serbia actually helped maintain a semi-totalitarian dis-order. It could be said that by forcing the majority of the population into an exclusive concern with the "practices of everyday life," Milošević's regime kept a sufficient plurality of people at least temporarily blind to alternatives and thus insured their support for the status quo. Immersion in everyday tactics was at least partially responsible for the increased opacity that society assumed for the majority of ordinary people. This opaqueness, among other things, then stimulated the people's urge to attempt to see through it by means of conspiracy theories which laid the blame for the catastrophic situation on all kinds of actors, international and domestic, thus helping the regime deflect the blame from itself.

The complementary (or contradictory) perception that the regime is all-powerful and that Milošević calls all the shots could also be seen as a conspiracy theory. It has been argued that by positing all-powerful cabals, conspiracy theories induce helplessness, resignation, and despair and thus obstruct organized political action. But, as Knight argues, they "hold somebody responsible" (Knight 1999:45). Dinkić's analysis of the hyperinflation, for instance, could be seen as a conspiracy theory in a social scientific disguise.[7] He argued that a small group of people in the power elite purposefully created the inflationary chaos for its own purposes. His book, after all, was subtitled "The Great Robbery of the People." One could argue that accounts like this only confirm the omnipotence of the regime and drive home the lesson of who holds the levers of power.[8] It is true that even the opposition sometimes endowed the regime with infinite power and cunning that induced resignation. I would suggest, however, that all theories, scientific or popular, that laid the blame for Serbia's predicaments squarely at Milošević's regime were, if not outright truth, then surely a "paranoia within reason" (Marcus 1999) and that, by holding an identifiable group responsible, they did a better job of mobilizing political action than conspiracies involving international agents or domestic surrogates and enemies.

Incisive and sober analyses like that of Dinkić and other commentators and social scientists were perhaps the best antidote to the paralyzing bewilderment combined with the false sense of understanding fostered by the regime-disseminated conspiracy theories. No amount of clear-headed analysis, however, will ever make the society completely transparent to its members. Human collective life, says Simmel, "requires a certain measure of secrecy which merely changes its topics: while leaving one of them, social life seizes upon another, and in all this alternation it preserves an unchanged quantity of secrecy" (1950:335–336). Secrecy, or what I prefer to call "social opacity," is actually an unavoidable, and in a particular Simmelian twist, even a positive phenomenon. A worthwhile question is then whether the conspiracy theories that arise as a way of dealing with this opacity "change their topics" from society to society in a way that illuminates something important about these societies. In a word, do the conspiracy theories, notwithstanding their cognitive "garbledness," and perhaps precisely in virtue of this "garbledness," aspire to a certain "poetic truth."

CONSPIRACY THEORIES AS POETICS OF OPACITY

Milja Vujanović's shows were a prime example of how conspiracy theories played on a strong need of a pariah or "rogue" state to manage its spoiled identity. Paranoia about world conspiracy situated Serbia at the center of that world. Serbia was the "rock" against which the "cart of the New World Order" would break, as the local phrase would have it. There must be something very valuable here in Serbia, so the conspiracy theories implied, if the whole (evil) world conspires to destroy us.

However fantastic these theories appear to be, and notwithstanding their obvious usefulness for Milošević's regime, they could nevertheless be seen as containing a kernel of poetic truth. In the tense weeks before NATO started bombing Yugoslavia in the spring of 1999, a graffiti from a Belgrade wall quickly spread through the Internet circuits. It said: "Mulder, come back—we believe it all."[9] A major locus of American conspiracy theorizing, the X-Files, derived much of its appeal from intentional epistemological ambiguity—always shimmering between credulity and ironic distance. Here it was equally ambiguously and ironically appropriated by a periphery which found itself at the center of the world's attention, as the "largest military alliance in world history" bombed it for more than two months. The idiom was taken from the center, but the viewpoint was peripheral. The message hinted that the truth (about international relations) is "out there" (in Washington, D.C.) and that the paranoia of the periphery might not even be a poetic truth but rather a prosaic commonsense.

On a more micro-social level, in everyday interactions, the persuasive telling of conspiracy theories can endow a teller with a certain authority. Authoritative accounts of the regime's secretive dealings imply that, even as an ordinary citizen not implicated in them, the teller can claim to be close to those supposedly privy to such secret information and thus, by definition, powerful.

Conspiracy theories often work on several levels, which sometimes endows them with multivalency that might justify calling them a poetic genre. At one level, they are stories about the incomprehensible world forces, and about finding human agency and willful action behind these forces. When told by members of a "rogue" or "pariah" state, they usually contain both a claim to victimhood and the perverse pride of being singled out for punishment. Conspiracy theories often imply abdication of personal responsibility and endow secretive authorities with seemingly indestructible power, but they can also provoke action aimed at crushing perceived conspiracies (those local ones, that is, which seem within reach). Conspiracy theories seem to promise great revelations, but they never satisfy. That is why they are so protean. The smugness and authority of a know-it-all (typically a "tavern philosopher") must be constantly undermined by a sense of not understanding and not being in control. Conspiracy theorizing is a futile attempt to master an uncontrollable or incomprehensible situation. It postulates agency everywhere and at the same time bespeaks the real lack of agency experienced by the ordinary citizens of Milošević's (rogue) state.

Poetics also reside in the possibility that the very form of conspiracy theorizing (their "logic") is in some way "functionally autosymbolic" of the social predicament that gives rise to it. "Functional autosymbolism" is the term coined by Herbert Silberer for "the tendency of sleep onset imagery to present not only what one is thinking about (material autosymbols) but formal features of one's cognitive functioning (Hunt 1989:149). In his best-known example, Silberer describes how, while trying to sort out the theories of Kant and Schopenhauer on time, his increasing drowsiness leads him to forget first one, then the other conception. Suddenly he experiences a dreamlike image in which he is asking a morose and uncommunicative secretary for a certain file, which he does not get. (Ibid.:149)

This is, Hunt says, "an excellent metaphor not of his thoughts about time, but of the failure of memory itself" (1989:149). Functional auto-symbolism, in short, is an imagistic self-referential presentation of the mind's own working. In that sense, "much mythology is functionally autosymbolic for the workings of the mind"—an insight shared, as Hunt reminds us, by Freud, Lévi-Strauss, and Jung, among others (150).

Silberer was extremely drowsy when he tried to solve a complex philosophical problem. The dream image that popped into his mind as an autosymbol of this cognitively deficient state was of a typical Central European morose and uncooperative bureaucrat, a figure Kafka made into a famous cypher. Frantic immersion in the everyday of Milošević's Serbia could be seen as a collective equivalent of this cognitively deficient state. You were trying to figure out the convoluted play of politics by simultaneously holding in your mind the gyrations of multiple political actors but you were dreadfully drowsy . . . baroque and bizarre conspiracy theories were then what popped out among the people made "drowsy" in Milošević's Serbia as, among other things, an imagistic self-referential presentation of society's own working. It is in this sense—as a form of communication in which form and content augment each other in ways that cannot be fully explicated—that conspiracy theories could be seen as exhibiting a certain "poetic of opacity."

POSTSCRIPT

The thirteen-year rule of Slobodan Milošević came to an end with the sweeping opposition victory in the September 24, 2000, elections in Yugoslavia, followed by the mass popular protests on October 5 that forced the regime to concede defeat. At first the October Revolution seemed to promise an "unwarping" of the social world and a transition from the poetic genres of baroque conspiracy theories, Jeremiads, and magical realism to the boring prose of the relatively undistorted normal life.

And yet, by 2005, two years after the assassination of Prime Minister Zoran Djindjić, and under the presidency of Vojislav Koštunica, dreamlike images autosymbolizing social opacity seemed to persist. In the *Peščanik* (*The Hourglass*), a weekly Belgrade Radio B92 show that provided a community of commiseration for the marginalized anti-nationalist, decidedly pro-European intelligentsia, the following comment was made on September 16, 2005, regarding the then current slew of government scandals, including high-level corruption in the army, the sacking of a Supreme Court judge, and the trial of Prime Minister Djindjić's assassins. Biljana Kovačević Vučo summarized the situation in an odd image: authorities are throwing sand in the eyes of the public, while whole "logs" (of scandalous doings) fly by us. Far worse, she added, the public, including the parliamentary opposition, wouldn't cry out even if all the "logs" were thrown openly at it. Having sand thrown into their eyes, of course, means that citizens have only the most blurred understanding of what is going on. "We can only guess at [what's really going on], Vučo says,

> but even this vague hint horrifies us while, if we really knew what's going on, I think we'd all emigrate. We are all a bit insane here—we behave so freely because we don't know what's really behind all of this. Sounds like conspiracy theory, but isn't. Otherwise, would this system persist as it is, would we remain as if in Munch's "Scream," always trying to say something, but no sound comes out, or it does come out but produces no effect.

And she then recounts a dream:

> I dreamt of a good friend the other day and I told him—I dreamt of you, we were in some demonstrations, and then you suddenly turned into a little baby . . . and you tried to say something. Something was coming out, I understood him, but it wasn't really articulated. And then I realized that this wasn't my friend, that this was Serbia. We are constantly emitting those screams which just shatter, disappear, produce no effect.

The Hourglass is often rich in metaphors, and this radio commentary was no exception. The editor and host Svetlana Lukić opened it, as usual, with a short gloss on current affairs. The situation Vučo figured as the speck of dust thrown into our eyes by the authorities [so we'll miss the logs flying by us], Lukić describes as our inability to distinguish real bombs from smoke bombs [thrown by the same authorities]. "Is there anyone here, in this little, revolting statelet (*u ovoj maloj, gadnoj zemljici*) who knows what's going on?" she agonizes, and then comes up with this nightmarish image:

> I have to confess I no longer understand. Just when I think I have a key of sorts that could clarify something, it turns out this key isn't opening any doors. I am thinking of that fable about a castle with a thousand rooms, a key in front of every one of them, but the key for some other door. That is, in this parable, no key is wrong, but the problem is we don't know which doors they open, all the keys have been switched around, and so . . . [who wouldn't go insane].

A castle with a thousand rooms and a thousand mismatched keys, a Rubik's cube and a cast of surrogates playing musical chairs, a horrified driver headed for the ditch, silent screaming, mists, slush, and gelatin . . . Stories abounded in Serbia. Some posited entirely reasonable or quite far-fetched conspiracies; others proposed scientific models; and still others proliferated metaphors of inchoateness. Everyone, from the granny in the food line to sophisticated political analysts, wanted to know what was really, really happening. Nobody knew, as if we were all from Kazakhstan . . . or dreaming and trying to wake up.

TEN

Mille vs. Transition

A Super Informant in the Slushy Swamp of Serbian Politics

The temporal "navel" of my research in Serbia was in 1994 and 1995, the time when Milošević decided to force the Bosnian Serbs to consolidate their territorial gains and press for peace. This 180-degree turn toward peace culminated in his signing of the Dayton Peace Accord at the end of 1995. During that period both Jeremiads and conspiracy theories proliferated. Proponents of the theories of "Serbs as the most ancient people" and neo-Byzantinism briefly flourished and then quietly left the limelight around that time, and the culture wars were fought fiercely over turbo-folk. The late 1990s brought the escalation of the Kosovo conflict, massive popular protests against Milošević, and finally the 1999 NATO bombing of Serbia. Milošević was ousted in October 2000 and sent to The Hague. For a while the mood became hopeful. It seemed that Serbia was on its way to normalcy and Europe. This was the time when transition, already under way for more than a decade in the rest of East Europe, started to claim the attention of people in Serbia after having been pushed into the background by the problems of war and national borders. But the shocking assassination of Prime Minister Zoran Djindjić in 2003, coupled with President Koštunica's inability or unwillingness to effect a clear break with the corruption and isolationism of Milošević's regime in the aftermath of the assassination, brought back from the shadows many of the former regime's prominent actors and ushered in what was felt as a return to (or the continuation of) Milošević's "twilight zone" in which criminals were hard to distinguish from businessmen, where the main levers of power were felt to still reside in the hands of state security, and where the pro-European, civic option that felt it had won the day in 2000 again felt increasingly marginalized and threatened. The new conservative nationalist-democratic bloc headed by Koštunica was in rapprochement with the extremely nationalist Serbian Radical Party, and the most conservative currents of the Serbian Orthodox Church were gaining in power and influence. It seemed that bad times were back, that Serbia was (again) stuck in a bad eternity, and Jeremiads proliferated once again. Just when I thought my research into Milošević's Serbia had safely transitioned into the realm of history, Serbia seemed to experience a déjà vu of the 1990s. One aspect, however, was definitely different. New wars were inconceivable, and the really authoritarian regime was definitely out (Milošević died in The Hague in 2006). Kosovo finally declared independence in 2008, but the attempt of Koštunica and his Radical Party allies to whip up nationalist sentiment couldn't quite distract the majority of people from the mundane problems of daily survival. Kosovo was gone, perhaps to remain a sort of "phantom limb" of the national imaginary, but the (delayed) Serbian transition was more directly palpable. When Koštunica and the Radicals were defeated in the 2008 elections by the Democratic Party, and after Radovan Karadžić was subsequently caught and sent to The Hague, the Serbian road to Europe finally seemed at least partially cleared. I will not speculate, however, on where Serbia is headed. Instead, as a kind of coda to this account of Milošević's years, I offer one more glimpse into Serbia wrestling with its transition after Djindjić's assassination. I will introduce a fictional TV character who could serve not only as an avatar of this whole period but also, in a sense, as my most perfect informant. This, moreover, is an opportunity to add a final trope to my tropology— that of "indeterminate irony."

Radio B92, a hero of the anti-Milošević resistance, was a recognized bastion of the anti-nationalist, pro-European segment of the Serbian political spectrum.[1] In 2003 their TV channel started a series called "Mille vs. Transition" that was partially funded by the ProMedia Serbia project sponsored by the U.S. Agency for International Development (USAID) through the International Research and Exchange Board (IREX).[2] The initial series of fifteen-minute episodes written by Srdjan Andjelić, directed by Raša Andrić, and starring the popular actor Zoran Cvijanović as "Mille from Čubura," succeeded beyond expectations. Mille's adventures, idiosyncrasies, and colorful expressions instantly passed into everyday speech, while public intellectuals seized upon Mille in some quite acrimonious polemics about grand issues of national identity and destiny.[3]

Ironies attract sociological imagination. They appear when irresolvable incompatibilities demand to be held together. To social scientists, moreover, they offer an opportunity to show hidden contradictions or unintended consequences of social action and to thus legitimate themselves as revealers of "deeper realities" (see Brown 1997:172–220). The Mille phenomenon caught my attention both because it seemed to present a case of unintended consequences, and because it entailed what Nadkarni (2007) labeled a "refusal of irony." I had already noted such refusal of irony in the way the originator of the term "turbo-folk"— Rambo Amadeus—undermined ironic readings of his unmistakably parodic performances (see Živković 2011), and to detect another refusal of irony in Serbia seemed to point to a trend or a useful diagnostic for that hard-to-characterize state that Serbia found itself in after Milošević's fall in 2000 and Prime Minister Zoran Djindjić's assassination in 2003. It is with an eye on such diagnostic potential that I will try to unpack Mille from Čubura as a hieroglyph of post-Djindjić Serbia.

In the opening episode of the series, we see how the camera crew enters Mille's apartment and finds him lovingly cleaning his favorite armchair—looted from the Parliament building during the "October Revolution" of 2000 that removed Milošević from power. The armchair sports a seatbelt from a car that Mille installed so he could prevent himself from destroying his precious TV set when he gets upset by the program. At the same time, however, he refuses to wear a seatbelt in his run-down Renault 4, as civilized Europe now demands. Instead, he sews a seatbelt onto his T-shirt to fool the cops and sells it on the street. Consistency is not Mille's strong suit.

He lives in Čubura, one of the central parts of Belgrade near the largest Belgrade farmer's market—the *Kalenić pijaca*. He has a plump wife and a baby son. He often assaults the camera in fits of rage, only to reappear on the screen after he "resets" himself by dangling a pair of traditional Serbian peasant leather sandals (*opanci*) in front of his eyes like a hypnotist's watch. He is outraged and insulted by this *new* thing called "transition." He was, he says often, against the *old* order, of course, but this *new* one is so disappointing, so demeaning, so threatening and bad that he has to exclaim: "It was better when it was worse!" That "worse" is, of course, the often unnamed but clearly indicated Milošević period.

Mille is shocked to learn in the news that the sacred word *inat* (obstinacy, doing things for spite, just to act contrary, often with obvious harmful consequences) that denotes the very core of the Unique Serbian Character is now officially purged from the vocabulary.[4] He then successfully promotes the equivalent Serbian word, since, after all, *inat* is a Turkish loanword—the new word is a rather rude version of what in English would be "cockiness" with the same etymology (*kurčenje*).

Like some local Don Quixote, Mille takes on Transition head-on, sometimes single-handedly and sometimes with the help of sympathetic neighbors and fellow citizens similarly stricken. In the first episode he mounts a campaign to obstruct the conversion of Deutsche Marks into Euros; in another he tries, but finally gives up, studying English, since the damn foreigners actually understand Serbian—if you only talk to them very slowly and loudly. Mille is highly suspicious when his otherwise uncouth, gruff fellow citizens suddenly start behaving super politely—for to behave in such a "European" way is to betray our own national character. He is intensely nostalgic for numerous state holidays of Tito's era and shamelessly indulges in Yugonostalgia. Instead of watching Latin American telenovellas like everyone else, he is addicted to the interminable TV coverage of The Hague tribunal that induces a nightmare where he finds himself in the same cell with Milošević as his accomplice.

The series took off in a way that must have surprised the authors. Overnight Mille became a sort of national hero; his tricks and turns of phrase become part of everyday speech. A curious thing seems to have happened. Mille was explicitly intended as a parody. As the actor who plays Mille—Zoran Cvijanović—said in an interview, "Our aim was to combine all the worst traits of our mentality in Mille. We wanted people to recognize themselves in Mille's traits and to warn them, in an entertaining way, not to give in to those traits, not to lose control and become—Mille" (Cvijanović 2005). This parodic intent of the series, however, seemed to have offered a point around which playing with a variety of ironic positions became a great communicative resource—a way for many to nuance their own position in the Serbian "quality space" and put down opponents with nimble footwork. The following schema of typical positionings toward Mille, which I distilled from the B92 Internet forum discussion of the series, will help make sense of what this footwork entailed.[5]

1. The first position puts down the masses who supposedly don't get the message of the series. The masses are seen as seriously embracing their own caricature, and the series' authors are criticized for overestimating the intelligence of their own audience.

1a. A more sophisticated variant of this position imputes this view to others, not oneself. For instance, someone will report that his father (in his sixties) is worried that the people will actually follow Mille's advice and resist change (such as accepting various European Union standards of behavior). The writer's position remains unstated—it is not clear whether he thinks the masses are or are not "that stupid." This is a clever position, because it allows a rather simple elitist position—"masses are literal-minded"—to be unloaded onto the older generation while the speaker is free to adopt a more flexible position (such as 2 or 4 below).

2. The series is vulgar, in bad taste, the script and acting are bad, and so on. This is a move in a Bourdieuian game of distinction that puts the author of such judgments of taste above even the B92 authors in terms of cultural capital. Since B92 is considered to be at the far extreme of urban, pro-European cosmopolitanism, this position entails that even B92 is not cosmopolitan enough.

3. A stance that takes Mille as yet another indicator of the way the urban cosmopolitan intelligentsia (exemplified by B92) shows how much they despise their own people. This is the stance that in its more extreme variants sees B92 as a "missionizing" elite, deracinated traitors to the nation and mercenaries of the West. This position is more characteristic of serious public debates than of Internet forums, and it usually entails a rhetorical identification with Mille but no real enjoyment, or playful idolizing, of his character.

4. "I love Mille, I can't help it. Let someone lend me more brains so I can see what Mille looks like from the viewpoint of an intelligent

person."[6] This is a dig at position 1 above. Here is a joyful embrace of Mille and mock acceptance of the "stupid Serbian everyman who takes Mille seriously" persona. It punctures elitist pretensions of positions 1 and 2, without getting into the serious populist positioning and conspiracy theorizing of position 3. In many variants of this position Mille is embraced with a kind of defiant enthusiasm and exaggeration that suggests ironic or parodic distancing. Yet the irony is not aimed at the simpleton who doesn't get Mille as ironically intended but rather at those who get the ironic intent of B92 but claim that the masses don't. This is also potentially a position of those who realize that any simple positioning is not adequate to the morally ambiguous Serbian situation. We can call this position (or family of positions) *indeterminate irony.* Its adroit oscillation between irony and its refusal exhibits certain affinities with other idioms of coping with the murkiness of the Serbian situation. Mille apparently lent himself admiringly to these types of footwork and that's probably one of the secrets of his unforeseen success.

The Mille phenomenon was debated not only on Internet forums such as the one on the B92 website but also on the pages of serious periodicals such as *Nova srpska politička misao (New Serbian Political Thought)*[7] and *Vreme*. The absolute virtuoso of scorn for all that Mille stood for must certainly be the social commentator from the weekly *Vreme*, Teofil Pančić, the sarcastic champion of precisely the political option embodied in B92. In the January 15, 2004, issue of *Vreme* Teofil devotes a whole column to Mille, titled "Mille from Čubura in the Government." The thesis is that even though the actual Mille on TV, "is constantly frustrated, nervous, shouting, lonely and misunderstood, like some Last Mohican of the 'Old World Order'—in the actual Serbian reality "Mille's agenda is faring not so badly at all." The Serbian collective-Mille is wooed by most politicians, and he "generously returns their compliments with his votes." So in the last elections, "the Mille-voter voted for those who promised him that we actually don't need any transition, or that it would be done painlessly, so that he, Mille, doesn't feel a thing" (Pančić 2004).

In Mille's head is "piled up the *nuclear waste* of the brainwashing nineties." Soon, Teofil says, "if this geometrical progression of *legitimization of organized stupidity as incomparable killing machine* continues,

Those Who Are Not Mille will again become just a stray sect, a miniature island in the ocean of *neochuburian zombies*" (Pančić 2004).

Exactly a year later, at the conclusion of the first series, Teofil produced a more in-depth analysis of Mille. He trusts no one who arrogantly claims zero percentage of Mille in his blood: "We are all, at least a little bit, infected by that virus, the only thing is whether we are trying to cure ourselves or are perfectly happy to be as we are." Mille is "(anti)stylized and exaggerated but is much closer to the 'realistic' photo robot of 'Our Man, here & now' than any previous comic embodiment of the national character. He does not 'resemble' any single individual—confess, you've never met a colorful cretin of such caliber before—but in what he's saying and what he's indicating as our Sore Spot, he becomes an unpolished relative of 'all of us,' more or less" (Pančić 2005).

> Mille is a reflection of a dominant *conformist eclecticism:* dabble-pondering[8] everything in this post-ideological era, he picks a little here, a little there, resembling a merry fellow who likes both wine and beer, and so layers one with another until he pukes. (Ibid.)

Beer and wine do not mix according to the native ethno-physiology of drinking, and one could easily point to "puking" as Teofil's own (metaphoric) gut reaction to the mixing of unmixables that functions as a move in a Bourdieuian game of distinction (the masses mix, the cultured discriminate). I actually think that Teofil's footwork is sufficiently nimble to allow him to dance away from the extremes of the elitist position I labeled as No. 1, because his colorful exaggerations could be interpreted as subtly ironic. Nevertheless, his position has been taken as a blatant example of the "missionizing" elite stance of despising the Serbian everyman. Teofil's analysis of Mille thus offered a pretext for yet another salvo in the war of words provoked by Slobodan Antonić's article, "The Missionizing Intelligentsia in Contemporary Serbia" (Antonić 2003).[9]

Without going into arcane details of Serbian politics, I summarize this polemic as being essentially about elite being (or not being) in tune with their own people (in the double meaning of both ethnic nation and the common folk conveyed by the single Serbian word *narod*). People like Teofil were accused of having a lower opinion of their own people than even the colonizing missionaries had of savages they had set out to deliver from their primitive, pagan ways. So angry were the Serb "missionaries" when their own people failed to appreciate their efforts, Antonić argued, that "they would go so far as to openly invite occupation by 'civilized foreigners'" (Antonić 2003). The "missionizing" intelligentsia, according to Antonić, thinks that their own people is essentially primitive, anti-modern, and non-European that it collectively suffers from nationalism, and that this sickness may require drastic cures—from book banning and imprisonment to foreign intervention. Instead, Antonić, and those affiliated with his position at the political science journal *New Serbian Political Thought,* advocate a "truly democratic pluralism" that would tolerate all the various manifestations of Serbian national ideology in the name of freedom of speech. Missionaries are proclaimed dogmatic and intolerant (even likened to old-time Communists) when they denounce excesses of Serbian nationalism. The problem is that these excesses include the promotion of openly fascistic ideologies and, most important, serious war crimes. In short, Antonić et al., try to present the "missionizing intelligentsia" as, at best, hysterical despisers of their own people and, at worst, betrayers of their nation.[10] For one side, to be truly democratic is to be anti-nationalistic and European; for the other side, sometimes labeled "national democrats," democracy is only true if it is true to a particular people/nation and its "national interests." For the "missionaries," however, "national democracy" is a dangerously misleading oxymoron; it is an ideology more dangerous than outspoken Serbian nationalism, because it presents the same extreme values under the guise of moderation and rationality.

It should now be clearer why Mille could act as a "lightning rod" in a political arena vexed by such dilemmas. If you see him as a "neo-chuburian zombie" you are clearly a condescending "missionary," and if you rhetorically identify with him, you are on the side of true national democracy and in tune with *vox populi.*[11]

MILLE SETS AN INDETERMINATE IRONY IN MOTION

Most of those who used Mille in everyday conversations, I would say, found him such an apt figure, so rich as a communicative resource, not just because of the content of what he does and says but because of the ironic play he affords. It is precisely this ambiguity, this *indeterminate irony,* that makes him such an icon of Serbia's predicaments of that time.

Asserting identity or solidarity with Mille among those who have certain cultural capital could be read both as irony or as camp—thus as a condescension toward, and implicit criticism of, all that Mille stands for, on the one hand, or as *complicity* nested within that condescension and critique, on the other. Indeterminate irony is an elusive beast—it involves both the practitioners and their audience in an irresolvable loop that could perhaps be formulated as the following chiasmus—critique of complicity/complicity of critique.

Perhaps this is the irony of complicity that involves the complicity of irony—for isn't that one of the possible interpretations of what Burke called the true or classic irony, the one "based upon a sense of fundamental kinship with the enemy, as one needs him, is indebted, is not merely outside him as an observer but contains him within, being consubstantial with him" (Burke 1969:514). What if Mille is our enemy, but we also suspect that we have a fundamental kinship with him, that we have more than a zero content of Mille in our blood, as Teofil would say? Are we then not also complicit with Mille even as we pour our sarcastic scorn upon him?

Teofil exploits the rhetorical resources of such ambiguous positioning, playing with the possibility that even he might have some Mille in his blood. His sarcasm might then also be layered with a dose of Burke's humble irony. Beyond that ironic ambiguity and perhaps even beyond camp, there lies the move Nadkarni (2007) calls "refusal of irony." This is a position that implies the sophistication of the ironist but snubs his elitism. The joyful embrace of Mille in Serbia then exhibits a pleasure that to a large extent seems to consist not so much in watching Mille but in "watching ourselves enjoying him—enjoying him as if he were authentic" (Nadkarni 2007:623).

Mille seems to offer himself to such ambiguous ironic uses. And it is because he seems to readily generate these ambiguities that he can be used as a figure of what is perceived as a particularly ambiguous political situation. Indeterminate irony is a symptom of a certain state of social being. Just as there was something in the way of being of socialism that spawned such rich a harvest of convoluted irony in literature,[12] so post-Milošević, post-Djindjić Serbia seems to have spawned the Mille phenomenon. This is more than just a symptom, a diagnostic. It is also a trope, a way such societies spontaneously fashion or latch onto figures for their own inchoately felt predicaments. Mille is thus a figure, not just a metaphor but something more complex, perhaps an ironic chiasmus, for the social realities of present-day Serbia. In the very formal structure of the indeterminate irony it has set in motion, moreover, the Mille phenomenon parallels that of other tropes or idioms people in Serbia have been using to make sense of their social reality.

A lot of these tropes or idioms turn out to be bizarre, outlandish, and strange. Conspiracy theories and tropes of amorphous substances, for instance, were a way to figure the "opacity of Milošević's Serbia." Amorphous substances like mud, slush, mists, and gelatin were often overdetermined as metaphors—that is, they figured both the "opacity of the political life" and another genre—that of the peculiar in-betweenness felt so often in the peripheries of Europe (and elsewhere). The spatial idioms of this in-betweenness underlie Serbian "symbolic geography," while the temporal idioms abound with images of "missing the [Euro] train, "catching up," and, in the Serbian case, most often of being "stuck" in some sort of twilight state of "bad eternity." These figures often try to capture a peculiar sense of being in the neither-here-nor-there state rather than of inhabiting the extremes of any "metaphoric continua" (Fernandez 1986). Thus the ubiquitous fairy-tale image of the "castle neither in the sky nor on the ground" (*čardak ni na nebu ni na zemlji*), the whole family of "half-bakedness" tropes, the notion of the Bearable Evil of Tito's communism or Milošević's rule, and the images of slumber—neither fully asleep nor fully awake. Teofil's columns are rife with these idioms. Recall the *"neochuburian zombies"* besieging the small stray sect of "Those Who Are Not Mille," in the post-Djindjić "swamp full of croaking dwarfs" where "there is no more space for an honest, spectacular fall—only for quiet, eternal rotting" (Pančić 2004).

A METHODOLOGICAL POSTSCRIPT: MILLE AS A
ONE-MAN PUBLIC OPINION AND A SUPER INFORMANT

In an episode titled "Public Opinion," Mille complains that nobody polls him, nobody phones to ask his opinion. At the end of the episode he succeeds beyond expectations—he becomes the *only* person public opinion surveyors call. Blissful, surrounded by telephones that constantly ring, he becomes a one-man Serbian public opinion. Being a photo-robot, the ultimate eclectic, as Teofil would say, Mille is then a generator of all the possible positions a citizen of Serbia might have on any burning question of the day. Obviously a sting aimed at polling and public opinion research, this episode could also be seen as aimed at ethnographic research and its fetishization of the native informant.

Mille is (supposedly) an impossible combination of contradictory traits; he is an *everyman,* a *conformist eclectic* merrily combining wine and beer until he pukes. He is a *photo-robot* of the Homo Serbicus Vulgaris, whether you despise him or identify with him. Isn't he then a kind of super informant? If some Boasians, in their more extreme moods, claimed that they could distill a whole culture out of a single informant, perhaps the whole of Serbia's social and political life in the last twenty or so years could be distilled from Mille.

Though individual stories and positionings I encountered were in one sense quite particular, even sometimes surprising in their idiosyncrasy, in another sense they were variations that combined a finite number of prefabricated elements that were more or less easily traceable to the output of mass media. Creativity and uniqueness belonged to the individual bricoleurs, but the junkyard Serbia was a common source for the individual projects of all.

Mille is perhaps, among other things, a good figure to think with or ponder what it is that anthropologists expect from their informants. Here he is, utterly ordinary and average, in his home and neighborhood, his natural everyday habitat, talking often in fits of impotent rage about important things that bother him. And he is a human kaleidoscope of media fragments that settle in different patterns according to the situation. There is hardly a cliché current in Serbia of the last twenty years that he doesn't use, hardly a conspiracy theory he doesn't subscribe to, a form of nostalgia he doesn't espouse at one moment or another. A human chameleon, he is both against Milošević and rooting for him, both against that Old Order when it was much worse and at the same time complaining that it was better when it was worse. He was obviously meant to be tongue-in-cheek, but he offered unexpected possibilities of ambiguous, indeterminately ironic identifications. And that indeterminately ironic play, nausea-producing as it might be, offers such a good parallel to the very pragmatics of taking a stance in a morally murky, twilight, neither-here-nor-there situation, a veritable "slushy zombie marsh of eternal torpor and rotting," as Serbia was so often portrayed by its (more verbally creative) citizens.

In fact, my research in Milošević's and post-Milošević Serbia drove home to me that the ability to simultaneously hold incompatible views is a normal human situation. It is only a special training in, and sustained focus on, coherence that makes incoherence induce symptoms of motion sickness. In the end I suspected that most people, most of the time, are in fact rather like Mille. In politically extremely unsettled situations like the one in Serbia, and particularly in the acts of political self-position-ing, our minds are perhaps like kaleidoscopes, filled not with regularly shaped colored glass but with irregularly shaped pieces of conspiracy theories, incompatible ideologies, and various other media junk, with the prism itself irregular and changing, so that the result is not beautiful configurations but different grotesqueries. These grotesqueries, however, in their very form, could also be seen as poetic statements on the inco-herence, opacity, and grotesqueness of the social world or, alternatively, as its dreamlike functional autosymbols.

Conclusion

Chrono-tropes and Awakenings

In conclusion, if I had to summarize in one sentence, I would say that it has all been about an exaggerated, larger-than-life, megalomaniacal story of Serbian innocent victimhood. It started with Kosovo and it ended in Kosovo—Kosovo as both a concrete place and the central imaginary topos of the Serbian ethnonationalist myth. This story should not be seen as a prime mover with a force of its own but rather as the main source of slogans for political rhetoric. It was promoted by identifiable individuals and served mundane political agendas that, given the context, have to be seen as instrumentally rational. The mythical victimhood story rested on real Serbian grievances and claims which, in the context of the unraveling common state, had been as legitimate as competing grievances and claims of other national groups in Yugoslavia. This exaggerated sense of victimhood, however, and especially the unwillingness to recognize the suffering of others, helped the Serbian authorities legitimate the violence in Croatia, Bosnia, and, finally, in Kosovo itself, at least to their own population.

That a sufficient majority was sufficiently enthralled by such a victimization tale to invest a communist apparatchik with the charisma of a savior, bring him to power in the late 1980s, and give him enough votes in the next twelve or so years to keep him more or less legitimately in the saddle is something that people in Serbia still have to come to terms with. There has been, fortunately, no lack of voices in Serbia throughout this period who called on their fellow citizens to find the responsibility for the disaster much closer to home rather than in some worldwide conspiracy.

Perhaps the central story of the whole Milošević period was a tale of how an obsession with big stories led to disaster. Big myths and ideological concepts have almost always been harmful to normal human beings, notes Vladimir Pištalo.

> They produce phrases which suffocate life. There is an amusing anecdote from the First World War. When the fighting started, French intellectuals hurried to the front lines to talk to soldiers who "actually experienced" the war. The wounded soldiers, however, responded not with what they actually experienced but with phrases they picked up from the newspapers. We are ourselves such sloganeering casualties (*ranjenici koji fraziraju*). (interview in *Vreme*, no. 304)

The word "phraseologize," or "sloganeer" (*frazirati*), of course, first of all recalls the empty and circumlocutory double-talk of the communist years. The fiery slogans coined by nationalist poets and writers were initially seen by many as a powerful antidote to that double-talk, but they turned out to be as life-suffocating, and certainly more dangerous than the communist ones.

A megalomaniacal obsession with History and Destiny is often seen as an ineradicable Serbian national trait. In that, Serbs often implicitly or explicitly contrast themselves with Czechs, who bow down and preserve life rather than make suicidal choices. Serbs are enamored of the grandeur of lost battles; Czechs attend to the "small work" of everyday life. This notion is well encapsulated in one of the rare pithy phrases that actually comes from Milošević himself rather than from the professional wordsmiths. In a meeting with municipality leaders in 1991, at the moment his power was threatened for the first time (with the March 9 demonstrations), Milošević famously said: "If we don't know how to work, at least we'll know how to fight" (*Ako ne umemo da radimo i privredjujemo, bar ćemo znati dobro da se tučemo*). In the aftermath of the 1999 NATO bombing, Stojan Cerović, perhaps the best social analyst of the period, provided a fitting postmortem to the whole Serbian "lost decade" by inverting Milošević's statement. After the bombing, he said,

The deepest, most important experience will be something that could be called the exit from history . . . Serbia will have nothing great to say to the world, there will be no reasons for big sacrifices and privations, which means that the profits of patriotic business will fall, and citizens will slowly learn to pay attention to things like taxes and interest rates. Absence of history will cause an abstinence crisis for a while, and everything will look trivial, small-minded, and meaningless to Serbs, but we should get used to that . . . Finally, isn't it high time, after all, for Serbs to show what they can do, when [they have proven that] they don't know how to fight? (*Najzad, zar nije vreme da Srbi pokažu šta umeju, kad već ne umeju da se biju?*). (Cerović 1999)

Anthropological accounts often derive their appeal from presenting a potentially edifying story of a consistent but different way a certain group of people copes with exigencies of life. Occasionally these exigencies become so extreme as to constitute a kind of "natural sociological experiment" that should teach us something significant about the human condition. Serbia of the 1990s has arguably presented such an experiment, but I find it hard to derive an edifying story from it. There is, consequently, no simple closure to my "story." In this sense, this whole book could be read as yet another Serbian Jeremiad.

This lack of narrative closure characteristic of Serbian Jeremiads, however, could also be seen as a chrono-trope—a way in which what we social scientists abstractly call "temporality" manifests itself in everyday life.[1] And just as different narrative shapes are a way of figuring shapes of lived time, so, too, can various temporalities be discerned in the whole family of sleep-dream-awakening tropes, and this is one of the reasons why Serbian imaginary may be seen as a "dreambook."

This dreambook opened with a Belgrade man waking up one morning in early July 1975 to the rasping voice of Duško Radović, who congratulated him on this great accomplishment and assured him he need not do anything else this day—it is plenty enough just to have awakened in Belgrade. In 1938, some thirty-seven years before that morning of 1975, in his *Essay on the Belgrade Man,* Vladimir Velmar-Janković compared Belgrade to a mill for producing a Belgrade Man out of a Serbian peasant, a mill that is "not up to speed, with new additives constantly tried out, the miller himself still at a loss, the grindstone not yet of the right weight and properly adjusted" (1992:32).

Those lucky to wake up in Belgrade in 1975 were, by implication, the relatively recent arrivals from the countryside. There is a sense in Radović's gentle rebuke that they are quite at ease with themselves—they have arrived, they have accommodated. It seems that, by 1975, the miller has adjusted his grindstone and that it is now up to speed. But other grindstones, in 1975, are grinding away in the distance as our Belgrade newcomer wakes up from his sweet dreams. According to Verdery, this is precisely the time when socialist elites discover the foreign loans. It is also the moment in capitalism's own cyclicity that makes the West eager to lend. This fateful interface with capitalism, Verdery argues, was crucial for the fall of socialism. The gears of capitalism were speeding up, and when the ever so slow gears of socialism engaged them, the result was a sort of asynchrony within socialism itself. It was as if the internal cogs of socialism started spinning at different speeds. Socialism fell, says Verdery, because of "the collision of two differently constituted temporal orders, together with the notions of person and activity proper to them . . . Because the leaders accepted Western temporal hegemony, socialism's messianic time proved apocalyptic" (1996:37).

In Yugoslavia, its own particular version of socialist temporalities gave way to the temporalities of nationalistic mobilization in the late 1980s and to temporalities of war in the 1990s. The citizens of Serbia also experienced the utterly bewildering temporalities of one of the highest hyperinflations in recorded history. Finally, in 2000, as Milošević's regime fell, they emerged into transition proper, a decade after the rest of East Europe. At the beginning of the twenty-first century these temporalities coexisted in Serbia—the nationalist phantasmagorias, socialist nostalgias, delayed transition. Catching up with Europe seemed near at hand in the first euphoria after Milošević's fall, but then, after the 2003 assassination of the Prime Minister Zoran Djindjić, it seemed as though the undead of the previous era were back again. How were the collisions of these temporalities experienced?

First a brief and quite provisional classification of temporalities. When Verdery talks of the two temporal orders, she means something like the large-scale rhythms and schedules of production, consumption, or leisure, and how they relate to individual subjectivity. If we distinguish between socialist and capitalist, and between societal and personal rhythms, we can ask how the collision of the large-scale temporalities of capitalism and socialism affects the individual insofar as the individual sense of person, agency, and subjectivity is influenced by their daily rhythms and schedules. In my metaphor, as the large cogwheels (and cogwheels within cogwheels) of capitalism and socialism mesh together more or less asynchronously, they grind the little man between their teeth. How does it feel to be ground up in that way?

On the other hand, Verdery mentions messianic and apocalyptic times of socialism. This type of temporality is a narrative shape rather than a matter of daily rhythms and schedules—a kind of "national biography" with Golden Ages, Falls from Grace, Exoduses, and other Tragic Travails, Valiant Struggles, Resurrections, Redemptions, and Radiant Futures forever threatened with Apocalypses. These are grand historical narratives that live in history textbooks, public commemorations, in the landscape, museums, and monuments. Our personal narratives, however, are anchored in collective frameworks of memory—a realm we should distinguish from official national biography or history. Svetlana Boym, for instance, distinguishes collective memory, "the common landmarks of everyday life," from national memory, even if they may "share images and quotations" (Boym 2001:53).

The newcomer to Belgrade who woke up to Radović's *Good Morning, Belgrade* in 1975 had internalized the rhythms and schedules of Tito's socialist Yugoslavia. Life to him appeared more or less "normal." This sense of normalcy gets disrupted in decades to come in various ways— both by the grindstones of capitalist rhythms and by the changes in national narrative shapes.

One of the main slogans of Milošević's national mobilization campaign in the late eighties was "Serbia has risen" (*Srbija je ustala*). The word, just as in English, can mean both to literally get up and stand straight or to get up after sleep. This "rise," in retrospect, proved to be an "awakening" into a nightmare, a nightmare that, in its turn, required a very different kind of "awakening." Urging this kind of awakening from the mythical narrative of the nation, a slogan from the 1996–97 anti-Milošević demonstrations in Serbia ironically suggested: "Serbia has risen—brew her some coffee!" (*Ustala je Srbija. Skuvajte joj kafu!*).

Instead of getting up and drinking a good cup of black Turkish coffee in order to get ready for the rhythms of flexible capitalism that (delayed) transition now demanded of Serbian citizens, our Belgrade man was treated to yet another round of national agonizing over the loss of Kosovo, refusals to hand over war-crime suspects to The Hague, interminable trials for Djindjić's assassins, and so on.

When in that atmosphere Biljana Kovačević Vučo told her dream about a friend turning into a baby on the *Hourglass* radio show in 2005, the important part was not so much the dream itself but the way it was used to express something about "Serbia." Something about Serbia at that moment made Vučo identify it with the screaming baby deprived of articulation in her dream. Svetlana Lukić's castle with a thousand rooms and a thousand scrambled keys could also perhaps be seen as a dream image.

The typical guests of *Hourglass,* as a particular type of European-oriented humanistic intellectual elite, tended to feel they were caught in a nightmare and wanted to wake up. They were forever searching for appropriate keys to open the thousand locked doors of the castle neither in the sky nor on the ground called Serbia. They posited themselves as awakeners of the slumbering masses toward whom they expressed an ambivalent mixture of anger, contempt, and compassion. For these were the masses of ordinary citizens who, in their struggle for everyday existence, had gotten used to the scandalous incongruities of life in Serbia and no longer noticed that anything was amiss (or so the awakeners liked to think). The *Hourglass* guests are also ordinary citizens subject to the same sleeping potions, but, as the opposition intelligentsia, they feel a duty to constantly pinch themselves in order to stay awake in the country of the slumbering—for who else will be left to shout that this is all indeed a bad dream.

And the time to finally wake up is running out, as the very symbol of the hourglass suggests. Awaken to what? Not to the national destiny obscured by fifty years of communist ideology or by globalizing forces of the New World Order. This type of awakening was the self-appointed task of the nationalist intelligentsia. The awakening that *Hourglass* guests have in mind is precisely to awake from these grand myths of national destiny and enter some sort of European Union temporality. To awake into this temporality, however, is to awake "downstream," as Fabian (1983) puts it, in regard to this idealized Europe that is always ahead, impossible to catch up to. Laments are then born about Serbia being forever stuck in time, "mired in bad eternity." This stasis temporality corresponds, then, to the intermediary states between sleep/dream and waking—a family of slumber or torpor metaphors.

We often get our metaphors from machines we make, but we also tend to use these metaphors long after the machines themselves had become obsolete. Velmar-Janković talked of mills and grindstones in an age of gears; I talked of gears in the age of transistors; and we are now in the age of computers, and yet it is trains[2] and cars that still supply us with our most trusted metaphors for synchronies and asynchronies.

Tamara Milekić (2004) plays both on cars and tropes of twilight, slumber and nightmare, in her essay, "Serbia Is a Big Trouble" (*Srbija je velika nevolja*). "Serbia has arrived at a tacit agreement," she writes, "to rest a little bit longer, to let pass yet another circle in the race it dropped out of, anyway, a long time ago.

> It is natural to feel sick to your stomach when you are put on the starting line of a race you never ran before, that everything depends on, and for which you are very badly prepared. You know you have to run, as slug-gish and clumsy as you are, while beside you, all turbo-monsters with a thousand kilometers in their feet. It is normal to want to run away back to your cozy warm hole . . . It is so childish to think that it is enough to close your eyes, curl up in your doll house, and everything will pass . . . It's impossible that Serbs don't know this, yet, nevertheless, they have decided to try it one more time. Imagine a Formula 1 race driver who enters his box to change tires, and then, elegantly, opens his doors, gets out of the car, and with a nonchalant gesture calms down his panicked team—Lay off with these stopwatches. Let's relax a little, let's have a bite and a drink. Cool off kids, it's not that the house is burning! And then, leaning on the fence and gazing at the racecourse, he notices something nobody has noticed before. That everyone anyway drives in circles. And that therefore it makes no difference when he'll rejoin the race. In five seconds or five minutes, it doesn't matter, when he is ready, when he is not sleepy, when his stomach stops hurting, when he gathers his determination, then he will join in. (Milekić 2004)

The engineer Margulies from Kataev's 1932 social-realist novel *Time, Forward!* always gets up at six in the morning, and he doesn't need the alarm clock. He is an exemplary shock worker, disdaining the mere ra-tional time-discipline of capitalism (Kataev 1933; also in Hanson 1997). Our Serbian man addressed by Milekić has long forgotten the Yugoslav equivalent of storming from the period of socialist "renewal and rebuilding" (*obnova i izgradnja*) of the 1940s and 1950s. He was most likely not even born then, but it is quite possible that he was contentedly waking up in Belgrade at 8:00 AM to the sound of Radović's *Good Morning, Belgrade* in 1975. And if he was preparing to go to school on that morning in 1975, he is now approximately the age of Mille from Čubura.

In the episode titled "Bensedin" Mille bemoans the worst knockout blow that the transition has delivered to date—the beloved tranquilizer Bensedin is no longer available over the counter (as it is heavily addictive). This, he says, was the only thing that helped us survive all these years. How easy it was then to climb to his apartment on the fourth floor, he reminisces, as he chews black market Bensedin and knocks down "Pino Silvestre" after-shave as a substitute. This goes on for minutes and minutes, while he is talking, gesticulating and climbing a dilapidated (but beautiful) circular staircase in the twilight. And he arrives, exhausted, at the second floor, and then, after a lot more climbing, he arrives at—the second floor, and then again at the second floor, in a Kafkaesque approximation to the unreachable Castle. They gave me the Chinese (ersatz Bensedin), he finally concludes. But it is not the bad drug that's the point here, it is the image of time.

In the episode "A Campaign against Violence," Mille plans to use a technique suggested by a friend in order to put his little baby son to sleep—a little poke between the eyes with a small rubber hammer that will "reset" him. The baby falls asleep at the mere sight of the hammer, "as if by remote," Mille notices with awe. However, after the baby starts screaming again, joined by his wife from the bedroom, and after the Milošević-era TV news jingles arranged in an endless video loop (guaranteed to put you into a trance) fail to put the baby to sleep, out of sheer exasperation Mille hits himself between the eyes so as to reset.

With resetting, we have finally arrived at a more contemporary kind of metaphor. Instead of grindstones and gears, hourglasses and alarm clocks, instead of trains and cars—the computers. The computer Mille invokes is a notoriously jury-rigged PC, most likely full of pirated software and riddled with viruses.[3] It constantly crashes and freezes. Mille's head is full of socialist and nationalist narratives layered atop one another. Moreover, his rhythms and daily schedules are changing. He anxiously feels that the transition is pushing him to the "starting line of a race he has never run before, that everything depends on, and for which he is very badly prepared." If only he could reset and wake up one morning in Belgrade as a fully adjusted citizen of the European Union—he would then feel that he has accomplished enough in his life for that day. To insist on something else in addition would be immodest.

NOTES

Introduction

1. See, among others, Glenny 1992; Thompson 1992; Cohen 1993; Woodward 1995; Silber and Little 1996; Allcock 2000; Nikolić 2002; Gagnon 2004; Cohen and Soso 2008; and Jović 2009.

2. I do this in some detail in Živković 2006a.

3. My short account in Živković 2006a of the vicissitudes of dream in the history of anthropology offers some glimpses into such mappings.

4. For predicaments of native ethnographers, see Abu-Lughod 1991; Altorki and El-Solh 1988; Barrios 1994; Bennoune 1985; Brettell 1993; Fahim 1982; Kondo 1990; Messerschmidt 1981; Narayan 1993; Ohnuki-Tierney 1984; and Srnivas 1967. See also Živković 2000.

5. In their highly acclaimed book on the criminal underworld two journalists characterized Belgrade of the 1990s as a city that "fused together Chicago of the 1920s, the economic crisis of Berlin in the 1930s, the espionage intrigues of Casablanca in the 1940s, and the cataclysmic hedonism of Vietnam in the 1960s" (Knežević and Tufegžić 1995). Gangsterism combined with hyperinflation, murky behind-the-scenes dealings, and desperate merriment on the brink of catastrophe. Now these are all time-worn journalistic clichés. To claim that Belgrade of the 1990s condensed them all was to combine rueful self-criticism with a sort of perverse pride. The situation was bad, but in that badness there was something colorful, exotic, or even grand—a claim to fame even if that fame was based on infamy.

6. I mix metaphors purposely. As Dale Pesmen put it: "Once a metaphor has been predicated, engaging in another image-union seems to adulterate the first world, diminishing its realism, that is, its ability to persuade us. After several such leaps, critics of mixed metaphor move from moral censure to motion sickness, alleging nauseating ontological and rhetorical shiftiness . . . Foucault says that Borges' "Chinese encyclopedia's" juxtaposed points of view make us aware of *our* thought's limitations. Mixed metaphor's images similarly defy us to understand "where we stand," as Foucault calls it, *the site* on which propinquity of these things would be possible. But maybe we're never standing like that anyway. Maybe where we're standing, legs aren't enough (Pesmen 2000: 3–4; see also Pesmen 1991 & 2000a). By mixing metaphors I want to signal that I too, as well as my informants may not have had a "place to stand" in Serbia.

1. Belgrade

1. *Sat, čarape, papuče, sapun, česma, džezva, kafa, šećer, kašika, čizme, burek, jogurt, pare, džep, kusur, dućan, duvan, torba, kafana, rakija, sevdah.* These words either have no other equivalents in Serbian and are normally not perceived as Turkish, or sound more natural, ordinary, and intimate than their Slavic or non-Turkish synonyms.

2. Serbia's Position in European Geopolitical Imaginings

1. Between 1941 and 1944 Velmar-Janković held a high position in the Ministry of Education of the German-installed Serbian government of Milan Nedić. He died in a car accident in Barcelona where he lived most of his life in exile.

2. Not the least of these advantages was the ethnic homogeneity of Poland, Hungary, and the Czech Republic. Despite the lip service paid by Western democracies to the ideals of multiculturalism, one could argue that they perceived ethnic homogeneity as a significant asset.

3. A movement started by Nehru, Nasser, and Tito at the 1955 Bandung Conference to provide an organizational framework for countries seeking to avoid an alliance with either of the two Cold War blocs. The organization now claims 118 countries and 15 observers but has lost most of its appeal after the end of the Cold War as well as because of previous internal conflicts (particularly over the 1979 Soviet invasion of Afghanistan).

4. Witness the scandal over the art installation commissioned by the Czech government to mark the start of its six-month presidency of the European Union in January 2009. The Czech artist David Cerny, with a few collaborators, constructed a 170-square-foot puzzle in front of the European Council building in Brussels depicting European Union member countries in terms of crude stereotypes. The depiction of Bulgaria as a network of "Turkish" squat toilets enraged the Bulgarian government which logged an official protest. A Bulgarian artist, Petko Stoyanov, accused Cerny of "identifying with the rich people and laughing at the poor ones" and compared his attitude with that of a preschooler laughing at someone because "he is fat, has lop [sic] ears or is wearing glasses" (http://entropa2.blogspot.com [accessed February 28, 2010]). Another Bulgarian, however, wrote that "the Socialist-Monarchist-Turkofill" [sic] Bulgarian government has indeed been "effectively transforming Bulgaria into toilets" (Neytcho Iltchev, January 21, 2009, comment on "david cerny's entropa" posted on http://frankgerlitzki.blogspot.com/2009/01/david-cernys-entropa.html [accessed February 28, 2010]). Other responses from Bulgarian citizens gleaned from a cursory exploration of Internet posts and articles, as well as some personal correspondence, included embarrassment at the Bulgarian government's official protest and oscillation between laughing and feeling offended.

5. The assassin, Gavrilo Princip, is a hero of Serbian history with streets and elementary schools named after him.

6. Vojvodina, extending north of the Danube, was part of the Austro-Hungarian Monarchy until 1918. Zemun is a city in Vojvodina that lies on the Danube's northern bank right across from Belgrade and today constitutes one of its municipalities. Although Zemun and Vojvodina passed back and forth between Ottomans

and Habsburgs several times, this remark relies on a widespread sense that the Danube formed the divide between the two empires and, by extension, two civilizations.

7. Stef Jansen (2002) follows this fruitful strategy in his excellent account of "the experience of 'Balkan' and 'Europe' in Beograd and Zagreb" that could be seen as a companion to this chapter. I consider it one of the best corroborations as well as augmentations of my arguments here.

8. In Croatian literature, Rihtman Auguštin writes, "Krleža has accomplished the most interesting, I would say, anthropological study of the Balkans as a metaphor and a stereotype. In addition, he described the Balkan mentality on two levels, as we see it, and the Balkan as others see it/us. In essence Krleža's attitude towards the Balkans is ambivalent: he condemns the Balkan mentality, and at the same time he to some extent admires it, as if he envied its unscrupulous efficiency" (1997:32).

9. In the 1996 movie, *Broken English* (Nicholas 1996), the father of a Croatian family that had fled war in Croatia and relocated to New Zealand (played by Rade Šerbedžija, one of the most famous Yugoslav actors) is depicted as extremely patriarchal, bigoted, and violent. In one scene he drives a large wooden stake through a huge pig as he prepares it for roasting so that it enters its anus and comes out of its mouth. He does that with a sensual glee and explains to a boy of about five who is watching that this is "how the Turks impaled us [obviously meaning Croats]. A man could live for three days thus impaled!" From a far away enough perspective, Croats and Serbs become indistinguishably Balkan—beastly, oriental violence they have been subjected to makes them equally violent in turn.

10. Turkish coffee is essentially a mode of sociality and its "Oriental" character might be seen, among other things, in a certain "dilation" of time encompassed by the ritual. Sipping coffee and chatting (exchanging gossip) is meant to create a protected enclave where time flows more slowly than during the rest of the day.

11. *Palanka* used to be a neutral term for a small town but probably as early as the turn of the century it acquired derogatory connotations of small-mindedness, backwardness, and a mixture of provincial fear of the world and parvenu snobbishness. The locus classicus for the contemporary analysis of this kind of mentality is Radomir Konstantinović's *Filosofija palanke* (*Small Town Philosophy*) (Konstantinović 1991).

12. The term *čaršija* was defined in chapter 1.

13. Traditional peasant leather footwear with the characteristic tip that curves upward. It is a prime diacritic for Serbian peasantry, often used together with *šubara,* the traditional headgear, or *gunjče,* the short, sheepskin jacket, as in the famous phrase *gunjče i opanak* that summarized the political agenda of Radicals, the peasant party that dominated Serbian and later Yugoslav politics (see Stokes 1990).

14. Derogatory term for a peasant.

15. *Narod* means people, folk, and nation at the same time.

16. From *memli* (Tur.)—dankness, in Serbian epic poetry especially associated with Turkish dungeons.

17. Brigandry. From *hajduk* (Tur.)—an outlaw, highway robber, brigand, but, with South Slavs, also a fighter for national freedom against the Turks.

18. *Buljuk* (Tur.)—a military unit, a company, acquired the meaning of a crowd, a mass, a large undifferentiated group of people with a slight derogatory connotation. Here the best translation is probably "legion."

19. He was returning from Ukraine, where he visited Kiev, Zhitomir, and Lvov. Even though deadly tired, he immediately launched, without any prompting, into a monologue that didn't stop for the entire seven hours that the journey took. It was hard to say whether he was a sober, down-to-earth person or a mythomaniac, a narrow-minded provincial or open-minded cosmopolitan, a democrat or an authoritarian. Some of the typical Serbian myths he accepted fully, some he criticized as "invented traditions" in a surprisingly sophisticated manner which showed that he had read some critical historiography. He would brag like Münchausen one moment and be self-effacing the next; he would profess high moral standards, and then boast of being a thief; he was a peasant and an urbanite, he sincerely praised Albanians and seriously advocated polygamy. He talked at length with a completely straight face of how he will "climb"—become the president of Serbia and what he will do then. His personal manner of communicating was of a know-it-all, a tavern philosopher. In a manner of speaking, he was my "best informant." He exemplified what I came to adopt as my methodological principle: that individuals can tell the most amazingly surprising stories but that the stories tend to be composed of a finite number of prefabricated elements of identifiable provenance and genealogy. In other words, the creativity of the individual bricoleurs might be infinite, but by far the majority of elements they used came from just a few "junkyards" that comprised the Serbian "cultural apparatus."

20. See Mattijs van de Port's work that focuses precisely on the Serbian attitudes toward Gypsies, particularly in the city of Novi Sad where he did his fieldwork in the early 1990s (van de Port 1998, 1999, 1999a). His work gives a much more ethnographically thick and nuanced account of the Gypsy trope in Serbia than I can provide here.

21. Commentary on soccer matches with Germans is a classical site for those distinctions. German teams are relentlessly efficient but soulless machines. They cannot match us in creativity, dazzling improvisation, and in our irresistible, but, alas, all too unpredictable and unreliable outbursts of sheer genius.

22. See, for instance, Mitrović 1996:10.

23. Thanks to Victor Friedman for drawing my attention to this possibility.

24. See Pesmen 2000.

25. Fonvisin asked: "How can we remedy the two contradictory and most harmful prejudices: the first, that everything with us is awful, while in foreign lands everything is good; the second, that in foreign lands everything is awful, and with us everything is good?" This was the dilemma on which the construction of the Russian national identity was predicated (Greenfeld 1992:223).

26. See note 13 above.

27. Internationally acclaimed novels of Milorad Pavić (who liked to see himself as a Balkan Borges) are probably the best examples of such neo-Byzantine exoticism (See Pavić 1988, 1990, 1993).

28. "Barbarogenius" (*barbarogenije*) is a term coined by Ljubomir Micić (1895–1971), a leftist poet and founder of the Zenitist avant-garde art movement in the 1920s. Barbarogenius was for Micić an embodiment of the idealized Balkan spirit as a rejuvenator of decadent Europe that he fashioned into a character in his novel *Barbarogenius, the Decivilizer* (*Barbarognije decivilizator* in Serbian, and *Barbarogénie le décivilisateur* in the 1938 French original (Micić 1993).

29. See a discussion on Bond's avoidance of Yugoslavia in Thompson 1992:47.

30. See Bjelić and Savić 2002; Todorova 1997; Bakić-Hayden and Hayden 1992; and Bakić-Hayden 1995.

31. "All those things that are primary values from the standpoint of comfort are relegated in the world of amorphous civilizations to secondary position. For, if they had primary value, it would have been normal to make concrete paths in parks and village backyards, and one wouldn't have stomped in mud for centuries. And one wouldn't shit in the cornfield but in water-closets" (Pavlović 1992:31).

32. Erasure is the process whereby "facts that are inconsistent with the ideological scheme either go unnoticed or get explained away" (Irvine and Gal 2000: 38).

33. As Carrier puts it, "signs of similarity become embarrassments, ignored or explained away in terms that maintain the purity of Us and Them. In a sense, signs of similarity become polluting, Mary Douglas's "matter out of place" (Carrier 1992:203).

3. Highlanders and Lowlanders

1. Now that the Serbs are largely cleansed from Croatia, it is the internal Croatian highlanders that are blamed for everything by the ordinary Zagreb citizen rather than the Serbs. "Give us back our Serbs, take our Herzegovinians" declare graffiti on Zagreb walls according to the Zagreb correspondent of the Belgrade weekly *NIN* (Stanivuković 1998:52).

2. Cvijić, like Dvorniković after him, thought of himself as a Yugoslav and believed that Yugoslav national consciousness would eventually emerge from the crucible of a new state of South Slavs, yet he extolled the virtues associated mainly with Serbs. This was resented by Croats who were quick to see expansionism beneath any of Serbian Yugoslav unity rhetoric. To emphasize the state-building capacities of the Dinarics was, for Croats like Tomašić, tantamount to a barely concealed claim for Serbian supremacy and the inherent right to rule over other Slavs united in the new state, some of which, like Croats and Slovenes, considered themselves more cultured and civilized than the Serbs.

3. "Even before migration to the Balkans, the ancestors of South Slavs (Serbs and Croats) might have belonged to the Carpathian branch of Ur-Slavs. So they might have had some highlanders' accumulated energy prior to coming to the mountains of the Balkans" (Dvorniković 1939:284).

4. In 1988 Belgrade literary critic Petar Džadžić took out those passages from Cvijić's work that were critical of Dinarics and assembled them together with selected critical passages from Ivo Andrić into a highly successful book (Cvijić and Andrić 1988).

5. "Prečani," however, also refers to the Serbs from across the Sava River that once marked the boundary between Serbia proper and Austro-Hungarian territories. These "prečani" were the principal bearers of Central European culture and institutions in the new Serbian state (see Jovanović 1925; see also in chapter 2 in this volume).

6. The only mountain in otherwise completely flat Vojvodina region.

7. Note how Novaković reverses Dvorniković's valuation of the way highlanders speak. He presents the sound of their speech as sharp and hard. That hardness,

however, is not an iconic sign of their manliness, hardness, and ultimately "state-building capacity" as something positive but, on the contrary, it is a sign of barbarity. Implied here is that the relative softness of Novaković's peasants is a sign of their higher civilizational level.

8. Insinuating that highlander immigrants are Communists. Like Danko Popović, Novaković emphasizes the fact that the new Communist elite, which disinherited and physically purged the old bourgeoisie in Serbia after World War II, was largely composed of the Dinaric Highlanders from outside Serbia proper.

9. I owe this phrase to Professor Raymond Fogelson, who suggested it as a logical fourth term in the tripartite classification of types I initially proposed consisting of (1) the (Šumadija) solid peasant, (2) the cosmopolitan-urbanite, and (3) the peasant-urbanite halfling. At that time I couldn't find an example of the peasant-cosmopolitan, but I have since realized that, in addition to Novaković, such influential writers as Danko Popović and Dobrica Ćosić are actually attributing a peculiar kind of "cosmopolitanism" to their idealized peasant characters.

10. An important mediating term between mountains and mentality is, of course, "pastoralism." The contrast between (stereotypically conceived) pastoralism and agriculture has been the popular fuel for ethnopsychological speculation and invidious comparisons of national characters worldwide. One of the best examples of scholarship on the Balkans using that scheme is Ramet 1986.

11. Writing about violence as a psychological trait of the Dinaric Serbs, Cvijić says that he picked that trait, among other reasons, because it is, "perhaps better than in any other poem, phenomenon or event, expressed in the poem 'Wedding of Maksim Crnojević'" (in Džadžić 1988:65).

12. See also the expanded version in Lauer 1995. The latest systematic effort to construct an account of the "Serbian culture of violence" along similar lines is *Heavenly Serbia: From Myth to Genocide* (Anzulović 1999).

13. The one-stringed lute-like instrument played with a fiddle to accompany the singing of heroic or epic songs.

14. With a background in German philology and ethnology, Gerhard Gesemann (1888–1948) came to Belgrade in 1914, on the eve of World War I, to study Slavic languages and literature. Instead of returning to his native Germany after the war broke out, he joined with the Serbian Army as a paramedic and survived the army's horrible retreat through Albania. The focus of his research was Serbian and South Slavic epic poetry which he extended into ethnopsychological studies (influenced by Cvijić's method) such as this one on the Montenegrian heroism, *Heroische Lebensform: Zur Literatur und Wesenskunde der Balkanichen Patriarchalität,* first published in Prague in 1934.

15. Although sometimes bitter enemies, Albanians belonged to the same heroic life form as Montenegrins, and Miljanov concedes that their adherence to a code of honor was even stricter than that among the Montenegrins.

16. Miljanov learned to write only when he was of advanced age, and I tried to preserve his archaic and somewhat awkward style in this English translation.

17. In the broadest sense, the fallacies involved in claiming a direct link between mountains, epic poetry, or, more generally, "violent mentality" and the Yugoslav wars belong to the Orientalist or Balkanist discourses. Such discourses posit a polity moved by entrenched, unchanging, unconscious, and irrational impulses

as opposed to the predictable, flexible, and rational calculations that supposedly guide Western polities.

18. Ivan Čolović (1993, 1994, 2002, 2006) and Ivo Žanić (2007), among others, have amply documented and brilliantly analyzed the folkloric elements in the warmongering rhetoric in both Serbia and Croatia. Cathy Carmichael (2002) and Xavier Bougarel (1998), to name only two, have carefully and complexly related the highlander/lowlander ideology with mass atrocities committed during the wars of Yugoslav succession.

4. Tender-hearted Criminals and the Reverse Pygmalion

1. The true story was published as "Eight Days in a Tunnel" in the Belgrade periodical *Duga*. Its author, Vanja Bulić, was the host of a popular TV show titled "Black Gems" (*Crni biseri*), which might have provided a template for the imaginary TV show "Pulse of the Asphalt" in Dragojević's *Wounds*.

2. Although the term was used for Balkan guerilla bands even before World War I, the contemporary use comes from the name assumed by the royalist forces loyal to the government in exile in the Axis-occupied Yugoslavia during World War II led by Draža Mihailović under the official name of the Yugoslav Army in the Fatherland. As the war progressed, these royalist forces increasingly turned from resisting the Axis occupiers to collaborating with them in fighting Tito's Partisans. The initial Allied support to Chetniks was eventually shifted to the Partisans. Mihailović was caught and executed by the new Communist regime in 1946. Chetniks were Serbian nationalists who committed large-scale atrocities against non-Serbs in Bosnia and Croatia during World War II. During the 1990s several of the Serbian paramilitary formations identified explicitly with the World War II Chetniks, using their emblems, singing their songs, and wearing their signature beards. Both Vojislav Šešelj's Serbian Radical Party and Vuk Drašković's Serbian Renewal Movement—at times quite strong and bitterly rivalrous opposition parties in Milošević's Serbia—claimed Chetnik identity. During the wars in Croatia and Bosnia there was a strong tendency among non-Serbs to call all Serbs Chetniks. In contemporary Serbia history was significantly revised to minimize the Chetnik collaborationist taint (i.e., the 2004 law equalizing former Partisans' and Chetniks' right to war pensions or the revised history textbooks). The ideological opposition of "Partisans" and "Chetniks" in Serbia still flares up, sometimes virulently, more than sixty years after their mutual slaughter in the Second World War. Dragojević masterfully re-creates this opposition by including, in his microcosmic band of Serbian fighters besieged in the tunnel, both an old Yugoslav army officer played by Bata Živojinović, the iconic hero of countless Partisan movies, and a bearded neo-Chetnik.

3. As Misha Glenny wrote in his review of the film in *Sight and Sound*, "Živojinović bravely undermines almost the entire body of his film work hitherto" (1996:12).

4. The documentary was followed by a companion book (Knežević and Tufegdžić 1995).

5. The two main characters in the *Underground*, Blacky and Marko, are both petty criminals turned into patriotic fighters against Germans in occupied Belgrade.

6. Two highly prominent "legends of the Belgrade asphalt," Branislav Matić-Beli and Djordje Božović-Giška (nicknames are important trademarks of crimi-

nals) were, in 1991, heavily involved in the formation of the first Serbian para-military organization, the Serbian Guard (*Srpska garda*) under the auspices of the oppositional Serbian Renewal Movement (*Srpski pokret obnove, SPO*) of Vuk Drašković. Beli was assassinated in front of his house in August 1991, and Giška was killed a month and half later on the front line in Croatia. The most plausible theories link both assassinations to the growing alarm of Milošević's regime at the prospect of having an opposition party command thousands of armed volunteers. The most prominent criminal in charge of paramilitaries was, of course, Željko Ražnjatović-Arkan, and, in his case, there was no doubt of his loyalty to the Serbian regime.

7. In the U.S. version "Kure" is felicitously rendered as "Dicky," thus translating the pun intended in the original (another possibility would have been "Cocky").

8. As the documentary *See You in the Obituary* shows, Belgrade criminals do try to emulate the stereotype or at least present themselves in such terms—as Noble Criminals of urban legends. In everyday life, among ordinary people, even to hint that one knows or associates with "tough" guys confers a certain macho aura and could be properly counted as belonging to the "poetics of manhood" genre.

9. The only interesting twist introduced in the *Officer* is that there are two girls vying for the love of the Partisan commissar (who is also from Zagreb, but the working-class, not the burgher's, Zagreb)—one a peasant girl, the other an older, sophisticated upper-class woman. Although both are beautiful, the officer falls for the cultured one. Culture is sexy for the primitive macho male, and machismo is sexy for the sophisticated, cultured female.

10. On the other hand, it is he who cringes when she swears. His is, however, not a Henry Higgins attitude. It is just that the "honor and shame" society from which he hails as a typical montagnard is generally much more careful about swearing and insults. When opposed to his urban girlfriend he stands for a certain purity and naiveté, that is to say, naturalness, but without the concomitant rough and violent machismo. In this opposition, the city comes out as an immoral, loose place where girls rival drunken sailors in uttering obscenities.

11. Danko Popović (1994) talks about Tito's victorious Partisans as wild highlanders who claimed the girls from Serbia's heartland region, Šumadija, as war booty in a manner similar to the way their *hajduk* (brigand) ancestors abducted the womenfolk of "agas and beys" during the Ottoman times. Counterposed to communist highlanders stand both the Šumadija girls (by implication, peasants) and the cultivated bourgeois girls from Belgrade and larger cities. In the behavior of Šumadija and Belgrade girls toward these new brigands with red stars on their caps, Popović says, one can see "a strange mix of epic romanticism and modern 'adaptation' to the new situation" (Popović 1994:232–233).

12. Another movie by the director of *The Melody, Three Is Needed for Happiness* (*Za sreću je potrebno troje*), is one possible counterexample I am aware of (Grlić 1985). A simple working girl from Zagreb falls in love with a handsome intellectual just released from prison for a minor robbery. A Bosnian warehouse guard from her shoe factory is in love with her and wants her to marry him. In a tense scene where both men are sitting in her kitchen, the working girl pointedly asks the ex-con if he went to the university. His affirmative answer unmistakably signals to the Bosnian warehouse guard that he has lost out. In this case, the cultural capital of the male is

seen as sexy by a lower-class female. The ex-con is played by Miki Manojlović, and he is again a moody, difficult, conflicted, unpredictable (but very charming) type, but for all his educational advantage he is not really playing Pygmalion to the working girl; he is no self-confident Higgins. On the contrary, in a sense, it is the working girl who will ultimately pull him down to her social level. Perhaps the reversal of what I claim is the dominant pattern could be traced to the fact that the screenplay was coauthored by the Croatian feminist writer Dubravka Ugrešić.

13. See chapter 2, note 28, in this volume.

14. Thus when Serbs lose a soccer match to Germans, rarely if ever is this expressed as anything like "the Germans screwed us." It is always their machine-like conditioning or some such product of their superior rationality that (temporarily) triumphs over our (fickle but ultimately superior) irrational inspiration. Only those perceived as lower on the civilizational scale could be (grudgingly and between ourselves) admitted to have metaphorically "screwed us over," that is, the Turks or Albanians.

15. The film title comes from the centerpiece of this street "theater"—a police cordon that started blocking a short street that leads to the main Belgrade square (see chapter 1 for a short description of this episode).

16. Mazaj (2007) performs an interesting analysis of tunnels, cellars, and trenches as spatial figures in *Pretty Village, Pretty Flame,* Kusturica's 1995 *Underground,* and Tanović's 2001 *No Man's Land.* Buses, too, could be included in this list of claustrophobic "other" spaces of Yugoslav and Serbian cinema of the last decade or so.

17. The lack of catharsis and moral transformation that I noted in the films examined in this chapter seems to be sending the metaphoric meta-message—the fact that nobody changes in the film, and that there's no resolution is an icon of Serbdom as a whole forever condemned to a bad eternity and eternal repetition. *The Cordon,* however, makes its temporality more of a question mark than a bold statement, food for thought rather than an anguished lament.

18. They were all published in the *Nationalities Papers* 34 (3) (July 2006).

5. Serbian Jeremiads

The epigraph is in Arnold 1993:21.

1. The most developed theory of rayah mentality (*rajinski mentalitet*) comes from Jovan Cvijić. See chapter 3 for his view on this character trait.

2. David Rieff, for instance, wrote in 1993 that, "if anything, it is the Bosnians of Sarajevo, with their fierce devotion to the idea of a multi-confessional, multicultural state, rather than the Serbs or the Croats, who are the real Europeans of the former Yugoslavia" (10). "Modern Turkey," he continued, "has moved on from the Balkans, but the Balkans have not necessarily moved on from the Ottoman legacy." And then he clinched it: "The Ottoman empire at its most bloodthirsty and caricatural lives on more completely in the Serb Republic of Bosnia than anywhere in Anatolia" (13).

3. And there was no need to remove any physical reminders of Ottoman rule, since, by and large, they are already long gone. Out of some eighty mosques that existed in Belgrade during Ottoman rule, for instance, only one remains standing today.

4. At the time run by a more or less independent TV channel—NTV Studio B —the *Impression of the Week* was a very popular show with the following format: three guests in the studio talk about what impressed them the most in the previous week. They were usually well-known public figures—leaders of political parties, scientists, artists, and intellectuals chosen so as to represent different, sometimes even violently opposed agendas. The "impressions of the week" were presented as ten short video clips of the previous week's programming. Most of them were about the current political situation, with a few "human interest" items thrown in, for instance, the birth of a baby elephant in the Belgrade Zoo. After the impressions were presented, viewers would call in with their votes and comments. Each caller gives one "black" and one "white" vote. In the studio, the guests discuss the hot topics of the day, push their agendas, and argue for a good hour before finally giving their votes and thus clinching that week's winners—the worst (the blackest) and the best (the whitest) impression of the week.

5. They got closer again later and even ended as cellmates at the Scheveningen prison in The Hague where for a while they still officially presided over their respective parties that often collaborated on the Serbian political scene between Milošević's fall in 2000 and his death in 2006.

6. This is a paraphrase of the famous call from Karadjordje, the leader of the First Serbian Uprising in 1804, to all the local leaders to start the uprising in the face of *dahia* terror.

7. For the role of Dragoš Kalajić, see chapter 6.

8. The text is titled "Janissaries from my alley," where the word he used for "alley" is "sokak"—a Turkism with very intimate connotations.

9. Gostuški refers to the role the Serbian Army played in the breaking of the so-called Salonika (Thessaloniki) front as part of the Allied offensive in 1918. The Serbian Army had been decimated and forced to retreat through Albania in 1916. It then recuperated on Greek islands (mostly Corfu) before joining the allies at the Salonika front. This breakthrough where the Serbian Army displayed great initiative, heroism, and endurance, is celebrated as one of the most glorious moments of modern Serbian history.

10. Here is Danojlić writing about his own persecution at the hands of the Communist regime: "The persecution unleashed against *Trouble With Words* seemed pretty shoddy, and when I talk about it today, I feel boundless boredom and sadness. Few were the persecutions in those years that resembled real persecutions: the ruling ideology was dying, and everything it was undertaking against the unfaithful, resembled a burlesque or caricature rather than true oppression . . . Post-Stalinism was a lousy shadow of Stalinism, and its persecutions shared that quality: they were shoddy, fretful, without passion or conviction" (Danojlić 1990:113–114).

11. By conflating High Byzantine culture (the spiritual music that he sings) with "ancient folk music," that is, the music of the ordinary people, Aksentijević actually put himself in a position very similar to that of the "mad painter" Milić of Mačva (see chapter 6).

12. A prominent cultural figure in Belgrade, Jerotić (b. 1924) has been giving innumerable well-attended public lectures on literature, psychology, philosophy, and theology, for more than thirty years. A Jungian of great erudition and humanistic/literary bent, he combined clinical practice with teaching pastoral psychology

at the Belgrade Theological Faculty since 1984. He is a member of both the Serbian Writers' Association and the Serbian Academy of Arts and Sciences.

13. He was a literary critic, one of the founders of the literary journal *Srpski književni glasnik,* and the so-called Belgrade literary style—all institutions of pivotal importance for Serbian culture in the first half of twentieth century. The essay in question was originally a lecture delivered to a group of Serbian students at Oxford University in June 1918. The title in Serbian, "Šta Srbi imaju da nauče od Engleza," could be rendered both as "What Serbs *Could,* and What Serbs *Should* Learn from the English."

14. The conference was organized by the newly formed Democratic Center, a nonparty organization led by Dragoljub Mićunović, and was held on the first two days of March in 1995, at the Belgrade Student Cultural Center.

15. Personal communication. Latinka Perović was a prominent member of the so-called Serbian Liberals who were purged from the leadership of the Serbian League of Communists in the early 1970s by Tito. After being ousted, she became a highly respected historian.

16. Elsewhere I advance a different reading of this situation in a paper devoted to Rambo Amadeus as a hero of "oscillating" or "indeterminate" irony (Živković 2011). In discussing his role in simultaneously parodying and embracing Serbian epic poetry (especially as performed by *guslari* [Balkan epic singers]), I also raise the possibility that many turbo-folk performers actually engaged in self-irony. With his "turbo-epics," just as with turbo-folk, Rambo's irony cut both ways— against the supposedly deadly serious turbo-folkers, on the one hand, and, on the other, the deadly serious intellectuals who were denouncing them.

17. The term *narodnjaci* can refer both to the musical genre and the type of people who consume it. The term has been given the status of a code word in the 1990s by the popular ballad singer Djordje Balašević in his song "Narodnjaci," where he defines them (with true sociological precision) as "a hybrid class half-way between village and city." The English translation "folkniks" was suggested by Victor Friedman (personal communication).

18. Never mind that the Lepenski vir culture had nothing to do with the Serbs. In this case, however, the campaign designers were probably not embracing the theories of "Serbs as the Most Ancient People," discussed in chapter 6, but only branding their product with a recognizable label that indexed something "ancient"—a very prominent component of the local sense of what "culture" is all about. When I mentioned that I studied "cultures," my interlocutors in Serbia would often immediately connect that to "Athens" and ancient Greeks, for instance.

19. Both "where you belong" and "what you should" use the same word "*nado*" in Russian—"gde *nado,*" and "shto *nado,*" respectively. In Serbian both would be rendered, respectively, as "gde *treba*" and "šta *treba.*" The relevant passage in Richard Lourie's English translation of the book is in Voinovich (1998:193–194).

6. Glorious Pasts and Imagined Continuities

1. Ostap Bender was the lovable resourceful crook, con man and self-styled "great combinator" hero of Ilf and Petrov's *The Twelve Chairs* and *The Little Golden*

Calf—novels that satirized the USSR's New Economic Policy (NEP) of the 1920s. (Il'f and Petrov 1961, 1962). Because of the enormous popularity of these novels in the Soviet World (and to some extent in the former Yugoslavia as well) Ostap Bender became an eponym for crooks and con artists in general.

2. Slapšak's "Mexican charlatan" is Roberto Salinas Price, a wealthy hotelier who turned revisionist Homeric scholar in the 1960s, and has since published a number of works trying to prove that both the *Iliad* and the *Odyssey* took place along the Croatian Dalmatian Coast and Neretva River in Herzegovina. His views are presented at http://www.homer.com.mx (accessed April 2010), and his books are published by Scylax Press (http://www.scylaxpress.com). Since I have no expertise to judge his theories, I am here deferring to Slapšak's judgment, since she is a classicist of international repute associated with institutions of impeccable credibility (Rutgers and Ljubljana Universities, Max Planck Institute, Centre National de la Recherche Scientifique, and Berghahn).

3. Roberto Salinas Price revisited Serbia in 2002, and in 2007 he promoted his new book, *Homeric Whispers* (*Homerska šaputanja*) in Belgrade (see Jovanović 2002; and Matović 2007). He also revisited Bosnia in 2006 reiterating his theories while at the same time contesting the notorious theories of the Bosnian entrepreneur and amateur archaeologist Semir Osmanagić who has claimed, since 2005, that three hills near Visoko in Bosnia are twelve-thousand-year-old human-built pyramids (see Bohannon 2008). The so-called Bosnian Pyramids are a fascinating new case of anchoring a desirable imaginary ancient past in a "place of power" that seems to vastly surpass the Salinas Price phenomenon in political weight and the stakes involved. The Bosnian Pyramids deserve a thorough investigation and analysis I am not in the position to offer here.

4. *I Even Met Happy Gypsies,* a film discussed in chapter 2 (see Petrović 1967).

5. *Inat* is indeed of Arabic origin but it entered Serbo-Croatian through Turkish.

6. Srbenda is augmentative of Srbin (a Serb), and in the usage established, according to Skerlić (1925:169–170) in the mid-nineteenth century, it denotes someone who is thoroughly and uncompromisingly devoted to everything Serbian, an "autochthonous, raw Serb without a trace of anything foreign" (Skerlić 1925:167). To this day, "Srbenda" carries the connotations of rusticity, simplicity, and traditional patriarchal values—the opposite of high culture polish and cosmopolitan sophistication. This equation of a mythological being from the Vedas with the romanticized rusticity of the Serbian variant of the Noble Savage is especially piquant.

7. Here the key evidence is found not in etymology and toponymy but mostly in the supposed scripts discovered in Lepenski Vir and the later Starčevo culture sites, especially that of Vinča near Belgrade. In Vinča marks were found on the pottery that could be interpreted as some sort of script. Official archaeology (Srejović) claimed that these marks were no more than personal seals of potters, but some, like Radivoje Pešić, claimed it was a full blown alphabetical script. Another researcher of ancient scripts, Svetislav Bilbija, claims to have deciphered Etruscan script on the basis of the Cyrillic script. The chain is now complete. From its origins in Lepenski Vir and Vinča (perhaps by detour through India), this script begets both that of Etruscans (who were actually "Rascians," that is, Serbs) and that of mysterious Pelasgians. It is thus the basis of the ancient Greek scripts, from which modern Latin and Greek develop. Therefore, when Serbs got their Cyrillic script,

which was adapted from Greek in the ninth century, they were just reclaiming by detour what they themselves had originated!

8. He was seriously ill from lung cancer and he died only three months later at the age of sixty-five, so it was my last chance to talk to a man who was not only the dean of Serbian archaeology and a world-famous archaeologist but a cultural institution in his own right.

9. The string of honorifics he attached to his name gives a good taste of his eccentricity. In an interview he gave in *Duga* (no. 463, November 23, 1991), he called himself "Milić, the General of Lepenski Vir, the Knight of Machva, the skeleton of Radovan, the Heliocentric, the grandson of Pantelija, the Serbian barbarogenius, the ancestor of Serb vampire wayside tombstones (*krajputaša*), the one who periodically rises from the grave and opposes mathematics."

10. A certain level of spiritual purity, including vows of chastity comparable to that of monks, is demanded from the painters, and the rules of representing religious themes and personages have been passed down for centuries without much change (see Florensky 1996).

11. At that time, however, the official Serbian Orthodox Church did not show its support by sending representatives to the grand opening. Only an excommunicated priest, Žarko Gavrilović, was present.

12. "The great tradition," according to Robert Redfield, "is cultivated in schools or temples; the little tradition works itself out and keeps itself going in the lives of the unlettered in their village communities. The tradition of the philosopher, theologian, and literary man is a tradition consciously cultivated and handed down; that of the little people is for the most part taken for granted and not submitted to much scrutiny or considered refinement and improvement" (1989:42). I have borrowed these terms from Redfield as a useful shorthand while aware of their problematic nature.

13. The solution to the puzzle of why this small group that proclaimed itself "rightist" and openly aligned itself with racist and fascist ideologies was not only tolerated but actively promoted by the nominally "leftist" regime of the Socialist Party of Serbia in the early 1990s lies in one important tenet they both shared—anti-liberalism and anti-capitalism.

14. The local term for the constellation of the Big Dipper is "*Velika kola*," which translates as Big Cart or Great Wagon (cf. British usage, The Wain).

15. Nemanja's youngest son, Rastko, who adopted the name Sava after becoming a monk, established the independent Serbian Church and became its first archbishop. Under the influence of Sava, Nemanja took monastic orders in Studenica, when he assumed the name Simeon, and then retired to Chilandar Monastery on Mt. Athos. After he died in Chilandar, Sava brought his relics to Studenica where their cult still thrives. Simeon was canonized as St. Simeon Myrobliptos (Sv. Simeon Mirotočivi). Because of its special connection to the sanctified Nemanjić dynasty and St. Sava, the founder of the Serbian Church, the Studenica Monastery always held a special place in the hierarchy of Serbian monasteries. Its central Church of the Virgin is an architectural masterpiece, and its frescoes are among the most beautiful on the territory of Serbia.

16. A relative from Israel related a similar demonstration to me in 1988, at the site of a stone inscription at least twenty-five hundred years old. When he toured

Israel some years before, the guide seated the group in front of that inscription and took about fifteen minutes to instruct all these speakers of modern Hebrew how to read it—thus demonstrating the continuity spanning thousands of years.

17. It took another three years, however, and the firm establishment of Milošević in power, before the turn was completed: when new elementary school readers were published in the summer of 1990, instead of Tito, it was Vuk Karadžić who peered out from the first page.

18. Such eclecticism could be seen not only as a sign of confusion (or of the spuriousness of such instrumentalization of tradition) but also as a marketing strategy designed to reach as many different constituencies as possible by broadcasting on a wide band.

19. Basara saw himself as leading a cultural crusade against the Serbian literary establishment and its "godfather," Dobrica Ćosić, on behalf of the new generation of "postmodernist" writers. The polemic offers a good example of Serbian cultural ideology cleavages but, as is usual in this genre, it relies heavily on readers being able to decipher veiled insinuations based on their connoisseurship of the Serbian literary scene.

20. An essay written in 1919 for the *Commission for the Preservation of Art and Antiquities of the Sergiei's Church of the Trinity* and presented in 1920 at a meeting of the Byzantine Section of the Moscow Institute for the Historical-Artistic Researches and Museology attached to the Russian Academy of the History of Material Culture.

21. Written in 1922, the essay was translated into English for the first time in 1996 (Florensky 1996).

7. Narrative Cycles

1. There are a number of good sources in English about Milošević's political career: Cohen 1993, 1997, and especially 2001; Djilas 1993; Vujačić 1995; Woodward 1995; Silber 1996; Budding 1998; Gordy 1999; Djukić 1992, 2001; Nikolić 2002; Stevanović 2004; Clark 2008; Vladisavljević 2008; and Jović 2009.

2. Milošević befriended Stambolić while still a student at the Belgrade Faculty of Law. As Stambolić rapidly ascended the rungs of political power in Serbia, he would typically arrange for his protégé to succeed him in his previous position. When Stambolić became president of the Serbian League of Communists in 1984, he appointed Milošević as the head of the Belgrade party committee, and when he became the president of Serbia, Milošević succeeded him as a chief of the Serbian Party.

3. Over the years speculation abounded as to why this particular, seemingly innocuous sentence had such an impact. I agree with Eric Gordy that the very simplicity of the sentence had a shock value compared to the usual "doubletalk" of communist functionaries. "This was one of the first instances," Gordy writes, "in which a leading politician had spoken in public and offered an idea that everybody could understand and who went so far as to encapsulate the message in a single comprehensible sentence. After years of progressively more incomprehensible and dense babble purporting to explain Yugoslavia's unnervingly opaque system of 'workers' self-management,' such an event was beyond memory for people who

opposed Milošević as well as those who supported him" (1999:26). This, however, should not lead us to agree with a widespread popular view of Milošević's language as inherently direct and refreshingly free of muddled socialist phrasings. Even a cursory inspection of his speeches reveals that they carried not a little trace of the socialist doubletalk. The perception of Milošević as a clear and persuasive speaker is rather a phenomenon that belongs to the mystique of the irrational relationship between the leader and the masses.

4. "The mass movement of Kosovo Serbs . . . was not openly anticommunist, though it could easily have become so. Milošević only gradually overcame his caution and started supporting it, but he was nonetheless the first leading communist to do so. With the help of the party-controlled media and the party machinery, he soon dominated the movement, discovering in the process that the best way to escape the wrath of the masses was to lead them. It was an act of political cannibalism. The opponent, Serbian nationalism, was devoured and its spirit permeated the eater. Milošević reinvigorated the party by forcing it to embrace nationalism" (Djilas 1993:87).

5. On the use of surrogates in Milošević's technology of rule, see Gordy 1999:17.

6. The ten-syllable meter characterizes most of Serbian (as well as Croatian and Bosnian Muslim) epic poetry (see Lord 2000).

7. Vlachs are Aromunian-speaking pastoralists who were assimilated into the surrounding Slavic population as either Catholic or Orthodox. The term was, however, used pejoratively by Catholics and Muslims to refer to the Orthodox (identified with Serbs) in general. Recursively Catholic urbanites would refer to non-urbanite newcomers as Vlachs regardless of their faith (or ethnic identity). Vlach thus embraces the meanings of pastoralist and highlander, and of Eastern as opposed to Western, uncivilized as opposed to civilized. Thus the equation with Serbs.

8. That Bosnia, here labeled "Eastern" by someone residing in Belgrade at the moment of speaking, is geographically to the *west* of Serbia only brings into sharper relief this instance of Serbian Orientalism.

9. His métier is the analysis of contemporary urban folklore, and various para-literary genres such as obituaries and epitaphs, graffiti and slogans, sport journalism and soccer fan folklore, lyrics of newly composed folk songs, tabloids, and so on—the genres he likes to call "wild literature" (*divlja književnost*).

10. June 28 (June 15, according to the old calendar), the day when the battle was fought. Starting with the five hundredth anniversary of the battle in 1889, St. Vitus's Day (*Vidovdan*) was formally celebrated by the newly established Serbian Kingdom and became an official state holiday in 1914 (after Kosovo became a part of Serbia in 1912). See Zirojević 2000; Djordjević 1991; and Durković-Jakšić 1989.

11. A typical Bećković neologism—*onebesiti*—literally, "to be made heavenly," implies both "to send to heavens," that is, to kill, and to make someone sacred, "of havens."

12. After the battle, Prince Lazar's remains were first kept in Priština in Kosovo. They were then removed to the Ravanica Monastery in 1390–91. The Great Migration of Serbs under the Patriarch Arsenije Čarnojević, in 1690, brought Lazar's remains to Szent Endre near Budapest. In 1697 they were transferred to the Vrdnik Monastery in Srem (in Croatia), where they rested until World War II. They were

then removed from Croatian territory to Belgrade during the war. In 1988–89 they were finally returned to the Gračanica Monastery in Kosovo after first traveling through Serb-populated areas of Croatia and Bosnia-Herzegovina (see Djordjević 1991:311–312).

13. The following joke that I heard in Serbia attests to the notoriety of this formula while providing a highly ironic and self-reflexive commentary on the whole graves = territory logic: A Bosnian spaceship lands on the Moon. The Bosnian space team is comprised of three delegations, Croat, Muslim, and Serb, and they have to stake their claims to the Moon territory. "We are used to mountains," say the Muslims, "so we will take all the mountains." "We cannot live without the sea," the Croats say, "so we will take all the Moon seas." Nothing is left for the Serbs. One of them takes out his gun and shoots his fellow Serb. "Where there are Serbian graves, that's Serbia," he says and takes it all.

14. This comes out very clearly in the collection of his replies to his critics (Drašković 1987), where the above argument of justifiability of revenge is elaborated in greater detail. When all is said and done, the main message remains: the Muslims were the first to commit unspeakable evil against innocent and defenseless Serbs in the Independent State of Croatia during World War II, and the Četnik revenge in the form of massacres of Muslims could never be made morally equal to Ustaša massacres, as proclaimed in the official Yugoslav doctrine of "symmetry" (Četnik crimes = Ustaša crimes). There is no symmetry between victims (Serbs) and perpetrators (Ustaša, Muslims), Drašković is saying, and the victims are justified in exacting revenge.

15. Indeed, both the Old Testament motifs of a Covenant of the people with God (and of the Chosen People) and the New Testament motifs of the Last Supper, Judas's betrayal, and especially Christ's choice of the Heavenly over the Earthly Kingdom are at the core of the Kosovo myth. A detailed examination of all these motifs and themes, some of which exist in quite complex and sometimes contradictory relationships, is something I cannot undertake here (excellent sources include Antonijević 1989; Brkić 1961; Delić 1990; Djurić 1990; Dragnich and Todorovich 1984; Durković-Jakšić 1989; Gojković 1995; Gorup 1991; Jevtić 1989; Kalezić 1989; Krstić 1991; Ljubinković 1989; Mihaljčić 1989; Popović 1998; Tomashevich 1991; Trebješanin 1989; Vucinich and Emmert 1991; Vukadinović 1989; and Zirojević 2000).

16. A detachment of the Serbian Army under the command of Major Dragutin Gavrilović was left to defend Belgrade against Austrian attack in 1915. Knowing that they would all die, Gavrilović delivered his famous speech that, at some point, everyone going to school in Serbia had to memorize. It ended in these words: "Soldiers, heroes! The Headquarters have erased our platoon from its evidence, our platoon has been sacrificed for the honor of Belgrade and our fatherland. You don't have to worry about your lives anymore. Thus forward into glory! For the King and the country! Long live the King! Long live Belgrade" (*Vojnici! Junaci! Vrhovna komanda izbrisala je naš puk iz svog brojnog stanja, naš puk žrtvovan je za čast Beograda i otadžbine . . . Vi nemate više da se brinete za svoje živote koji više ne postoje . . . Zato napred u slavu! Za kralja i otadžbinu! živeo kralj! . . . živeo Beograd!*)

17. It comes as a shock to someone, who had to memorize Gavrilović's speech in school and still chokes with emotion when he recalls it, that Gavrilović actually survived the war and died in Belgrade in 1945! Somehow this fact, though not actively repressed, managed to remain concealed for generations and generations who grew up on this example of suicidal heroism.

18. It is important to note that the historical experience of Serbs includes an instance in which the whole army, the government, and a large number of the civilian population could in fact be made to leave the country altogether. It is thus entirely conceivable for Serbs to be completely overrun by a foreign power and practically kicked out of their state. I would argue that, however many instructive parallels one can make with Russian history and Tolstoy's *War and Peace,* there is that profound difference in historical experience between Russia and Serbia that has to be borne in mind. I doubt that it is conceivable to the Russian mind that a foreign force, no matter how formidable, could kick the Russians out of their homeland, or completely overrun it. Both Napoleon and Hitler got bogged down in the Russian winter and lost in the Russian vastness. Size does matter (in national imaginary)!

19. Vuk Drašković, who had in the meantime publicly renounced his 1980s nationalist rhetoric, appealed to that counter-script as the deputy prime minister on the eve of the 1999 bombing of Serbia in his call for accommodation with the overwhelming force of NATO. That many Serbs saw this as a betrayal attests to the power of the Last Stand mentality that thrived as never before under the NATO bombing.

20. Čolović analyzes extensively this contrast between the Czechs who systematically avoided battles and Serbs who systematically opted for enormous sacrifices of life in the work of Mihailo Marković, a prominent philosopher associated with the Praxis group in the 1960s who became one of the chief ideologues of Milošević's Socialist Party in the 1990s (Čolović 2002:71–72).

21. Da se nije boj ni jedan bio
    Bilo bi nas više, ali koga?
    I bilo bi bolje, ali kome?
These lines are from Bećković's poem "Lelek mene" published in his 1978 collection *Lele i kuku.* Parts of this poem were reproduced in Djurić 1990:593.

8. "The Wish to Be a Jew"; or, The Power of the Jewish Trope

The chapter title is an allusion to Kafka's enigmatic short story "The Wish to be a Red Indian" (Kafka 1972 [1946]).

1. In the wake of the Cankarjev dom incident, the Federation of Jewish Communities of Yugoslavia, as an official representative of all the Yugoslav Jewish communities with its seat in Belgrade, was faced with a delicate situation. Reacting too strongly against the Slovenes could be interpreted as Jewish support for the Serbian regime, especially as it would come from Belgrade, but, on the other hand, there was an urge to react officially and demand that the Jews and their suffering be left out of Yugoslav squabbles. After a period of agonizing over what the right and properly diplomatic response to the abuses in the Cankarjev dom should be, the Federation issued its public protestation. The Slovenian Youth Organization was reminded that during the war Jews were wearing that same Star of David while

being taken to concentration camps and gas chambers, and that there were no gas chambers in Kosovo. The Federation saw such political uses as trivializing and debasing symbols burdened with heavy associations to an all too real experience of suffering.

2. Originally a supporter of Israel's independence, Tito's Yugoslavia broke diplomatic relations with Israel after the 1967 War and, as a leader of the Non-Aligned Movement, sided firmly with the Arab states and the Palestinian cause. Despite this official anti-Israel policy, the Yugoslav Jewish community was allowed to keep its contacts with Israel with the tacit agreement that it stays low key and minds its own business (see Gordiejew 1999).

3. Theodor Barth, who studied the Zagreb Jewish community in the late 1990s, points out that even in Croatia there was some identification with the Jewish position. He says that "the role model of the 'Jew' as the epitome of historical victim and suffering was elaborated in Croatia beyond the simple rhetorical use of the comparison. Quite a few Croatians were serious about this. And in a number of cases the yearning for things Jewish crossed the threshold of hostility, or remained ambiguously defined in terms of philo- and anti-Semitism: the stronger the silence on Jasenovac, the stronger the desire" (Barth 1999:215).

4. The main sources include Browning 1985; Romano 1980; Hilberg 1985; and *Encyclopedia of the Holocaust* 1990.

5. I was present at one meeting at the Jewish Community Center in Belgrade where these issues were debated. The faction of mostly older members who were in favor of more vocal support of Serbs in the current media war were using the old Jewish argument that history teaches us that you never know how things might turn for the Jews (meaning, we are now safe in Serbia, but it may turn ugly). The then president of the Community first disputed the idea of Jews offering any kind of support that would end up implicitly endorsing Serbian quisling authorities like General Nedić or Ljotić, for both were indeed anti-Semites and did indeed help the Germans in carrying out the extermination of Serbia's Jews. Second, he said, it is true that "you never know" how it may turn, but what history teaches us is that no show of loyalty to the regime ever made any difference when things indeed changed for the worse. And if expressing loyalty to the regime has absolutely no influence on whether the Jews will be left in peace or persecuted, then why compromise one's integrity and offer support to Milošević?

6. However, a number of Jewish intellectuals offered a dissenting view. Rather than the strengthening of memory, they saw the Holocaust Museum as a domestication, an Americanization, and ultimately as "the taming of the Holocaust." "I see the existence of the museum as a statement of raw power, and that's the only thing I like about it," wrote Melvin Jules Bukiet in the *New York Times* (April 18, 1993), "a blatant kowtowing to the position the survivors have attained in contemporary society. Unfortunately, the museum will not spur the remembrance the donors seek, but will finally permit this country to forget."

7. "His Family's Refugee Past Is Said to Inspire NATO's Commander" by Elizabeth Becker. The blurb says: "Some say General Clark's roots give him empathy for Kosovo's victims" (*New York Times* May 3, 1999).

8. For the role the Holocaust plays in the American imagination, see Peter Novick 1999.

9. That Sekelj was very far from Jews living in Serbia who tended to endorse the regime's position was perhaps best proved by the fact that the Serbian-Jewish Friendship Society sued him for slander, which allegedly appeared in his book *The Time of Infamy* (*Vreme beščašća*) (Sekelj 1995; see also Sekelj 1997).

10. I was able to trace this theory to Dejan Lučić, the author of such best sellers as *The Secrets of the Albanian Mafia* (*Tajne Albanske mafije*) and *The Rulers from the Shadow* (*Vladari iz senke*). Described on the "Bad Serb Club" website as "a cult writer for all those who are looking for the essence behind the politics that we see," Dejan Lučić is reported to have attributed the NATO aggression against Yugoslavia to "the rulers from the shadow, thirteen of them, [who] are planning to bring 'the new world order' by the year 2000."

9. Garbled Genres

1. For the role of Jasenovac in Serbian victimhood rhetoric, see chapter 7.

2. Facing imminent air attacks on their positions, the military commanders of Republika Srpska captured more than a hundred United Nations Protection Force (UNPROFOR) personnel and tied them to strategic military installations as human shields on May 27, 1995. The hostages were released on June 2.

3. For popular accounts of higher dimensions, see Abbott 2002; Banchoff 1990; Kaku 1994; Pickover 1999; and Rucker 1984.

4. Dinkić led the expert team "G17" that advised Serbian opposition, and he became the Yugoslav National Bank Governor in December 2000, after the opposition victory in the October elections.

5. Such rapid issuance of new banknotes did alleviate the sheer physical problems usually associated with such hyperinflation. Even though one often needed a ridiculously bulky wad of banknotes to buy trifles, people usually didn't have to carry bagfuls. Larger transactions, in any case, were conducted in hard currency (Deutsche Marks predominantly). The problem was that after a while the shapes and colors of banknotes blurred in one's mind, and even the most astute found it hard to deal with everyday transactions.

6. In an unpublished paper Stef Jansen (2008) noted how the inhabitants of the Sarajevo suburb of Dobrinja responded to the total disruption of their everyday life during the siege of the city by spontaneously evolving various "grids" in order to organize activities that were previously organized by the state (transportation, education, etc.). He makes a point of contrasting such desire for rational ordering among Sarajevans with the critique of the state and its top-down planning (i.e., in James Scott's work).

7. I am grateful to Paul Silverstein for pointing this out to me.

8. Dinkić himself, however, is not overly guilty of portraying the "robbers" as infinitely clever or omnipotent. He clearly points out that some of the inflation-producing mechanisms which in retrospect looked like inventions of malevolent geniuses were, in fact, arrived at only by a lucky stroke or after a number of failures to lure hard currency out of people's straw mattresses.

9. Mulder, an FBI agent in the American science fiction TV series the *X-Files* (1993–2002), believes in aliens and the paranormal, and becomes a pawn in government conspiracies.

10. Mille vs. Transition

1. See Collin 2002, for a sympathetic journalistic account.

2. See http://www.irex.org/newsroom/news/2004/0413-mdd-mile.asp (accessed April 2010) for the IREX blurb on the series.

3. Mille is a very common Serbian name. I am deliberately spelling it "Mille" to avoid the native English speaker's tendency to read "Mile" as a unit of length (thus something like "Kilometer vs. Transition). Thanks to Bruce Grant for pointing this out to me.

4. For the importance of *inat* as a secret to Serbian mentality, see the farmer's market vignette in chapter 5 that, coincidentally, took place at the *Kalenić pijaca* (just across the street from where Mille lives).

5. A good sample of this discussion that I consider fairly representative of the kinds of positions I encountered in everyday conversations is available at http://forum.b92.net/index.php?showtopic=7833&st=60 (accessed April 2010).

6. http://forum.b92.net/index.php?showtopic=7833&st=60 (accessed April 2010).

7. The Serbian site is at http://www.nspm.rs; the site in English is at http://www.nspm.rs/nspm-in-english; and the old site is at http://starisajt.nspm.rs/indexs.htm (accessed August 2010).

8. Teofil here creatively modifies the verb *mozgati*—literally "to brain," to think or ponder, in a way that suggests dabbling, stuttering, or birdlike pecking—coining a new verb, *mozguckajuci,* that means something like "birdlike superficial mentation."

9. The whole polemic is accessible (in Serbian) at http://starisajt.nspm.rs/PrenetiTekstovi/antonic_polemika_vreme2.htm (accessed April 2010).

10. And in a move typical of domestic conspiracy theories, its stark incongruity overlooked, this "missionizing" intelligentsia is often accused of both a Stalinist mind-set (and pedigree) and of being mercenaries of NATO, the West, and the New World Order.

11. Such rhetorical identification is most clear in an angry rejoinder to Teofil's second analysis of Mille by Dragan Milosavljević, a journalist who often participates in polemics on the *New Serbian Political Thought* website on the side of "national democrats" who battle the "missionizing" intelligentsia. See http://starisajt.nspm.rs/komentari2005/2005_dm_mile_1.htm (accessed August 2010). See also the whole polemic about Mille at http://starisajt.nspm.rs/Intervjui/kulturna_politika.htm (accessed April 2010).

12. My favorite is Haraszti's *Velvet Prison* (1987).

Conclusion

1. The term was suggested by James W. Fernandez (personal communication).

2. The need to synchronize train schedules provided the impetus for standardizing time zones. The train journey offered the most vivid example of the shock of modernity's acceleration (see Schivelbusch 1986). Regularity or irregularity of national train schedules is used to characterize a nation's rationality and closeness to modernity. Einstein used trains to explain his relativity theory. In

Serbia, to say "southern railroad track" (*južna pruga*) is to evoke a wealth of associations with backwardness and slowness; indeed, Milošević promised fast trains at
the end of his rule to signal his embrace of European values. The most ubiquitous
phrase expressing the inability of peripheries to "catch up" with the metropolis is to
say that they fail to "catch the train" or that they should strive to jump into the last
rail car (on the road to modernity).

    3. I discussed the tropes of jury-rigging, in detail, as a commentary on the
makeshift, crooked, improvised, and messy nature of the social world in Serbia at
the panel in honor of Daphne Berdahl in 2008 (Živković 2008). Although I focus
on car maintenance and restoration as the primary site of jury-rigging or jerry-
building (*budženje* in Serbian), which is then metaphorically extended to the whole
of society, one could argue that houses, too, and especially computers, offer rich
loci for these practices and the tropes they produce.

BIBLIOGRAPHY

Abbott, Edwin A., and Ian Stewart. 2002. *The Annotated Flatland: A Romance of Many Dimensions.* Cambridge, Mass.: Perseus.

Abu-Lughod, Lila. 1991. "Writing Against Culture." In *Recapturing Anthropology: Working in the Present,* ed. R. G. Fox. Santa Fe: School of American Research Press.

Adamović, Vladimir. 1991. "Dinarski i moravski tip: sličnosti i razlike." In *Etnopsihologija danas,* ed. B. Jovanović. Beograd: Dom kulture "Studentski grad."

Aksentijević, Pavle. 1994. Statement in the column "Ljudi i vreme." *Vreme,* August 8.

Allcock, John B. 2000. *Explaining Yugoslavia.* New York: Columbia University Press.

Altorki, Soraya, and Cammilia Fawzi El-Solh, eds. 1988. *Arab Women in the Field: Studying Your Own Society.* Syracuse, N.Y.: Syracuse University Press.

Anderson, Benedict. 1991. *Imagined Communities: Reflections on the Origin and Spread of Nationalism.* Rev. ed. London: Verso.

Antonić, Slobodan. 2002. *Zarobljena zemlja: Srbija za vlade Slobodana Miloševića.* Beograd: Otkrovenje.

———. 2003. "Misionarska inteligencija u današnjoj Srbiji." *Vreme,* February 5. Available at http://www.vreme.com/cms/view.php?id=332405 or http://starisajt.nspm.rs/Komentari/komentarilantmisionarskantelig.htm (accessed April 2010).

Antonijević, Dragoslav. 1989. "Kult kneza Lazara u folklornoj tradiciji." In *Kosovska bitka 1389. godine i njene posledice: Medjunarodni simpozijum, Himelstir, 1989,* ed. N. Tasić. Beograd: Srpska akademija nauka i umetnosti (SANU).

Anzulović, Branimir. 1999. *Heavenly Serbia: From Myth to Genocide.* New York: New York University Press.

Appadurai, Arjun. 1986. "Theory in Anthropology: Center and Periphery." *Comparative Studies in Society and History* 28 (2): 356–361.

Arnold, Matthew. 1993. "Democracy (1861)." In *Culture and Anarchy and Other Writings,* ed. S. Collini. Cambridge: Cambridge University Press.

Arthur, Brian W. 1990. "Positive Feedbacks in the Economy." *Scientific American,* 92–99.

Bakhtin, Mikhail Mikhailovich. 1994. *The Dialogic Imagination: Four Essays.* Austin: University of Texas Press.

Bakić-Hayden, Milica, and Robert Hayden. 1992. "Orientalist Variations on the Theme 'Balkans': Symbolic Geography in Recent Yugoslav Cultural Politics." *Slavic Review* 51 (1): 1–15.

Bakić-Hayden, Milica. 1995. "Nesting Orientalisms: The Case of Former Yugoslavia." *Slavic Review* 54 (4): 917–931.

———. 1997. "Devastating Victory and Glorious Defeat: The Mahabharata and Kosovo in National Imaginings." Ph. D. dissertation, Department of South Asian Languages and Civilizations, University of Chicago.

Banac, Ivo. 1984. *The National Question in Yugoslavia: Origins, History, Politics.* Ithaca, N.Y.: Cornell University Press.

Banchoff, Thomas F. 1990. *Beyond the Third Dimension: Geometry, Computer Graphics, and Higher Dimensions.* New York: Scientific American Library.

Banfield, Edward C. 1958. *The Moral Basis of a Backward Society.* Glencoe: Free Press.

Barrios, Elisa M. 1994. "The Return of the Native Point of View to Anthropology: From Authenticity to Professional Authority in 'Native' Anthropology." Master's thesis, Department of Anthropology, University of Chicago.

Barth, Frederik. 1981. "Ethnic Groups and Boundaries." In *Process and Form in Social Life: Selected Essays of Frederik Barth.* London: Routledge & Kegan Paul.

Barth, Theodor. 1999. "Ben Zug—Jewish Identity: The Books of Zagreb and Sarajevo." In *Collective Identity and Citizenship in Europe: Fields of Access and Exclusion,* ed. T. Barth and M. Enzell. Oslo: ARENA/The Van Leer Institute.

Bećković, Matija. 1989. "Kosovo je najskuplja srpska reč." *Glas crkve: časopis za hrišćansku kulturu i crkveni život (Vidovdanski broj),* 19–28.

———. 1989a. "Kalendar 1982–1989." In *Serbia i komentari za 1988/89,* ed. Z. Stojković. Beograd: Zadužbina Miloša Crnjanskog.

———. 1990. *Služba.* Beograd: Srpska književna zadruga.

Bennoune, Mahfoud. 1985. What Does It Mean to Be a Third World Anthropologist? *Dialectical Anthropology* 9:357–364.

Biševac, Safeta. 1997. "Ima li antisemitizma u Jugoslaviji: Ovde, za mržnju, Jevreji nisu neophodni." *Naša Borba,* March 26.

Bjelić, Dušan I., and Obrad Savić, eds. 2002. *Balkan as Metaphor: Between Globalization and Fragmentation.* Cambridge, Mass.: MIT Press.

Blagojević, Slobodan. 1991. "Dnevnik o Dvornikoviću." *Delo* 37 (9–12): 3–25.

Bogdanović, Bogdan. 1993. "Murder of the City." *New York Review of Books,* May 27, p. 20.

Bogert, Ralph. 1991. "Paradigm of Defeat or Victory? The Kosovo Myth vs. the Kosovo Covenant in Fiction." In *Kosovo: Legacy of a Medieval Battle,* ed. W. S. Vucinich and T. A. Emmert. Minneapolis: University of Minnesota Press.

Bohannon, John. 2008. "The Man Who Went Up a Hill and Came Down a Pyramid." *Discover.* Published online October 2, 2008. Available at http://discovermagazine.com/2008/nov/22-the-man-who-went-up-a-hill-and-came-down-a-pyramid/article_view?b_start:int=2&-C= (accessed February 23, 2009).

Booth, Wayne C. 1974. *A Rhetoric of Irony.* Chicago: University of Chicago Press.

Bougarel, Xavier. 1998. "Yugoslav Wars: The 'Revenge of the Countryside,' Between Sociological Reality and Nationalist Myth." Paper read at Annual Meeting of the American Association for the Advancement of Slavic Studies (AAASS), Boca Raton, Florida.

Bourdieu, Pierre. 1966. "The Sentiment of Honor in Kabyle Society." In *Honor and Shame: The Values of Mediterranean Society,* ed. J. G. Peristany. Chicago: University of Chicago Press.

———. 1977. *Outline of a Theory of Practice.* Cambridge: Cambridge University Press.

———. 1984. *Distinction: A Social Critique of the Judgement of Taste.* Cambridge, Mass.: Harvard University Press.

Boym, Svetlana. 2001. *The Future of Nostalgia.* New York: Basic Books.

Brandt, Erik. 1997. "Myths of Innocence: War and Anthropological Discourse, the Case of the Former Yugoslavia." Paper read at The Second Conference of the Association for Balkan Anthropology (ABA), September 4–7, Bucharest, Romania.

Branković, Srbobran. 1995. *Serbia at War with Itself: Political Choice in Serbia, 1990–1994.* Translated by Mary Thompson-Popović and Mira Poznanović. Beograd: Sociological Society of Serbia.

Brettell, Caroline B, ed. 1993. *When They Read What We Write: The Politics of Ethnography.* Westport, Conn.: Bergin & Garvey.

Briggs, Charles L., and Richard Bauman. 1992. "Genre, Intertextuality, and Social Power." *Journal of Linguistic Anthropology* 2 (2): 131–172.

Brkić, Jovan. 1961. *Moral Concepts in Traditional Serbian Epic Poetry.* Slavistic Printings and Reprintings 24. The Hague: Mouton.

Brown, Keith. 2003. *The Past in Question: Modern Macedonia and the Uncertainties of Nation.* Princeton, N.J.: Princeton University Press.

Brown, Richard Harvey. 1977. *A Poetic for Sociology: Toward a Logic of Discovery for the Human Science.* Cambridge: Cambridge University Press.

Browning, Christopher R. 1985. *Fateful Months: Essays on the Emergence of the Final Solution.* New York: Holmes & Meier.

Bruner, Edward M., and Phyllis Gorfain. 1984. "Dialogic Narration and the Paradoxes of Masada." In *Text, Play, and Story: The Construction and Reconstruction of Self and Society,* ed. S. Plattner and E. Bruner. Washington, D.C.: American Ethnological Society.

Budding, Audrey Helfant. 1998. "Serb Intellectuals and the National Question, 1961–1991." Ph.D. diss., History Department, Harvard University, Cambridge, Mass.

Burgess, Anthony. 1986. *A Clockwork Orange.* New York: Norton.

Burke, Kenneth. 1969. *A Grammar of Motives.* Berkeley: University of California Press.

Burke, Peter. 1978. *Popular Culture in Early Modern Europe.* New York: Harper and Row.

Byrnes, Robert F., ed. 1976. *Communal Families in the Balkans: The Zadruga. Essays By Philip E. Mosely and Essays in His Honor.* South Bend, Ind.: University of Notre Dame Press.

Čajkanović, Veselin. 1973. *Mit i religija u Srba: izabrane studije,* ed. V. Djurić. Beograd: Srpska književna zadruga.

———. 1985. *O magiji i religiji.* Beograd: Prosveta.

Čanak, Nenad. 1994. "Janičari iz mog sokaka." *Nedeljna Borba,* June 11.

Carmichael, Cathie. 2002. *Ethnic Cleansing in the Balkans: Nationalism and the Destruction of Tradition.* London: Routledge.

Carrier, James G. 1992. "Occidentalism: The World Turned Upside Down." *American Ethnologist* 19:195–212,

Cassirer, Ernst. 1946. *The Myth of the State*. New Haven, Conn.: Yale University Press.

Castoriadis, Cornelius. 1987. *The Imaginary Institution of Society*. Cambridge, Mass.: MIT Press.

Cerović, Stojan. 1994. "Beogradska južna pruga." *Vreme*, September 12.

———. 1995. "Policijska bajka." *Vreme*, June 12.

———.1999. "Duh izgubljene decenije: Izlazak iz istorije." *Vreme*, August 28.

Certeau, Michel de. 1988. *The Practice of Everyday Life*. Berkeley: University of California Press.

Chambers, Ross. 2001. "Narrative and the Imaginary: A Review of Gilbert Durand's *The Anthropological Structures of the Imaginary*." *Narrative* 9 (1): 100–109.

Clark, Janine N. 2008. *Serbia in the Shadow of Milošević: The Legacy of Conflict in the Balkans*. London: Tauris.

Cohen, Lenard. 1993. *Broken Bonds: The Disintegration of Yugoslavia*. Boulder, Colo.: Westview.

———. 1997. "Slobodan Milosevic." In *The Serbs and Their Leaders in the Twentieth Century*, ed. P. Radan and A. Pavković. Aldershot: Ashgate.

———. 2001. *Serpent in the Bosom: The Rise and Fall of Slobodan Milosevic*. Boulder, Colo.: Westview.

Cohen, Leonard J., and Jasna Dragović-Soso, eds. 2008. *State Collapse in South-Eastern Europe: New Perspectives on Yugoslavia's Disintegration*. Lafayette, Ind.: Purdue University Press.

Cohen, Philip J. 1996. *Serbia's Secret War: Propaganda and the Deceit of History*. Eastern European Studies 2. College Station: Texas A&M University Press.

Collin, Matthew. 2002. *Guerrilla Radio: Rock 'N' Roll Radio and Serbia's Underground Resistance*. New York: Thunder's Mouth.

Čolović, Ivan. 1985. *Divlja književnost: Etnolingvističko proučavanje paraliterature*. Beograd: Nolit.

———. 1993. "The Propaganda of War: Its Strategies." In *Yugoslavia: Collapse, War, Crimes*, ed. S. Biserko. Belgrade: Centre for Anti-War Action: Association of Independent Intellectuals "Belgrade Circle."

———. 1994. *Bordel ratnika: folklor, politika i rat*. Beograd: Biblioteka XX vek.

———. 1994a. *Pucanje od zdravlja*. Beograd: Beogradski krug.

———. 1996. "Sozercanje." *Naša Borba*, August 10.

———. 1997. *Politika simbola: Ogledi o političkoj antropologiji*. Beograd: Radio B92.

———. 2002. *Politics of Identity in Serbia: Essays in Political Anthropology*. Translated by C. Hawkesworth. New York: New York University Press.

Comaroff, Jean, and John Comaroff. 2003. "Transparent Fictions; or, The Conspiracies of a Liberal Imagination: An Afterword." In *Transparency and Conspiracy: Ethnographies of Suspicion in the New World Order*, ed. H. G. West and T. Sanders. Durham, N.C.: Duke University Press.

Ćosić, Dobrica. 1978. *A Time of Death*. Translated by Muriel Heppell. New York: Harcourt Brace Jovanovich.

Cvijanović, Zoran. 2005. Intervju—Zoran Cvijanović: Espreso bato. *Vreme*, January 27. Available at http://www.vreme.com/cms/view.php?id=404318 (accessed April 2010)

Cvijić, Jovan, and Ivo Andrić. 1988. *O balkanskim psihičkim tipovima.* Edited by Petar Džadžić. Beograd: Prosveta.

Cvijić, Jovan. 1987a. *Antropogeografski i etnografski spisi.* Vol. 4 (I), *Sabrana dela.* Beograd: Srpska akademija nauka i umetnosti (SANU), Književne Novine & Zavod za udžbenike.

———. 1987b. *Balkansko poluostrvo.* Vol. 2, *Sabrana dela.* Beograd: Srpska akademija nauka i umetnosti (SANU), Književne Novine & Zavod za udžbenike.

———. 1930. Studies in Jugoslav Psychology. *Slavonic Review* 9 (26): 375–390.

Danojlić, Milovan. 1990 [1977]. *Muka s rečima.* 5th ed. Beograd: Biblioteka XX vek.

David, Filip. 2000. "Antisemitizam medju nama." *Danas (Vikend),* January 6–9.

Delić, Jovan. 1990. "Ustaničko vaskresenje kosovskog mita prema Vukovom Srpskom rječniku." In *Tradicija i Vuk Stef. Karadžić.* Beograd: BIGZ.

Denich, Bette S. 1974. "Sex and Power in the Balkans." In *Woman, Culture, and Society,* ed. M. Z. Rosaldo and L. Lamphere. Stanford. Calif.: Stanford University Press.

———. 1994. "Dismembering Yugoslavia: Nationalist Ideologies and the Symbolic Revival of Genocide." *American Ethnologist* 21 (2): 367–390.

Dimova, Rozita. 2006. "Modern Masculinities: Ethnicity, Education, and Gender in Macedonia." *Nationalities Papers* 34 (3): 305–320.

Dinkić, Mladjan. 1995. *Ekonomija destrukcije: velika pljačka naroda.* Beograd: VIN.

Djilas, Aleksa. 1991. *The Contested Country: Yugoslav Unity and Communist Revolution, 1919–1953.* Cambridge, Mass.: Harvard University Press.

———. 1993. "A Profile of Slobodan Milošević." *Foreign Affairs* 72 (3): 81–96.

Djordjević, Dimitrije. 1991. "The Tradition of Kosovo in the Formation of Modern Serbian Statehood in the Nineteenth Century." In *Kosovo: Legacy of a Medieval Battle,* ed. W. S. Vucinich and T. A. Emmert. Minneapolis: University of Minnesota Press.

Djordjević, Mirko. 1995. "Književnost populističkog talasa." *Republika,* March 31.

———. 1996. "Matija Bećković—pesnik i propovednik." *Republika,* November 16–30.

———. 1996a. "Povratak propovednika." *Republika,* July 1–31.

Djukič, Slavoljub. 1992. *Kako se dogodio vodja: borbe za vlast u Srbiji posle Josipa Broza, Biblioteka posebnih izdanja.* Beograd: Filip Višnjić.

———. 1994. *Izmedju slave i anateme: politička biografija Slobodana Miloševića.* Beograd: Filip Višnjić.

———. 2001. *Milošević and Marković: A Lust for Power.* Montreal: McGill-Queen's University Press.

Djurić, Vojislav, ed. 1990. *Kosovski boj u srpskoj knjizevnosti.* Beograd: Srpska književna zadruga.

Doniger, Wendy. 1984. *Dreams, Illusion, and Other Realities.* Chicago: University of Chicago Press.

Dragičevic-Šešić, Milena. 1995. "Kulturna politika sada i ovde." Beograd: TV Politika.

Dragnich, Alex N., and Slavko Todorovich. 1984. *The Saga of Kosovo: Focus on Serbian-Albanian Relations.* Boulder, Colo.: East European Monographs.

Dragojević, Srdjan. 1998. Interview. *Vreme,* June 6.

Drakulić, Slavenka. 1993. *How We Survived Communism and Even Laughed.* New York: Norton.

Drašković, Danica. 1994. "Svaka svoga da ubije dahiju." *Nedeljna Borba*, July 30.

Drašković, Vuk. 1982. *Nož*. Beograd: Zapis.

———. 1985. *Molitva*. 2 vols. Beograd: Nova knjiga.

———. 1987. *Odgovori*. Beograd: Glas.

———. 1990. *Koekude Srbijo*. 4th ed. Beograd: Nova knjiga.

Dumont, Louis. 1994. *German Ideology: From France to Germany and Back*. Chicago: University of Chicago Press.

Durković-Jakšić, Ljubomir. 1989. "Ustanovljenje u vaskrsloj Srbiji 1889. Vidovdana za državni praznik." In *Sveti knez Lazar: Spomenica o šestoj stogodišnjici kosovskog boja 1389–1989*. Beograd: Sveti Arhijerejski Sinod Srpske pravoslavne crkve.

Dvorniković, Vladimir. 1939. *Karakterologija Jugoslovena*. Beograd: Geca Kon A. D.

Džadžić, Petar. 1994. *Homo balcanicus, homo heroicus*. 2 vols. Beograd: Prosveta.

———. 1988. "Jovan Cvijić i balkanski psihički tipovi." Introductory essay in *Jovan Cvijić/Ivo Andrić: O balkanskim psihičkim tipovima*, ed. P. Džadžić. Beograd: Prosveta.

Elias, Norbert. 1994. *The Civilizing Process: The History of Manners and State Formation and Civilization*. Oxford: Blackwell.

———. 1996. *The Germans: Power Struggles and the Development of Habitus in the Nineteenth and Twentieth Centuries*. New York: Columbia University Press.

Emmert, Thomas A. 1996. "Milos Obilic and the Hero Myth." Serbian Studies, *Journal of the North American Society for Serbian Studies* 10.

Encyclopedia of the Holocaust. London: Collier Macmillan, 1990.

Fahim, Hussein, ed. 1982. *Indigenous Anthropology in Non-Western Countries: Proceedings of a Burg Wartenstein Symposium*. Durham, N.C.: Carolina Academic Press.

Fernandez, James W. 1986. *Persuasions and Performances: The Play of Tropes in Culture*. Bloomington: Indiana University Press.

———. 1988. "Andalusia on Our Minds: Two Contrasting Places in Spain as Seen in a Vernacular Poetic Duel of the Late 19th Century." *Cultural Anthropology* Vol. 3 (1): 21–35.

———. 1997. "The North-South Axis in European Popular Cosmologies and the Dynamic of the Categorical." *American Anthropologist* 99 (4): 725–730.

Florensky, Pavel. 1996. *Iconostasis*. Translated by Donald Sheehan and Olga Andrejev. Crestwood, N.Y.: St. Vladimir's Seminary Press.

Fortis, Alberto. 1778. *Travels into Dalmatia; containing general observations on the natural history of that country and the neighbouring islands; the natural productions, arts, manners and customs of the inhabitants: in a series of letters from Abbe Alberto Fortis, to the Earl of Bute, the Bishop of Londonderry, John Strange, Esq. &c. &c. To which are added by the same author, Observations on the island of Cherso and Osero. Translated from the Italian under the author's inspection. With an appendix, and other considerable additions, never before printed. Illustrated with twenty copper plates*. London: Printed for J. Robson.

Freidenreich, Harriet Pass. 1979. *The Jews of Yugoslavia: A Quest for Community*. Philadelphia, Pa.: Jewish Publication Society of America.

Gagnon, V. P., Jr. 2004. *The Myth of Ethnic War: Serbia and Croatia in the 1990s*. Ithaca, N.Y.: Cornell University Press.

Gal, Susan. 1991. "Bartók's Funeral: Representations of Europe in Hungarian Political Rhetoric." *American Ethnologist,* 18 (3): 440–458.

Gal, Susan, and Judith T. Irvine. 1995. "The Boundaries of Languages and Disciplines: How Ideologies Construct Difference." *Social Research* 62 (4): 967–1001.

Garton Ash, Timothy. 1989. "Does Central Europe Exist?" In *The Uses of Adversity: Essays on the Fate of Central Europe.* New York: Random House.

———. 1997. "Eastern Europe's Paradox—Why Some Nations Prosper while Others Decline." *Washington Post,* October 5, C01.

Gesemann, Gerhard. 1968 [1943]. *Čojstvo i junaštvo starih Crnogoraca* (Translated from the original German: *Heroische lebensform: Zur Literatur und Wesenskunde der Balkanichen Patriarchalität*). Cetinje: Obod.

Ginzburg, Carlo. 1979. "Clues: Roots of a Scientific Paradigm." *Theory and Society* 7 (3): 273–288.

———. 1984. "Clues: Morelli, Freud, and Sherlock Holmes." In *The Sign of Three: Dupin, Holmes, Peirce,* ed. Umberto Eco and Thomas A. Sebeok. Bloomington: Indiana University Press.

Glenny, Misha. 1992. *The Fall of Yugoslavia: The Third Balkan War.* London: Penguin.

———. 1996. "If You Are Not For Us." *Sight and Sound,* 10–13.

Glišić, Milivoje. 1995. "Lepota života." *NIN,* March 24, p. 25.

Goffman, Erving. 1959. *The Presentation of Self in Everyday Life.* Garden City, N.Y.: Doubleday Anchor Books.

———. 1963. *Stigma: Notes on the Management of Spoiled Identity.* Englewood Cliffs, N.J.: Prentice Hall.

Gojković, Drinka. 1995. "Trauma bez katarze: Udruženje književnika Srbije: Radjanje nacionalizma iz duha demokratije." *Republika,* June 16–30.

Goldsworthy, Vesna. 1998. *Inventing Ruritania: The Imperialism of the Imagination.* New Haven, Conn.: Yale University Press.

Gordiejew, Paul Benjamin. 1999. *Voices of Yugoslav Jewry.* Albany: State University of New York Press.

Gordy, Eric. 1999. *The Culture of Power in Serbia: Nationalism and the Destruction of Alternatives.* University Park: Pennsylvania State University Press.

Gorup, Radmila J. 1991. "Kosovo and Epic Poetry." In *Kosovo: Legacy of a Medieval Battle,* ed. W. S. Vucinich and T. A. Emmert. Minneapolis: University of Minnesota Press.

Gourgouris, Stathis. 1996. *Dream Nation: Enlightenment, Colonization, and the Institution of Modern Greece.* Stanford, Calif.: Stanford University Press.

Greenfeld, Liah. 1992. *Nationalism: Five Roads to Modernity.* Cambridge, Mass.: Harvard University Press.

Greer, Charles. 1997. "Vuk Karadžić on How to Make a Language: Representing Language Conflict, Serbia, 1818." Unpublished manuscript, Linguistics Department, University of California, Berkeley.

Hall, Brian. 1995. *The Impossible Country: A Journey through the Last Days of Yugoslavia.* New York: Penguin Books.

Halpern, Joel, and Eugene Hammel. 1969. "Observations on the Intellectual History of Ethnology and Other Social Sciences in Yugoslavia." *Comparative Studies in Society and History* 11 (1): 17–26.

Hannerz, Ulf. 1992. *Cultural Complexity: Studies in the Social Organization of Meaning.* New York: Columbia University Press.

Hanson, Stephen E. 1997. *Time and Revolution: Marxism and the Design of Soviet Institutions.* Chapel Hill: University of North Carolina Press.

Harazsti, Miklos. 1987. *The Velvet Prison: Artists under State Socialism.* New York: Basic Books.

Havel, Vaclav. 1986. *Living in Truth.* London: Faber and Faber.

Hayden, Robert. 1994. "Recounting the Dead: The Discovery and Redefinition of Wartime Massacres in Late- and Post-Communist Yugoslavia." In *Memory, History, and Opposition under State Socialism,* ed. R. S. Watson. Santa Fe, N.M.: School of American Research Press.

——. 1996. "Schindler's Fate: Genocide, Ethnic Cleansing, and Population Transfers." *Slavic Review* 55 (4): 727–748.

——. 1999. *Blueprints for a House Divided: The Constitutional Logic of the Yugoslav Conflicts.* Ann Arbor: University of Michigan Press.

Herzfeld, Michael. 1985. *The Poetics of Manhood: Contest and Identity in a Cretan Mountain Village.* Princeton, N.J.: Princeton University Press.

——. 1987. *Anthropology through the Looking Glass: Critical Ethnography in the Margins of Europe.* Cambridge: Cambridge University Press.

——. 1997. *Cultural Intimacy: Social Poetics in the Nation-State.* New York: Routledge.

——. 2001. "Irony and Power: Toward a Politics of Mockery in Greece." In *Irony in Action: Anthropology, Practice, and the Moral Imagination,* ed. James W. Fernandez and Mary Taylor Huber. Chicago: University of Chicago Press.

Hilberg, Raul. 1985. *The Destruction of the European Jews.* New York: Holmes & Meier.

Hofstadter, Richard. 1965. *The Paranoid Style in American Politics and Other Essays.* New York: Knopf.

Hunt, Harry T. 1989. *The Multiplicity of Dreams: Memory, Imagination, and Consciousness.* New Haven, Conn.: Yale University Press.

Huntington, Samuel P. 1993. "The Clash of Civilizations?" *Foreign Affairs* 72 (3): 22–49.

Il'f, Il'a, and Evgenii Petrov. 1961. *The Twelve Chairs.* Translated by J. H. C. Richardson. New York: Vintage Books. Original edition, *Dvenadtsat' stul'ev.*

——. 1962. *The Golden Calf.* Translated by J. H. C. Richardson. London: F. Muller. Original edition, *Zolotoi Telenok.*

Iordanova, Dina. 1996. "Conceptualizing the Balkans in Film." *Slavic Review* 55 (4): 882–890.

——. 1996a. "Balkan Film Representations since 1989: The Quest for Admissibility." *Historical Journal of Film, Radio, and TV* 18 (2): 263–280.

——. 2001. *Cinema of Flames: Balkan Film, Culture, and the Media.* London: British Film Institute.

Irvine, Judith T., and Susan Gal. 2000. "Language Ideology and Linguistic Differentiation." In *Regimes of Language: Ideologies, Polities, and Identities,* ed. P. V. Kroskrity. Santa Fe, N.M.: School of American Research.

Ivy, Marilyn. 1995. *Discourses of the Vanishing: Modernity, Phantasm, Japan.* Chicago: University of Chicago Press.

Jameson, Fredric. 1988. "Cognitive Mapping." In *Marxism and the Interpretation of Culture*, ed. C. Nelson and L. Grossberg. Urbana: University of Illinois Press.

Jansen, Stef. 2002. "Svakodnevni orijentalizam: dozivljaj 'Balkana'/'Evrope' u Beogradu i Zagrebu." *Filozofija i društvo* 18:33–71.

———. 2008. "Looking for a Bus: How Certain Schemes to Improve the Suburban Condition Have Been Hailed." Paper read at Critical Spaces of Hope: Locating Postsocialism and the Future in Post-Yugoslav Anthropology, at the University of Chicago.

Jevtić, Atanasije. 1987. *Od Kosova do Jadovna*. Biblioteka "Glas Crkve": Posebna izdanja; knjiga 5. Šabac: Glas Crkve. Available at http://www.rastko.rs/kosovo /istorija/kosovo-jadovno_c.html (accessed April 2010)

———. 1989. "Kosovsko opredeljenje za carstvo nebesko u istorijskoj sudbini srpskog naroda." In *Sveti knez Lazar: Spomenica o šestoj stogodišnjici kosovskog boja 1389–1989*. Beograd: Sveti Arhijerejski Sinod Srpske pravoslavne crkve.

———. 1992. *Sveti Sava i kosovski zavet*. Beograd: Srpska književna zadruga.

Jovanović, Bojan, ed. 1992. *Karakterologija Srba*. Beograd: Naučna knjiga.

Jovanović, Dragan. 1995. "Metaekologija: Ljudi od blata." *NIN*, December 15, p. 64.

———. 2002. "Vraćanje Troji." *NIN*, July 25. Available at http://www.nin.co.yu/ 2002-07/25/24262.html (accessed April 2010).

Jovanović, Slobodan. 1925. *Ustavobranitelji i njihova vlada (1838–1858)*. 2nd ed. Beograd: Izdavačka knjižarnica Napredak.

———. 1991. "Jedan predlog za proučavanje srpskog nacionalnog karaktera." *Duga*, March 16–30, pp. 82–90.

———. 1992. "Srpski nacionalni karakter." In *Karakterologija Srba*, ed. B. Jovanović. Beograd: Naučna knjiga.

Jović, Dejan. 2009. *Yugoslavia: A State That Withered Away*. West Lafayette, Ind.: Purdue University Press.

Kafka, Franz. 1972 [1946]. *The Complete Stories*. New York: Schocken Books.

Kaku, Michio. 1994. *Hyperspace: A Scientific Odyssey through Parallel Universes, Time Warps, and The Tenth Dimension*. New York: Oxford University Press.

Kalajić, Dragoš. 1990. "Srpska odbrana Evrope." *Duga*, no. 427.

———. 1995. "Škola za nove janičare." *Oslobodjenje*, March 21, p. 3.

Kalezić, Dimitrije M. 1989. "Religioznofilosofske dimenzije kosovske tradicije." In *Sveti knez Lazar: Spomenica o šestoj stogodišnjici kosovskog boja 1389–1989*. Beograd: Sveti Arhijerejski Sinod Srpske pravoslavne crkve.

Kaplan, Robert D. 1993. *Balkan Ghosts: A Journey through History*. New York: St. Martin's.

Kataev, Valentin. 1933. *Time, Forward!* Translated by C. Malamuth. New York: Farrar & Rinehart.

Kifner, John. 1994. "Through the Serbian Mind's Eye." *New York Times*, Sunday, April 10.

Kinzer, Stephen. 1993. "The Nightmare's Roots: The Dream World Called Serbia." *New York Times*, Sunday, May 16, pp. 1, 5.

Knežević, Aleksandar, and Vojislav Tufegdžić. 1995. *Kriminal koji je izmenio Srbiju*. Beograd: Radio B-92.

Knight, Peter. 1999. "'A Plague of Paranoia': Theories of Conspiracy Theory since the 1960s." In *Fear Itself: Enemies Real and Imagined in American Culture,* ed. N. L. Schultz. West Lafayette, Ind.: Purdue University Press.

Koljević, Nikola. 1991. "Srbi i Srbija." *NIN,* May 17, p. 42.

Komnenić, Milan. 1989. "Šest stotina naših kosovdana." *Glas crkve (Vidovdanski broj),* 33–38.

Kondo, Dorinne. 1990. *Crafting Selves: Power, Gender, and Discourses of Identity in a Japanese Workplace.* Chicago: University of Chicago Press.

Konstantinović, Radomir. 1991. *Filosofija palanke.* 2nd ed. Beograd: Nolit.

Krleža, Miroslav. 1982. *Zastave.* 3rd ed. Vol. 1. Sarajevo: NIŠRO Oslobodjenje.

Krstić, Dragan. 1991. "Obretenje Lazarevo." In *Naučni sastanak slavista u Vukove dane,* 19/1. Beograd: MSC.

Kundera, Milan. 1991. [1984]. "The Tragedy of Central Europe." In *From Stalinism to Pluralism: A Documentary History of Eastern Europe since 1945,* ed. G. Stokes. New York: Oxford University Press.

Lauer, Reinhard, and Werner Lehfeldt, eds. 1995. *Das jugoslawische Desaster: historische, sprachliche und ideologische Hintergründe, Sammlung Harrassowitz.* Wiesbaden: Harrassowitz.

Lauer, Reinhard. 1993. "Aus Mördern werden Helden: Serbische Heldendichtung." *Frankfurter Allgemeine Zeitung.*

Laušević, Mirjana. 1994. "Music and Politics in Bosnia." Paper read at the Annual Meeting of the Society for Ethnomusicology (with American Folklore Society), October 1994, Milwaukee, Wisconsin.

Lindstrom, Nicole, and Maple Razsa. 1998. "'Balkan is Beautiful': Examining the Role of 'Balkanism' in the Construction of Croatian National Identity." Paper read at the Slavic Forum, April 18, University of Chicago.

Ljubinković, Nenad, ed. 1989. *Kosovo u pamćenju i stvaralaštvu.* Beograd: Narodna biblioteka "Vuk Karadžić."

Lomnitz-Adler, Claudio. 1992. *Exits from the Labyrinth: Culture and Ideology in the Mexican National Space.* Berkeley: University of California Press.

Lord, Albert B. 2000. *The Singer of Tales.* Cambridge, Mass.: Harvard University Press.

Luković-Pjanović, Olga. 1988. *Srbi . . . narod najstariji.* Indianapolis: Glas Srba (also 1990 Beograd: Dosije; and 1993, 1994, and 2003 Beograd: Miroslav).

Marcus, George E., ed. 1999. *Paranoia Within Reason: A Casebook in Conspiracy as Explanation.* Late Editions: Cultural Studies for the End of the Century 6. Chicago: University of Chicago Press.

Marković, Zoran M. 1996. "Nacija—žrtva i osveta (prema revijalnoj štampi u Srbiji, 1987–1991)." *Republika,* May 1–15.

Matić, Jovanka. 1996. "The Media and Ethnic Mobilization: The Formula of Kosovo." In *Ethnicity in Postcommunism.* Beograd: Institute of Social Sciences: Forum for Ethnic Relations: International Network Europe and the Balkans.

Matović, D. 2007. Balkanci su jedan narod. *Večernje novosti online.* October 16. Available at http://www.novosti.rs/code/navigate.php?Id=12&status=jedna&vest=109954&datum=2007-10-16 (accessed April 2010).

Matvejević, Predrag. 1989. "Central Europe Seen from the East of Europe. In *In Search of Central Europe,* ed. G. Schöpflin and N. Wood. Cambridge: Polity.

Mazaj, Meta. 2007. "Tunnels, Trenches, Cellars: Nation and Heterotopia in Post-Yugoslav Film." In *Mythistory and Narratives of the Nation in the Balkans,* ed. T. Aleksić. Newcastle: Cambridge Scholars.

Messerschmidt, Donald A, ed. 1981. *Anthropologists at Home in North America: Methods and Issues in the Study of One's Own Society.* Cambridge: Cambridge University Press.

Meštrović, Stjepan G., S. Letica, and M. Goreta. 1993. *Habits of the Balkan Heart: Social Character and the Fall of Communism.* College Station: Texas A & M University Press.

Micić, Ljubomir. 1993. *Barbarogenije decivilizator.* Translated from French by Radmila Jovanović. Beograd: Filip Višnjić.

Mihailović, Milica, and Srećko Mihailović. 1996. "Anti-Semitism in the Nineties." In *Ethnicity in Postcommunism,* ed. D. Janić and S. Bianchini. Beograd: Institute of Social Sciences: Forum for Ethnic Relations: International Network Europe and the Balkans.

Mihaljčić, Rade. 1989. *The Battle of Kosovo in History and in Popular Tradition.* Belgrade: BIGZ.

Milekić, Tamara. 2004. "Srbija je golema nevolja." *Profil* 45, pp. 26–34.

Milinković, Branko, ed. 1994. *Govor mržnje: analiza sadržaja domaćih medija u prvoj polovini 1993. godine.* Beograd: Centar za antiratnu akciju.

Miljanov, Marko. 1967. *Sabrana djela.* 5 vols. Titograd: Grafički zavod.

Milosavljević, Olga. 1995. "Upotreba autoriteta nauke: Javna politička delatnost Srpske akademije nauka i umetnosti (1986–1992)." *Republika* 119–120: i–xxx.

Mišić, Zoran. 1990. "Šta je to kosovsko opredeljenje: odgovor na jedno pitanje Marka Ristića." In *Kosovski boj u srpskoj književnosti.* Beograd: Srpska književna zadruga.

Mitrović, Andrej, et al. 1996. *Srbi o Nemcima..* Beograd: DBR International.

Mitrović, Andrej. 1996. "Predgovor: Srbi o Nemcima." In Andrej Mitrović et al., *Srbi o Nemcima.* Beograd: DBR International.

Nadkarni, Maya. 2007. "The Master's Voice: Authenticity, Nostalgia, and the Refusal of Irony in Postsocialist Hungary." *Social Identities* 13 (5): 611–626.

Narayan, Kirin. 1993. "How Native Is a 'Native' Anthropologist?" *American Anthropologist* 95 (3): 671–686.

Naumović, Slobodan. 1994. "Upotreba tradicije: politicka tranzicija i promena odnosa prema nacionalnim vrednostima u Srbiji 1987–1990." In *Kulture u tranziciji,* ed. M. Prošić-Dvornić. Beograd: Plato.

———. 1995. "Ustaj seljo, ustaj rode: Simbolika seljaštva i politička komunikacija u novijoj istoriji Srbije." *Godišnjak za društvenu istoriju* 1:39–63.

Nenadović, Aleksandar. 2000. "*Politika* in the Storm of Nationalism." In *The Road to War in Serbia: Trauma and Catharsis,* ed. N. Popov. Budapest: Central European University Press.

Nikolić, Milan, ed. 1995. *Šta je stvarno rekao Dobrica Cosić.* Beograd: Bodeks.

Nikolić, Miloš. 2002. *The Tragedy of Yugoslavia.* Baden-Baden: Nomos Verlagsgesellschaft.

Njegoš, Petar II. Petrović. 1989. *The Mountain Wreath.* Translated by Vasa D. Mihailović. Beograd: Vajat.

Novaković, Nikola J. 1994. "Premeštanje prema rasporedu svetlosti." *Naša Borba,*
    Sunday, December 24.
Novick, Peter. 1999. *The Holocaust in American Life.* Boston York: Houghton Mifflin.
Ohnuki-Tierney, Emiko. 1984. "Native Anthropologists." *American Ethnologist* 11
    (3): 584–586.
Pančić, Teofil. 1998. "Rane: Brlja, krv, *utoka,* kokain." *Vreme,* June 6.
———. 2004. "Mile sa Čubure u Vladi." *Vreme,* January 15. Available at http://www
    .vreme.com/cms/view.php?id=364193 (accessed April 2010).
———. 2005. "Mile protiv tranzicije—koplje u trnje: Nacionalna klasa." *Vreme,* Janu-
    ary 27. Available at http://www.vreme.com/cms/view.php?id=404318 (accessed
    April 2010).
Parker, Martin. 2001. "Human Science as Conspiracy Theory." In *The Age of Anxi-
    ety: Conspiracy Theory and the Human Sciences,* ed. J. Parish and M. Parker.
    Oxford: Blackwell.
Pavić, Milorad. 1988. *Dictionary of the Khazars: A Lexicon Novel in 100,000 Words.*
    New York: Knopf.
———. 1990. *Landscape Painted with Tea.* New York: Knopf.
———. 1993. *The Inner Side of the Wind; or, The Novel of Hero and Leander.* New
    York: Knopf.
———. 1998. *A Short History of Belgrade.* Translated by C. Pribičević-Zorić.
    Beograd: Dereta. Original edition, *Kratka istorija Beograda.*
Pavlović, Živojin, and Dušanka Milanović-Zeković. 1992. *Ludilo u ogledalu: Razgo-
    vori o civilizacijama, o religijama, o čoveku, o životu i smrti, o mržnji, o ljubavi.*
    Beograd: Srpska književna zadruga.
Pawlikowski, Paul. 1992. *Serbian Epics.* A "Bookmarks" series documentary. Lon-
    don: BBC.
Perec, Georges. 1999. *Species of Spaces and Other Pieces.* Translated by J. Sturrock.
    London: Penguin.
Pesmen, Dale. 1991. "Reasonable and Unreasonable Worlds: Some Expectations
    of Coherence in Culture Implied by the Prohibition of Mixed Metaphor." In
    Beyond Metaphor: The Theory of Tropes in Anthropology, ed. J. W. Fernandez.
    Stanford, Calif.: Stanford University Press.
———. 1998. "The Russian Soul: Ethnography and Metaphysics." Ph. D. disserta-
    tion, Department of Anthropology, University of Chicago.
———. 2000. *Russia and Soul: An Exploration.* Ithaca, N.Y.: Cornell University
    Press.
———. 2000a. "'A boggy, soggy, squitchy picture, truly': Notes on Image-Making in
    Anthropology and Elsewhere. *Anthropology and Humanism* 25 (2): 111–119.
Pickover, Clifford, A. 1999. *Surfin through Hyperspace: Understanding Higher Uni-
    verses in Six Easy Lessons.* New York: Oxford University Press.
Pištalo, Vladimir. Interview. *Vreme,* August 17.
Polanyi, Michael. 1958. *Personal Knowledge: Towards a Post-Critical Philosophy.*
    Chicago: University of Chicago Press.
Popadić, Dragan. 2000. "O mentalnom zdravlju naroda." *Republika* 233:21–28.
Popov, Nebojša. 1993. "Srpski populizam: Od marginalne do dominantne pojave."
    Vreme (special issue), May 24.

Popov, Nebojša, ed. 2000. *The Road to War in Serbia: Trauma and Catharsis.* Budapest: Central European University Press.

Popović, Bogdan. 1929. "Šta Srbi imaju da nauče od Engleza." *Srpski književni glasnik* 26 (April):252–266.

Popović, Danko. 1985. *Knjiga o Milutinu.* Beograd: Književne novine.

———. 1994. *Nespokoji.* Beograd: I. P. "Beograd" D.D.

Popović, Miodrag. 1998. *Vidovdan i časni krst: Ogledi iz književne arheologije.* Beograd: Biblioteka XX vek.

Popović, Nebojša. 1997. *Jevreji u Srbiji 1918–1941.* Beograd: Institut za savremenu instoriju.

Port, Mattijs van de. 1998. *Gypsies, Wars, and Other Instances of the Wild: Civilization and Its Discontents in a Serbian Town.* Amsterdam: Amsterdam University Press.

———. 1999. "The Articulation of Soul: Gypsy Musicians and the Serbian Other." *Popular Music* 18 (3): 291–308.

———. 1999a. "'It Takes a Serb to Know a Serb': Uncovering the Roots of Obstinate Otherness in Serbia." *Critique of Anthropology* 19 (1): 7–30.

Pozzi, Henri. 1994 [1935]. *Black Hand over Europe.* Translated by Ksenija Horvat. Zagreb: Croatian Information Centre.

Prodanović, Mileta. 2002. *Stariji i lepši Beograd.* Beograd: Stubovi kulture.

Radić, Radmila. 2000. "The Church and the 'Serbian Question.'" In *The Road to War in Serbia: Trauma and Catharsis,* ed. N. Popov. Budapest: Central European University Press.

Radović, Dušan. 1975. *Beograde dobro jutro.* Beograd: BIGZ.

Ramet, Sabrina P. 1996. *Balkan Babel: The Disintegration of Yugoslavia from the Death of Tito to Ethnic War.* 2nd ed. Boulder, Colo.: Westview.

Redfield, Robert. 1989. *The Little Community and Peasant Society and Culture.* Midway Reprint. Chicago: University of Chicago Press.

Rieff, David. 1993. "Notes on the Ottoman Legacy Written in a Time of War." *Salmagundi,* 3–15.

Ries, Nancy. 1997. *Russian Talk: Culture and Conversation during Perestroika.* Ithaca, N.Y.: Cornell University Press.

Rihtman Auguštin, Dunja. 1997. "Zasto i otkad se grozimo Balkana?" *Erasmus* 19:27–35.

Romano, Jaša. 1980. *Jevreji Jugoslavije 1941–1945, žrtve genocida i ucesnici NOR.* Beograd: Savez Jevrejskih opstina Jugoslavije.

Rucker, Rudy. 1984. *The Fourth Dimension: A Guided Tour of the Higher Universes.* Boston: Houghton Mifflin.

Rupnik, Jacques. 1994. "Europe's New Frontiers: Remapping Europe." *Daedalus* 123 (3): 91–114,

Sapir, Edward. 1924. "Culture, Genuine and Spurious." *American Journal of Sociology* 29:401–429.

Šćekić, Draško. 1994. *Sorabi: istoriopis.* Beograd: Sfairos/Timor.

Schivelbusch, Wolfgang. 1986. *The Railway Journey: The Industrialization of Time and Space in the Nineteenth Century.* Berkeley: University of California Press.

Schöpflin, George, and Nancy Wood, eds. 1989. *In Search of Central Europe.* Cambridge: Polity.

Schutz, Alfred. 1970. *On Phenomenology and Social Relations: Selected Writings.* Chicago: University of Chicago Press.

Selimović, Meša. 1977. *Sjećanja.* Beograd: Sloboda.

———. 1970. *Za i protiv Vuka.* Sarajevo: Svjetlost.

Sekelj, Laslo. 1993. *Yugoslavia: The Process of Disintegration.* Boulder, Colo.: Social Science Monographs and Atlantic Research and Publications.

———. 1995. *Vreme beščašća.* Beograd: Akademija Nova.

———. 1997. "Antisemitism and Jewish Identity in Serbia after the 1991 Collapse of the Yugoslav State." *Analysis of Current Trends in Antisemitism, acta no. 12.* Jerusalem: Hebrew University of Jerusalem.

Sekulić, Isidora. 2001. *Zapisi o mome narodu.* Edited by Z. Gluščević and M. Josimčević. Vol. 5, *Sabrana dela Isidore Sekulić.* Novi Sad: Stylos.

Silber, Laura, and Allan Little. 1996. *Yugoslavia: Death of a Nation.* TV Books, Penguin USA.

Simic, Andrei. 1973. *The Peasant Urbanites: A Study of Rural-Urban Mobility in Serbia.* New York: Seminar.

———. 1976. "Country 'N' Western Yugoslav Style: Contemporary Folk Music as a Mirror of Social Sentiment." *Journal of Popular Culture* 1 (1): 156–166.

———. 1979. "Commercial Folk Music in Yugoslavia: Idealization and Reality." *Journal of The Association of Graduate Dance Ethnologists, UCLA* 2:25–37.

———. 1979a. "Sevdah: The Ritual Containment of Machismo in the Balkans." *Journal of the Association of Graduate Dance Ethnologists, UCLA* 3:26–37.

———. 1983. "Machismo and Cryptomatriarchy: Power, Affect, and Authority in the Contemporary Yugoslav Family." *Ethos* 11 (1–2): 66–86.

Simis, Konstantin M. 1982. *USSR: The Corrupt Society: The Secret World of Soviet Capitalism.* New York: Simon and Schuster.

Simmel, Georg. 1950. *The Sociology of Georg Simmel.* Translated, edited, and with an introduction by Kurt H. Wolff. New York: Free Press.

Škaljić, Abdulah. 1989. *Turcizmi u srpskohrvatskom jeziku.* 6th ed. Sarajevo: Svetlost.

Skerlić, Jovan. 1925. *Omladina i njena književnost (1848–1871): izučavanja o nacionalnom i književnom romantizmu kod Srba.* Beograd: Izdavačka knjižara Napredak.

Slapšak, Svetlana. 1994. *Ogledi o bezbrižnostii.* Beograd: Radio B92.

Spark, Alasdair. 2001. *Conspiracy Thinking and Conspiracy Studying.* Available at http://www2.winchester.ac.uk/ccc/resources/essays/thinkstudy.htm (accessed April 2010).

Srejović, Dragoslav. 1972. *Europe's First Monumental Sculpture: New Discoveries at Lepenski Vir.* New York: Stein and Day.

Srnivas, M. N. 1967. "Some Thoughts on the Study of One's Own Society." In M. N. Srnivas, *Social Change in Modern India.* Berkeley: University of California Press.

Stanivuković, Zorica. 1998. "Hrvatska: Predrasude s kamatama." *NIN,* March 19, pp. 52–53.

Stanojčić, Vojislav. 1995. "TV prenosi iz Skupstine: Pet Vekova SPS-a." *Naša Borba,* March 30.

Stefanović, Nenad. 1993. "Srpska patriotska geografija: Beogradska dvojka na južnoj pruzi." *Duga* 516:13–15.

———. 1994. "Svić, crvene magle." *Duga* 525:14–16.

Stevanovic, Vidosav. 2004. *Milosevic: The People's Tyrant*. London: I. B. Taurus.

Stokes, Gale. 1990. *Politics as Development: The Emergence of Political Parties in Nineteenth-century Serbia*. Durham, N.C.: Duke University Press.

Thompson, Mark. 1992. *A Paper House: The Ending of Yugoslavia*. New York: Pantheon Books.

———. 1994. *Forging War: The Media in Serbia, Croatia, and Bosnia-Herzegovina*. London: Article 19.

Todorova, Maria. 1997. *Imagining the Balkans*. New York: Oxford University Press.

Tomashevich, George Vid. 1991. "The Battle of Kosovo and the Serbian Church." In *Kosovo: Legacy of a Medieval Battle*, ed. W. S. Vucinich and T. A. Emmert. Minneapolis: University of Minnesota.

Tomašić, Dinko. 1941. "Sociology in Yugoslavia." *American Journal of Sociology* 47:53–69.

———. 1948. *Personality and Culture in Eastern European Politics*. New York: George W. Stewart.

Trebješanin, Žarko. 1989. "Značaj kosovskog mita za socijalizaciju u srpskoj patrijarhalnoj kulturi." *Etnološke sveske* 10:113–116.

———. 1995. *Duša i politika: psihopatologija nesvakidasnjeg života*. Beograd: Vreme knjige.

Tucaković, Dinko. 1998. Simbolične i druge rane. *Vreme*, June 6.

Vasiljević, Vladan. 1992. "Intelektualna provincija Srbija." In *Druga Srbija*. Beograd: Plato, Beogradski krug, Borba.

Velmar-Janković, Vladimir. 1992. *Pogled s Kalemegdana: Ogled o beogradskom čoveku*. Beograd: Biblioteka grada Beograda.

Verdery, Katherine. 1991. *National Ideology under Socialism: Identity and Cultural Politics in Ceausescu's Romania*. Berkeley: University of California Press.

———. 1996. *What Was Socialism, and What Comes Next?* Princeton, N.J.: Princeton University Press.

———. 1999. *The Political Life of Dead Bodies: Reburial and Postsocialist Change*. New York: Columbia University Press.

Veselinov, Dragan. 1992. "Iseljavanje iz Vojvodine." In *Druga Srbija*. Beograd: Plato, Beogradski krug, Borba.

Vladisavljević, Nebojša. 2008. *Serbia's Antibureaucratic Revolution: Milošević, the Fall of Communism, and Nationalist Mobilization*. Houndmills, Hampshire: Palgrave Macmillan.

Voinovich, V. N. 1975. *Zhizn' i neobychainye prikliucheniia soldata Ivana Chonkina: Roman-anekdot v piati chastiakh*. Paris: YMCA-PRESS.

———. 1998. *The Life and Extraordinary Adventures of Private Ivan Chonkin*. Translated by R. Lourie. Evanston, Ill.: Northwestern University Press.

Vucinich, Wayne S., and Thomas A. Emmert, eds. 1991. *Kosovo: Legacy of a Medieval Battle*. Minnesota Mediterranean and East European Monographs. Minneapolis: University of Minnesota.

Vujačić, Veljko Marko. 1995. "Communism and Nationalism in Russia and Serbia." Ph. D. dissertation, Department of Sociology, University of California, Berkeley.

Vukadinović, Alek, ed. 1989. "Kosovo, 1389–1989." *Serbian Literary Quarterly,* 1–3 (special edition on the occasion of the six hundredth anniversary of the Battle of Kosovo). Beograde: Association of Serbian Writers.

Vuković, Tomislav, and Edo Bojović. 1992. *Pregled srpskog antisemitizma.* Zagreb: Altair.

Vygotsky, Lev. 1986. *Thought and Language.* Translated by Alex Kozulin. Cambridge, Mass.: MIT Press.

Wachtel, Andrew. 1998. *Making a Nation, Breaking a Nation: Literature and Cultural Politics in Yugoslavia.* Stanford. Calif.: Stanford University Press.

Watzlawick, Paul. 1977. *How Real Is Real? Confusion, Disinformation, Communication.* New York: Vintage Books.

West, Rebecca. 1969. *Black Lamb and Grey Falcon: A Journey through Yugoslavia.* Harmondsworth, Middlesex: Penguin Books.

White, Hayden. 1999. "Freud's Topology of Dreaming." In *Figural Realism: Studies in the Mimesis Effect.* Baltimore, Md.: Johns Hopkins University Press.

Williams, Raymond. 1993. *Keywords: A Vocabulary of Culture and Society.* Oxford: Oxford University Press.

Williams, Robert C. 1970. "The Russian Soul: A Study in European Thought and Non-European Nationalism." *Journal of the History of Ideas* 31 (4): 573–588,

Wolff, Larry. 1994. *Inventing Eastern Europe: The Map of Civilization on the Mind of the Enlightenment.* Stanford, Calif.: Stanford University Press.

———. 2001. *Venice and the Slavs: The Discovery of Dalmatia in the Age of Enlightenment.* Stanford, Calif.: Stanford University Press.

Woodward, Susan L. 1995. *Balkan Tragedy: Chaos and Dissolution after the Cold War.* Washington, D.C.: Brookings Institution.

Žanić, Ivo. 2007. *Flag on the Mountain: A Political Anthropology of the War in Croatia and Bosnia-Herzegovina, 1990–1995.* Translated by Graham McMaster and Celia Hawkesworth. London: SAQUI, in association with the Bosnian Institute.

Zerubavel, Eviatar. 1981. *Hidden Rhythms: Schedules and Calendars in Social Life.* Chicago: University of Chicago Press.

Zirojević, Olga. 2000. "Kosovo in the Collective Memory." In *The Road to War in Serbia: Trauma and Catharsis,* ed. N. Popov. Budapest: Central European University Press.

Živković, Marko. 1990. "Representing the Balkans: Symbolic Geography of the South-Eastern Margins of Europe." Unpublished ms., Department of Anthropology, University of Chicago.

———. 2000. "Telling Stories of Serbia: Native and Other Dilemmas on the Edge of Chaos." In *Fieldwork Dilemmas: Anthropologists in Postsocialist Societies,* ed. H. G. De Soto and N. Dudwick. Madison: University of Wisconsin Press.

———. 2001. "Jelly, Slush, and Red Mists: Poetics of Amorphous Substances in Serbian Jeremiads of the 1990s." *Anthropology and Humanism* 25 (2): 168–182.

———. 2006. "Ex-Yugoslav Masculinities under the Female Gaze; or, Why Men Skin Cats, Beat Up Gays, and Go to War." *Nationalities Papers* 34 (3): 257–263.

———. 2006a. "Sueños dentro-fuera: algunos usos del sueño en la teoría social y la investigación etnográfica" (Dreams inside-out: Some uses of dream in social theory and ethnographic inquiry). *Revista de Antropolog'a Social* 15:139–171.

———. 2007. "Cordon." *Cineaste* 32 (3): 53–54.

———. 2008. "Tales of Mega Jury-Rigging: Trabi, Fića and Diana in Comparative Perspective." Paper read at the 107th American Anthropological Association Annual Meeting, November 19–23, San Francisco. Available, as video, at http://www.gmclasses.com/anthropology/wp-content/uploads/2010/03/Marko-Zivkovic.mov (accessed April 2010).

———. 2011. "Serbian Turbo-Epics: Genres, Intertextuality, and the Play of Ironies." In *Balkan Epic: Song, History, Modernity,* ed. P. V. Bohlman and N. Petković. Lanham, Md.: Scarecrow.

Žižek, Slavoj. 1997. Uživanje u pokornosti i sluganstvu. *Naša Borba,* January 5.

FILMOGRAPHY

Bringa, Tone. 1992. *We Are All Neighbors: Bosnia.* Granada Television. 52 min.

Dragojević, Srdjan. 1996. *Lepa sela lepo gore (Pretty Village, Pretty Flame).* Feature film. Beograd: Cobra Film, RTV Serbia.

———. 1998. *Rane (The Wounds).* Feature film. Beograd and Frankfurt: Cobra Film; Pandora Film.

Grlić, Rajko. 1981. *Samo jednom se ljubi (The Melody Hunts My Reverie).* Feature film. Zagreb: Jadran Film.

———. 1985. *Za sreću je potrebno troje (Three Are Needed for Love).* Feature film. Beograd; Zagreb: Centar Film; Jadran Film.

Karanović, Srdjan. 1983. *Nešto izmedju (Something In-Between).* Feature film. Beograd: Union Film.

Knežević, Aleksandar, and Vojislav Tufegdžić. 1995. *Vidimo se u čitulji (The Crime That Changed Serbia).* Documentary film. Beograd: Radio B92.

Kusturica, Emir. 1989. *Dom za vešanje (Time of the Gypsies).* Feature film. Sarajevo: Forum Film.

———. 1995. *Underground (Bila jednom jedna zemlja).* Feature film. Yugoslavia, France, and Germany: CiBy 2000, Komuna & Pandora.

Lekić, Miroslav. 1993. *Bolje od bekstva.* FR Yugoslavia: Cobra Film.

Lotianu, Emil. 1975. *Tabor ukhodit v nebo* (a.k.a *Gypsies Are Found Near Heaven, Gypsy Camp Vanishes into the Blue, or Queen of the Gypsies).* USSR: Mosfilm.

Marković, Goran. 1977. *Specijalno vaspitanje (Special Education).* Yugoslavia: Centar Film.

———. 1979. *Nacionalna klasa do 785 ccm (National Class Category up to 785 ccm).* Yugoslavia: Centar Film.

———. 1981. *Variola Vera.* Yugoslavia: Art Film 80.

———. 1982. *Tito i ja (Tito and Me).* Yugoslavia: Avala Film.

———. 1997. *Poludeli ljudi.* FR Yugoslavia: Radio B92.

———. 2002. *The Cordon (Kordon).* Serbia: RTS, RTB, Viktoria Film.

Mitić, Boris. 2003. *Pretty Dyana: A Gypsy Recycling Saga.* Dribbling Pictures. Downloadable at http://video.google.com/videoplay?docid=-2181669920911563723# (accessed April 2010).

Nicholas, Gregor. 1996. *Broken English.* Feature film. New Zealand.

Pawlikowski, Paul. 1992. *Serbian Epics.* London: BBC Documentary.

Petrović, Aleksandar. 1967. *Skupljači perja* (*I Even Met Happy Gypsies*). Feature film. Beograd: Avala Film.

Skerlić, Slobodan-Boban. 1997. *Do koske* (*Rage*). Feature film. Beograd: Monte Royal Pictures; RTV Serbia; Avala Film.

Sorak, Dejan. 1987. *Oficir s ružom* (*Officer with a Rose*). Feature film. Beograd; Zagreb: Centar Film; Jadran Film.

Tanović, Danis. 2001. *No Man's Land* (*Ničija zemlja*). Bosnia-Herzegovina, Slovenia, Italy, France, Belgium, and the UK.

Šotra, Zdravko. 1994. *Dnevnik Uvreda '93*. FR Yugoslavia: RTS, Dan Film and Avala Film.

Stojanović, Gorčin. 1995. *Ubistvo s predumišljajem* (*Premeditated Murder*). Feature film. Beograd: Cinema Design.

INDEX

Italicized page numbers refer to illustrations.

NEW ANTHROPOLOGIES OF EUROPE

*Daphne Berdahl, Matti Bunzl, and
Michael Herzfeld, founding editors*

MARKO ŽIVKOVIĆ
*is Assistant Professor of Anthropology
at the University of Alberta.*